CONSUMER GUIDE®

1994 CARS

S0-BTP-288

CONTENTS

INTRODUCTION

1994 Cars covers more than 150 passenger cars, minivans, and sport-utility vehicles. Major changes, key features, and latest available prices are included for each model, along with ratings for the specific model tested by the auto editors of Consumer Guide®.

To help readers compare competitors, vehicles are divided into 10 model groups based on their size, price, and market position. A complete list of model groups, including vehicles not covered in this issue, follows the Shopping Tips. Each report lists the model group to which the vehicle belongs, as well as similar vehicles built from the same design.

How Cars Are Rated

The Rating Guide with each report has numerical ratings in 16 categories. These ratings apply only to the vehicle as it was tested by the editors. For example, the ratings for the Acura Integra apply only to the GS-R 3-door hatchback, which has standard anti-lock brakes (ABS) and a more powerful engine than other Integras. An Integra without ABS and the base engine may not score as highly in braking or acceleration. The chart below the Rating Guide lists major specifications for the tested vehicle.

In addition to the ratings, the editors have selected Best Buys in each of the 10 model groups as the best overall choices. In some groups, there are models labeled Recommended and Budget Buy that also are worthy of attention. Road test results play a major role in the editors' decisions. Other factors include price, cost of ownership, reputation for reliability and durability, warranties, and safety features.

Price Information

The latest available prices are provided for all models (and their optional equipment) included in this issue. In most cases, this includes dealer invoice prices and our estimated fair price. In some cases, only suggested retail prices were available; with some models that hadn't yet gone on sale (such as the 1995 Oldsmobile Aurora), no prices were available.

Two federal taxes affect car prices. First, a gas-guzzler tax is levied on cars that attain less than 22.5 mpg in combined city/highway mileage based on EPA estimates. Some manufacturers include the gas-guzzler tax in the base prices; others list it separately. Guzzler taxes range from $1000 to more than $5000, so they can have a substantial impact on the purchase price.

Second, a 10 percent "luxury tax" is levied on cars selling for more than $32,000. The tax applies only to the amount over $32,000, so a car that sells for $38,000 will carry a tax of $600 and one that sells for $50,000 will be hit with a $1800 tax. Note that the tax applies to the *transaction* price, not the suggested retail price, and any trade-in would be subtracted from the total cost before the tax was figured.

The dealer invoice prices are what the dealer pays the manufacturer for the car, including its factory- or port-installed options. The dealer's cost of preparing a car for delivery to the consumer is included in the invoice price of all domestic cars. On some imported vehicles, this cost may not be included in the dealer invoice. The destination charge is not included in either the suggested retail or dealer invoice prices (except where noted), so it must be added to the total cost of the vehicle.

The fair prices listed in this book are estimates based on national market conditions for each model. Since market conditions can vary greatly in different parts of the country, the fair prices should only be used as a guide. If possible, it's best to price the same car at three or more dealers to get a better idea of the fair price in your area.

Fair prices aren't listed for some models because of insufficient information about market conditions for that particular vehicle.

While we have done all we can to see that the prices in this issue are accurate, car companies are free to change their prices at any time. Most car companies have raised prices more than once during recent model years, so don't automatically assume that a dealer is lying if they claim these prices are out of date.

However, many dealers routinely tell our readers that the prices we publish are incorrect so they can eliminate dealer-invoice price from consideration. Once they accomplish that, then they're back in the driver's seat on price negotiations.

If a dealer claims our prices are incorrect or the information in this issue doesn't match what you see in showrooms, contact us and we'll do our best to help you out.

Advertising fees are not included in the price lists because they vary greatly in different parts of the country and not all dealers try to charge their customers for advertising. We think it's unfair for consumers to reimburse dealers for their advertising expenses, so we strongly suggest you argue against paying such a fee. It's their cost of doing business, not yours.

The editors invite your questions and comments. Address them to:

Consumer Guide®
7373 N. Cicero Ave.
Lincolnwood, IL 60646

KEY TO SPECIFICATIONS

Dimensions and capacities are supplied by the manufacturers. **Body types: notchback** = coupe or sedan with a separate trunk; **hatchback** = coupe or sedan with a rear liftgate. **Wheelbase** = distance between the front and rear wheels. **Curb weight** = weight of base models, not including optional equipment. **Engine types: ohv** = overhead valve; **ohc** = overhead camshaft; **dohc** = dual overhead camshafts; **I** = inline cylinders; **V** = cylinders in V configuration; **flat** = horizontally opposed cylinders. **Engine size (l/cu. in.)** = liters/cubic inches. **Rpm** = revolutions per minute. **Brakes: ABS** = anti-lock braking system. **NA** = not available.

SHOPPING TIPS ——————

Before you venture out to test drive and comparison shop the new models, here are some suggestions to get you started on the right road:

● Determine how much you are willing to pay—or can afford to pay. If you plan on buying a car (instead of leasing) you should shop for a loan at a bank or other lending institution before you shop for a car. It's better to figure out how much you can afford at a bank than in a dealer's showroom, where they can juggle numbers faster than you can count.

● Decide which vehicle or type of vehicle best suits your needs and pocketbook. If you're single and seldom carry more than one passenger, a small car or even a 2-seater can be perfect. If you're married and have three children, you should be looking at larger cars or minivans.

● If you have an old car you intend to sell, you'll almost always get more money by selling it yourself instead of trading it in. Dealers want to make money on your old car, so they'll only give you wholesale value or less. You might be able to sell it for close to its retail value, which can easily put hundreds of dollars into your pocket.

Showroom Strategies

If you intend to buy a new vehicle instead of leasing one, here are some suggestions for planning your shopping strategy:

● There are no formulas for calculating a "good deal." You can't just "knock 10 percent off the sticker." It all depends on supply and demand for a particular model in your area and how much competition there is among dealers.

● Don't tell a car salesman how much you're willing to pay. Your price might be higher than what others are paying. Even if it's right on target, a salesman might reject it by saying, "We couldn't possibly sell it for that."

It's their job to price the products they sell. It's your privilege to accept or reject their price.

● Once you've settled on a car, shop at least three dealers—more if you can—to compare prices on the same model with the same equipment. Let them know you're comparison shopping and that you'll buy from the dealer who gives you the lowest price and the best treatment.

● Get written price quotes that are good next week, not just today. If a dealer won't give you a price in writing, take your business elsewhere. They're not being straight with you if they offer you a verbal quote that's "good for today only."

Take your time and think about it at home. Don't be pressured into making a snap decision in the showroom.

● Don't put a deposit on a car just to get a price quote or a test drive.

Dealers want to get a deposit because then you've made a commitment to them and you're less likely to keep shopping. Go to another dealer instead.

• Don't shop for a monthly payment. Dealers will try to convince you to buy a car you can't afford by stretching the payments from 48 months to 60 months. That lowers your monthly payment, but it means you'll pay more interest and be in hock longer.

For example, if you borrow $15,000 for 48 months at eight percent interest, you'll pay $366 per month, or $17,568 in total.

If you borrow $15,000 for 60 months you'll likely pay a higher interest rate, say, 8.5 percent. Your monthly payment drops to $308.25, but you'll pay $18,495 over the 5-year life of the loan. That's $927 more in interest than you'll pay on a 4-year loan.

• Keep your trade-in out of the new-car price. If you're thinking about trading in your old vehicle, get a written trade-in value *after* you settle on a price for the new car.

When the dealer asks if you're trading in your old car, tell him, "Maybe. We can talk about that later." Some dealers will try to lure you with the offer of a high trade-in allowance and then inflate the price of the new vehicle.

"One-Price" Models

If you're uneasy—or terrified—about negotiating a price from a dealer, then shop for a "one-price" model, such as an Oldsmobile Achieva Special Edition or a Saturn, or go to dealers that advertise "no-dicker" sales practices. "One-price" isn't necessarily the lowest price for a particular car, but it can reduce the stress and let you concentrate on finding the model that best meets your needs.

In addition to Saturn and Oldsmobile, Buick, Chevrolet, Ford, Mercury, and others this year offer one-price and so-called "value-priced" models that typically have more standard features for less money than a base model.

For example, the Achieva S coupe, the base model, has a list price of $14,075 and a destination charge of $485. The Achieva Special Edition comes with air conditioning and an automatic transmission, which would cost $1385 as individual options, and includes the destination charge for a total of $13,995. In addition, Oldsmobile positions the Special Edition as a one-price model, eliminating the need to dicker over price.

Lease Instead of Buy?

Leasing has become a popular alternative to buying as tax laws have changed, eliminating deductions for interest on car loans. Also, prices of new cars have soared to where many people can no longer afford to buy.

Recent estimates indicate that leases account for 20 to 25 percent of new car sales overall and well over 50 percent of luxury models that cost $30,000 or more.

Is leasing right for you? It depends on your particular financial situation, so sit down with an accountant or tax adviser for a heart-to-heart talk on whether leasing is the best way to go. Some people still buy simply because they're more comfortable with "owning" a vehicle than "renting" one. However, some financial advisers argue that most advantages to owning a car have disappeared, making leasing more attractive.

Here are some guidelines to help you decide whether you should lease or buy:

• One of leasing's major advantages is that a large down payment isn't needed, though some leases require a substantial initial payment (sometimes couched in terms like "capital cost reduction"). Also, monthly lease payments are generally lower than the monthly loan payment for an equivalent car.

When you buy a car, lenders typically want a down payment of at least 20 percent. With the average price of a new car approaching $18,000, that requires $4500 in cash or trade-in value on a used car. If you don't have that much, then leasing might be a better bet.

• The major disadvantage to leasing is that unless you eventually buy a car, you'll always be making a monthly payment. At the end of a lease you have the option of giving it back to the leasing company or buying it. Either way, you're going to have to dig into your pocket again to keep a car in your driveway.

Think ahead two or three years. Will your financial situation allow you to lease another new car or take out a loan to buy one?

• While the monthly payments may be lower on a lease, in the long run it is usually cheaper to buy if you keep cars five years or longer. For example, if you pay off a car loan in four years and keep the car another three years, your only expenses once the car is paid for will be for maintenance and repairs.

If your car needs few repairs—and that can be a big "if"—then you'll be thousands of dollars ahead because you won't be making a monthly payment.

• On the other hand, would you rather drive a 7-year-old car or a much newer one? A 2- or 3-year lease gives you the option of having a new car more often. The car you drive will always be under warranty and you don't have the hassle of selling or trading in an old car. After two or three years, you simply turn it in to the leasing agent.

• Leasing generally used to be cheaper than buying for those who claimed their car as a business expense because of tax advantages. Tax laws have changed so the advantages may be greatly reduced for some people.

How do you find out? Talk to your accountant or financial adviser—not the guy next door. Because everyone has a different situation, leasing can be a great deal for your next-door neighbor but of no real benefit to you.

MODEL GROUPS

Subcompact Cars
Chevrolet Cavalier
Dodge Colt
Dodge Neon
Dodge Shadow
Eagle Summit
Eagle Summit Wagon
Ford Aspire
Ford Escort
Geo Metro
Geo Prizm
Honda Civic
Hyundai Elantra
Hyundai Excel
Kia Sephia
Mazda 323/Protege
Mercury Tracer
Mitsubishi Expo LRV
Mitsubishi Mirage
Nissan Sentra
Plymouth Colt
Plymouth Colt Vista
Plymouth Neon
Plymouth Sundance
Pontiac Sunbird
Saturn Sedan/Wagon
Subaru Impreza
Subaru Justy
Subaru Loyale
Suzuki Swift
Toyota Corolla
Toyota Tercel
Volkswagen Golf/Jetta

Compact Cars
Buick Skylark
Chevrolet Corsica
Chrysler LeBaron
Dodge Spirit
Ford Tempo
Mazda 626
Mercury Topaz
Mitsubishi Expo
Mitsubishi Galant
Nissan Altima
Oldsmobile Achieva
Plymouth Acclaim
Pontiac Grand Am

Subaru Legacy
Toyota Camry
Volkswagen Passat

Mid-size Cars
Buick Century
Buick Regal
Chevrolet Lumina
Ford Taurus
Ford Thunderbird
Honda Accord
Hyundai Sonata
Mercury Cougar
Mercury Sable
Oldsmobile Cutlass Ciera
Oldsmobile Cutlass Supreme
Pontiac Grand Prix

Full-size Cars
Buick LeSabre
Buick Roadmaster
Chevrolet Caprice
Chrysler Concorde
Dodge Intrepid
Eagle Vision
Ford Crown Victoria
Mercury Grand Marquis
Oldsmobile Eighty Eight
Pontiac Bonneville

Premium Coupes
Acura Legend
Audi Cabriolet
BMW 8-Series
Cadillac Eldorado
Jaguar XJS
Lexus SC 300/400
Lincoln Mark VIII
Mercedes-Benz E320
Mercedes-Benz SL
Mercedes-Benz S500/600

Premium Sedans
Acura Legend
Acura Vigor
Audi V8 Quattro
Audi 90
Audi 100/S4
BMW 3-Series

BMW 5-Series
BMW 7-Series
Buick Park Avenue
Cadillac De Ville/Concours
Cadillac Fleetwood
Cadillac Seville
Chrysler New Yorker/LHS
Infiniti G20
Infiniti J30
Infiniti Q45
Jaguar Sedan
Lexus ES 300
Lexus GS 300
Lexus LS 400
Lincoln Continental
Lincoln Town Car
Mazda 929
Mercedes-Benz C-Class
Mercedes-Benz E-Class
Mercedes-Benz S-Class
Mitsubishi Diamante
Nissan Maxima
Oldsmobile Aurora
Oldsmobile Ninety Eight
Saab 900
Saab 9000
Volvo 850
Volvo 940/960

Sports Coupes
Acura Integra
Chevrolet Beretta
Eagle Talon
Ford Probe
Honda Civic del Sol
Honda Prelude
Hyundai Scoupe
Mazda MX-3
Mazda MX-6
Mercury Capri
Mitsubishi Eclipse
Nissan 240SX
Plymouth Laser
Saturn SC1/SC2
Toyota Celica
Toyota Paseo

Sports and GT Cars
Acura NSX
Chevrolet Camaro
Chevrolet Corvette

Dodge Stealth
Dodge Viper
Ford Mustang
Mazda Miata
Mazda RX-7
Mitsubishi 3000GT
Nissan 300ZX
Pontiac Firebird
Subaru SVX
Toyota MR2
Toyota Supra
Volkswagen Corrado

Sport-Utility Vehicles
Chevrolet S10 Blazer
Ford Explorer
Geo Tracker
GMC Jimmy
Isuzu Amigo
Isuzu Rodeo
Isuzu Trooper
Jeep Cherokee
Jeep Grand Cherokee
Jeep Wrangler
Kia Sportage
Land Rover Defender
Mazda Navajo
Mitsubishi Montero
Nissan Pathfinder
Oldsmobile Bravada
Range Rover
Suzuki Samurai
Suzuki Sidekick
Toyota Land Cruiser
Toyota 4Runner

Minivans
Chevrolet Astro
Chevrolet Lumina Minivan
Chrysler Town & Country
Dodge Caravan
Ford Aerostar
GMC Safari
Mazda MPV
Mercury Villager
Nissan Quest
Oldsmobile Silhouette
Plymouth Voyager
Pontiac Trans Sport
Toyota Previa
Volkswagen EuroVan

ACURA INTEGRA — RECOMMENDED
Built in Japan.

Acura Integra GS-R 3-door

SPORTS COUPE

Integra has been redesigned for 1994 and, like the previous generation, it has front-wheel drive and comes in 3-door hatchback coupe and 4-door sedan styling. Among the new features are standard dual air bags, which replace motorized front shoulder belts. Acura is the luxury division of Honda and Integra is its least-expensive model. Though the 1994 Integras have new styling, they've changed little in size and weight. Both body styles come in base RS, luxury LS, and sporty GS-R price levels. The GS-R series previously was limited to the coupe. The RS and LS come with a 142-horsepower 1.8-liter 4-cylinder, essentially last year's engine with two more horsepower. GS-R models have a new 1.8-liter 4-cylinder with Honda's variable valve timing and 170 horsepower. A 5-speed manual transmission is standard on the RS and LS and an electronic 4-speed automatic is optional. The GS-R models come only with a 5-speed manual. Four-wheel disc brakes are standard across the board, and the LS and GS-R also have a standard anti-lock system. The anti-lock feature isn't available on RS models. The 1994 Integra is better than its predecessor in most ways, but only the manual-transmission RS lists for less $15,000, so it's not a great value even with this year's standard dual air bags. However, like previous Integras, the new one has commendable assembly quality and should be reliable. You should also expect high resale value. The hatchback has a cramped rear seat that won't suit most adults. The 4-door sedan has a longer wheelbase and a roomier rear seat, making it a better choice for those who carry more than one passenger.

Acura Integra prices are on page 244.

ACURA INTEGRA GS-R

Rating Guide	1	2	3	4	5
Performance					
Acceleration	▮▮▮▮▮▮▮▮▮				
Economy	▮▮▮▮▮▮▮▮▮				
Driveability	▮▮▮▮▮▮▮▮▮				
Ride	▮▮▮▮▮▮▮▮				
Steering/handling	▮▮▮▮▮▮▮▮▮				
Braking	▮▮▮▮▮▮▮▮▮▮▮				
Noise	▮▮▮▮▮▮▮				
Accommodations					
Driver seating	▮▮▮▮▮▮▮▮				
Instruments/controls	▮▮▮▮▮▮▮▮				
Visibility	▮▮▮▮▮▮▮▮				
Room/comfort	▮▮▮▮▮▮▮				
Entry/exit	▮▮▮▮▮▮▮				
Cargo room	▮▮▮▮▮▮▮				
Workmanship					
Exterior	▮▮▮▮▮▮▮▮				
Interior	▮▮▮▮▮▮▮▮				
Value	▮▮▮▮▮▮▮				

Total Points 60

Specifications

Body type	3-door hatchback	Engine type	dohc I-4
Wheelbase (in.)	101.2	Engine size (l/cu. in.)	1.8/109
Overall length (in.)	172.4	Horsepower @ rpm	170 @ 7600
Overall width (in.)	67.5	Torque @ rpm	128 @ 6200
Overall height (in.)	52.6	Transmission	manual/5-sp.
Curb weight (lbs.)	2560	Drive wheels	front
Seating capacity	4	Brakes, F/R	disc/disc (ABS)
Front head room (in.)	38.5	Tire size	195/55VR15
Max. front leg room (in.)	42.7	Fuel tank capacity (gal.)	13.2
Rear head room (in.)	35.0	EPA city/highway mpg	25/31
Min. rear leg room (in.)	28.1	Test mileage (mpg)	28.4
Cargo volume (cu. ft.)	13.3		

Warranties The entire car is covered for 4 years/50,000 miles. Body perforation rust is covered for 4 years/unlimited miles.

Rating scale 5=Exceptional; 4=Above average; 3=Average; 2=Below average; 1=Poor

ACURA LEGEND

Built in Japan.

Acura Legend Sedan GS

PREMIUM SEDAN/COUPE

All members of the Legend line get a power tilt/telescopic steering column as a new standard feature and there's a new GS 4-door as the top-shelf sedan. Acura is the luxury division of Honda. The new steering column automatically tilts up when the ignition key is removed to make exiting easier and returns to its original position when the key is inserted again. The steering wheel position is included in the standard driver's seat memory system. In addition to the GS sedan, Legend comes as a 4-door sedan and 2-door coupe in L and LS price levels. The base 4-door has been dropped. The GS comes with the 230-horsepower 3.2-liter V-6 and 6-speed manual transmission that were introduced on last year's coupes. The GS sedan also has some features previously exclusive to the LS coupe, including traction control, a sport suspension, 16-inch tires (versus 15-inch on other models), and a body-color grille. The L models and LS sedan retain a 200-horsepower 3.2-liter V-6 and a standard 5-speed manual. A 4-speed automatic transmission is optional across the board. All models have front-wheel drive, driver- and passenger-side air bags, and anti-lock brakes. Legend's appearance is freshened by a restyled grille, front bumpers, and lower air intakes. Legend prices have climbed so that this is no longer an outstanding dollar value. The Legend sedan is still a good choice because of its strong performance, roomy and plush accommodations, high quality, and good resale value. Because there's so much competition in the $30,000 to $40,000 range, Acura dealers should be offering big discounts and attractive leases on both the sedan and coupe.

Acura Legend prices are on page 244.

ACURA LEGEND SEDAN LS

Rating Guide	1	2	3	4	5

Performance

Acceleration					
Economy					
Driveability					
Ride					
Steering/handling					
Braking					
Noise					

Accommodations

Driver seating					
Instruments/controls					
Visibility					
Room/comfort					
Entry/exit					
Cargo room					

Workmanship

Exterior					
Interior					

Value

Total Points..63

Specifications

Body type ....4-door notchback	Engine type......................ohc V-6
Wheelbase (in.) 114.6	Engine size (l/cu. in.).........3.2/196
Overall length (in.)...............194.9	Horsepower @ rpm ...200 @ 5500
Overall width (in.) 71.3	Torque @ rpm ....210 @ 4500
Overall height (in.)..................55.1	Transmission.................auto/4-sp.
Curb weight (lbs.) 3516	Drive wheels ....front
Seating capacity.........................5	Brakes, F/R...........disc/disc (ABS)
Front head room (in.) 38.5	Tire size....................205/60VR15
Max. front leg room (in.) 42.7	Fuel tank capacity (gal.) 18.0
Rear head room (in.) 36.5	EPA city/highway mpg 19/24
Min. rear leg room (in.) 33.5	Test mileage (mpg) 20.2
Cargo volume (cu. ft.).............14.8	

Warranties The entire car is covered for 4 years/50,000 miles. Body perforation rust is covered for 4 years/unlimited miles.

Rating scale 5=Exceptional; 4=Above average; 3=Average; 2=Below average; 1=Poor

ACURA VIGOR

Built in Japan.

Acura Vigor LS

PREMIUM SEDAN

All 1994 versions of Acura's mid-level sedan have dual air bags and the top-line GS model has a dashboard-mounted CD player as a new standard feature. Acura is the luxury division of Honda, and the front-drive Vigor is sized and priced between the flagship Legend and entry-level Integra sedans. The base Vigor LS catches up to the GS by getting a standard passenger-side air bag. The GS gained that feature last year. Both have had a driver-side air bag since the Vigor was introduced as a 1992 model. Anti-lock brakes also are standard on both models. The big change for the GS is a new sound system with a cassette player and a CD player. The CD player is in lieu of the "Digital Signal Processor" that allowed changing the sound to match venues such as concert halls, cathedrals, and nightclubs. The only other announced change is a switch from Zebra wood interior trim to burled-type wood. Vigor has a 2.5-liter 5-cylinder engine. A 5-speed manual transmission is standard and a 4-speed electronic automatic is optional. The Vigor is derived from the 1990-93 Accord. Since the Accord has been redesigned for 1994, a replacement for the Vigor is expected for the 1995 model year. Vigor has all the safety, comfort, and convenience features expected of a "near-luxury" sedan but is short of interior space for its exterior size. Its 5-cylinder engine isn't as smooth or refined as the V-6 in the rival Lexus ES 300. Because this car hasn't sold well, Acura dealers are giving big discounts and Acura has been offering cut-rate lease programs.

Acura Vigor prices are on page 245.

ACURA VIGOR LS

Rating Guide	1	2	3	4	5

Performance

Acceleration	▮▮▮▮▮ (4)
Economy	▮▮▮ (3)
Driveability	▮▮▮ (3)
Ride	▮▮▮ (3)
Steering/handling	▮▮▮▮ (4)
Braking	▮▮▮▮▮ (5)
Noise	▮▮▮ (3)

Accommodations

Driver seating	▮▮▮ (3)
Instruments/controls	▮▮▮▮ (4)
Visibility	▮▮▮ (3)
Room/comfort	▮▮▮ (3)
Entry/exit	▮▮▮ (3)
Cargo room	▮▮▮ (3)

Workmanship

Exterior	▮▮▮▮ (4)
Interior	▮▮▮▮▮ (5)

Value

Value	▮▮▮ (3)

Total Points..58

Specifications

Body type	4-door notchback	Engine type	ohc I-5
Wheelbase (in.)	110.4	Engine size (l/cu. in.)	2.5/150
Overall length (in.)	190.4	Horsepower @ rpm	176 @ 6300
Overall width (in.)	70.1	Torque @ rpm	170 @ 3900
Overall height (in.)	52.0	Transmission	auto/5-sp.
Curb weight (lbs.)	3197	Drive wheels	front
Seating capacity	5	Brakes, F/R	disc/disc (ABS)
Front head room (in.)	38.8	Tire size	205/60HR15
Max. front leg room (in.)	43.7	Fuel tank capacity (gal.)	17.2
Rear head room (in.)	36.2	EPA city/highway mpg	20/26
Min. rear leg room (in.)	30.3	Test mileage (mpg)	23.7
Cargo volume (cu. ft.)	14.2		

Warranties The entire car is covered for 4 years/50,000 miles. Body perforation rust is covered for 4 years/unlimited miles.

Rating scale 5=Exceptional; 4=Above average; 3=Average; 2=Below average; 1=Poor

AUDI 90/CABRIOLET

Built in Germany.

Audi 90 S

PREMIUM SEDAN

Audi joins the *alfresco* set for 1994 with its first convertible. Simply called Cabriolet, it is based on the 90-Series sedan, which was redesigned last year. The 90-Series sedan, which had a driver-side air bag last year, gains a passenger-side air bag as its major change for 1994. The Cabriolet also has dual air bags. It is 2.2 inches shorter in wheelbase and 4.3 inches shorter in overall length than the sedan, and it seats four rather than five. All models have a 172-horsepower 2.8-liter V-6 and standard anti-lock brakes. All models also have front-wheel drive except the 90 Quattro Sport, which has permanently engaged all-wheel drive and comes only with a 5-speed manual transmission. On the 90 S and 90 CS, a 5-speed manual is standard and a 4-speed automatic is optional. The Cabriolet comes only with the automatic. The automatic transmission requires the driver to apply the brake pedal and push down on the shift lever to shift from park. Other than the passenger-side air bag, the only changes for the sedan this year are that leather upholstery and a power tilt/slide sunroof have been added as new options for the 90 S. We haven't tested the Cabriolet yet. Though we find the 90 sedan enjoyable to drive, we think the firm suspension makes it better suited to driving on the German Autobahn than on American interstates. We've been impressed by the assembly quality of 90 models we've driven, testament to Audi's continuing efforts to attract customers. However, rivals in the same price range, such as the Lexus ES 300, offer even better quality, as well as smoother, quieter performance and higher resale value.

Audi 90/Cabriolet prices are on page 246.

AUDI 90 S

Rating Guide	1	2	3	4	5
Performance					
Acceleration					
Economy					
Driveability					
Ride					
Steering/handling					
Braking					
Noise					
Accommodations					
Driver seating					
Instruments/controls					
Visibility					
Room/comfort					
Entry/exit					
Cargo room					
Workmanship					
Exterior					
Interior					
Value					

Total Points **57**

Specifications

Body type	4-door notchback	Engine type	ohc V-6
Wheelbase (in.)	102.8	Engine size (l/cu. in.)	2.8/169
Overall length (in.)	180.3	Horsepower @ rpm	172 @ 5500
Overall width (in.)	66.7	Torque @ rpm	184 @ 3000
Overall height (in.)	54.3	Transmission	auto/4-sp.
Curb weight (lbs.)	3197	Drive wheels	front
Seating capacity	5	Brakes, F/R	disc/disc (ABS)
Front head room (in.)	37.8	Tire size	195/65HR15
Max. front leg room (in.)	42.4	Fuel tank capacity (gal.)	17.4.2
Rear head room (in.)	37.2	EPA city/highway mpg	18/26
Min. rear leg room (in.)	32.5	Test mileage (mpg)	18.7
Cargo volume (cu. ft.)	14.0		

Warranties The entire car is covered for 3 years/50,000 miles. Body perforation rust is covered for 10 years/unlimited miles.

Rating scale 5=Exceptional; 4=Above average; 3=Average; 2=Below average; 1=Poor

AUDI 100/S4 ————————

Built in Germany.

Audi 100 S 4-door

PREMIUM SEDAN

Audi has added a front-drive version of the 100-Series 5-door wagon and dropped the base 4-door notchback sedan. For 1994, front-drive models include an S sedan and wagon and a CS sedan. Models with permanently engaged all-wheel drive include the CS Quattro sedan and wagon and high-performance S4 sedan. The sedan seats five and the wagon adds a 2-place rear seat for 7-passenger capacity. All models come with dual air bags and anti-lock brakes. All models except the S4 come with a 172-horsepower 2.8-liter V-6. A 5-speed manual transmission is standard on both S models and the CS Quattro sedan. A 4-speed automatic transmission is optional on those models. The automatic is standard on the CS Quattro wagon and, in a change for 1994, also on the CS sedan. The electronic automatic transmission has recalibrated shift points and a new feature that momentarily reduces engine power to provide smoother shifts. The automatic has a shift interlock that requires applying the brake pedal to shift out of park. In addition, the driver has to press down on the shift lever. The limited-production S4 sedan packs a turbocharged 2.2-liter 5-cylinder engine with 227 horsepower. It comes only with a 5-speed manual transmission. The 100 is a well-equipped car that matches rivals such as the Acura Legend and Lexus ES 300 in features and accommodations but falls behind in overall performance and refinement. Audi is struggling to win back customers in the U.S., so dealers should be offering big discounts whether you're buying or leasing.

Audi 100/S4 prices are on page 247.

AUDI 100 S

Rating Guide	1	2	3	4	5
Performance					
Acceleration					
Economy					
Driveability					
Ride					
Steering/handling					
Braking					
Noise					
Accommodations					
Driver seating					
Instruments/controls					
Visibility					
Room/comfort					
Entry/exit					
Cargo room					
Workmanship					
Exterior					
Interior					
Value					

Total Points 60

Specifications

Body type ....4-door notchback	Engine type......................ohc V-6
Wheelbase (in.) 105.8	Engine size (l/cu. in.).........2.8/169
Overall length (in.)................192.6	Horsepower @ rpm ...172 @ 5500
Overall width (in.) 70.0	Torque @ rpm ....184 @ 3000
Overall height (in.)..................56.3	Transmission.................auto/4-sp.
Curb weight (lbs.)..................3363	Drive wheels ....front
Seating capacity.........................5	Brakes, F/R..........disc/disc (ABS)
Front head room (in.) 38.4	Tire size 195/65HR15
Max. front leg room (in.) 42.2	Fuel tank capacity (gal.) 21.1
Rear head room (in.) 37.6	EPA city/highway mpg 18/24
Min. rear leg room (in.)...........34.8	Test mileage (mpg) 20.5
Cargo volume (cu. ft.).............16.8	

Warranties The entire car is covered for 3 years/50,000 miles. Body perforation rust is covered for 10 years/unlimited miles.

Rating scale 5=Exceptional; 4=Above average; 3=Average; 2=Below average; 1=Poor

BMW 3-SERIES

Built in Germany.

BMW 325i

PREMIUM SEDAN

Anew convertible bowed during the summer to complete the overhaul of BMW's 3-Series line that began with the 1992 sedans and continued last year with the coupes. All 3-Series models gain a passenger-side air bag as a new standard feature this year. A driver-side air bag and anti-lock brakes already were standard. The new ragtop shares the coupe's lower-body styling but has unique rear sheetmetal. For now it comes only as the 325iC with the 189-horsepower 2.5-liter 6-cylinder engine used in the 325 coupe and sedan. A 318iC convertible should arrive during 1994 with the same 138-horsepower 1.8-liter 4-cylinder as the 318 coupe and sedan. A new option for the convertible is a "Rollover Protection System," a pair of roll bars that pop up from behind the back seat in 0.3-second if a sensor detects the vehicle is about to tip over. BMW claims this system meets the federal rollover standard for hardtops. Among other changes for 1994, BMW's ASC+T traction control system is a new option for 6-cylinder models, and a redesigned front spoiler graces the 318is, 325i, and 325is. All models have rear-wheel drive and a standard 5-speed manual transmission. A 4-speed automatic is optional across the board. We're impressed by the convertible and have even higher regard for the 6-cylinder coupe and sedan, which offer strong performance, good assembly quality, and roomy interiors. The 318 models are geared toward enthusiasts who prefer a manual transmission. We recommend you compare the 3-Series cars to the Lexus ES 300, and then choose between BMW's sporty approach to the more luxurious Lexus approach.

BMW 3-Series prices are on page 248.

BMW 325i

Rating Guide	1	2	3	4	5
Performance					
Acceleration	▓▓▓▓▓▓▓▓▓▓▓▓▓▓▓▓				
Economy	▓▓▓▓▓▓▓▓				
Driveability	▓▓▓▓▓▓▓▓▓▓▓▓▓▓▓▓				
Ride	▓▓▓▓▓▓▓▓▓▓▓▓▓▓▓▓				
Steering/handling	▓▓▓▓▓▓▓▓▓▓▓▓▓▓▓▓				
Braking	▓▓▓▓▓▓▓▓▓▓▓▓▓▓▓▓▓▓▓▓				
Noise	▓▓▓▓▓▓▓▓▓▓▓▓				
Accommodations					
Driver seating	▓▓▓▓▓▓▓▓▓▓▓▓▓▓▓▓				
Instruments/controls	▓▓▓▓▓▓▓▓▓▓▓▓▓▓▓▓				
Visibility	▓▓▓▓▓▓▓▓▓▓▓▓▓▓▓▓				
Room/comfort	▓▓▓▓▓▓▓▓▓▓▓▓▓▓▓▓				
Entry/exit	▓▓▓▓▓▓▓▓▓▓▓▓▓▓▓▓				
Cargo room	▓▓▓▓▓▓▓▓▓▓▓▓▓▓▓▓				
Workmanship					
Exterior	▓▓▓▓▓▓▓▓▓▓▓▓▓▓▓▓				
Interior	▓▓▓▓▓▓▓▓▓▓▓▓▓▓▓▓				
Value	▓▓▓▓▓▓▓▓▓▓▓▓▓				

Total Points..60

Specifications

Body type ....4-door notchback	Engine type ....dohc I-6
Wheelbase (in.) 106.3	Engine size (l/cu. in.).........2.5/162
Overall length (in.)................174.5	Horsepower @ rpm ...189 @ 5900
Overall width (in.) 66.8	Torque @ rpm ....181 @ 4200
Overall height (in.) 54.8	Transmission ....manual/5-sp.
Curb weight (lbs.) 2866	Drive wheels ....rear
Seating capacity.........................5	Brakes, F/R.............disc/disc (ABS)
Front head room (in.) 37.8	Tire size 205/60HR15
Max. front leg room (in.) 40.9	Fuel tank capacity (gal.) 17.2
Rear head room (in.) 37.3	EPA city/highway mpg 19/28
Min. rear leg room (in.) 34.1	Test mileage (mpg) 20.5
Cargo volume (cu. ft.).............15.4	

Warranties The entire car is covered for 4 years/50,000 miles. Body perforation rust is covered for 6 years/unlimited miles.

Rating scale 5=Exceptional; 4=Above average; 3=Average; 2=Below average; 1=Poor

BMW 5-SERIES

Built in Germany.

BMW 540i

PREMIUM SEDAN

BMW started the new model year last spring by adding the V-8 powered 530i and 540i to its rear-drive 5-Series line and calling them 1994s. This fall, the big news is a passenger-side air bag as a new standard feature for all models in BMW's mid-level range. A driver-side air bag and anti-lock brakes already were standard. The 6-cylinder 535i sedan has been dropped, leaving the 525i sedan and 525i Touring wagon as the only models in the lineup with fewer than eight cylinders. Both have a 189-horsepower 2.5-liter inline six. The sedan comes with a 5-speed manual standard and a 4-speed automatic optional, and the wagon comes only with the automatic. The 525i and 525i Touring gain the ellipsoid headlamps and 250-watt stereo previously found only on the V-8 models. The Touring adds leather upholstery as standard equipment and the 525i adds ASC+T traction control as a new option. V-8 models include the 530i sedan and 530i Touring with a 215-horsepower 3.0-liter engine, and the 540i sedan with a 282-horsepower 4.0-liter engine, the same V-8 used in the larger 740i/740iL. A 5-speed manual transmission is standard on the 530i and a 5-speed automatic is optional. The automatic is standard on the other V-8 models. In addition to the potent V-8s, the 5-Series now has more competitive prices against rivals such as the Infiniti Q45 and Lexus LS 400. The 6-cylinder 535i was overpriced, but the 540i is less expensive than its Japanese competitors. We still give Infiniti and Lexus the edge in overall quality and value. However, BMW's V-8-power 5-Series cars are well worth considering as alternatives.

BMW 5-Series prices are on page 249.

BMW 540i

Rating Guide	1	2	3	4	5
Performance					
Acceleration	||||||||||||||||||||||||||||||||||||||||
Economy	|||||||||||||||||
Driveability	||||||||||||||||||||||||||||||||||||||||
Ride	||||||||||||||||||||||||||||||||||||||||
Steering/handling	||||||||||||||||||||||||||||||||||||||||
Braking	|||||||||||||||||||||||||||||||||||||||||||||
Noise	|||||||||||||||||||||||||||||||
Accommodations					
Driver seating	|||||||||||||||||||||||||||||||
Instruments/controls	||||||||||||||||||||||||||||||||||
Visibility	|||||||||||||||||||||||||||
Room/comfort	||||||||||||||||||||||||||||||
Entry/exit	||||||||||||||||||||||||||||
Cargo room	||||||||||||||||||||||||||||
Workmanship					
Exterior	||||||||||||||||||||||||||||||||||||||||
Interior	||||||||||||||||||||||||||||||||||||||||
Value	|||||||||||||||||||||||||||||||
Total Points					**61**

Specifications

Body type ....4-door notchback
Wheelbase (in.) 108.7
Overall length (in.)................185.8
Overall width (in.) 68.9
Overall height (in.)..................55.6
Curb weight (lbs.) 3804
Seating capacity.........................5
Front head room (in.) 38.5
Max. front leg room (in.) 42.0
Rear head room (in.) 37.4
Min. rear leg room (in.).........25.5
Cargo volume (cu. ft.).............16.2

Engine type.....................dohc V-8
Engine size (l/cu. in.)......4.0/243
Horsepower @ rpm ...282 @ 5800
Torque @ rpm ....295 @ 4500
Transmission.................auto/5-sp.
Drive wheels ....rear
Brakes, F/R...........disc/disc (ABS)
Tire size.....................225/60ZR15
Fuel tank capacity (gal.).........21.1
EPA city/highway mpg 16/23
Test mileage (mpg) 15.7

Warranties The entire car is covered for 4 years/50,000 miles. Body perforation rust is covered for 6 years/unlimited miles.

Rating scale 5=Exceptional; 4=Above average; 3=Average; 2=Below average; 1=Poor

BMW 7-SERIES

Built in Germany.

BMW 740i

PREMIUM SEDAN

BMW upgraded its flagship sedan last year with a new 4.0-liter V-8 to create 740i and 740iL models as replacements for the 6-cylinder 735i and 735iL. Those models and the V-12 750iL are unchanged for 1994. Reason: The Bavarian automaker is finalizing a new third-generation 7-Series that should appear in Europe next spring and in the U.S. next fall. In the current generation, the 740i has a 111.5-inch wheelbase and the 740iL and 750iL have a 116-inch wheelbase, with the additional length added to the rear seat. The 4.0-liter V-8 is rated at 282 horsepower and comes with a 5-speed automatic transmission. The 5.0-liter V-12 used in the 750iL is rated at 296 horsepower and comes with a 4-speed automatic. All models have rear-wheel drive. The 5-speed automatic has electronic controls that have Economy, Sport, and Winter shift modes. In Winter, the transmission starts in third gear to minimize wheel slip on slippery surfaces. Dual air bags and anti-lock brakes are standard on all models. Standard equipment on the 750iL includes ASC+T, BMW's traction-control system. ASC+T is optional on the 740i and 740iL. Electronic Damping Control, an electronic suspension system, is optional on all 7-Series models. The V-8 engine makes the 7-Series sedans much more competitive in performance with cars such as the Infiniti Q45 and Lexus LS 400, but the starting price of nearly $56,000 is higher than all rivals except those from Mercedes-Benz. In addition, you can get the same 4.0-liter V-8 in the less-expensive BMW 5-Series. Hefty discounts should be available on all 7-Series models.

BMW 7-Series prices are on page 250.

BMW 740i

Rating Guide	1	2	3	4	5
Performance					
Acceleration					▓
Economy	▓				
Driveability				▓	
Ride				▓	
Steering/handling				▓	
Braking					▓
Noise				▓	
Accommodations					
Driver seating				▓	
Instruments/controls				▓	
Visibility			▓		
Room/comfort			▓		
Entry/exit			▓		
Cargo room				▓	
Workmanship					
Exterior					▓
Interior					▓
Value				▓	
Total Points					**64**

Specifications

Body type ....4-door notchback	Engine type ....dohc V-8
Wheelbase (in.) 111.5	Engine size (l/cu. in.).........4.0/243
Overall length (in.)................193.3	Horsepower @ rpm ...282 @ 5800
Overall width (in.) 72.6	Torque @ rpm ....295 @ 4500
Overall height (in.)..................55.6	Transmission.................auto/5-sp.
Curb weight (lbs.) 4002	Drive wheels ....rear
Seating capacity.........................5	Brakes, F/R..........disc/disc (ABS)
Front head room (in.) 38.3	Tire size.....................225/60ZR15
Max. front leg room (in.) 44.3	Fuel tank capacity (gal.) 21.5
Rear head room (in.) 37.2	EPA city/highway mpg 16/23
Min. rear leg room (in.)...........38.8	Test mileage (mpg) 17.7
Cargo volume (cu. ft.)............17.6	

Warranties The entire car is covered for 4 years/50,000 miles. Body perforation rust is covered for 6 years/unlimited miles.

Rating scale 5=Exceptional; 4=Above average; 3=Average; 2=Below average; 1=Poor

BUICK CENTURY/ BUDGET BUY
OLDSMOBILE CUTLASS CIERA

Built in Oklahoma City, Okla., and Mexico.

Buick Century Special 4-door

MID-SIZE

A driver-side air bag and anti-lock brakes are standard on all Century and Cutlass Ciera models, and there are two new engines for these front-drive, mid-size cars, which are built from the same design. Last year, the air bag was standard on upscale versions and optional on the base models. Anti-lock brakes are a new feature for 1994. A 120-horsepower 2.2-liter 4-cylinder engine is standard on all Centurys and the Ciera S sedan, replacing a 110-horsepower 2.2-liter. Optional on all Centurys and standard on the Cutlass Cruiser wagon is a 160-horsepower 3.1-liter V-6, which replaces a 3.3-liter V-6. The 4-cylinder comes with a 3-speed automatic and the V-6 with an electronic 4-speed automatic. All models come with automatic power door locks that lock when the transmission is shifted into a drive gear. A new feature this year automatically unlocks the doors when the transmission is shifted into park. The bulk of Cutlass Ciera sales are expected to be one-price Special Edition versions of the sedan and wagon that have more standard equipment and lower prices than regular S models. Buick offers a similar one-price Special wagon in California. Buick and Oldsmobile introduced these cars in the 1982 model year, so they're ancient compared to other mid-size cars. Drawbacks include old-fashioned styling, dated interior design, and mediocre ride and handling. In addition, the suspension allows too much bouncing and body lean. However, they have good acceleration with the V-6, ample passenger and cargo room, and a standard driver-side air bag and anti-lock brakes—all at reasonable prices.

Buick Century prices are on page 251;
Oldsmobile Cutlass Ciera prices are on page 395.

BUICK CENTURY SPECIAL

Rating Guide	1	2	3	4	5
Performance					
Acceleration	▓▓▓▓▓▓▓░				
Economy	▓▓▓▓░				
Driveability	▓▓▓▓▓▓▓▓				
Ride	▓▓▓▓▓▓▓▓				
Steering/handling	▓▓▓▓▓▓▓				
Braking	▓▓▓▓▓▓▓▓▓▓				
Noise	▓▓▓▓▓▓▓				
Accommodations					
Driver seating	▓▓▓▓▓▓				
Instruments/controls	▓▓▓▓▓▓				
Visibility	▓▓▓▓▓▓▓				
Room/comfort	▓▓▓▓▓▓▓				
Entry/exit	▓▓▓▓▓▓▓				
Cargo room	▓▓▓▓▓▓▓				
Workmanship					
Exterior	▓▓▓▓▓▓▓				
Interior	▓▓▓▓▓▓▓▓				
Value	▓▓▓▓▓▓▓				
Total Points					**58**

Specifications

Body type	4-door notchback	Engine type	ohv V-6
Wheelbase (in.)	104.9	Engine size (l/cu. in.)	3.1/191
Overall length (in.)	189.1	Horsepower @ rpm	160 @ 5200
Overall width (in.)	69.4	Torque @ rpm	185 @ 4000
Overall height (in.)	54.2	Transmission	auto/4-sp.
Curb weight (lbs.)	2974	Drive wheels	front
Seating capacity	6	Brakes, F/R	disc/disc (ABS)
Front head room (in.)	38.6	Tire size	185/75R14
Max. front leg room (in.)	42.1	Fuel tank capacity (gal.)	16.5
Rear head room (in.)	38.3	EPA city/highway mpg	19/29
Min. rear leg room (in.)	35.9	Test mileage (mpg)	NA
Cargo volume (cu. ft.)	16.2		

Warranties The entire car is covered for 3 years/36,000 miles. Body perforation rust is covered for 6 years/100,000 miles.

Rating scale 5=Exceptional; 4=Above average; 3=Average; 2=Below average; 1=Poor

BUICK LE SABRE/ RECOMMENDED
OLDSMOBILE EIGHTY EIGHT

Built in Flint, Mich., and Wentzville, Mo.

Buick LeSabre Limited

FULL-SIZE

A passenger-side air bag is a new standard feature as the major change for LeSabre and Eighty Eight, full-size cars that are built from the same design but have different styling and interior features. The similar Pontiac Bonneville also gets the passenger-side air bag (see separate report). A driver-side air bag has been standard on these cars since 1992 and anti-lock brakes were made standard on all models last year. The Eighty Eight gets a new dashboard this year that has a more compact control layout and far fewer buttons than the previous one. Both LeSabre and Eighty Eight come only as 4-door sedans with a 170-horsepower 3.8-liter V-6 engine and a 4-speed electronic automatic transmission. LeSabre comes in Custom and Limited price levels, and as a one-price ($19,995) Custom in California. The Eighty Eight lineup includes a base sedan, a more-luxurious LS version, and one-price Special Edition versions of both that are available nationally. The $19,995 Special Edition has more standard features than the base sedan yet is priced nearly $1500 less. There also are specially equipped California versions of the base Eighty Eight and a sporty LSS model. We still rate these cars highly, though they have been eclipsed by the Chrysler LH sedans (Chrysler Concorde, Dodge Intrepid, and Eagle Vision) in overall execution. GM's full-size front-drive sedans are still good choices, especially the one-price models. You can buy a fully-equipped Eighty Eight Special Edition, for example, for thousands less than a loaded Toyota Camry, a compact sedan.

Buick LeSabre prices are on page 253;
Oldsmobile Eighty Eight prices are on page 400.

BUICK LE SABRE

Rating Guide	1	2	3	4	5

Performance

Acceleration	▮▮▮▮▮ (5)
Economy	▮▮ (2)
Driveability	▮▮▮▮▮ (5)
Ride	▮▮▮▮▮ (5)
Steering/handling	▮▮▮ (3)
Braking	▮▮▮▮▮ (5)
Noise	▮▮▮▮ (4)

Accommodations

Driver seating	▮▮▮▮ (4)
Instruments/controls	▮▮▮▮ (4)
Visibility	▮▮▮▮ (4)
Room/comfort	▮▮▮▮ (4)
Entry/exit	▮▮▮▮ (4)
Cargo room	▮▮▮▮ (4)

Workmanship

Exterior	▮▮▮▮▮ (5)
Interior	▮▮▮▮ (4)

Value ▮▮▮▮ (4)

Total Points......63

Specifications

Body type	4-door notchback
Wheelbase (in.)	110.8
Overall length (in.)	200.0
Overall width (in.)	73.6
Overall height (in.)	55.7
Curb weight (lbs.)	3449
Seating capacity	6
Front head room (in.)	38.8
Max. front leg room (in.)	42.5
Rear head room (in.)	37.8
Min. rear leg room (in.)	40.4
Cargo volume (cu. ft.)	17.1
Engine type	ohv V-6
Engine size (l/cu. in.)	3.8/231
Horsepower @ rpm	170 @ 4800
Torque @ rpm	225 @ 3200
Transmission	auto/4-sp.
Drive wheels	front
Brakes, F/R	disc/drum (ABS)
Tire size	205/70R14
Fuel tank capacity (gal.)	18.0
EPA city/highway mpg	19/28
Test mileage (mpg)	19.3

Warranties The entire car is covered for 3 years/36,000 miles. Body perforation rust is covered for 6 years/100,000 miles.

Rating scale 5=Exceptional; 4=Above average; 3=Average; 2=Below average; 1=Poor

BUICK PARK AVENUE/ OLDSMOBILE NINETY EIGHT

Built in Wentzville, Mo., and Orion, Mich.

Buick Park Avenue Ultra

PREMIUM SEDAN

These similar front-drive luxury sedans gain a standard passenger-side air bag and 20 horsepower for their optional supercharged engine. A driver-side air bag and anti-lock brakes have been standard on Park Avenue and Ninety Eight since they were redesigned for the 1991 model year. Along with the passenger-side air bag, the Ninety Eight has a new dashboard. These cars are built from the same design but have different styling and interior features. Park Avenue returns in base and Ultra price levels. Oldsmobile has dropped its Touring Sedan model, leaving base Regency and more-expensive Elite models. In addition, there are a one-price ($24,999) California model and a one-price ($24,995) Special Edition available in other states. A 170-horsepower 3.8-liter V-6 engine and 4-speed electronic automatic are standard on all models except the Park Avenue Ultra. The supercharged 3.8-liter V-6, standard on the Ultra and optional on the Elite, gains 20 horsepower and 15 pounds/feet of torque from changes to the supercharger and induction system. Though we prefer the Park Avenue's exterior styling, we think the Ninety Eight's new dashboard is a huge improvement in ergonomics over the previous one, and more convenient than Buick's. The base engine provides strong performance, but the 225 horsepower supercharged engine provides a big improvement in acceleration. Step on the gas and there's an instant and satisfying response from the engine. Unfortunately, the supercharged engine uses more gas and requires more-expensive premium fuel.

Buick Park Avenue prices are on page 254;
Oldsmobile Ninety Eight prices are on page 402.

BUICK PARK AVENUE ULTRA

Rating Guide	1	2	3	4	5
Performance					
Acceleration	▓▓▓▓▓▓▓▓▓▓▓▓▓▓▓▓▓▓▓				
Economy	▓▓▓▓▓				
Driveability	▓▓▓▓▓▓▓▓▓▓▓▓▓▓▓				
Ride	▓▓▓▓▓▓▓				
Steering/handling	▓▓▓▓▓▓▓▓▓▓				
Braking	▓▓▓▓▓▓▓▓▓▓				
Noise	▓▓▓▓▓▓▓▓				
Accommodations					
Driver seating	▓▓▓▓▓▓▓▓▓▓				
Instruments/controls	▓▓▓▓▓▓▓▓▓▓				
Visibility	▓▓▓▓▓▓▓▓				
Room/comfort	▓▓▓▓▓▓▓▓▓▓				
Entry/exit	▓▓▓▓▓▓▓▓▓▓				
Cargo room	▓▓▓▓▓▓▓▓				
Workmanship					
Exterior	▓▓▓▓▓▓▓▓▓▓▓▓▓▓▓▓▓▓▓				
Interior	▓▓▓▓▓▓▓▓▓▓▓▓				
Value	▓▓▓▓▓▓▓▓▓				

Total Points...63

Specifications

Body type ....4-door notchback
Wheelbase (in.) 110.8
Overall length (in.) 205.3
Overall width (in.) 73.6
Overall height (in.) 55.1
Curb weight (lbs.) 3536
Seating capacity 6
Front head room (in.) 38.8
Max. front leg room (in.) 42.7
Rear head room (in.) 37.8
Min. rear leg room (in.) 40.7
Cargo volume (cu. ft.).............20.3

Engine ......Supercharged ohv V-6
Engine size (l/cu. in.).........3.8/231
Horsepower @ rpm ...225 @ 5000
Torque @ rpm ....275 @ 3200
Transmission ....auto/4-sp.
Drive wheels ....front
Brakes, F/R ....disc/drum (ABS)
Tire size 215/70R15
Fuel tank capacity (gal.) 18.0
EPA city/highway mpg 17/27
Test mileage (mpg) 19.8

Warranties The entire car is covered for 3 years/36,000 miles. Body perforation rust is covered for 6 years/100,000 miles.

Rating scale 5=Exceptional; 4=Above average; 3=Average; 2=Below average; 1=Poor

BUICK REGAL

Built in Canada.

Buick Regal Gran Sport 4-door

MID-SIZE

A driver-side air bag is a new standard feature on Regal, a front-drive mid-size car that returns in 2- and 4-door styling. Regal previously met the federal requirement for passive restraints with automatic front seat belts, which are retained for 1994. Anti-lock brakes are now standard instead of optional on the base Custom model. They already were standard on the Limited and Gran Sport models. The Custom and Gran Sport come in both body styles and the Limited only as a 4-door sedan. In addition, there are one-price versions of both body styles available in California. The base engine this year is a new 160-horsepower 3.1-liter V-6, which replaces a 140-horsepower V-6 of the same size. A 170-horsepower 3.8-liter V-6 is standard on the Limited and Gran Sport, and optional on the Custom. Both engines come with an electronic 4-speed automatic transmission. The standard power locks have a new feature that automatically unlocks them when the transmission is shifted into park. Regal is built from the same design as the Chevrolet Lumina, Oldsmobile Cutlass Supreme, and Pontiac Grand Prix. Each car has its own styling and interior features. Regal is the only one of this group to offer the 3.8-liter V-6. This year's revamped 3.1-liter V-6 is not only stronger but also smoother and quieter than last year's. We still prefer the 3.8-liter V-6, which delivers strong acceleration and swift, safe passing. Though Regal is more appealing this year with the addition of a standard driver-side air bag, there are several rivals with dual air bags, including the new Honda Accord and the Ford Taurus.

Buick Regal prices are on page 256.

BUICK REGAL GRAN SPORT

Rating Guide	1	2	3	4	5
Performance					
Acceleration	▓▓▓▓▓▓▓▓▓▓▓▓▓▓▓▓▓░				
Economy	▓▓▓▓▓░				
Driveability	▓▓▓▓▓▓▓▓▓▓▓▓▓▓▓▓▓▓▓				
Ride	▓▓▓▓▓▓▓▓▓▓▓░				
Steering/handling	▓▓▓▓▓▓▓▓▓▓▓▓░				
Braking	▓▓▓▓▓▓▓▓▓▓▓▓▓▓▓▓▓				
Noise	▓▓▓▓▓▓▓▓▓▓▓░				
Accommodations					
Driver seating	▓▓▓▓▓▓▓▓▓▓▓▓▓▓				
Instruments/controls	▓▓▓▓▓▓▓▓▓▓▓▓				
Visibility	▓▓▓▓▓▓▓▓▓▓▓▓▓				
Room/comfort	▓▓▓▓▓▓▓▓▓▓▓▓▓				
Entry/exit	▓▓▓▓▓▓▓▓▓▓▓▓▓▓				
Cargo room	▓▓▓▓▓▓▓▓▓▓▓░				
Workmanship					
Exterior	▓▓▓▓▓▓▓▓▓▓▓▓▓				
Interior	▓▓▓▓▓▓▓▓▓▓▓▓▓				
Value	▓▓▓▓▓▓▓▓▓▓▓░				

Total Points...**58**

Specifications

Body type ....4-door notchback	Engine type......................ohv V-6
Wheelbase (in.) 107.5	Engine size (l/cu. in.).........3.8/231
Overall length (in.)................194.8	Horsepower @ rpm ...170 @ 4800
Overall width (in.) 72.5	Torque @ rpm ....225 @ 3200
Overall height (in.) 54.5	Transmission.................auto/4-sp.
Curb weight (lbs.) 3340	Drive wheels ....front
Seating capacity......................5	Brakes, F/R..........disc/disc (ABS)
Front head room (in.) 38.5	Tire size 225/60R16
Max. front leg room (in.) 42.4	Fuel tank capacity (gal.) 16.5
Rear head room (in.) 37.8	EPA city/highway mpg 19/28
Min. rear leg room (in.)...........36.2	Test mileage (mpg) 17.3
Cargo volume (cu. ft.).............15.9	

Warranties The entire car is covered for 3 years/36,000 miles. Body perforation rust is covered for 6 years/100,000 miles.

Rating scale 5=Exceptional; 4=Above average; 3=Average; 2=Below average; 1=Poor

CADILLAC DE VILLE/ ——
CONCOURS

Built in Hamtramck, Mich.

Cadillac De Ville Concours

PREMIUM SEDAN

Cadillac's best-selling model has been redesigned for 1994 and comes in two distinct versions. The base model is called Sedan de Ville and the top-of-the line version is called De Ville Concours. Both are 4-door sedans built on the same front-drive platform used for the Cadillac Seville, but the wheelbase has been stretched from 111 inches to 113.8 on the De Ville models. Concours comes with two features that weren't offered on last year's models—Cadillac's 4.6-liter Northstar engine and Road Sensing Suspension (RSS). The Northstar, which has dual overhead camshafts, is rated at 270 horsepower in the Concours. RSS is a computer-controlled suspension that adjusts firmness in milliseconds based on vehicle speed and road conditions. The Sedan de Ville comes with a 200-horsepower 4.9-liter V-8, an overhead-valve engine used in last year's models, and Speed Sensitive Suspension, which adjusts suspension firmness to one of three levels based on vehicle speed. Cadillac says the dual front air bags standard on the 1994 models are designed to protect three front-seat occupants. Though the new De Ville's styling is conservative in the Cadillac tradition, the 1994 models boast substantial improvements over the previous generation. The Concours has the more impressive performance, thanks to the potent, smooth Northstar engine and sophisticated RSS. However, the Sedan de Ville is a bargain in the luxury sedan field. The base price of $32,990 is unchanged from last year even with the addition of new standard features such as a passenger-side air bag and a remote keyless entry system.

Cadillac De Ville/Concours prices are on page 263.

CADILLAC DE VILLE CONCOURS

Rating Guide	1	2	3	4	5
Performance					
Acceleration					
Economy					
Driveability					
Ride					
Steering/handling					
Braking					
Noise					
Accommodations					
Driver seating					
Instruments/controls					
Visibility					
Room/comfort					
Entry/exit					
Cargo room					
Workmanship					
Exterior					
Interior					
Value					

Total Points...**64**

Specifications

Body type ....4-door notchback	Engine type....................dohc V-8
Wheelbase (in.) 113.8	Engine size (l/cu. in.)........4.6/279
Overall length (in.)................209.2	Horsepower @ rpm ...270 @ 5600
Overall width (in.) 76.6	Torque @ rpm ....300 @ 4000
Overall height (in.)..................56.3	Transmission.................auto/4-sp.
Curb weight (lbs.) 3758	Drive wheels ....front
Seating capacity.........................6	Brakes, F/R..........disc/disc (ABS)
Front head room (in.) 38.5	Tire size 225/60HR16
Max. front leg room (in.) 42.6	Fuel tank capacity (gal.) 20.0
Rear head room (in.) 38.4	EPA city/highway mpg 16/25
Min. rear leg room (in.)...........43.3	Test mileage (mpg) ....NA
Cargo volume (cu. ft.).............20.0	

Warranties The entire car is covered for 4 years/50,000 miles. Body perforation rust is covered for 6 years/100,000 miles.

Rating scale 5=Exceptional; 4=Above average; 3=Average; 2=Below average; 1=Poor

CADILLAC FLEETWOOD

Built in Arlington, Tex.

Cadillac Fleetwood

PREMIUM SEDAN

Fleetwood, Cadillac's rear-drive sedan, has a new standard engine, a 260-horsepower 5.7-liter V-8. It is based on the LT1 V-8 used in the Chevrolet Corvette. Among new features on Cadillac's version is sequential fuel injection with one injector for each cylinder. The LT1 replaces a 180-horsepower 5.7-liter V-8 that had one injector mounted on the intake manifold. Fleetwood also has a new transmission, a 4-speed automatic with electronic shift controls that replaces a hydraulically controlled 4-speed automatic. The new 5.7-liter engine also is standard this year on the Buick Roadmaster and optional on the Chevrolet Caprice. Fleetwood was redesigned last year, when it gained standard traction control, anti-lock brakes, and dual air bags. At 225 inches overall, it is the longest production car built in the U.S. It comes only as a 4-door sedan. The LT1 V-8 makes the 1994 model a much fleeter Fleetwood. The new engine provides quick takeoffs and delivers strong passing power with only a little more pressure on the gas pedal. Cadillac claims that 60 mph can be reached in just 8.5 seconds this year, two seconds faster than last year. We haven't had a chance to measure fuel economy but we imagine it will be as bad as before—maybe worse. We averaged just 14.8 mpg with a 1993 model from urban driving. Cadillac has updated its rear-drive sedan considerably over the past two years with fresher styling, air bags, and more power. Though it's still too big and clumsy for our tastes, it's now a much better car and a good choice over the rival Lincoln Town Car. The best news is that the base price of $33,990 is unchanged from 1993.

Cadillac Fleetwood prices are on page 265.

CADILLAC FLEETWOOD

Rating Guide	1	2	3	4	5
Performance					
Acceleration	‖‖‖‖‖‖‖‖‖‖‖‖‖‖‖‖‖‖‖‖‖‖‖‖‖‖‖‖‖‖				
Economy	‖‖‖‖‖‖‖‖‖				
Driveability	‖‖‖‖‖‖‖‖‖‖‖‖‖‖‖‖‖‖‖‖‖‖‖‖‖‖				
Ride	‖‖‖‖‖‖‖‖‖‖‖‖‖‖‖‖‖‖‖‖‖‖‖				
Steering/handling	‖‖‖‖‖‖‖‖‖‖‖‖‖‖‖‖‖‖‖‖‖‖‖				
Braking	‖‖‖‖‖‖‖‖‖‖‖‖‖‖‖‖‖‖‖‖‖‖‖‖‖‖				
Noise	‖‖‖‖‖‖‖‖‖‖‖‖‖‖‖‖‖‖‖‖‖‖‖				
Accommodations					
Driver seating	‖‖‖‖‖‖‖‖‖‖‖‖‖‖‖‖‖‖‖‖‖‖‖				
Instruments/controls	‖‖‖‖‖‖‖‖‖‖‖‖‖‖‖‖‖‖‖‖‖‖‖				
Visibility	‖‖‖‖‖‖‖‖‖‖‖‖‖‖‖‖‖‖‖‖‖‖‖				
Room/comfort	‖‖‖‖‖‖‖‖‖‖‖‖‖‖‖‖‖‖‖‖‖‖‖‖‖‖				
Entry/exit	‖‖‖‖‖‖‖‖‖‖‖‖‖‖‖‖‖‖‖‖‖‖‖‖‖‖				
Cargo room	‖‖‖‖‖‖‖‖‖‖‖‖‖‖‖‖‖‖‖‖‖‖‖‖‖‖				
Workmanship					
Exterior	‖‖‖‖‖‖‖‖‖‖‖‖‖‖‖‖‖‖‖‖‖‖‖				
Interior	‖‖‖‖‖‖‖‖‖‖‖‖‖‖‖‖‖‖‖‖‖‖‖				
Value	‖‖‖‖‖‖‖‖‖‖‖‖‖‖‖‖‖‖‖‖‖‖‖				
Total Points					**59**

Specifications

Body type	4-door notchback	Engine type	ohv V-8
Wheelbase (in.)	121.5	Engine size (l/cu. in.)	5.7/350
Overall length (in.)	225.0	Horsepower @ rpm	260 @ 5000
Overall width (in.)	78.0	Torque @ rpm	335 @ 2400
Overall height (in.)	57.1	Transmission	auto/4-sp.
Curb weight (lbs.)	4477	Drive wheels	rear
Seating capacity	6	Brakes, F/R	disc/drum (ABS)
Front head room (in.)	38.7	Tire size	235/70R15
Max. front leg room (in.)	42.5	Fuel tank capacity (gal.)	23.0
Rear head room (in.)	39.1	EPA city/highway mpg	17/25
Min. rear leg room (in.)	43.9	Test mileage (mpg)	NA
Cargo volume (cu. ft.)	21.1		

Warranties The entire car is covered for 4 years/50,000 miles. Body perforation rust is covered for 6 years/100,000 miles.

Rating scale 5=Exceptional; 4=Above average; 3=Average; 2=Below average; 1=Poor

CADILLAC SEVILLE/— RECOMMENDED
ELDORADO

Built in Hamtramck, Mich.

Cadillac Seville STS

PREMIUM SEDAN (Seville)/PREMIUM COUPE (Eldorado)

The Northstar V-8 engine is standard on all Seville and Eldorado models this year. Last year, the base models came with a 200-horsepower 4.9-liter overhead valve V-8. This year, they have a 270-horsepower version of the 4.6-liter Northstar, which has dual overhead camshafts. The Seville Touring Sedan (STS) and Eldorado Touring Coupe use a 295-horsepower version of the Northstar. The base Seville is called Seville Luxury Sedan (SLS) this year. Seville is a 4-door and Eldorado a 2-door coupe built from the same front-drive design but with a shorter wheelbase and different styling. Dual air bags and anti-lock brakes are standard on both. The SLS and base Eldorado also add as standard traction control and Road Sensing Suspension (RSS), which adjusts suspension firmness based on road conditions and vehicle speed. A Security Package that was optional on the base models last year is standard this year. It includes remote keyless entry, central unlocking, and a new anti-lockout feature. Seville and Eldorado are worthy alternatives to Japanese and European luxury cars. In the Seville line, last year the STS held a clear performance advantage over the base model. This year, the gap is considerably narrower. Though the STS has impressive handling, it also has stiff tires (rated for over 149 mph) that ride harshly compared to the SLS's. Though Seville's base prices have escalated to nearly $41,000 for the SLS and nearly $45,000 for the STS, that's still much less than a Lexus LS 400 or Infiniti Q45.

Cadillac Eldorado prices are on page 264;
Cadillac Seville prices are on page 266.

CADILLAC SEVILLE STS

Rating Guide	1	2	3	4	5
Performance					
Acceleration					▌
Economy	▌				
Driveability				▌	
Ride			▌		
Steering/handling				▌	
Braking					▌
Noise				▌	
Accommodations					
Driver seating				▌	
Instruments/controls			▌		
Visibility			▌		
Room/comfort				▌	
Entry/exit				▌	
Cargo room			▌		
Workmanship					
Exterior					▌
Interior				▌	
Value				▌	

Total Points..61

Specifications

Body type ....4-door notchback	Engine type.....................dohc V-8
Wheelbase (in.) 111.0	Engine size (l/cu. in.).........4.6/279
Overall length (in.)...............204.4	Horsepower @ rpm ...295 @ 6000
Overall width (in.) 74.2	Torque @ rpm ....290 @ 4400
Overall height (in.)..................54.5	Transmission.................auto/4-sp.
Curb weight (lbs.) 3830	Drive wheels ....front
Seating capacity.........................5	Brakes, F/R...........disc/disc (ABS)
Front head room (in.) 38.0	Tire size....................225/60ZR16
Max. front leg room (in.) 43.0	Fuel tank capacity (gal.) 20.0
Rear head room (in.) 38.3	EPA city/highway mpg 16/25
Min. rear leg room (in.)...........39.1	Test mileage (mpg) 16.8
Cargo volume (cu. ft.).............14.4	

Warranties The entire car is covered for 4 years/50,000 miles. Body perforation rust is covered for 6 years/100,000 miles.

Rating scale 5=Exceptional; 4=Above average; 3=Average; 2=Below average; 1=Poor

CHEVROLET BERETTA/ ——
CORSICA

Built in Wilmington, Del.

Chevrolet Beretta

SPORTS COUPE (Beretta)/COMPACT (Corsica)

Chevrolet's front-drive sports coupe and similar compact sedan get more power, a new automatic transmission, standard automatic power locks, and a new model lineup for Beretta. Corsica comes in only one trim level, while the Beretta comes in base and new Z26 versions, the latter replacing last year's GT and GTZ models. There also are one-price versions of both cars available only in California. A driver-side air bag, door-mounted front shoulder belts, and anti-lock brakes are standard across the board. Standard on Corsica and the base Beretta is a 2.2-liter 4-cylinder engine with 120 horsepower, 10 more than before. The Z26 comes standard with the Quad 4 engine, a 170-horsepower 2.3-liter dual-cam 4-cylinder. Optional on all is a new 3.1-liter V-6 with 160 horsepower, 20 more than last year's 3.1-liter. On the Beretta, the 4-cylinders come with a standard 5-speed manual. A 3-speed automatic is optional with the 2.2-liter on the Beretta and standard on the Corsica. A new electronic 4-speed automatic is the only transmission available with the V-6. The 2.2-liter 4-cylinder provides adequate but noisy acceleration, making the stronger, quieter 3.1-liter V-6 well worth the extra money. The Z26's Quad 4 engine is potent at high speeds, but it's also quite noisy and requires premium fuel, so we recommend the V-6 in that model, too. Neither car matches the tight assembly quality and refinement of Japanese rivals, but they are among the least expensive cars available with a V-6, air bag, and anti-lock brakes.

Chevrolet Beretta prices are on page 267;
Chevrolet Corsica prices are on page 274.

CHEVROLET BERETTA

Rating Guide	1	2	3	4	5
Performance					
Acceleration	▓▓▓▓▓▓▓▓▓▓▓▓▓▓				
Economy	▓▓▓▓▓▓▓				
Driveability	▓▓▓▓▓▓▓▓▓▓				
Ride	▓▓▓▓▓▓▓▓				
Steering/handling	▓▓▓▓▓▓▓▓▓▓▓▓				
Braking	▓▓▓▓▓▓▓▓▓▓▓▓▓▓▓▓▓				
Noise	▓▓▓▓▓▓▓▓▓				
Accommodations					
Driver seating	▓▓▓▓▓▓▓▓▓▓▓▓				
Instruments/controls	▓▓▓▓▓▓▓▓				
Visibility	▓▓▓▓▓▓▓▓▓▓▓▓				
Room/comfort	▓▓▓▓▓▓▓▓▓▓				
Entry/exit	▓▓▓▓▓▓▓▓▓▓				
Cargo room	▓▓▓▓▓▓▓▓▓▓				
Workmanship					
Exterior	▓▓▓▓▓▓▓▓▓▓▓▓▓▓				
Interior	▓▓▓▓▓▓▓▓▓▓				
Value	▓▓▓▓▓▓▓▓				

Total Points...**54**

Specifications

Body type ....2-door notchback	Engine type........................ohv V-6
Wheelbase (in.) 103.4	Engine size (l/cu. in.)..........3.1/191
Overall length (in.)................183.4	Horsepower @ rpm ...160 @ 5200
Overall width (in.) 68.2	Torque @ rpm ....185 @ 4000
Overall height (in.)..................56.2	Transmission................auto/4-sp.
Curb weight (lbs.) 2649	Drive wheels ....front
Seating capacity..........................5	Brakes, F/R ....disc/drum (ABS)
Front head room (in.) 38.1	Tire size 205/60R15
Max. front leg room (in.) 43.4	Fuel tank capacity (gal.) 15.6
Rear head room (in.) 37.4	EPA city/highway mpg 21/29
Min. rear leg room (in.)...........35.0	Test mileage (mpg) ....NA
Cargo volume (cu. ft.).............13.4	

Warranties The entire car is covered for 3 years/36,000 miles. Body perforation rust is covered for 6 years/100,000 miles.

Rating scale 5=Exceptional; 4=Above average; 3=Average; 2=Below average; 1=Poor

CHEVROLET CAMARO/
PONTIAC FIREBIRD `RECOMMENDED`

Built in Canada.

Chevrolet Camaro Z28 3-door

SPORTS AND GT

The 1994 versions of the rear-drive Camaro and Firebird get revised transmissions, an optional traction-control system, and a new convertible body style. The Camaro convertible went on sale in late fall and the Firebird ragtop is supposed to arrive in the spring. Dual air bags and anti-lock brakes are standard across the board. The Camaro 3-door hatchback and convertible are available in base and high-performance Z28 trim. Firebird comes in base, Formula, Trans Am, and new Trans Am GT models. Base models of both cars use a 160-horsepower 3.4-liter V-6. All others have a 275-horsepower 5.7-liter V-8 that requires premium fuel. A 5-speed manual transmission is standard with the V-6. The 6-speed manual standard with the V-8 gains Computer-Aided Gear Selection, which forces a first-to-fourth-gear shift under light acceleration. Optional with both engines is an electronic 4-speed automatic. Traction control is due as a midyear option for V-8s with automatic. The V-8 models offer great acceleration with either transmission, though we'll welcome the optional traction control for driving in rain and snow. Handling is of a high order, but V-8 models ride stiffly with the optional Z-rated tires. These cars are impractical as ever. Front passenger foot space is scarce, the rear seats suit only children, and cargo space is barely adequate. These cars offer lots of performance, style, and standard safety features at reasonable prices but can be costly to insure. See our report on the arch rival Ford Mustang; which has been redesigned.

Chevrolet Camaro prices are on page 269;
Pontiac Firebird prices are on page 418.

CHEVROLET CAMARO Z28

Rating Guide	1	2	3	4	5
Performance					
Acceleration	▓▓▓▓▓▓▓▓▓▓▓▓▓▓▓▓▓▓▓▓▓▓▓▓
Economy	▓▓▓▓▓▓
Driveability	▓▓▓▓▓▓▓▓▓▓▓▓▓▓▓
Ride	▓▓▓▓▓▓▓▓▓
Steering/handling	▓▓▓▓▓▓▓▓▓▓▓▓
Braking	▓▓▓▓▓▓▓▓▓▓▓▓▓▓▓▓▓▓▓▓▓▓▓▓
Noise	▓▓▓▓▓▓▓▓▓
Accommodations					
Driver seating	▓▓▓▓▓▓▓▓▓▓▓▓▓▓▓
Instruments/controls	▓▓▓▓▓▓▓▓▓▓▓▓▓▓▓▓▓
Visibility	▓▓▓▓▓▓▓▓▓
Room/comfort	▓▓▓▓▓▓▓▓▓
Entry/exit	▓▓▓▓▓▓▓▓▓
Cargo room	▓▓▓▓▓▓▓▓▓▓▓▓
Workmanship					
Exterior	▓▓▓▓▓▓▓▓▓▓▓▓
Interior	▓▓▓▓▓▓▓▓▓▓▓▓
Value	▓▓▓▓▓▓▓▓▓▓▓▓

Total Points..53

Specifications

Body type	3-door hatchback	Engine type	ohv V-8
Wheelbase (in.)	101.1	Engine size (l/cu. in.)	5.7/350
Overall length (in.)	193.2	Horsepower @ rpm	275 @ 5000
Overall width (in.)	74.1	Torque @ rpm	325 @ 2400
Overall height (in.)	51.3	Transmission	auto/4-sp.
Curb weight (lbs.)	3373	Drive wheels	rear
Seating capacity	4	Brakes, F/R	disc/disc (ABS)
Front head room (in.)	37.2	Tire size	245/50ZR16
Max. front leg room (in.)	43.0	Fuel tank capacity (gal.)	15.5
Rear head room (in.)	35.3	EPA city/highway mpg	17/24
Min. rear leg room (in.)	26.8	Test mileage (mpg)	17.4
Cargo volume (cu. ft.)	12.9		

Warranties The entire car is covered for 3 years/36,000 miles. Body perforation rust is covered for 6 years/100,000 miles.

Rating scale 5=Exceptional; 4=Above average; 3=Average; 2=Below average; 1=Poor

CHEVROLET CAPRICE/———
BUICK ROADMASTER

Built in Arlington, Tex.

Chevrolet Caprice Classic 4-door

FULL-SIZE

Caprice and Roadmaster share their rear-drive chassis, though they differ in styling and interior features. For 1994, both get a passenger-side air bag to complement the previously standard driver-side air bag. Anti-lock brakes also are standard. Both also get new engines, restyled interiors, and General Motors' Pass-Key II theft-deterrent system as a new standard feature. Standard on the Roadmaster and optional on the Caprice is the LT1 engine, a 5.7-liter V-8 with 260 horsepower, 80 more than last year's 5.7-liter. Caprice's standard engine is a new 4.3-liter V-8 that produces 200 horsepower. A new 4-speed electronic automatic is the only transmission offered. Both Caprice and Roadmaster come in 4-door sedan and 5-door wagon body styles. Later in the year, a new Impala SS is due to join the Caprice line, resurrecting a name used on performance Chevys during the 1960s. Both V-8s are smooth, strong performers. They're thirsty around town but get decent mileage out on the open road. Base suspensions are relatively soft, though firm enough that these full-size cars aren't bouncing all over the road. All have cavernous interiors with room for six in the sedans and eight in the Caprice wagon, though the passengers in the middle must straddle a driveline hump. Overall, we prefer GM's front-drive full-size cars, but none offers a station wagon and they can't match the 5000-pound towing capacity of the Caprice and Roadmaster. The only full-size, rear-drive alternatives are the Ford Crown Victoria and Mercury Grand Marquis sedans.

Buick Roadmaster prices are on page 259;
Chevrolet Caprice prices are on page 270.

CHEVROLET CAPRICE CLASSIC

Rating Guide	1	2	3	4	5
Performance					
Acceleration	||||||||||||||||||||||||||||||||||||||||||||||||| |||||| |||||| |||||| ||||||
Economy	||||||||||||||||||||||||				
Driveability	|||||||||||||||||||||||||||||||||||||||| ||||||		
Ride	||||||||||||||||||||||||||||||||||||			
Steering/handling	||||||||||||||||||||||||||||||||||||||||			
Braking	||||||||||||||||||||||||||||||||||||||||			
Noise	||||||||||||||||||||||||||||||||			
Accommodations					
Driver seating	||||||||||||||||||||||||||||||||||||||||			
Instruments/controls	||||||||||||||||||||||||||||||||||||||||			
Visibility	||||||||||||||||||||||||||||||||||||||||			
Room/comfort	|||||||||||||||||||||||||||||||||||||||||||||||||||		
Entry/exit	|||||||||||||||||||||||||||||||||||||||||||||||||||		
Cargo room	||||||||||||||||||||||||||||||||||||||||			
Workmanship					
Exterior	||||||||||||||||||||||||||||||||||||||||			
Interior	||||||||||||||||||||||||||||||||||||||||			
Value	||||||||||||||||||||||||||||||||			

Total Points...61

Specifications

Body type ....4-door notchback	Engine type......................ohv V-8
Wheelbase (in.) 115.9	Engine size (l/cu. in.).........5.7/350
Overall length (in.)................214.1	Horsepower @ rpm ...260 @ 5000
Overall width (in.) 77.0	Torque @ rpm ....330 @ 3200
Overall height (in.)..................55.7	Transmission.................auto/4-sp.
Curb weight (lbs.) 4036	Drive wheels ....rear
Seating capacity.........................6	Brakes, F/R...........disc/disc (ABS)
Front head room (in.) 39.2	Tire size.....................195/60VR14
Max. front leg room (in.).........42.2	Fuel tank capacity (gal.) 13.2
Rear head room (in.) 39.7	EPA city/highway mpg 17/25
Min. rear leg room (in.)...........39.5	Test mileage (mpg) 25.7
Cargo volume (cu. ft.).............20.4	

Warranties The entire car is covered for 3 years/36,000 miles. Body per-foration rust is covered for 6 years/100,000 miles.

Rating scale 5=Exceptional; 4=Above average; 3=Average; 2=Below average; 1=Poor

CHEVROLET CAVALIER/———
PONTIAC SUNBIRD

Built in Lordstown, Ohio.

Chevrolet Cavalier VL 2-door

SUBCOMPACT

The front-drive Cavalier and Sunbird see only minor revisions for 1994 because redesigned models are due next year. Cavalier gains a stronger base engine and a new unlock feature for its standard automatic door locks. Sunbird also gets the unlock feature and loses some models, while the remaining ones gain standard equipment. Cavalier comes in four body styles: 2-door coupe in VL, RS, and Z24 trim; 4-door sedan in VL and RS trim; 5-door wagon in base trim; and convertible in RS and Z24 trim. Sunbird comes in the same body styles except the wagon. Sunbird comes in LE trim in all three body styles and in SE trim as a coupe. Cavalier and Sunbird have standard anti-lock brakes and door-mounted front seat belts that can be left buckled to automatically deploy when the doors are closed. The standard engine for VL and RS Cavaliers is a 2.2-liter 4-cylinder with 120 horsepower, 10 more than in 1993. All Sunbirds but the SE come with a 110-horsepower 2.0-liter 4-cylinder. A 140-horsepower 3.1-liter V-6 is standard on the Cavalier Z24 and Sunbird SE and optional on all others but the Cavalier VL. A 5-speed manual transmission is standard on all except the Cavalier RS sedan, RS convertible, and wagon. They come with a 3-speed automatic that's optional on all other Cavaliers and Sunbirds. Cavalier and Sunbird are ancient cars introduced in 1982—and it shows. They survive by offering great value for the money. Most competitors are more refined and have at least a driver-side air bag, but few offer anti-lock brakes at such a low price.

Chevrolet Cavalier prices are on page 273;
Pontiac Sunbird prices are on page 424.

CHEVROLET CAVALIER VL

Rating Guide	1	2	3	4	5
Performance					
Acceleration	||||||||||||||||||||||||||||||||		
Economy	|||||||||||||||||||||||||||||||||||||||		
Driveability	||||||||||||||||||||||||||||		
Ride	||||||||||||||||||||||||||||		
Steering/handling	||||||||||||||||||||||||||||		
Braking	|||||||||||||||||||||||||||||||||||||||||||||||	
Noise	||||||||||||||||||||||||			
Accommodations					
Driver seating	||||||||||||||||||||||||||||		
Instruments/controls	||||||||||||||||||||||||||||		
Visibility	|||||||||||||||||||||||||||||||||||||||||||||||	
Room/comfort	||||||||||||||||||||||||||||		
Entry/exit	||||||||||||||||||||||||||||		
Cargo room	||||||||||||||||||||||||||||		
Workmanship					
Exterior	|||||||||||||||||||||||||||||||||||||||		
Interior	||||||||||||||||||||||||||||		
Value	|||||||||||||||||||||||||||||||||||||||		
Total Points					**54**

Specifications

Body type ....2-door notchback	Engine type ....ohv I-4
Wheelbase (in.) 101.3	Engine size (l/cu. in.)........2.2/133
Overall length (in.)................182.3	Horsepower @ rpm ...120 @ 5200
Overall width (in.) 66.3	Torque @ rpm ....130 @ 4000
Overall height (in.)..................52.0	Transmission ....manual/5-sp.
Curb weight (lbs.)..................2509	Drive wheels ....front
Seating capacity...........................5	Brakes, F/R ....disc/drum (ABS)
Front head room (in.) 37.8	Tire size 185/75R14
Max. front leg room (in.).........42.6	Fuel tank capacity (gal.) 15.2
Rear head room (in.) 36.1	EPA city/highway mpg 25/36
Min. rear leg room (in.)...........31.2	Test mileage (mpg) ....NA
Cargo volume (cu. ft.).............13.2	

Warranties The entire car is covered for 3 years/36,000 miles. Body perforation rust is covered for 6 years/100,000 miles.

Rating scale 5=Exceptional; 4=Above average; 3=Average; 2=Below average; 1=Poor

CHEVROLET CORVETTE

Built in Bowling Green, Ky.

Chevrolet Corvette convertible

SPORTS AND GT

A passenger-side air bag joins a driver-side air bag in this 2-seat, rear-drive sports car. Corvette comes in hatchback and convertible body styles. Standard engine remains the 300-horsepower 5.7-liter LT1 V-8, offered with a choice of 4-speed automatic or 6-speed manual transmissions at the same price. Optional on coupes is the ZR-1 package, which includes a 405-horsepower 5.7-liter V-8 with dual overhead camshafts, the LT5. It comes only with the 6-speed manual. Anti-lock disc brakes and Acceleration Slip Regulation, a traction control system, are standard, as is leather upholstery. Other changes include a standard heated glass rear window for the convertible, which previously had a plastic rear window. There are softer springs for the Selective Ride Control system, an adjustable suspension that's optional on the base coupe and convertible and included in the ZR-1 equipment. The ZR-1 also gets new 5-spoke aluminum wheels. Corvette has become more civilized in recent years. Suspensions no longer jar your teeth over bumps and improved assembly quality has reduced rattles and squeaks. The addition of standard traction control is a big help in wet-weather driving. Ingress/egress is still awkward, primarily due to the low seating position, high door sills. and protruding dash. However, Corvette handles like a race car and boasts magnificent acceleration. There's a performance advantage with the ZR-1 package but not enough to justify its stiff price. Though rivals such as the Nissan 300ZX Turbo and Toyota Supra Turbo are more refined, they don't match the 'Vette's macho flavor.

Chevrolet Corvette prices are on page 275.

CHEVROLET CORVETTE CONVERTIBLE

Rating Guide	1	2	3	4	5
Performance					
Acceleration	▮▮▮▮▮				■
Economy	▮▮				
Driveability	▮▮▮▮				
Ride	▮▮▮				
Steering/handling	▮▮▮▮▮				
Braking	▮▮▮▮				
Noise	▮▮▮				
Accommodations					
Driver seating	▮▮▮▮				
Instruments/controls	▮▮▮▮				
Visibility	▮▮▮				
Room/comfort	▮▮▮▮				
Entry/exit	▮▮				
Cargo room	▮▮				
Workmanship					
Exterior	▮▮▮▮				
Interior	▮▮▮▮				
Value	▮▮▮				
Total Points **47**					

Specifications

Body type ....2-door convertible	Engine type ....ohv V-8
Wheelbase (in.) 96.2	Engine size (l/cu. in.).........5.7/350
Overall length (in.)................178.5	Horsepower @ rpm ...300 @ 5000
Overall width (in.) 70.7	Torque @ rpm ....340 @ 3600
Overall height (in.) 47.3	Transmission ....auto/4-sp.
Curb weight (lbs.) 3383	Drive wheels ....rear
Seating capacity 2	Brakes, F/R ....disc/disc (ABS)
Front head room (in.) 36.5	Tire size....................285/40ZR17
Max. front leg room (in.) 42.0	Fuel tank capacity (gal.) 20.0
Rear head room (in.) ....—	EPA city/highway mpg 17/24
Min. rear leg room (in.) ....—	Test mileage (mpg) 16.6
Cargo volume (cu. ft.)...............6.6	

Warranties The entire car is covered for 3 years/36,000 miles. Body perforation rust is covered for 6 years/100,000 miles.

Rating scale 5=Exceptional; 4=Above average; 3=Average; 2=Below average; 1=Poor

CHEVROLET LUMINA

Built in Canada.

Chevrolet Lumina Euro 3.4 Sedan

MID-SIZE Similar to Buick Regal, Oldsmobile Cutlass Supreme, and Pontiac Grand Prix

The mid-size front-wheel-drive Lumina sees few changes this fall because a replacement is due in the spring. The current version has door-mounted front seat belts that can be left buckled to automatically deploy when the doors are closed. Its siblings at Buick, Olds, and Pontiac get a standard driver-side air bag for 1994, and the Grand Prix also gets a passenger-side air bag. The redesigned Lumina, due as an early 1995 model, is expected to have dual air bags and new styling. Lumina returns for 1994 as a 2-door coupe and a 4-door sedan. The base coupe has been dropped, leaving Euro and Z34 coupes. The sedan continues in base and Euro models. Standard on the base sedan and Euro models is a 140-horsepower 3.1-liter V-6. A 210-horsepower 3.4-liter V-6 with dual overhead camshafts is standard on the Z34 coupe and included in the Euro 3.4 Sedan option package. The only transmission offered is a new electronic 4-speed automatic. Anti-lock brakes are standard on all Luminas except the base sedan, where they are optional. Standard power door locks automatically lock all doors when the transmission is shifted out of park. They must be unlocked manually. Lumina is competitive in price with the Ford Taurus and other mid-size rivals, but the absence of air bags is a drawback and the dashboard is poorly laid out. Acceleration is adequate with the 3.1-liter V-6 and brisk with the 3.4-liter. Chevy is offering California buyers a special "value-priced" Lumina Euro Sedan. We think your best bet is to wait a few months for the redesigned 1995 model.

Chevrolet Lumina prices are on page 276.

CHEVROLET LUMINA EURO 3.4 SEDAN

Rating Guide	1	2	3	4	5
Performance					
Acceleration	▓	▓	▓	▓	▓
Economy	▓	▓			
Driveability	▓	▓	▓	▓	
Ride	▓	▓	▓		
Steering/handling	▓	▓	▓	▓	
Braking	▓	▓	▓	▓	▓
Noise	▓	▓	▓		
Accommodations					
Driver seating	▓	▓	▓	▓	
Instruments/controls	▓	▓	▓	▓	
Visibility	▓	▓	▓	▓	
Room/comfort	▓	▓	▓	▓	
Entry/exit	▓	▓	▓	▓	
Cargo room	▓	▓	▓	▓	
Workmanship					
Exterior	▓	▓	▓		
Interior	▓	▓	▓		
Value	▓	▓	▓		

Total Points...59

Specifications

Body type ....4-door notchback	Engine type.....................dohc V-6
Wheelbase (in.) 107.5	Engine size (l/cu. in.).........3.4/207
Overall length (in.)................198.3	Horsepower @ rpm ...210 @ 5200
Overall width (in.) 71.0	Torque @ rpm ....215 @ 4000
Overall height (in.) 53.6	Transmission.................auto/4-sp.
Curb weight (lbs.) 3516	Drive wheels ....front
Seating capacity.........................5	Brakes, F/R...........disc/disc (ABS)
Front head room (in.) 38.7	Tire size 215/60R16
Max. front leg room (in.) 42.4	Fuel tank capacity (gal.).........17.1
Rear head room (in.) 38.0	EPA city/highway mpg 17/26
Min. rear leg room (in.)...........36.9	Test mileage (mpg) 17.2
Cargo volume (cu. ft.).............15.7	

Warranties The entire car is covered for 3 years/36,000 miles. Body perforation rust is covered for 6 years/100,000 miles.

Rating scale 5=Exceptional; 4=Above average; 3=Average; 2=Below average; 1=Poor

CHEVROLET LUMINA— BUDGET BUY
MINIVAN/OLDSMOBILE
SILHOUETTE/PONTIAC
TRANS SPORT

Built in Tarrytown, N.Y.

Chevrolet Lumina Minivan LS

MINIVAN

The Lumina Minivan (formerly called APV) and Trans Sport have shorter noses this year, and all three of GM's front-drive, plastic-bodied minivans gain a standard driver-side air bag. New options include a power sliding side door, child-safety seats, an automatic door-locking system, and later in the year, traction control. Anti-lock brakes are standard on all. Also standard across the board are a 120-horsepower 3.1-liter V-6 engine and 3-speed automatic transmission. The optional powertrain is a 170-horsepower 3.8-liter V-6 mated to a 4-speed automatic. Lumina and Trans Sport have standard seats for five. Seats for seven are standard on Silhouette and optional on the other two. The middle and rear buckets have quick-release latches for easy removal. Two integrated child safety seats (for toddlers between 20 and 40 pounds) that fold out of the backrests in the middle row are a new option on 7-passenger models. The base 3.1-liter V-6 is adequate when pulling light loads, but heavier work requires the optional 3.8-liter engine, which gives these minivans brisk acceleration. With the standard driver-side air bag and anti-lock brakes, and options such as child safety seats and power sliding side door, this trio is well worth considering. All three have one-price models in California, and Olds also offers one nationally, that offer a lot of features at reasonable cost.

Chevrolet Lumina Minivan prices are on page 278;
Oldsmobile Silhouette prices are on page 404;
and Pontiac Trans Sport prices are on page 426.

CHEVROLET LUMINA MINIVAN LS

Rating Guide	1	2	3	4	5
Performance					
Acceleration				▌	
Economy	▌				
Driveability			▌		
Ride			▌		
Steering/handling			▌		
Braking				▌	
Noise			▌		
Accommodations					
Driver seating			▌		
Instruments/controls			▌		
Visibility		▌			
Room/comfort				▌	
Entry/exit			▌		
Cargo room				▌	
Workmanship					
Exterior			▌		
Interior			▌		
Value			▌		

Total Points...**60**

Specifications

Body type ....4-door van
Wheelbase (in.) 109.8
Overall length (in.)................191.5
Overall width (in.) 73.9
Overall height (in.).................65.7
Curb weight (lbs.) 3554
Seating capacity........................7
Front head room (in.) 39.2
Max. front leg room (in.) 40.1
Rear head room (in.) 38.7
Min. rear leg room (in.)...........36.9
Cargo volume (cu. ft.)...........112.6

Engine type ....ohv V-6
Engine size (l/cu. in.).........3.8/231
Horsepower @ rpm ...170 @ 4800
Torque @ rpm ....225 @ 3200
Transmission ....auto/4-sp.
Drive wheels ....front
Brakes, F/R ....disc/drum (ABS)
Tire size 205/70R15
Fuel tank capacity (gal.) 20.0
EPA city/highway mpg 17/25
Test mileage (mpg) 19.0

Warranties The entire vehicle is covered for 3 years/36,000 miles. Body perforation rust is covered for 6 years/100,000 miles.

Rating scale 5=Exceptional; 4=Above average; 3=Average; 2=Below average; 1=Poor

CHEVROLET S10 BLAZER/ GMC JIMMY/OLDSMOBILE BRAVADA

Built in Pontiac, Mich., and Moraine, Ohio.

Chevrolet S10 Blazer 5-door

SPORT-UTILITY VEHICLE

With a redesigned compact sport-utility due next summer, this trio carries on for 1994 with few changes, though GMC's high-performance Typhoon, with its turbocharged engine, has been dropped. Blazer and Jimmy come in 3- and 5-door models with rear-wheel drive or "shift-on-the-fly" 4-wheel drive. Bravada comes only as a 5-door with permanently engaged 4WD. Four-wheel anti-lock brakes that work in both 2WD and 4WD are standard on all. New safety features include side door guard beams and a center high-mounted stoplamp. All are powered by a 4.3-liter V-6. The standard engine in Blazer and Jimmy makes 165 horsepower and comes with a 5-speed manual transmission. An optional 200-horsepower version comes only with a 4-speed automatic; this is the standard powertrain for Bravada. A 60/40 split front seat is now standard on 5-door models of the Blazer and Jimmy. These vehicles are showing their age against the newer, roomier, and more refined Ford Explorer and Jeep Grand Cherokee. In their defense, the 4.3-liter V-6 is a strong if noisy engine, and the 4-wheel anti-lock feature and convenient shift-on-the-fly 4WD (and Bravada's permanent 4WD) are appealing. However, the Blazer/Jimmy suspension is still among the least compliant in the class, so you'll bounce and bang over bumpy roads. Except for price, we rate the Explorer and Grand Cherokee as better choices.

Chevrolet S10 Blazer prices are on page 280; GMC Jimmy prices are on page 329; and Oldsmobile Bravada prices are on page 395.

CHEVROLET S10 BLAZER

Rating Guide	1	2	3	4	5
Performance					
Acceleration					
Economy					
Driveability					
Ride					
Steering/handling					
Braking					
Noise					
Accommodations					
Driver seating					
Instruments/controls					
Visibility					
Room/comfort					
Entry/exit					
Cargo room					
Workmanship					
Exterior					
Interior					
Value					

Total Points...53

Specifications

Body type ....5-door wagon
Wheelbase (in.) 107.0
Overall length (in.) 176.8
Overall width (in.) 65.4
Overall height (in.) 64.1
Curb weight (lbs.) 3776
Seating capacity 6
Front head room (in.) 39.1
Max. front leg room (in.) 42.5
Rear head room (in.) 38.8
Min. rear leg room (in.) 36.5
Cargo volume (cu. ft.).............74.3

Engine type ....ohv V-6
Engine size (l/cu. in.).........4.3/262
Horsepower @ rpm ...200 @ 4500
Torque @ rpm ....260 @ 3600
Transmission ....auto/4-sp.
Drive wheels......................rear/all
Brakes, F/R ....disc/drum (ABS)
Tire size 205/75R15
Fuel tank capacity (gal.) 20.0
EPA city/highway mpg 16/22
Test mileage (mpg) 18.4

Warranties The entire vehicle is covered for 3 years/36,000 miles. Body perforation rust is covered for 6 years/100,000 miles.

Rating scale 5=Exceptional; 4=Above average; 3=Average; 2=Below average; 1=Poor

CHRYSLER CONCORDE

Built in Canada.

Chrysler Concorde

FULL-SIZE Similar to Dodge Intrepid and Eagle Vision

The front-wheel-drive Concorde was introduced last year to much critical acclaim. For 1994, the base engine gets more power, a front bench seat is available, and the touring suspension is standard instead of optional. Dual air bags and anti-lock brakes are again standard. The base 3.3-liter V-6 gains eight horsepower this year, to 161. Optional is an overhead-camshaft 3.5-liter V-6 with 214 horsepower. Both engines team with a 4-speed automatic transmission. A flexible-fuel version of the 3.3-liter V-6 that can run on gasoline or a blend of gas and up to 85 percent methanol (M85) is a new no-cost option in all states except California. A power moonroof and a security alarm are new options. Concorde and its LH sedan siblings impress us with their modern design, roomy interiors, lively performance, standard safety and convenience features, and attractive pricing, though Chrysler keeps upping the ante. The base 3.3-liter V-6 furnishes adequate acceleration, while the 3.5-liter has a lot more zip in all situations. While the 3.5-liter is listed as a $725 option, to get it you must also purchase an option package that costs more than $1200. Wide door openings, generous passenger space, and a user-friendly dashboard are among Concorde's assets. Last year's base suspension was softer than the touring suspension that is standard this year, but the ride isn't harsh. Concorde feels secure on the road and corners like a sports sedan. Some of the interior trim is too plasticky and road noise remains too high for this price level. Still, this is an impressive sedan with far more positive points than negatives.

Chrysler Concorde prices are on page 283.

CHRYSLER CONCORDE

Rating Guide	1	2	3	4	5
Performance					
Acceleration	▓▓▓▓▓▓▓▓▓▓				
Economy	▓▓▓▓▓				
Driveability	▓▓▓▓▓▓				
Ride	▓▓▓▓▓▓▓				
Steering/handling	▓▓▓▓▓▓▓				
Braking	▓▓▓▓▓▓▓▓▓▓▓▓▓				
Noise	▓▓▓▓▓				
Accommodations					
Driver seating	▓▓▓▓▓▓				
Instruments/controls	▓▓▓▓▓▓				
Visibility	▓▓▓▓▓▓				
Room/comfort	▓▓▓▓▓▓▓▓▓▓				
Entry/exit	▓▓▓▓▓▓▓				
Cargo room	▓▓▓▓▓▓▓▓▓▓				
Workmanship					
Exterior	▓▓▓▓▓▓				
Interior	▓▓▓▓▓▓				
Value	▓▓▓▓▓▓				
Total Points					**63**

Specifications

Body type	4-door notchback	Engine type	ohc V-6
Wheelbase (in.)	113.0	Engine size (l/cu. in.)	3.5/215
Overall length (in.)	202.8	Horsepower @ rpm	214 @ 5800
Overall width (in.)	74.4	Torque @ rpm	221 @ 2800
Overall height (in.)	56.3	Transmission	auto/4-sp.
Curb weight (lbs.)	3379	Drive wheels	front
Seating capacity	5	Brakes, F/R	disc/disc (ABS)
Front head room (in.)	38.4	Tire size	205/70R15
Max. front leg room (in.)	42.3	Fuel tank capacity (gal.)	18.0
Rear head room (in.)	37.3	EPA city/highway mpg	18/26
Min. rear leg room (in.)	38.7	Test mileage (mpg)	19.1
Cargo volume (cu. ft.)	16.7		

Warranties Customer's choice of 3-year/36,000-mile warranty or 1-year/12,000 mile basic warranty with 7-year/70,000-mile powertrain warranty. Body perforation rust is covered for 7 years/100,000 miles.

Rating scale 5=Exceptional; 4=Above average; 3=Average; 2=Below average; 1=Poor

CHRYSLER LE BARON

Built in Newark, Del., and Mexico.

Chrysler LeBaron GTC convertible

COMPACT Sedan similar to Dodge Spirit/Plymouth Acclaim

The slow-selling coupe has been dropped for 1994, leaving two very different front-wheel-drive LeBarons: a 2-door convertible and a 4-door sedan. The sedan has a longer wheelbase than the convertible (103.5 inches versus 100.6), and different styling. A new Chrysler coupe is expected later this year but probably won't use the LeBaron name. For 1994, the convertible comes as a single GTC model that adds a standard passenger-side air bag to the driver-side air bag that was already standard. The LeBaron 4-door returns in two models, LE and Landau. Both sedans have a standard driver-side air bag with a motorized belt for the front passenger. Anti-lock brakes are optional all LeBarons. The only engine is now a 141-horsepower 3.0-liter V-6 built in Japan by Mitsubishi. A 4-speed automatic transmission is standard on the convertible and optional on the sedan. The sedan comes standard with a 3-speed automatic. Nothing here measures up to the quality of Japanese rivals, but neither do the prices. The convertible, with its standard V-6, automatic transmission, dual air bags, power top, and attractive styling, is competitive in dollar value. The 3.0-liter V-6 with 4-speed automatic provides more than adequate acceleration. On the down side, the LeBaron ragtop's body seems to twist and flex more than most convertibles. There's room for 6-footers in front, but the rear seat is no place for adults on long trips and the trunk is small. The LeBaron sedan is a roomy compact, but it's nothing more than a plusher version of the Dodge Spirit/Plymouth Acclaim, so see the report on those cars for more information.

Chrysler LeBaron prices are on page 285.

CHRYSLER LE BARON GTC CONVERTIBLE

Rating Guide	1	2	3	4	5
Performance					
Acceleration	▮▮▮▮▮▮▮▮▮▮▮▮▮▮▮▮▮▮				
Economy	▮▮▮▮▮▮▮				
Driveability	▮▮▮▮▮▮▮▮▮▮▮▮▮				
Ride	▮▮▮▮▮▮▮▮▮▮▮				
Steering/handling	▮▮▮▮▮▮▮▮▮▮▮▮				
Braking	▮▮▮▮▮▮▮▮▮▮▮▮▮▮▮▮▮▮▮				
Noise	▮▮▮▮▮▮▮				
Accommodations					
Driver seating	▮▮▮▮▮▮▮▮▮▮▮▮▮▮				
Instruments/controls	▮▮▮▮▮▮▮▮▮▮▮▮				
Visibility	▮▮▮▮▮▮▮▮▮▮				
Room/comfort	▮▮▮▮▮▮▮▮▮▮▮				
Entry/exit	▮▮▮▮▮▮▮▮▮▮				
Cargo room	▮▮▮▮▮▮▮				
Workmanship					
Exterior	▮▮▮▮▮▮▮▮▮▮▮▮▮▮				
Interior	▮▮▮▮▮▮▮▮▮▮▮▮				
Value	▮▮▮▮▮▮▮▮▮▮				

Total Points...52

Specifications

Body type ....2-door convertible		Engine type......................ohc V-6
Wheelbase (in.) 100.6		Engine size (l/cu. in.).........3.0/181
Overall length (in.)................184.8		Horsepower @ rpm ...141 @ 5000
Overall width (in.)...................69.2		Torque @ rpm ....171 @ 2400
Overall height (in.)..................52.4		Transmission................auto/4-sp.
Curb weight (lbs.) 3122		Drive wheels ....front
Seating capacity............................4		Brakes, F/R...........disc/disc (ABS)
Front head room (in.) 38.3		Tire size 205/60R15
Max. front leg room (in.) 42.5		Fuel tank capacity (gal.) 14.0
Rear head room (in.) 37.0		EPA city/highway mpg 20/28
Min. rear leg room (in.)...........33.0		Test mileage (mpg) 22.9
Cargo volume (cu. ft.)...............9.2		

Warranties Customer's choice of 3-year/36,000-mile warranty or 1-year/12,000-mile basic warranty with 7-year/70,000-mile powertrain warranty. Body perforation rust is covered for 7 years/100,000 miles.

Rating scale 5=Exceptional; 4=Above average; 3=Average; 2=Below average; 1=Poor

CHRYSLER NEW YORKER/LHS

Built in Canada.

Chrysler LHS

PREMIUM SEDAN Similar to Chrysler Concorde, Dodge Intrepid, and Eagle Vision

The New Yorker and sportier LHS debuted last spring as early 1994 models. In the fall, both gained variable-assist power steering as a new standard feature. Both are based on the Concorde LH sedan. However, the bodies of the New Yorker and LHS are five inches longer, resulting in more rear seat and trunk space, and their styling is different. New Yorker and LHS come with a 214-horsepower 3.5-liter V-6 engine and 4-speed electronic automatic transmission. Dual air bags and anti-lock brakes are standard. The new variable-assist feature reduces the turning effort required at low speeds to make parking easier. A security alarm, automatic headlamps, and automatic day/night mirror are new standard features on the LHS and new options on the New Yorker. A power moonroof, added to the LHS's standard equipment during the summer, is a new New Yorker option. Since these are really stretched LH sedans, they have all the same attributes, plus rear leg room that would do a limousine proud. The mid-level touring suspension is now standard on the New Yorker and we're not convinced it's a wise move. The softer base suspension and tires gave it a more comfortable ride without allowing floating or wallowing. Now, the New Yorker feels much like the firmer LHS, which isn't as stiff as some cars that try to be sport sedans, but still isn't as compliant as the best imports. Road noise that's prominent at highway speeds and restricted visibility to the rear from the narrow back window are our only other real gripes about these roomy and roadworthy sedans.

Chrysler New Yorker/LHS prices are on page 287.

CHRYSLER LHS

Rating Guide	1	2	3	4	5
Performance					
Acceleration				▓	
Economy	▓				
Driveability			▓		
Ride			▓		
Steering/handling			▓		
Braking					▓
Noise				▓	
Accommodations					
Driver seating			▓		
Instruments/controls			▓		
Visibility			▓		
Room/comfort				▓	
Entry/exit			▓		
Cargo room			▓		
Workmanship					
Exterior			▓		
Interior			▓		
Value				▓	
Total Points					**63**

Specifications

Body type	4-door notchback	Engine type	ohc V-6
Wheelbase (in.)	113.0	Engine size (l/cu. in.)	3.5/215
Overall length (in.)	207.4	Horsepower @ rpm	214 @ 5800
Overall width (in.)	74.4	Torque @ rpm	221 @ 2800
Overall height (in.)	56.3	Transmission	auto/4-sp.
Curb weight (lbs.)	3457	Drive wheels	front
Seating capacity	5	Brakes, F/R	disc/disc (ABS)
Front head room (in.)	39.3	Tire size	225/60R16
Max. front leg room (in.)	42.3	Fuel tank capacity (gal.)	18.0
Rear head room (in.)	37.8	EPA city/highway mpg	18/26
Min. rear leg room (in.)	40.6	Test mileage (mpg)	18.4
Cargo volume (cu. ft.)	16.7		

Warranties Customer's choice of 3-year/36,000-mile warranty or 1-year/12,000-mile basic warranty with 7-year/70,000-mile powertrain warranty. Body perforation rust is covered for 7 years/100,000 miles.

Rating scale 5=Exceptional; 4=Above average; 3=Average; 2=Below average; 1=Poor

DODGE CARAVAN/ CHRYSLER TOWN & COUNTRY/PLYMOUTH VOYAGER

Built in St. Louis, Mo., and Canada.

Plymouth Grand Voyager LE

MINIVAN

All versions of Chrysler Corporation's minivan add a passenger-side air bag, side door guard beams, and other changes that enable it to meet all passenger car safety requirements through 1998. The Chrysler Town & Country also gets a stronger standard engine. Caravan and Voyager come in standard-size and extended-length "Grand" models with a longer wheelbase and body. Town & Country comes only in the extended length. Both body styles come with front-wheel drive, but this year, only the extended-length models are available with permanently engaged all-wheel drive. A new 162-horsepower 3.8-liter V-6 is standard on Town & Country and optional on the Grand Caravan and Voyager. The base Caravan/Voyager engine is a 100-horsepower 2.5-liter 4-cylinder that's available only on standard-length versions. A 3.0-liter V-6 with 142 horsepower and a 3.3-liter V-6 with 162 horse-power (12 more than last year) are also available. Anti-lock brakes are standard on Town & Country and optional on all Caravans and Voyagers except the base models. Among other changes; the dashboard on all versions has been redesigned so that the radio is easier to reach. Chrysler also has made several changes this year that make these minivans much quieter. Chrysler's minivans still set the standard for this class with their car-like road manners, efficient use of interior space, and combination of features.

Chrysler Town & Country prices are on page 288; Dodge Caravan prices are on page 289; Plymouth Voyager prices are on page 410.

PLYMOUTH GRAND VOYAGER LE

Rating Guide	1	2	3	4	5
Performance					
Acceleration	▮▮▮▮				
Economy	▮▮				
Driveability	▮▮▮▮				
Ride	▮▮▮▮				
Steering/handling	▮▮▮▮				
Braking	▮▮▮▮▮				
Noise	▮▮▮▮				
Accommodations					
Driver seating	▮▮▮▮				
Instruments/controls	▮▮▮▮				
Visibility	▮▮▮				
Room/comfort	▮▮▮▮▮				
Entry/exit	▮▮▮				
Cargo room	▮▮▮▮▮				
Workmanship					
Exterior	▮▮▮▮				
Interior	▮▮▮▮				
Value	▮▮▮▮▮				

Total Points...63

Specifications

Body type	4-door van	Engine type	ohv V-6
Wheelbase (in.)	119.3	Engine size (l/cu. in.)	3.3/201
Overall length (in.)	192.8	Horsepower @ rpm	162 @ 4800
Overall width (in.)	72.0	Torque @ rpm	194 @ 3600
Overall height (in.)	66.7	Transmission	auto/4-sp.
Curb weight (lbs.)	3602	Drive wheels	front
Seating capacity	7	Brakes, F/R	disc/disc (ABS)
Front head room (in.)	39.1	Tire size	205/70R15
Max. front leg room (in.)	38.3	Fuel tank capacity (gal.)	20.0
Rear head room (in.)	38.7	EPA city/highway mpg	18/23
Min. rear leg room (in.)	37.7	Test mileage (mpg)	NA
Cargo volume (cu. ft.)	141.3		

Warranties Customer's choice of 3-year/36,000-mile warranty or 1-year/12,000-mile basic warranty with 7-year/70,000-mile powertrain warranty. Body perforation rust is covered for 7 years/100,000 miles.

DODGE/PLYMOUTH COLT AND EAGLE SUMMIT

Built in Japan.

Dodge Colt ES 2-door

SUBCOMPACT Similar to Mitsubishi Mirage

The Dodge and Plymouth Colt, along with the Eagle Summit, are similar front-drive subcompacts built in Japan by Mitsubishi, which sells its own version as the Mirage. All gain a standard driver-side air bag as their major new feature for 1994. They retain a motorized shoulder belt for the front passenger. The Dodge Colt comes as a 2-door coupe and 4-door sedan in base and ES price levels. The Plymouth Colt comes in the same body styles in base and GL trim. Ditto for the Eagle Summit, but its 2-door comes in DL and ES trim, while the 4-doors come in LX and ES trim. Though the model designations are different, the equipment and prices are the same for all three brands. Eagle and Plymouth also offer wagon versions that are similar to the Mitsubishi Expo (see separate report). Base engine is a 92-horsepower 1.5-liter 4-cylinder that comes with either a standard 5-speed manual transmission or optional 3-speed automatic. A 113-horsepower 1.8-liter 4-cylinder is standard on the 4-door models and a new option on top-line 2-doors. It comes with a standard 5-speed manual or optional 4-speed automatic. Anti-lock brakes are optional on top-line 4-door models. Acceleration with the 1.5-liter engine is modest and passing power with the automatic transmission is poor. With either transmission, the 1.8-liter models are quicker and nearly as economical. The front seats have adequate room but the back seat is cramped. Road and engine noise are prevalent on all models. If you're shopping for an economical subcompact, also look at the Saturn sedan and Toyota Tercel.

Dodge/Plymouth Colt prices are on page 294;
Eagle Summit prices are on page 303.

DODGE COLT ES

Rating Guide	1	2	3	4	5
Performance					
Acceleration	▮▮▮				
Economy	▮▮▮▮▮				
Driveability	▮▮▮				
Ride	▮▮▮				
Steering/handling	▮▮▮				
Braking	▮▮▮				
Noise	▮▮▮				
Accommodations					
Driver seating	▮▮▮				
Instruments/controls	▮▮▮▮				
Visibility	▮▮▮				
Room/comfort	▮▮▮				
Entry/exit	▮▮▮				
Cargo room	▮▮▮				
Workmanship					
Exterior	▮▮▮				
Interior	▮▮▮				
Value	▮▮▮				
Total Points **54**					

Specifications

Body type	2-door notchback	Engine type	ohc I-4
Wheelbase (in.)	96.1	Engine size (l/cu. in.)	1.5/90
Overall length (in.)	171.1	Horsepower @ rpm	92 @ 6000
Overall width (in.)	66.1	Torque @ rpm	93 @ 3000
Overall height (in.)	51.4	Transmission	manual/5-sp.
Curb weight (lbs.)	2085	Drive wheels	front
Seating capacity	5	Brakes, F/R	disc/drum
Front head room (in.)	38.6	Tire size	155/80R13
Max. front leg room (in.)	42.9	Fuel tank capacity (gal.)	13.2
Rear head room (in.)	36.4	EPA city/highway mpg	32/39
Min. rear leg room (in.)	31.1	Test mileage (mpg)	NA
Cargo volume (cu. ft.)	10.5		

Warranties Customer's choice of 3-year/36,000-mile basic warranty with 5-year/60,000-mile powertrain warranty or 1-year/12,000-mile basic warranty with 7-year/70,000-mile powertrain warranty. Body perforation rust is covered for 7 years/100,000 miles.

Rating scale 5=Exceptional; 4=Above average; 3=Average; 2=Below average; 1=Poor

DODGE INTREPID

Built in Canada.

Dodge Intrepid ES

FULL-SIZE Similar to Chrysler Concorde and Eagle Vision

Dodge's version of the front-drive LH sedan has a more powerful base engine and variable-assist power steering for its second season. Dual air bags are again standard and anti-lock brakes are optional on both the base model and the sportier ES. Horsepower on the standard 3.3-liter V-6 increases from 153 to 161 this year. The optional 3.5-liter V-6 returns with 214. Both engines come with an electronic 4-speed automatic transmission. A flexible-fuel version of the 3.3-liter V-6 that can run on gasoline or a blend of gas and up to 85 percent methanol (M85) is available in all states except California. Air conditioning goes from optional to standard on both models and a touring suspension, optional last year on the base Intrepid, is now standard on both. The variable-assist power steering (standard on ES, optional on base) provides more assist at low speeds to make parking easier. As with the other LH sedans, we have high regard for the Intrepid. There's generous leg and head room all around, the rear seat is wide enough for three adults, and the trunk is spacious. Instruments and controls are logically arranged, though reaching the climate system panel is a stretch. The standard 3.3-liter V-6 gives Intrepid adequate acceleration, while the optional 3.5-liter V-6 provides more snap for quick passing on highways. Among the few negatives, road noise is prominent at freeway speeds and the optional Performance Handling Group gives the ES a stiff ride. Since we're impressed with all the LH sedans, check out the others if you're shopping this league. Unfortunately, their prices have risen drastically in the past year.

Dodge Intrepid prices are on page 296.

DODGE INTREPID ES

Rating Guide	1	2	3	4	5
Performance					
Acceleration	▓▓▓▓▓▓				
Economy	▓▓▓▓▓				
Driveability	▓▓▓▓▓▓▓▓				
Ride	▓▓▓▓▓▓▓				
Steering/handling	▓▓▓▓▓▓				
Braking	▓▓▓▓▓▓▓▓▓▓				
Noise	▓▓▓▓▓▓				
Accommodations					
Driver seating	▓▓▓▓▓▓				
Instruments/controls	▓▓▓▓▓▓				
Visibility	▓▓▓▓▓▓				
Room/comfort	▓▓▓▓▓▓▓▓▓▓				
Entry/exit	▓▓▓▓▓▓▓				
Cargo room	▓▓▓▓▓▓				
Workmanship					
Exterior	▓▓▓▓▓▓▓▓				
Interior	▓▓▓▓▓▓▓▓				
Value	▓▓▓▓▓▓▓				
Total Points					**60**

Specifications

Body type	4-door notchback	Engine type	ohv V-6
Wheelbase (in.)	113.0	Engine size (l/cu. in.)	3.3/201
Overall length (in.)	201.7	Horsepower @ rpm	161 @ 5300
Overall width (in.)	74.4	Torque @ rpm	181 @ 3200
Overall height (in.)	56.3	Transmission	auto/4-sp.
Curb weight (lbs.)	3271	Drive wheels	front
Seating capacity	5	Brakes, F/R	disc/disc (ABS)
Front head room (in.)	38.4	Tire size	225/60R16
Max. front leg room (in.)	42.3	Fuel tank capacity (gal.)	18.0
Rear head room (in.)	37.2	EPA city/highway mpg	20/28
Min. rear leg room (in.)	38.7	Test mileage (mpg)	20.8
Cargo volume (cu. ft.)	16.7		

Warranties Customer's choice of 3-year/36,000-mile warranty or 1-year/12,000-mile basic warranty with 7-year/70,000-mile powertrain warranty. Body perforation rust is covered for 7 years/100,000 miles.

Rating scale 5=Exceptional; 4=Above average; 3=Average; 2=Below average; 1=Poor

DODGE/PLYMOUTH NEON

Built in Belvidere, Ill.

Dodge Neon

SUBCOMPACT

Chrysler Corporation says that the Neon will set new standards for small cars in performance, safety, design, and value when it is introduced in early 1994. This front-drive subcompact bows as a 1995 model and is pitched as a fun-to-drive small car that offers more interior space than comparably sized competitors. It is sold in identical form through Dodge and Plymouth dealers. Chrysler started with a clean sheet of paper in designing Neon, which has "cab-forward" styling like the full-size Chrysler LH sedans. Cab forward is the term Chrysler uses to describe how the wheels are pushed out to the ends of the car to create more passenger space. Initially, it comes only as a 4-door sedan with a new 2.0-liter 4-cylinder engine rated at 132 horsepower. A 5-speed manual transmission is standard and a 3-speed automatic is optional. Base and Sport models are offered. A 2-door coupe and a more powerful engine with dual overhead camshafts are expected to join the lineup in the fall of 1994. Compared to a Honda Civic sedan, Neon's 104-inch wheelbase is .8 of an inch longer while its 171.8-inch overall length is 1.2-inches shorter. A complete equipment list wasn't available. However, dual air bags are standard. Options include anti-lock brakes, power door locks, and an integrated child safety seat. Power windows and a sunroof won't be available for at least another year. Prices weren't announced in time for this issue, but Chrysler estimated Neon would start at about $8800 and that fully equipped models would sell for $11,000 to $11,500. We haven't driven a Neon so we cannot rate its performance.

Dodge/Plymouth Neon prices not available at time of publication.

DODGE NEON (Ratings Not Available)

Rating Guide	1	2	3	4	5
Performance					
Acceleration					
Economy					
Driveability					
Ride					
Steering/handling					
Braking					
Noise					
Accommodations					
Driver seating					
Instruments/controls					
Visibility					
Room/comfort					
Entry/exit					
Cargo room					
Workmanship					
Exterior					
Interior					
Value					
Total Points					

Specifications

Body type	4-door notchback	Engine type	ohc I-4
Wheelbase (in.)	104.0	Engine size (l/cu. in.)	2.0/121
Overall length (in.)	171.8	Horsepower @ rpm	132 @ 6000
Overall width (in.)	67.4	Torque @ rpm	129 @ 5000
Overall height (in.)	54.8	Transmission	manual/5-sp.
Curb weight (lbs.)	2320	Drive wheels	front
Seating capacity	5	Brakes, F/R	disc/drum
Front head room (in.)	39.6	Tire size	NA
Max. front leg room (in.)	42.5	Fuel tank capacity (gal.)	11.2
Rear head room (in.)	36.5	EPA city/highway mpg	NA
Min. rear leg room (in.)	35.1	Test mileage (mpg)	NA
Cargo volume (cu. ft.)	11.8		

Warranties Not Available.

Rating scale 5=Exceptional; 4=Above average; 3=Average; 2=Below average; 1=Poor

DODGE SPIRIT/ PLYMOUTH ACCLAIM

Built in Newark, Del.

Dodge Spirit

COMPACT Similar to Chrysler LeBaron Sedan

Both the Spirit and identical Acclaim now come in just one trim level and a motorized front passenger belt is the major new safety feature for 1994. A driver-side air bag has been standard since 1990. Anti-lock brakes are optional. Standard engine is a 100-horsepower 2.5-liter 4-cylinder that comes with a standard 5-speed manual transmission or optional 3-speed automatic. An optional 142-horsepower 3.0-liter V-6 comes with either the 3-speed automatic or a 4-speed automatic. A flexible-fuel version of the 4-cylinder engine that can run on gasoline or up to 85 percent methanol is available as a no-cost option. The V-6 is a strong performer in this car, though it's also rather noisy. Acceleration with the 4-cylinder is adequate off the line, but merging and passing power are poor. We averaged 22.3 mpg in our test of a 4-cylinder on a mix of highways and urban expressways. Engine and road noise intrude at highway speeds and wind noise is prominent around the side windows. The suspension feels stable on smooth roads but bangs and clunks harshly on rough surfaces. Spirit and Acclaim are the least-expensive 6-passenger cars you can buy. Cabin and cargo space are ample for the compact exterior dimensions. Head room is good front and rear, and there's sufficient back-seat leg room for adults to sit comfortably and the wide, tall doors allow easy entry/exit. The large trunk has a low liftover and a wide, flat floor that holds lots of luggage. Spirit and Acclaim are no match for newer, more refined Japanese compacts, but they offer good value for the money.

Dodge Spirit prices are on page 300;
Plymouth Acclaim prices are on page 405.

DODGE SPIRIT

Rating Guide	1	2	3	4	5
Performance					
Acceleration	▓▓▓▓▓▓▓▓▓▓▓▓▓▓				
Economy	▓▓▓▓▓▓▓▓▓▓▓▓▓				
Driveability	▓▓▓▓▓▓▓▓▓▓▓▓▓				
Ride	▓▓▓▓▓▓▓▓▓▓▓▓▓				
Steering/handling	▓▓▓▓▓▓▓▓▓▓▓▓▓				
Braking	▓▓▓▓▓▓▓▓▓▓▓▓▓				
Noise	▓▓▓▓▓▓▓▓▓▓▓				
Accommodations					
Driver seating	▓▓▓▓▓▓▓▓▓▓▓▓▓				
Instruments/controls	▓▓▓▓▓▓▓▓▓▓▓▓				
Visibility	▓▓▓▓▓▓▓▓▓▓▓▓▓▓				
Room/comfort	▓▓▓▓▓▓▓▓▓▓▓▓▓▓				
Entry/exit	▓▓▓▓▓▓▓▓▓▓▓▓▓▓				
Cargo room	▓▓▓▓▓▓▓▓▓▓▓▓▓▓				
Workmanship					
Exterior	▓▓▓▓▓▓▓▓▓▓▓▓▓				
Interior	▓▓▓▓▓▓▓▓▓▓▓▓▓				
Value	▓▓▓▓▓▓▓▓▓▓▓▓▓				

Total Points...55

Specifications

Body type	4-door notchback	Engine type	ohc I-4
Wheelbase (in.)	103.5	Engine size (l/cu. in.)	2.5/153
Overall length (in.)	181.2	Horsepower @ rpm	100 @ 4400
Overall width (in.)	68.1	Torque @ rpm	140 @ 2400
Overall height (in.)	53.5	Transmission	auto/3-sp.
Curb weight (lbs.)	2824	Drive wheels	front
Seating capacity	6	Brakes, F/R	disc/drum
Front head room (in.)	38.4	Tire size	185/70R14
Max. front leg room (in.)	41.9	Fuel tank capacity (gal.)	16.0
Rear head room (in.)	37.9	EPA city/highway mpg	22/27
Min. rear leg room (in.)	38.3	Test mileage (mpg)	22.3
Cargo volume (cu. ft.)	14.4		

Warranties Customer's choice of 3-year/36,000-mile warranty or 1-year/12,000-mile basic warranty with 7-year/70,000-mile powertrain warranty. Body perforation rust is covered for 7 years/100,000 miles.

Rating scale 5=Exceptional; 4=Above average; 3=Average; 2=Below average; 1=Poor

EAGLE VISION

Built in Canada.

Eagle Vision TSi

FULL-SIZE Similar to Chrysler Concorde and Dodge Intrepid

Vision, Eagle's version of Chrysler Corporation's front-drive LH sedan, comes in base ESi and sportier TSi models. The ESi now looks more like the TSi because it uses the same lower body cladding and fascias. Dual air bags are standard on both. Anti-lock brakes are standard on TSi and optional on ESi. Horsepower on the ESi's 3.3-liter V-6 increases from 153 to 161. The 3.5-liter V-6 standard on the TSi returns with 214 horsepower. A flexible-fuel version of the 3.3-liter that can run on gasoline or a blend of gas and up to 85 percent methanol (M85) is now offered in all states except California. An electronic 4-speed automatic is the only transmission. Both Visions gain a standard variable-assist feature for the power steering that makes parking easier. Vision offers outstanding cargo and passenger space. A convenient built-in child safety seat is optional. The dashboard is generally well laid out, though the climate controls are at the base of the dashboard and most drivers have to stretch to reach them. The ESi's 3.3-liter engine provides adequate acceleration, while the TSi's 3.5-liter is smoother and more potent. Handling and roadholding are top-notch, especially in the TSi. However, the TSi's optional performance suspension is too stiff, making the ride harsh. Both Visions suffer from too much road noise, though the TSi with its more aggressive tires is the bigger offender. The Vision and its LH siblings have a few flaws, but the pluses far outweigh the minuses, making them prime choices in this class.

Eagle Vision prices are on page 305.

EAGLE VISION TSi

Rating Guide	1	2	3	4	5
Performance					
Acceleration				▮	
Economy		▮			
Driveability				▮	
Ride			▮		
Steering/handling				▮	
Braking					▮
Noise			▮		
Accommodations					
Driver seating					▮
Instruments/controls					▮
Visibility				▮	
Room/comfort					▮
Entry/exit				▮	
Cargo room				▮	
Workmanship					
Exterior				▮	
Interior				▮	
Value				▮	

Total Points **61**

Specifications

Body type .... 4-door notchback
Wheelbase (in.) 113.0
Overall length (in.) 201.6
Overall width (in.) 74.4
Overall height (in.) 55.8
Curb weight (lbs.) 3344
Seating capacity 5
Front head room (in.) 38.4
Max. front leg room (in.) 42.3
Rear head room (in.) 37.2
Min. rear leg room (in.) 38.7
Cargo volume (cu. ft.) 16.6

Engine type .... ohc V-6
Engine size (l/cu. in.) 3.5/215
Horsepower @ rpm ... 214 @ 5800
Torque @ rpm .... 221 @ 2800
Transmission .... auto/4-sp.
Drive wheels .... front
Brakes, F/R .... disc/disc (ABS)
Tire size 225/60R16
Fuel tank capacity (gal.) 18.0
EPA city/highway mpg 18/26
Test mileage (mpg) 21.6

Warranties Customer's choice of 3-year/36,000-mile warranty or 1-year/12,000-mile basic warranty with 7-year/70,000-mile powertrain warranty. Body perforation rust is covered for 7 years/100,000 miles.

Rating scale 5=Exceptional; 4=Above average; 3=Average; 2=Below average; 1=Poor

FORD AEROSTAR

Built in St. Louis, Mo.

Ford Aerostar XLT Extended

MINIVAN

The addition of a center high-mounted stoplamp is among the few changes for Aerostar, which is in its final season. It will be replaced by a new front-drive minivan called Windstar next spring. Aerostar comes in regular- and extended-length bodies, both on a 118.9-inch wheelbase with a choice of rear- or permanently engaged 4-wheel drive. Standard on rear-drive models is a 3.0-liter V-6 with 135 horsepower. Optional on rear-drive extended versions and standard on 4WD models is a 4.0-liter V-6 with 155 horsepower. A 5-speed manual transmission is standard with the 3.0-liter. A 4-speed automatic is standard with the 4.0-liter and optional on the smaller V-6. All models have a standard driver-side air bag and anti-lock rear brakes. Seats for up to seven are available. Optional are two integrated child safety seats that fold out of the middle bench seat. The child seats have 5-point safety harnesses and are designed for children between 20 and 60 pounds. Aerostar's truck roots pay off in its ability to haul hefty loads and pull heavier trailers than lighter-duty front-drive minivans. Drawbacks include a high step-up into the cabin and a stiff suspension. Power is adequate with the base engine and robust with the 4.0-liter engine, though both use lots of gas. Lightly loaded rear-drive models can have poor traction in rain and snow, so consider 4WD if you live in the snow belt, though 4WD adds weight, hurting gas mileage even more. Aerostar has plenty of passenger space, but cargo room is scarce in the shorter model unless you remove the heavy rear seat. For a daily people hauler, we think a front-drive minivan is a better choice.

Ford Aerostar prices are on page 307.

FORD AEROSTAR EXTENDED 4WD

Rating Guide	1	2	3	4	5
Performance					
Acceleration	▓▓▓			
Economy	▓▓				
Driveability	▓▓▓			
Ride	▓▓▓			
Steering/handling	▓▓▓			
Braking	▓▓▓▓▓				
Noise	▓▓▓			
Accommodations					
Driver seating	▓▓▓▓			
Instruments/controls	▓▓▓			
Visibility	▓▓▓			
Room/comfort	▓▓▓▓			
Entry/exit	▓▓				
Cargo room	▓▓▓▓			
Workmanship					
Exterior	▓▓▓▓			
Interior	▓▓▓▓			
Value	▓▓▓			
Total Points					**53**

Specifications

Body type	4-door van	Engine type	ohv V-6
Wheelbase (in.)	118.9	Engine size (l/cu. in.)	4.0/245
Overall length (in.)	190.3	Horsepower @ rpm	155 @ 4000
Overall width (in.)	72.0	Torque @ rpm	230 @ 2400
Overall height (in.)	72.3	Transmission	auto/4-sp.
Curb weight (lbs.)	3955	Drive wheels	all
Seating capacity	7	Brakes, F/R	disc/drum (ABS)
Front head room (in.)	39.5	Tire size	215/70R14
Max. front leg room (in.)	41.4	Fuel tank capacity (gal.)	21.0
Rear head room (in.)	38.8	EPA city/highway mpg	15/20
Min. rear leg room (in.)	40.5	Test mileage (mpg)	15.4
Cargo volume (cu. ft.)	170.0		

Warranties The entire vehicle is covered for 3 years/36,000 miles. Body perforation rust is covered for 6 years/100,000 miles.

Rating scale 5=Exceptional; 4=Above average; 3=Average; 2=Below average; 1=Poor

FORD CROWN VICTORIA/ ──
MERCURY GRAND MARQUIS

Built in Canada.

Ford Crown Victoria LX

FULL-SIZE

A passenger-side air bag is standard instead of optional this year on Crown Victoria. It joins a driver-side air bag and gives the Ford version of this full-size, rear-drive sedan the same dual air bag setup that was already standard on the Grand Marquis. These cars differ only in interior and exterior trim. The sole powertrain is a 4.6-liter overhead-camshaft V-8 and 4-speed electronic automatic transmission. Standard horsepower is 190. Horsepower increases to 210 with the dual exhaust system included in the Trailer Towing and Handling and Performance option packages. Anti-lock brakes are optional on all models and team with a traction control system. The rear-drive Chevrolet Caprice and Buick Roadmaster, which also have standard dual air bags for 1994, are the only direct rivals. Crown Vic and Grand Marquis accelerate well off the line, but suffer lazy throttle response in the 30-to-50 mph range. In addition, the transmission is slow to downshift for passing. Though they have roomy interiors and big trunks, full-size, rear-drive cars such as these with V-8s and body-on-frame construction are dinosaurs among today's nimbler front-drive, V-6 competitors. That's why we prefer the likes of the Dodge Intrepid and Pontiac Bonneville and their siblings. They have less towing power than the rear-drive V-8 designs but comparable interior room and overall performance. The best deals on these cars are the one-price Special Value models, which include several optional features yet sell for less than base models without those fea-

Ford Crown Victoria prices are on page 309;
Mercury Grand Marquis prices are on page 370.

FORD CROWN VICTORIA LX

Rating Guide	1	2	3	4	5
Performance					
Acceleration	▓▓▓				
Economy	▓▓				
Driveability	▓▓▓				
Ride	▓▓▓				
Steering/handling	▓▓▓				
Braking	▓▓▓▓▓				
Noise	▓▓▓▓▓				
Accommodations					
Driver seating	▓▓▓				
Instruments/controls	▓▓▓				
Visibility	▓▓				
Room/comfort	▓▓▓▓				
Entry/exit	▓▓▓▓				
Cargo room	▓▓▓				
Workmanship					
Exterior	▓▓▓▓				
Interior	▓▓▓▓				
Value	▓▓▓				
Total Points					**61**

Specifications

Body type	4-door notchback	Engine	ohc V-8
Wheelbase (in.)	114.4	Engine size (l/cu. in.)	4.6/281
Overall length (in.)	212.4	Horsepower @ rpm	210 @ 4600
Overall width (in.)	77.8	Torque @ rpm	270 @ 3400
Overall height (in.)	56.8	Transmission	auto/4-sp.
Curb weight (lbs.)	3776	Drive wheels	rear
Seating capacity	6	Brakes, F/R	disc/disc (ABS)
Front head room (in.)	39.4	Tire size	225/60R15
Max. front leg room (in.)	42.5	Fuel tank capacity (gal.)	20.0
Rear head room (in.)	38.0	EPA city/highway mpg	18/25
Min. rear leg room (in.)	39.7	Test mileage (mpg)	17.3
Cargo volume (cu. ft.)	20.6		

Warranties The entire car is covered for 3 years/36,000 miles. Body perforation rust is covered for 6 years/100,000 miles.

Rating scale 5=Exceptional; 4=Above average; 3=Average; 2=Below average; 1=Poor

FORD ESCORT/ MERCURY TRACER

BUDGET BUY

Built in Wayne, Mich., and Mexico.

Ford Escort LX 4-door

SUBCOMPACT Similar to Mazda Protege

All versions of Escort and Tracer gain a standard driver-side air bag and anti-lock brakes (ABS) are a new option on sporty models. Escort and Tracer share a front-drive chassis that also is used for the Mazda Protege. Both the Ford and Mercury versions come in 4-door sedan and 5-door wagon body styles, with Escort also available as 3- and 5-door hatchbacks. An 88-horsepower 1.9-liter Ford 4-cylinder is the base engine. The sporty Escort GT hatchback and Tracer LTS 4-door have a 127-horsepower 1.8-liter Mazda 4-cylinder. On all models, a 5-speed manual transmission is standard and a 4-speed automatic is optional. ABS is a new option on the GT and the LTS. The air bag brings Escort and Tracer up to speed with most subcompact rivals, and the optional ABS is a safety feature already available elsewhere in this class. Escort and Tracer have adequate passenger and cargo room for their small exterior dimensions. Fuel economy is impressive. Performance is modest on the base models and lively on the GT and LTS. Escort and Tracer are far less refined than such competitors as the Geo Prizm, Honda Civic, and Toyota Corolla, which also have standard dual air bags. Escort and Tracer are attractively priced, however, and Ford says about 90 percent of Escorts are one-price LX models that carry a suggested retail of $11,395 with the manual transmission and $12,185 with automatic, including the destination charge, air conditioning, power steering, and other features. Tracer doesn't offer one-price models this year, but dealers should be discounting.

Ford Escort prices are on page 311;
Mercury Tracer prices are on page 375.

FORD ESCORT LX

Rating Guide	1	2	3	4	5
Performance					
Acceleration	▓▓▓▓▓▓				
Economy	▓▓▓▓▓▓▓▓				
Driveability	▓▓▓▓▓▓				
Ride	▓▓▓▓▓▓▓▓▓				
Steering/handling	▓▓▓▓▓▓				
Braking	▓▓▓▓▓▓▓				
Noise	▓▓▓▓▓▓				
Accommodations					
Driver seating	▓▓▓▓▓▓				
Instruments/controls	▓▓▓▓▓▓▓▓				
Visibility	▓▓▓▓▓▓▓▓▓▓				
Room/comfort	▓▓▓▓▓▓				
Entry/exit	▓▓▓▓▓▓▓				
Cargo room	▓▓▓▓▓▓▓				
Workmanship					
Exterior	▓▓▓▓▓▓▓				
Interior	▓▓▓▓▓▓▓				
Value	▓▓▓▓▓▓▓▓				

Total Points..**55**

Specifications

Body type ....4-door notchback	Engine type ....ohc I-4
Wheelbase (in.) 98.4	Engine size (l/cu. in.).........1.9/114
Overall length (in.)................170.9	Horsepower @ rpm .....88 @ 4400
Overall width (in.) 66.7	Torque @ rpm ....108 @ 3800
Overall height (in.)..................52.7	Transmission.................auto/4-sp.
Curb weight (lbs.) 2371	Drive wheels ....front
Seating capacity............................5	Brakes, F/R....................disc/drum
Front head room (in.) 38.4	Tire size 175/70R13
Max. front leg room (in.) 41.7	Fuel tank capacity (gal.) 11.9
Rear head room (in.) 37.4	EPA city/highway mpg 25/33
Min. rear leg room (in.)...........34.6	Test mileage (mpg) 27.4
Cargo volume (cu. ft.).............12.1	

Warranties The entire car is covered for 3 years/36,000 miles. Body perforation rust is covered for 6 years/100,000 miles.

Rating scale 5=Exceptional; 4=Above average; 3=Average; 2=Below average; 1=Poor

FORD EXPLORER/ MAZDA NAVAJO

Built in Louisville, Ky.

Ford Explorer XLT

SPORT-UTILITY VEHICLE

Explorer, America's best-selling sport-utility vehicle, gets only minor trim and option package changes for 1994. It comes in 3-door and 5-door wagon styling. Mazda purchases 3-door models from Ford, gives it different trim, and calls it the Navajo. Navajo gets restyled alloy wheels as its only change. All versions are available with 2-wheel drive or on-demand 4-wheel drive that's for use only on slippery surfaces. The only engine is a 160-horsepower 4.0-liter V-6 available with a standard 5-speed manual transmission or optional 4-speed automatic. Four-wheel anti-lock brakes that operate in both 2WD and 4WD are standard. Fog lamps are a new option for XL, XLT, and Eddie Bauer Explorers, and the XL's optional Power Equipment Group now includes a rear washer/wiper and defroster. Optional trailer-towing packages allow Explorer to pull up to 5600 pounds and Navajo up to 5400. A redesigned version of these trucks is due for 1995 with dual air bags. The ability to double as a roomy 4WD sport-utility and a handsome upscale family wagon earned Explorer the top-seller's crown. The 5-door model's long wheelbase gives it an expansive interior and a comfortable ride. A bouncier, choppier ride and poor rear-seat access is the penalty of the shorter wheelbase on the 3-door Explorer and the Navajo. Cargo space is generous. The engine is gruff but has good low-end torque and brisk acceleration. Explorer is roomier than its chief rival, the Jeep Grand Cherokee, but the Jeep has a driver-side air bag, more versatile 4WD systems, and an available V-8 engine.

Ford Explorer prices are on page 313;
Mazda Navajo prices are on page 360.

FORD EXPLORER

Rating Guide	1	2	3	4	5
Performance					
Acceleration	▓▓▓				
Economy	▓▓				
Driveability	▓▓▓				
Ride	▓▓▓				
Steering/handling	▓▓▓▓				
Braking	▓▓▓▓▓				
Noise	▓▓▓				
Accommodations					
Driver seating	▓▓▓				
Instruments/controls	▓▓▓				
Visibility	▓▓▓				
Room/comfort	▓▓▓				
Entry/exit	▓▓▓				
Cargo room	▓▓▓▓				
Workmanship					
Exterior	▓▓▓▓				
Interior	▓▓▓▓				
Value	▓▓▓▓				
Total Points **61**					

Specifications

Body type	5-door wagon	Engine type	ohv V-6
Wheelbase (in.)	111.9	Engine size (l/cu. in.)	4.0/245
Overall length (in.)	184.3	Horsepower @ rpm	160 @ 4400
Overall width (in.)	70.2	Torque @ rpm	220 @ 2800
Overall height (in.)	67.3	Transmission	auto/4-sp.
Curb weight (lbs.)	4053	Drive wheels	rear/all
Seating capacity	5	Brakes, F/R	disc/drum (ABS)
Front head room (in.)	39.9	Tire size	235/75R15
Max. front leg room (in.)	42.4	Fuel tank capacity (gal.)	19.0
Rear head room (in.)	39.3	EPA city/highway mpg	15/20
Min. rear leg room (in.)	37.7	Test mileage (mpg)	16.1
Cargo volume (cu. ft.)	81.6		

Warranties The entire car is covered for 3 years/36,000 miles. Body perforation rust is covered for 6 years/100,000 miles.

Rating scale 5=Exceptional; 4=Above average; 3=Average; 2=Below average; 1=Poor

FORD MUSTANG

Built in Dearborn, Mich.

Ford Mustang GT 2-door

SPORTS AND GT

Ford's rear-drive "ponycar" has been redesigned for the first time in 15 years, getting new sheetmetal and a new interior with dual air bags but retaining rear-wheel drive and an available V-8 engine. A 2-door coupe and convertible are available in base and GT form. Gone are the hatchback body style and mid-line LX models. Wheelbase increases 1.9 inches and overall length about one inch. A 145-horsepower 3.8-liter V-6 replaces a 105-horsepower 2.3-liter 4-cylinder as the base model's engine. Exclusive to the GT is a 5.0-liter V-8 with 215 horsepower, 10 more than last year's V-8. A 5-speed manual transmission is standard and a 4-speed automatic is optional with both. Four-wheel disc brakes are standard and anti-lock brakes (ABS) are available for the first time as an option on both models. A passenger-side air bag joins a previously standard driver-side air bag. The convertible has a power fabric top with a glass rear window. A removable fiberglass hardtop that weighs about 80 pounds is a new option. The new Mustang feels more solid than its predecessor and the dual air bags and available ABS are important safety advances. Compared to the arch-rival Chevrolet Camaro, Mustang has a softer ride and more body lean in corners, but neither car absorbs bumps well. The interior is more upright and airier than Camaro's yet just as tight in the rear seat. The base engine provides adequate acceleration. Though the GT has 60 fewer horsepower than the Camaro Z28, it can still smoke the rear tires off the line. Overall, Camaro has more performance and features for the money, but Mustang has a more user-friendly manner.

Ford Mustang prices are on page 316.

FORD MUSTANG GT

Rating Guide	1	2	3	4	5
Performance					
Acceleration	▮▮▮▮▮▮▮▮▮▮				
Economy	▮▮▮▮				
Driveability	▮▮▮▮▮▮				
Ride	▮▮▮▮▮▮				
Steering/handling	▮▮▮▮▮▮▮▮▮				
Braking	▮▮▮▮▮▮▮▮▮▮				
Noise	▮▮▮▮▮▮				
Accommodations					
Driver seating	▮▮▮▮▮▮▮				
Instruments/controls	▮▮▮▮▮▮▮▮				
Visibility	▮▮▮▮▮▮▮				
Room/comfort	▮▮▮▮▮▮				
Entry/exit	▮▮▮▮▮▮				
Cargo room	▮▮▮▮▮▮				
Workmanship					
Exterior	▮▮▮▮▮▮▮▮				
Interior	▮▮▮▮▮▮▮▮				
Value	▮▮▮▮▮▮▮				
Total Points					**51**

Specifications

Body type	2-door notchback
Wheelbase (in.)	101.3
Overall length (in.)	181.5
Overall width (in.)	71.8
Overall height (in.)	52.9
Curb weight (lbs.)	3341
Seating capacity	4
Front head room (in.)	38.1
Max. front leg room (in.)	42.6
Rear head room (in.)	35.9
Min. rear leg room (in.)	30.3
Cargo volume (cu. ft.)	10.0
Engine type	ohv V-8
Engine size (l/cu. in.)	5.0/302
Horsepower @ rpm	215 @ 4200
Torque @ rpm	285 @ 3400
Transmission	auto/4-sp.
Drive wheels	rear
Brakes, F/R	disc/disc (ABS)
Tire size	225/55ZR16
Fuel tank capacity (gal.)	15.4
EPA city/highway mpg	NA
Test mileage (mpg)	NA

Warranties The entire car is covered for 3 years/36,000 miles. Body perforation rust is covered for 6 years/100,000 miles.

Rating scale 5=Exceptional; 4=Above average; 3=Average; 2=Below average; 1=Poor

FORD PROBE

Built in Flat Rock, Mich.

Ford Probe GT

SPORTS COUPE Similar to Mazda MX-6

Ford's front-drive sports coupe adds a standard passenger-side air bag for 1994. Probe shares its major mechanical components with the Mazda MX-6, though each has unique styling and Probe is a 3-door hatchback, the MX-6 a 2-door notchback coupe. Both are built at a Michigan plant jointly owned by Ford and Mazda. The MX-6 also gets a second air bag this year (see separate report under Mazda 626/MX-6). The base Probe has a 115-horsepower 2.0-liter 4-cylinder engine. The GT has a 164-horsepower 2.5-liter V-6. A 5-speed manual transmission is standard and a 4-speed automatic is optional on both models, as are anti-lock brakes. A Sport Edition option package gives the base Probe an exterior appearance similar to that of the GT, which has been more popular than expected. Deleted from the base model's options list, however, are the GT's seats, leather upholstery, and power seats. On both models, cruise control and a remote keyless entry system are now available only as part of option packages. Probe is a smartly styled sports coupe that satisfies a range of tastes. The GT model has outstanding overall performance with the manual transmission, though it rides stiffly. Lower demand for the 4-cylinder version means bigger discounts on the base Probe, which has adequate overall performance. Unfortunately, the automatic transmission saps the verve of both engines. The interior has a convenient dashboard and plenty of room in front, but only children will be comfortable in the rear. The dashboard has a convenient design. Probe and the similar MX-6 are the top choices in the competitive sports coupe market.

Ford Probe prices are on page 318.

FORD PROBE GT

Rating Guide	1	2	3	4	5
Performance					
Acceleration	▓▓▓▓▓▓▓▓				
Economy	▓▓▓▓▓				
Driveability	▓▓▓▓▓▓▓				
Ride	▓▓▓▓▓				
Steering/handling	▓▓▓▓▓▓▓				
Braking	▓▓▓▓▓▓▓▓▓▓				
Noise	▓▓▓▓▓				
Accommodations					
Driver seating	▓▓▓▓▓▓▓				
Instruments/controls	▓▓▓▓▓▓▓				
Visibility	▓▓▓▓▓▓▓				
Room/comfort	▓▓▓▓▓				
Entry/exit	▓▓▓▓▓				
Cargo room	▓▓▓▓▓▓				
Workmanship					
Exterior	▓▓▓▓▓▓▓				
Interior	▓▓▓▓▓▓▓				
Value	▓▓▓▓▓▓▓				

Total Points..55

Specifications

Body type	3-door hatchback	Engine type	dohc V-6
Wheelbase (in.)	102.9	Engine size (l/cu. in.)	2.5/153
Overall length (in.)	178.9	Horsepower @ rpm	164 @ 5600
Overall width (in.)	69.8	Torque @ rpm	160 @ 4800
Overall height (in.)	51.6	Transmission	auto/4-sp.
Curb weight (lbs.)	2690	Drive wheels	front
Seating capacity	4	Brakes, F/R	disc/disc (ABS)
Front head room (in.)	37.8	Tire size	225/50VR16
Max. front leg room (in.)	43.1	Fuel tank capacity (gal.)	15.5
Rear head room (in.)	34.8	EPA city/highway mpg	20/26
Min. rear leg room (in.)	28.5	Test mileage (mpg)	22.2
Cargo volume (cu. ft.)	18.0		

Warranties The entire car is covered for 3 years/36,000 miles. Body perforation rust is covered for 6 years/100,000 miles.

Rating scale 5=Exceptional; 4=Above average; 3=Average; 2=Below average; 1=Poor

FORD TAURUS/ MERCURY SABLE

Built in Atlanta, Ga., and Chicago, Ill.

Ford Taurus LX 4-door

MID-SIZE

The passenger-side air bag moves from the options list to the standard-equipment roster as the main change for the Ford version of this popular front-drive intermediate. Taurus is built from the same design as the Mercury Sable, which got dual air bags as standard for 1993. Both return in 4-door sedan and 5-door wagon styling. Engine choices are V-6s of 3.0- or 3.8-liters; both have 140 horsepower, but the 3.8-liter makes more torque than the 3.0-liter, 215 pounds/feet to 165. A 4-speed automatic is the only transmission with these engines. The high-performance Taurus SHO sedan uses different V-6s, both with 220 horsepower. With the 5-speed manual transmission, SHO gets a 3.0-liter; with automatic it gets a 3.2-liter. Anti-lock brakes are standard on the SHO and optional on other Taurus and Sable models. A cellular telephone is a new option and all models get a new steering wheel in which the air-bag housing doubles as the horn pad. Taurus and Sable remain atop our ranking of mid-size cars because no rival offers their range of utility, performance, safety features, and quality at these prices. Dealers should be discounting prices and offering attractive leases on these roomy family cars. Acceleration with the base V-6 is more than adequate, while the 3.8-liter furnishes a better jump off the line and stronger passing power. Taurus and Sable are surefooted and agile in the manner of European sedans. The only major ergonomic problem is a stereo that has small buttons and is mounted too low to easily reach. If you're looking for a mid-size car, we recommend you start your shopping here.

Ford Taurus prices are on page 320;
Mercury Sable prices are on page 372.

FORD TAURUS LX

Rating Guide	1	2	3	4	5
Performance					
Acceleration	▒	▒	▒	▒	
Economy	▒	▒			
Driveability	▒	▒	▒		
Ride	▒	▒	▒	▒	
Steering/handling	▒	▒	▒	▒	
Braking	▒	▒	▒	▒	▒
Noise	▒	▒	▒		
Accommodations					
Driver seating	▒	▒	▒	▒	
Instruments/controls	▒	▒	▒	▒	
Visibility	▒	▒	▒		
Room/comfort	▒	▒	▒	▒	
Entry/exit	▒	▒	▒		
Cargo room	▒	▒	▒		
Workmanship					
Exterior	▒	▒	▒	▒	
Interior	▒	▒	▒	▒	
Value	▒	▒	▒	▒	▒

Total Points..59

Specifications

Body type	4-door notchback	Engine type	ohv V-6
Wheelbase (in.)	106.0	Engine size (l/cu. in.)	3.8/232
Overall length (in.)	192.0	Horsepower @ rpm	140 @ 3800
Overall width (in.)	70.7	Torque @ rpm	215 @ 2200
Overall height (in.)	54.1	Transmission	auto/4-sp.
Curb weight (lbs.)	3104	Drive wheels	front
Seating capacity	6	Brakes, F/R	disc/disc (ABS)
Front head room (in.)	38.3	Tire size	205/65R15
Max. front leg room (in.)	41.7	Fuel tank capacity (gal.)	16.0
Rear head room (in.)	37.6	EPA city/highway mpg	19/28
Min. rear leg room (in.)	37.5	Test mileage (mpg)	17.9
Cargo volume (cu. ft.)	18.0		

Warranties The entire car is covered for 3 years/36,000 miles. Body perforation rust is covered for 6 years/100,000 miles.

Rating scale 5=Exceptional; 4=Above average; 3=Average; 2=Below average; 1=Poor

FORD TEMPO/ ─────── MERCURY TOPAZ

Built in Kansas City, Mo., and Canada.

Ford Tempo LX

COMPACT

These front-drive 2- and 4-door sedans carry over with few changes as Ford prepares to replace them next spring with the Ford Contour and Mercury Mystique. Tempo and Topaz differ mainly in exterior styling, though Tempo offers two price series (GL and LX), while Mercury offers just one (GS). A 96-horsepower 2.3-liter 4-cylinder engine is standard on all models and a 135-horsepower 3.0-liter V-6 is optional. Both engines are available with a 5-speed manual or 3-speed automatic transmission. A driver-side air bag is optional on 4-cylinder models with the automatic transmission. This year, air-bag equipped models get a manual seat belt for the driver's seat, while the front passenger seat keeps a motorized shoulder belt with a manual lap belt. Anti-lock brakes aren't offered. The 1995 Contour and Mystique will have standard dual air bags, optional anti-lock brakes, and a roomier, more modern design. They can't arrive a moment too soon. Topaz and Tempo have been way behind most competitors in sophistication and refinement for some years, but they've also been beating a lot of rivals on price. If you're on a tight budget, there's good value here. Both engines are loud and coarse in even moderate work, but at least the V-6 supplies adequate acceleration in situations where the 4-cylinder is weak and unresponsive. Passing ability with either is slowed by the automatic transmission's reluctance to downshift unless you floor the throttle. Trunk space is adequate, and there's ample passenger room in front and an adequate amount in back.

Ford Tempo prices are on page 322;
Mercury Topaz prices are on page 374.

FORD TEMPO LX

Rating Guide	1	2	3	4	5
Performance					
Acceleration	▐▐▐▐▐▐▐▐▐▐▐▐▐▐▐				
Economy	▐▐▐▐▐▐▐▐▐▐▐▐				
Driveability	▐▐▐▐▐▐▐▐▐▐▐▐▐▐				
Ride	▐▐▐▐▐▐▐▐▐▐▐▐				
Steering/handling	▐▐▐▐▐▐▐▐▐▐▐▐▐				
Braking	▐▐▐▐▐▐▐▐▐▐▐▐▐▐				
Noise	▐▐▐▐▐▐▐▐				
Accommodations					
Driver seating	▐▐▐▐▐▐▐▐▐▐▐▐▐▐▐▐▐				
Instruments/controls	▐▐▐▐▐▐▐▐▐▐▐▐▐▐▐				
Visibility	▐▐▐▐▐▐▐▐▐▐▐▐▐▐				
Room/comfort	▐▐▐▐▐▐▐▐▐▐▐▐				
Entry/exit	▐▐▐▐▐▐▐▐▐▐▐▐				
Cargo room	▐▐▐▐▐▐▐▐▐▐				
Workmanship					
Exterior	▐▐▐▐▐▐▐▐▐▐▐▐▐▐▐				
Interior	▐▐▐▐▐▐▐▐▐▐▐▐▐▐▐				
Value	▐▐▐▐▐▐▐▐▐▐▐▐				
Total Points **53**					

Specifications

Body type	4-door notchback	Engine type	ohv V-6
Wheelbase (in.)	99.9	Engine size (l/cu. in.)	3.0/182
Overall length (in.)	177.0	Horsepower @ rpm	135 @ 4800
Overall width (in.)	68.3	Torque @ rpm	150 @ 4250
Overall height (in.)	52.8	Transmission	auto/3-sp.
Curb weight (lbs.)	2569	Drive wheels	front
Seating capacity	5	Brakes, F/R	disc/drum
Front head room (in.)	37.5	Tire size	185/70R14
Max. front leg room (in.)	41.5	Fuel tank capacity (gal.)	15.9
Rear head room (in.)	36.8	EPA city/highway mpg	20/23
Min. rear leg room (in.)	36.0	Test mileage (mpg)	21.0
Cargo volume (cu. ft.)	12.9		

Warranties The entire car is covered for 3 years/36,000 miles. Body perforation rust is covered for 6 years/100,000 miles.

Rating scale 5=Exceptional; 4=Above average; 3=Average; 2=Below average; 1=Poor

FORD THUNDERBIRD/——
MERCURY COUGAR

Built in Lorain, Ohio.

Ford Thunderbird LX

MID-SIZE

Dual air bags and a new V-8 are the key changes to these rear-drive coupes, which also get fresh front and rear styling. Thunderbird returns in LX and Super Coupe (SC) trim and Cougar only in XR7 trim. The T-Bird LX and Cougar have a standard 140-horsepower 3.8-liter V-6. Ford's overhead-cam 4.6-liter V-8 with 205 horsepower replaces a 200-horsepower overhead-valve 5.0-liter as the optional engine for the LX and Cougar. The SC continues with a 230-horsepower supercharged version of the V-6 and a 5-speed manual transmission. Optional on the SC and standard on the others is a 4-speed automatic. The automatic gains electronic shift controls and an overdrive lockout button that also triggers second-gear starts for better traction on slippery surfaces. In addition, traction control is a new option for the LX and Cougar and included with automatic transmission on the SC. Anti-lock brakes are again standard on the SC and optional on the others. The new driver- and passenger-side air bags reside in a much-improved dashboard and replace motorized shoulder belts and manual lap belts. The V-6 can't move them with any verve. The optional V-8 has good acceleration off the line and strong highway passing power, but unimpressive throttle response in the 30-50 mph range. The electronic automatic also is slow to downshift for passing. At around $17,000 for a car with standard air conditioning, AM/FM cassette, dual air bags, and more, the LX and Cougar are good deals. Pontiac also has a good deal on the 2-door Grand Prix, which gains dual air bags this year.

Ford Thunderbird prices are on page 324;
Mercury Cougar prices are on page 369.

FORD THUNDERBIRD LX

Rating Guide	1	2	3	4	5
Performance					
Acceleration					
Economy					
Driveability					
Ride					
Steering/handling					
Braking					
Noise					
Accommodations					
Driver seating					
Instruments/controls					
Visibility					
Room/comfort					
Entry/exit					
Cargo room					
Workmanship					
Exterior					
Interior					
Value					

Total Points...**57**

Specifications

Body type ....2-door notchback
Wheelbase (in.).....................113.0
Overall length (in.)................200.3
Overall width (in.) 72.7
Overall height (in.)..................52.5
Curb weight (lbs.) 3575
Seating capacity...........................5
Front head room (in.) 38.1
Max. front leg room (in.) 42.5
Rear head room (in.) 37.5
Min. rear leg room (in.)...........35.8
Cargo volume (cu. ft.).............15.1

Engine type.......................ohc V-8
Engine size (l/cu. in.).........4.6/281
Horsepower @ rpm ...205 @ 4500
Torque @ rpm ....265 @ 3300
Transmission.................auto/4-sp.
Drive wheels ....rear
Brakes, F/R...........disc/disc (ABS)
Tire size 215/70R15
Fuel tank capacity (gal.).........18.0
EPA city/highway mpg 18/25
Test mileage (mpg) 16.4

Warranties The entire car is covered for 3 years/36,000 miles. Body perforation rust is covered for 6 years/100,000 miles.

Rating scale 5=Exceptional; 4=Above average; 3=Average; 2=Below average; 1=Poor

GEO METRO

Built in Canada.

Geo Metro 3-door

SUBCOMPACT Similar to Suzuki Swift

The tiny front-drive Metro loses its convertible and upscale LSi hatchbacks for 1994 and gains CFC-free air conditioning. Metro comes as a 3-door hatchback in fuel-miser XFi and as 3- and 5-door hatchbacks in base trim. The only engine is a 1.0-liter 3-cylinder. In the XFi, it's rated at 49 horsepower and comes only with a 5-speed manual transmission. In the others, the engine is rated at 55 horsepower and comes with the 5-speed manual or an optional 3-speed automatic. The 5-door model is about four inches longer in wheelbase and overall length than the 3-door. Metro is built from the same design as the Suzuki Swift but has different styling and engines. Metro meets the passive-restraint requirements with door-mounted front seat belts that can be left buckled to automatically deploy when the doors are closed. All models also come with automatic front door locks that engage when vehicle speed reaches about eight mph; they must be unlocked manually. Though we averaged an impressive 38.5 mpg in rush-hour commuting in a test of a 5-speed 3-door model, that is largely due to the Metro's lightweight construction, which is evident in frail-feeling fenders and doors, thin interior panels, and tiny wheels and tires. Metro can keep pace with around-town traffic, but highway passing power is woefully lacking. Automatic transmission costs some mileage and acceleration, though not much. Tall drivers will find head room scarce and rear leg room in the 3-door is insufficient for adults. All models suffer a jarring ride and excessive engine, road, and wind noise. We'd consider the Metro only if fuel economy was the overwhelming priority.

Geo Metro prices are on page 326.

CONSUMER GUIDE®

GEO METRO

Rating Guide	1	2	3	4	5
Performance					
Acceleration	▓▓				
Economy	▓▓▓▓▓				
Driveability	▓▓▓				
Ride	▓▓▓				
Steering/handling	▓▓▓				
Braking	▓▓▓				
Noise	▓▓				
Accommodations					
Driver seating	▓▓▓				
Instruments/controls	▓▓▓▓				
Visibility	▓▓▓▓▓				
Room/comfort	▓▓▓				
Entry/exit	▓▓▓				
Cargo room	▓▓▓				
Workmanship					
Exterior	▓▓▓				
Interior	▓▓▓				
Value	▓▓▓				

Total Points 48

Specifications

Body type	3-door hatchback	Engine type	ohc I-3
Wheelbase (in.)	89.2	Engine size (l/cu. in.)	1.0/61
Overall length (in.)	147.4	Horsepower @ rpm	55 @ 5700
Overall width (in.)	62.7	Torque @ rpm	58 @ 3300
Overall height (in.)	52.4	Transmission	manual/5-sp.
Curb weight (lbs.)	1650	Drive wheels	front
Seating capacity	4	Brakes, F/R	disc/drum
Front head room (in.)	37.8	Tire size	145/80R12
Max. front leg room (in.)	42.5	Fuel tank capacity (gal.)	10.6
Rear head room (in.)	36.5	EPA city/highway mpg	46/49
Min. rear leg room (in.)	29.8	Test mileage (mpg)	38.5
Cargo volume (cu. ft.)	29.1		

Warranties The entire car is covered for 3 years/36,000 miles. Body perforation rust is covered for 6 years/100,000 miles.

Rating scale 5=Exceptional; 4=Above average; 3=Average; 2=Below average; 1=Poor

GEO PRIZM

Built in Fremont, Calif.

Geo Prizm LSi

SUBCOMPACT Similar to Toyota Corolla

A standard passenger-side air bag joins a driver-side air bag as the big news for Prizm, a front-drive subcompact that is a clone of the Toyota Corolla. Corolla also gains the second air bag this year. Prizm comes as a 4-door sedan in base and higher-priced LSi models. Both have a standard 108-horsepower 1.6-liter 4-cylinder available with a 5-speed manual transmission or optional 3-speed automatic. Optional on the LSi is a 115-horsepower 1.8-liter 4-cylinder that teams with a standard 5-speed manual or optional 4-speed automatic. Anti-lock brakes are optional on both models. Seat belts have been revised to make it easier to install child safety seats and the optional air conditioning now has CFC-free refrigerant. The 1.6-liter engine furnishes adequate acceleration, but the 1.8-liter provides noticeably more zip. Our 1.8-liter LSi with a 5-speed averaged well over 30 mpg in highway driving and posted an impressive 27.5 mpg in rush-hour suburban commuting. The Prizm LSi had more engine and road noise than a Corolla LE we drove, though it was still quieter than most small sedans. Ride comfort is impressive. There's ample room in the front seats. In back, medium-size adults find their knees pressed into the front seatbacks even when the front seats aren't all the way back, and head room is limited for taller people. The dashboard has clearly marked gauges and large climate controls. Among our few complaints: The radio is mounted too low in the center of the dashboard and the optional stereo with the CD player has too many small buttons. There are less-expensive small cars, but few are as polished as Prizm.

Geo Prizm prices are on page 327.

GEO PRIZM LSi

Rating Guide	1	2	3	4	5
Performance					
Acceleration				▓	
Economy				▓	
Driveability					▓
Ride				▓	
Steering/handling				▓	
Braking					▓
Noise				▓	
Accommodations					
Driver seating				▓	
Instruments/controls				▓	
Visibility				▓	
Room/comfort			▓		
Entry/exit			▓		
Cargo room			▓		
Workmanship					
Exterior				▓	
Interior				▓	
Value				▓	
Total Points					**59**

Specifications

Body type	4-door notchback	Engine type	dohc I-4
Wheelbase (in.)	97.0	Engine size (l/cu. in.)	1.8/110
Overall length (in.)	172.6	Horsepower @ rpm	115 @ 5800
Overall width (in.)	66.3	Torque @ rpm	115 @ 4800
Overall height (in.)	52.7	Transmission	manual/5-sp.
Curb weight (lbs.)	2347	Drive wheels	front
Seating capacity	5	Brakes, F/R	disc/drum (ABS)
Front head room (in.)	38.8	Tire size	185/65R14
Max. front leg room (in.)	42.4	Fuel tank capacity (gal.)	13.2
Rear head room (in.)	37.1	EPA city/highway mpg	28/34
Min. rear leg room (in.)	32.9	Test mileage (mpg)	29.7
Cargo volume (cu. ft.)	12.7		

Warranties The entire car is covered for 3 years/36,000 miles. Body perforation rust is covered for 6 years/100,000 miles.

Rating scale 5=Exceptional; 4=Above average; 3=Average; 2=Below average; 1=Poor

GEO TRACKER/
SUZUKI SIDEKICK

Built in Canada.

Geo Tracker convertible

SPORT-UTILITY VEHICLE

These two pint-sized sport-utility vehicles get a few equipment changes for 1994 and Tracker adds a new engine for California models. Tracker comes as a 2-door convertible and a 2-door hardtop. The convertible is available with either rear-wheel drive or part-time 4-wheel drive (not for use on dry pavement). The hardtop comes only with 4WD. Suzuki also sells a 2-door convertible but substitutes a 5-door wagon for Tracker's 2-door hardtop. Both Sidekick body styles are available with rear- or part-time 4-wheel drive. An 80-horsepower 1.6-liter 4-cylinder with two valves per cylinder remains standard on all 2-door Trackers and Sidekicks— except California-bound Trackers, which get a 95-horsepower version of that engine with four valves per cylinder. A 5-speed manual transmission is standard and a 3-speed automatic is optional. The Sidekick 5-door wagon has the 95-horsepower engine tied to either a 5-speed manual or 4-speed automatic transmission. Tracker and Sidekick now come with a center high-mounted stoplamp. Rear anti-lock brakes that function only in 2WD remain standard. Compared to the crude Jeep Wrangler, Tracker and Sidekick are more modern and refined. That's not to say, however, that we would recommend any of these mini sport-utilities for everyday driving. Though they make a strong fashion statement, they're poor substitutes for cars.

Geo Tracker prices are on page 328;
Suzuki Sidekick prices are on page 434.

GEO TRACKER CONVERTIBLE

Rating Guide	1	2	3	4	5
Performance					
Acceleration	▓▓▓▓▓▓▓▓				
Economy	▓▓▓▓▓▓▓▓				
Driveability	▓▓▓▓▓▓▓▓				
Ride	▓▓▓▓▓				
Steering/handling	▓▓▓▓▓				
Braking	▓▓▓▓▓▓▓▓▓				
Noise	▓▓▓				
Accommodations					
Driver seating	▓▓▓▓▓▓				
Instruments/controls	▓▓▓▓▓▓▓▓▓				
Visibility	▓▓▓▓▓▓▓				
Room/comfort	▓▓▓▓▓				
Entry/exit	▓▓▓▓▓▓▓				
Cargo room	▓▓▓▓▓				
Workmanship					
Exterior	▓▓▓▓▓▓▓				
Interior	▓▓▓▓▓▓▓				
Value	▓▓▓▓▓▓▓				

Total Points..**45**

Specifications

Body type	2-door convertible	Engine type	ohc I-4
Wheelbase (in.)	86.6	Engine size (l/cu. in.)	1.6/97
Overall length (in.)	142.5	Horsepower @ rpm	80 @ 5400
Overall width (in.)	64.2	Torque @ rpm	94 @ 3000
Overall height (in.)	65.6	Transmission	manual/5-sp.
Curb weight (lbs.)	2189	Drive wheels	rear/all
Seating capacity	4	Brakes, F/R	disc/drum (ABS)
Front head room (in.)	39.5	Tire size	205/75R15
Max. front leg room (in.)	42.1	Fuel tank capacity (gal.)	11.1
Rear head room (in.)	38.3	EPA city/highway mpg	25/27
Min. rear leg room (in.)	31.6	Test mileage (mpg)	22.8
Cargo volume (cu. ft.)	31.9		

Warranties The entire vehicle is covered for 3 years/36,000 miles. Body perforation rust is covered for 6 years/100,000 miles.

Rating scale 5=Exceptional; 4=Above average; 3=Average; 2=Below average; 1=Poor

HONDA ACCORD —

Built in Marysville, Ohio.

Honda Accord EX 4-door

MID-SIZE

Accord has been redesigned for 1994 and gets new styling, a larger interior, standard dual air bags, and more powerful 4-cylinder engines. The Accord again has front-wheel drive and comes as a 4-door sedan, 2-door coupe, and 5-door wagon. Wheelbase is about the same as before, but overall length is shorter by 1.2 inches while width grows by three inches. The sedan and coupe come in DX, LX, and EX price levels, the wagon in LX and EX. Accord has two new 2.2-liter 4-cylinder engines. DX and LX models use a 130-horsepower version and the EX has a 145-horsepower version. A 5-speed manual transmission is standard and an electronic 4-speed automatic is optional on all models. We tested an EX sedan with automatic transmission and though it was more than adequate in most situations, it felt lethargic when a quick burst of acceleration was needed. Our fuel economy ranged from the low 20s in the city to the low 30s on the highway. The new Accord feels poised in tight turns and grips the road well. Wind and tire noise are less evident than before, and ride quality is improved. There's ample room for four adults, though head room is reduced in front by the EX's standard power moonroof. A low dashboard and thin roof pillars create a commanding view of the road to the front and sides. The new Accord is a solid family car with a refined, sporty manner, but it needs a V-6 engine to compete head-on with its top rivals, the Toyota Camry and Ford Taurus (the V-6 is coming for 1995). Despite this year's improvements, base prices haven't gone up much, so Accord remains a good value.

Honda Accord prices are on page 334.

HONDA ACCORD EX

Rating Guide	1	2	3	4	5
Performance					
Acceleration	▮▮▮▮▮▮▮▮▮▮▮▮▮▮▮▮▮▮▮▮				
Economy	▮▮▮▮▮▮▮▮▮▮▮▮				
Driveability	▮▮▮▮▮▮▮▮▮▮▮▮				
Ride	▮▮▮▮▮▮▮▮▮▮▮▮▮▮				
Steering/handling	▮▮▮▮▮▮▮▮▮▮▮▮▮▮				
Braking	▮▮▮▮▮▮▮▮▮▮▮▮▮▮▮▮▮▮▮▮				
Noise	▮▮▮▮▮▮▮▮▮▮▮▮				
Accommodations					
Driver seating	▮▮▮▮▮▮▮▮▮▮▮▮▮▮▮▮				
Instruments/controls	▮▮▮▮▮▮▮▮▮▮▮▮▮▮▮▮				
Visibility	▮▮▮▮▮▮▮▮▮▮▮▮▮▮▮▮				
Room/comfort	▮▮▮▮▮▮▮▮▮▮▮▮▮▮▮▮				
Entry/exit	▮▮▮▮▮▮▮▮▮▮▮▮▮▮▮▮				
Cargo room	▮▮▮▮▮▮▮▮▮▮▮▮▮▮▮▮				
Workmanship					
Exterior	▮▮▮▮▮▮▮▮▮▮▮▮▮▮▮▮				
Interior	▮▮▮▮▮▮▮▮▮▮▮▮▮▮▮▮				
Value	▮▮▮▮▮▮▮▮▮▮▮▮▮▮▮▮				

Total Points...62

Specifications

Body type	4-door notchback	Engine type	ohc I-4
Wheelbase (in.)	106.9	Engine size (l/cu. in.)	2.2/132
Overall length (in.)	184.0	Horsepower @ rpm	145 @ 5500
Overall width (in.)	70.1	Torque @ rpm	147 @ 4500
Overall height (in.)	55.1	Transmission	auto/4-sp.
Curb weight (lbs.)	3075	Drive wheels	front
Seating capacity	5	Brakes, F/R	disc/disc (ABS)
Front head room (in.)	38.4	Tire size	195/60HR15
Max. front leg room (in.)	42.7	Fuel tank capacity (gal.)	17.0
Rear head room (in.)	36.7	EPA city/highway mpg	23/30
Min. rear leg room (in.)	34.3	Test mileage (mpg)	26.0
Cargo volume (cu. ft.)	13.0		

Warranties The entire car is covered for 3 years/36,000 miles. Body perforation rust is covered for 3 years/unlimited miles.

Rating scale 5=Exceptional; 4=Above average; 3=Average; 2=Below average; 1=Poor

HONDA CIVIC

Built in East Liberty, Ohio; Canada; and Japan.

 ✓ BEST BUY

Honda Civic EX 4-door

SUBCOMPACT

A passenger-side air bag joins a driver-side air bag as standard equipment on all 1994 Civics and anti-lock brakes (ABS) are available on three additional models. Civic is a front-drive subcompact available in three body styles. The hatchback comes in CX, VX, DX, and sporty Si price levels. The 4-door sedan and 2-door coupe return in DX and EX trim. The 4-door also comes in a mid-level LX trim. All DX and LX models have a 1.5-liter 4-cylinder engine with 102 horsepower. The CX 3-door continues with a 70-horsepower version of the 1.5-liter and the VX with a 92 horsepower version. EX and Si models have a 1.6-liter with 125 horsepower. A 5-speed manual transmission is standard on all models and a 4-speed automatic is optional on the DX, LX, and EX. Last year, ABS was standard on the EX sedan and not available on other Civics. This year, they're also optional on the LX sedan, EX coupe, and Si hatchback. Performance depends on powertrain in the Civic line. The EX and Si are best, while the low-power CX hatchback is more of an around-town shopper. The fuel-miser VX hatchback produces astounding EPA mileage but leisurely pickup. The Civic sedan has ride quality that rivals bigger cars and more interior space than some compacts. Unfortunately, the top-line EX 4-door costs as much as a low-end Accord when similarly equipped. However, all Civics are well-built, return good mileage, and should be reliable and have high resale value. Though they aren't the design and value leaders they once were, they remain excellent choices among subcompacts. The Toyota Corolla and similar Geo Prizm are Civic's most formidable rivals.

Honda Civic prices are on page 335.

CONSUMER GUIDE®

HONDA CIVIC EX

Rating Guide	1	2	3	4	5
Performance					
Acceleration	‖‖‖‖‖‖‖‖‖‖‖‖‖‖‖‖‖‖‖‖‖‖‖‖				
Economy	‖‖‖‖‖‖‖‖‖‖‖‖‖‖‖‖‖‖‖‖‖‖‖‖				
Driveability	‖‖‖‖‖‖‖‖‖‖‖‖‖‖‖‖‖				
Ride	‖‖‖‖‖‖‖‖‖‖‖‖‖‖‖‖‖				
Steering/handling	‖‖‖‖‖‖‖‖‖‖‖‖‖‖‖‖‖‖‖‖‖‖‖‖				
Braking	‖‖‖‖‖‖‖‖‖‖‖‖‖‖‖‖‖‖‖‖‖‖‖‖‖‖‖‖‖‖				
Noise	‖‖‖‖‖‖‖‖‖‖‖‖‖‖‖‖‖				
Accommodations					
Driver seating	‖‖‖‖‖‖‖‖‖‖‖‖‖‖‖‖‖‖‖‖‖‖‖‖				
Instruments/controls	‖‖‖‖‖‖‖‖‖‖‖‖‖‖‖‖‖‖‖‖‖‖‖‖				
Visibility	‖‖‖‖‖‖‖‖‖‖‖‖‖‖‖‖‖				
Room/comfort	‖‖‖‖‖‖‖‖‖‖‖‖‖‖‖‖‖‖‖‖‖‖‖‖				
Entry/exit	‖‖‖‖‖‖‖‖‖‖‖‖‖‖‖‖‖				
Cargo room	‖‖‖‖‖‖‖‖‖‖‖‖‖‖‖‖‖‖‖‖‖‖‖‖				
Workmanship					
Exterior	‖‖‖‖‖‖‖‖‖‖‖‖‖‖‖‖‖‖‖‖‖‖‖‖				
Interior	‖‖‖‖‖‖‖‖‖‖‖‖‖‖‖‖‖‖‖‖‖‖‖‖				
Value	‖‖‖‖‖‖‖‖‖‖‖‖‖‖‖‖‖‖‖‖‖‖‖‖				

Total Points...59

Specifications

Body type ....4-door notchback
Wheelbase (in.) 103.2
Overall length (in.) 173.0
Overall width (in.) 67.0
Overall height (in.) 51.7
Curb weight (lbs.) 2522
Seating capacity 5
Front head room (in.) 39.1
Max. front leg room (in.) 42.5
Rear head room (in.) 37.2
Min. rear leg room (in.) 32.8
Cargo volume (cu. ft.) 12.4

Engine type ....ohc I-4
Engine size (l/cu. in.) 1.6/97
Horsepower @ rpm ...125 @ 6600
Torque @ rpm ....106 @ 55200
Transmission ....manual/5-sp.
Drive wheels ....front
Brakes, F/R ....disc/disc (ABS)
Tire size 175/65R14
Fuel tank capacity (gal.) 11.9
EPA city/highway mpg 29/35
Test mileage (mpg) 30.7

Warranties The entire car is covered for 3 years/36,000 miles. Body perforation rust is covered for 3 years/unlimited miles.

Rating scale 5=Exceptional; 4=Above average; 3=Average; 2=Below average; 1=Poor

HONDA CIVIC DEL SOL

Built in Japan.

Honda Civic del Sol Si

SPORTS COUPE

A passenger-side air bag and a new model have been added to Honda's 2-seat, front-drive sports coupe, which comes with a removable aluminum roof panel that weighs 24 pounds and can be stored in a frame built into the trunk. The new model is called VTEC, Honda's name for its variable valve timing engine technology. The VTEC model joins returning S and Si models, all of which now have dual air bags. Anti-lock brakes aren't offered. The VTEC has a 1.6-liter 4-cylinder engine with dual overhead camshafts and 160 horsepower. The Si has a 1.6-liter with 125 horsepower and the base S model has a 102-horsepower 1.5-liter 4-cylinder. A 5-speed manual is standard and a 4-speed automatic is optional on the S and Si. All come with power side windows and a power rear window. Though it's fun to drive, del Sol is not a true sports car in the mold of the similarly priced Mazda Miata. Its flexibility to provide open-air motoring or fully enclosed security is one of its main attractions. With the roof panel off, the del Sol is remarkably free of the cockpit buffeting typical of convertibles, but it is prone to body flex and twisting—flaws that diminish with the roof panel in place. The lift-off top eats up about two cubic feet of trunk space, which leaves 8.3 cubic feet—barely enough to hold the stuff that two occupants need to take on a weekend trip. All three engines are fuel-efficient and acceleration ranges from good in the S model, to enthusiastic in the Si, and inspiring in the new VTEC. These engines perform best at high rpm, however, so they're considerably less lively with automatic transmission.

Honda Civic del Sol prices are on page 336.

HONDA CIVIC DEL SOL Si

Rating Guide	1	2	3	4	5
Performance					
Acceleration				▮	
Economy				▮	
Driveability				▮	
Ride			▮		
Steering/handling				▮	
Braking				▮	
Noise			▮		
Accommodations					
Driver seating				▮	
Instruments/controls				▮	
Visibility				▮	
Room/comfort				▮	
Entry/exit				▮	
Cargo room			▮		
Workmanship					
Exterior				▮	
Interior				▮	
Value				▮	

Total Points...56

Specifications

Body type ....2-door notchback	Engine type ....ohc I-4
Wheelbase (in.) 93.3	Engine size (l/cu. in.)...........1.6/97
Overall length (in.)................157.3	Horsepower @ rpm ...125 @ 6600
Overall width (in.) 66.7	Torque @ rpm ....106 @ 5200
Overall height (in.).................49.4	Transmission ....manual/5-sp.
Curb weight (lbs.) 2414	Drive wheels ....front
Seating capacity.........................2	Brakes, F/R ....disc/disc
Front head room (in.) 37.5	Tire size 185/60HR14
Max. front leg room (in.) 40.3	Fuel tank capacity (gal.) 11.9
Rear head room (in.) ....—	EPA city/highway mpg 29/35
Min. rear leg room (in.) ....—	Test mileage (mpg) 33.4
Cargo volume (cu. ft.).............10.5	

Warranties The entire car is covered for 3 years/36,000 miles. Body perforation rust is covered for 3 years/unlimited miles.

Rating scale 5=Exceptional; 4=Above average; 3=Average; 2=Below average; 1=Poor

HONDA PRELUDE

Built in Japan.

Honda Prelude Si

SPORTS COUPE

Like other 1994 Hondas, all Preludes come with standard dual air bags. Last year, all models had a driver-side air bag and only the Si 4WS and VTEC models had one for the front passenger. Leather upholstery, which wasn't previously offered, is standard this year on the Si 4WS and VTEC models. Other changes include a modestly restyled nose and turn signal lamps; cup holders and a storage compartment for the center console; and new vacuum-fluorescent gauges. The base S model has a 135-horsepower 2.2-liter 4-cylinder engine with a single overhead camshaft, while the Si and Si 4WS have a dual-camshaft 2.3-liter 4-cylinder with 160 horsepower. The top-line VTEC comes with a 190-horsepower 2.2-liter 4-cylinder with dual camshafts and Variable Timing and Lift Electronic Control, Honda's variable valve timing system. A 5-speed manual transmission is standard on all Preludes and a 4-speed automatic is optional on all except the VTEC. The Si 4WS has electronic 4-wheel steering that turns the rear wheels in the same direction as the fronts to improve cornering. Four-wheel disc brakes are standard on all Preludes and an anti-lock feature is standard on all except the S model. Prelude is well-made, fun to drive, and expensive. Only the S models are priced below $20,000 and that doesn't include air conditioning. Like most sports coupes, Prelude has a tiny back seat that makes it an impractical car for those who frequently carry more than one passenger. All three engines are smooth and economical, however, and Prelude should be reliable and have good resale value, compensating somewhat for the high prices.

Honda Prelude prices are on page 336.

HONDA PRELUDE Si

Rating Guide	1	2	3	4	5
Performance					
Acceleration	▐▐▐▐▐▐▐▐▐▐▐▐▐▐▐▐▐▐▐▐▐▐▐▐				
Economy	▐▐▐▐▐▐▐▐▐▐▐▐▐				
Driveability	▐▐▐▐▐▐▐▐▐▐▐▐▐▐▐▐				
Ride	▐▐▐▐▐▐▐▐▐▐▐▐▐▐				
Steering/handling	▐▐▐▐▐▐▐▐▐▐▐▐▐▐▐▐				
Braking	▐▐▐▐▐▐▐▐▐▐▐▐▐▐▐▐▐▐▐▐▐▐▐▐▐				
Noise	▐▐▐▐▐▐▐▐▐▐▐▐▐▐▐				
Accommodations					
Driver seating	▐▐▐▐▐▐▐▐▐▐▐▐▐▐▐▐▐▐				
Instruments/controls	▐▐▐▐▐▐▐▐▐▐▐▐▐▐▐▐				
Visibility	▐▐▐▐▐▐▐▐▐▐▐▐▐▐				
Room/comfort	▐▐▐▐▐▐▐▐▐▐▐				
Entry/exit	▐▐▐▐▐▐▐▐▐▐▐▐				
Cargo room	▐▐▐▐▐▐▐▐▐▐				
Workmanship					
Exterior	▐▐▐▐▐▐▐▐▐▐▐▐▐▐▐▐▐▐▐				
Interior	▐▐▐▐▐▐▐▐▐▐▐▐▐▐▐▐▐▐▐				
Value	▐▐▐▐▐▐▐▐▐▐▐▐▐				
Total Points					**54**

Specifications

Body type ....2-door notchback	Engine type ....dohc I-4
Wheelbase (in.) 100.4	Engine size (l/cu. in.)........2.3/138
Overall length (in.)................174.8	Horsepower @ rpm ...160 @ 5800
Overall width (in.) 69.5	Torque @ rpm ....156 @ 4500
Overall height (in.)..................50.8	Transmission ....manual/5-sp.
Curb weight (lbs.) 2866	Drive wheels ....front
Seating capacity............................4	Brakes, F/R...........disc/disc (ABS)
Front head room (in.) 38.0	Tire size....................205/55VR15
Max. front leg room (in.) 44.2	Fuel tank capacity (gal.) 15.9
Rear head room (in.) 35.1	EPA city/highway mpg 22/26
Min. rear leg room (in.)...........28.1	Test mileage (mpg) 22.5
Cargo volume (cu. ft.)...............7.9	

Warranties The entire car is covered for 3 years/36,000 miles. Body perforation rust is covered for 3 years/unlimited miles.

Rating scale 5=Exceptional; 4=Above average; 3=Average; 2=Below average; 1=Poor

HYUDAI ELANTRA

Built in South Korea.

Hyundai Elantra GLS

SUBCOMPACT

Elantra gets two important new safety features this year. Both the base and upscale GLS versions of this front-drive 4-door notchback gain a standard driver-side air bag, and the GLS adds anti-lock brakes to its options list. A 113-horsepower 1.6-liter 4-cylinder continues as standard in the base model with the 5-speed manual transmission. A 124-horsepower 1.8-liter 4-cylinder powers the base model with the optional 4-speed automatic and the GLS with either transmission. Elantra's styling is freshened with a new grille, headlamps, front bumper, and taillamps. Air conditioners now use CFC-free refrigerant. While we applaud the addition of the driver-side air bag, some rivals now have dual air bags. We also appreciate the new optional anti-lock brakes, which will improve Elantra's stopping ability in emergency braking. Unfortunately, Elantra is average to below average in other key areas. The ride is floaty on wavy surfaces yet stiff and jiggly on bumpy roads. Noise levels are high even for a lower-priced small car. Acceleration is mediocre with either engine and the automatic transmission tends to shifts harshly. On the other hand, Elantra offers more passenger and cargo space than some rivals, a good driving position with clear visibility to all directions, and functional instruments and controls. Hyundai includes free maintenance during the first two years of ownership and 5-year/60,000-mile powertrain coverage. Still, it's hard to recommend Elantra over better-built, more refined cars like the Honda Civic, Geo Prizm, and Toyota Corolla—except on price. Hyundai dealers should be discounting.

Hyundai Elantra prices are on page 337.

HYUNDAI ELANTRA GLS

Rating Guide	1	2	3	4	5
Performance					
Acceleration	▓▓▓▓▓▓▓▓▓				
Economy	▓▓▓▓▓▓▓▓▓▓				
Driveability	▓▓▓▓▓▓▓▓▓▓				
Ride	▓▓▓▓▓▓▓▓				
Steering/handling	▓▓▓▓▓▓▓▓▓				
Braking	▓▓▓▓▓▓▓▓▓				
Noise	▓▓▓▓▓▓▓				
Accommodations					
Driver seating	▓▓▓▓▓▓▓▓▓				
Instruments/controls	▓▓▓▓▓▓▓▓▓▓				
Visibility	▓▓▓▓▓▓▓▓▓▓				
Room/comfort	▓▓▓▓▓▓▓▓▓				
Entry/exit	▓▓▓▓▓▓▓▓▓				
Cargo room	▓▓▓▓▓▓▓▓				
Workmanship					
Exterior	▓▓▓▓▓▓▓▓▓				
Interior	▓▓▓▓▓▓▓▓▓▓				
Value	▓▓▓▓▓▓▓▓▓				

Total Points...51

Specifications

Body type	4-door notchback	Engine type	dohc I-4
Wheelbase (in.)	98.4	Engine size (l/cu. in.)	1.8/110
Overall length (in.)	172.8	Horsepower @ rpm	124 @ 6000
Overall width (in.)	66.1	Torque @ rpm	116 @ 4500
Overall height (in.)	52.0	Transmission	auto/4-sp.
Curb weight (lbs.)	2500	Drive wheels	front
Seating capacity	5	Brakes, F/R	disc/drum
Front head room (in.)	38.4	Tire size	185/60R14
Max. front leg room (in.)	42.6	Fuel tank capacity (gal.)	13.7
Rear head room (in.)	37.6	EPA city/highway mpg	23/28
Min. rear leg room (in.)	33.4	Test mileage (mpg)	NA
Cargo volume (cu. ft.)	11.8		

Warranties The entire car is covered for 3 years/36,000 miles. Major powertrain components are covered for 5 years/60,000 miles. Body perforation rust is covered for 5 years/100,000 miles.

Rating scale 5=Exceptional; 4=Above average; 3=Average; 2=Below average; 1=Poor

HYUNDAI EXCEL

Built in South Korea.

Hyundai Excel GS

SUBCOMPACT

A 5-speed manual transmission is now standard on all members of Hyundai's entry-level subcompact line. Previously, the base Excel 3-door hatchback sedan came with a 4-speed manual, while the 5-speed was standard on the higher-priced GS hatchback and GL sedan. Aside from that, the Korean-built Excel has only new wheel covers and interior fabrics, plus a CFC-free refrigerant for the optional air conditioning, as its changes for 1994. All models come with an 81-horsepower 1.5-liter 4-cylinder engine, which Hyundai builds under license from Mitsubishi. The Japanese automaker owns an equity interest in Hyundai, and the two companies share other components and some vehicles. A 4-speed automatic transmission with electronic controls is again optional across the board. All models have front-wheel drive. Excel meets the federal requirement for passive restraints with door-mounted front shoulder belts that can be left buckled to automatically deploy when the doors are closed. Separate lap belts buckle manually. Excel isn't as cheap as it was in the late 1980s, relative to other small cars, yet it remains near the bottom in price and market position. It's far from our first choice in today's highly competitive subcompact class. Ride comfort, handling, and braking are unexceptional, while noise levels are high and performance is low. We clocked an Excel at 13 seconds to 60 mph with the 5-speed manual and at nearly 15 seconds with the automatic. On the plus side, Excel offers good mileage and a comprehensive warranty plus free maintenance for two years. Excel makes passable sense as basic wheels for minimum money.

Hyundai Excel prices are on page 338.

HYUNDAI EXCEL GS

Rating Guide	1	2	3	4	5
Performance					
Acceleration	▓▓▓▓				
Economy	▓▓▓▓▓▓▓▓▓▓				
Driveability	▓▓▓▓▓▓				
Ride	▓▓▓▓▓▓				
Steering/handling	▓▓▓▓▓▓				
Braking	▓▓▓▓▓▓				
Noise	▓▓▓				
Accommodations					
Driver seating	▓▓▓▓▓▓▓▓				
Instruments/controls	▓▓▓▓▓▓				
Visibility	▓▓▓▓▓▓				
Room/comfort	▓▓▓▓▓▓				
Entry/exit	▓▓▓▓▓▓				
Cargo room	▓▓▓▓▓▓				
Workmanship					
Exterior	▓▓▓▓▓▓				
Interior	▓▓▓▓▓▓				
Value	▓▓▓▓▓▓				

Total Points..51

Specifications

Body type ....3-door hatchback
Wheelbase (in.) 93.8
Overall length (in.) 161.4
Overall width (in.) 63.3
Overall height (in.) 54.5
Curb weight (lbs.) 2150
Seating capacity...........................5
Front head room (in.) 37.8
Max. front leg room (in.) 41.7
Rear head room (in.) 37.6
Min. rear leg room (in.)...........33.1
Cargo volume (cu. ft.).............37.9

Engine type ....ohc I-4
Engine size (l/cu. in.)...........1.5/90
Horsepower @ rpm .....81 @ 5500
Torque @ rpm ....91 @ 3000
Transmission.................auto/4-sp.
Drive wheels ....front
Brakes, F/R....................disc/drum
Tire size 175/70R13
Fuel tank capacity (gal.).........11.9
EPA city/highway mpg 27/35
Test mileage (mpg) 28.4

Warranties The entire car is covered for 3 years/36,000 miles. Major powertrain components are covered for 5 years/60,000 miles. Body perforation rust is covered for 5 years/100,000 miles.

Rating scale 5=Exceptional; 4=Above average; 3=Average; 2=Below average; 1=Poor

HYUDAI SCOUPE

Built in South Korea.

Hyundai Scoupe Turbo

SPORTS COUPE

Hyundai's front-drive sports coupe gets only minor changes for 1994 after being given a facelift and more power last year. Scoupe returns in base and LS models with a 92-horsepower 1.5-liter 4-cylinder engine and as the Scoupe Turbo, which has a turbocharged version of this engine with 115 horsepower. A 5-speed manual transmission is standard on all models and a 4-speed automatic is optional on the base and LS. The 1994 Scoupe adopts CFC-free refrigerant for its optional air conditioning, there are new wheel covers for the base and LS models, spruced-up interior fabrics, and a different trim molding for the rear roof pillars. Neither an air bag nor anti-lock brakes are available. Scoupe is a sporty 2-door that can't hide its low-bucks design. Its biggest drawback is a general lack of polish. The chassis allows too much body lean in tight turns and too much bouncing and jiggling on anything but ultra-smooth roads. Performance is leisurely in the base and LS models. Though the Turbo manages decent acceleration, it's not that thrifty; we averaged a so-so 23.5 mpg overall. Both engines drone and throb like a mad threshing machine even at a moderate pace, and hard braking is compromised by wheel locking that increases stopping distances and diminishes directional control. The back seat is suitable only for pre-teens. On the plus side, driving tasks are simplified by a comfortable seating position, straightforward dashboard, and good visibility. Scoupe boasts a decent-sized trunk and one of the most comprehensive warranties around. Overall, it's worth considering if you're short on cash but crave a little flash.

Hyundai Scoupe prices are on page 339.

HYUNDAI SCOUPE TURBO

Rating Guide	1	2	3	4	5
Performance					
Acceleration	▓▓▓▓▓▓▓▓▓▓▓▓▓▓▓▓▓▓▓▓▓▓				
Economy	▓▓▓▓▓▓▓▓▓▓▓▓▓▓▓▓▓▓				
Driveability	▓▓▓▓▓▓▓▓▓▓▓▓▓				
Ride	▓▓▓▓▓▓▓▓▓▓▓▓▓▓▓				
Steering/handling	▓▓▓▓▓▓▓▓▓▓▓▓▓▓▓▓▓▓▓▓▓▓				
Braking	▓▓▓▓▓▓▓▓▓▓▓▓▓▓▓				
Noise	▓▓▓▓▓▓▓▓▓▓▓▓▓				
Accommodations					
Driver seating	▓▓▓▓▓▓▓▓▓▓▓▓▓▓▓▓▓▓				
Instruments/controls	▓▓▓▓▓▓▓▓▓▓▓▓▓▓▓▓▓▓				
Visibility	▓▓▓▓▓▓▓▓▓▓▓▓▓▓▓▓▓▓				
Room/comfort	▓▓▓▓▓▓▓▓▓▓▓▓▓				
Entry/exit	▓▓▓▓▓▓▓▓▓▓▓				
Cargo room	▓▓▓▓▓▓▓▓▓▓▓▓▓▓▓				
Workmanship					
Exterior	▓▓▓▓▓▓▓▓▓▓▓▓▓▓▓▓▓▓				
Interior	▓▓▓▓▓▓▓▓▓▓▓▓▓▓▓▓▓▓				
Value	▓▓▓▓▓▓▓▓▓▓▓▓▓▓▓				
Total Points					**49**

Specifications

Body type	2-door notchback	Engine type	Turbo ohc I-4
Wheelbase (in.)	93.8	Engine size (l/cu. in.)	1.5/90
Overall length (in.)	165.9	Horsepower @ rpm	115 @ 5500
Overall width (in.)	64.0	Torque @ rpm	123 @ 3000
Overall height (in.)	50.0	Transmission	manual/5-sp.
Curb weight (lbs.)	2119	Drive wheels	front
Seating capacity	4	Brakes, F/R	disc/drum
Front head room (in.)	38.1	Tire size	185/60HR14
Max. front leg room (in.)	42.8	Fuel tank capacity (gal.)	11.9
Rear head room (in.)	34.3	EPA city/highway mpg	26/31
Min. rear leg room (in.)	29.4	Test mileage (mpg)	23.5
Cargo volume (cu. ft.)	9.3		

Warranties The entire car is covered for 3 years/36,000 miles. Major powertrain components are covered for 5 years/60,000 miles. Body perforation rust is covered for 5 years/100,000 miles.

Rating scale 5=Exceptional; 4=Above average; 3=Average; 2=Below average; 1=Poor

HYUDAI SONATA

Built in South Korea.

Hyundai Sonata GLS

MID-SIZE

A redesigned Sonata is scheduled to go on sale in the U.S. in February as an early 1995 model. The new Sonata has a longer front-drive chassis, fresh styling, and dual front air bags as standard equipment. Prices weren't announced in time for this issue, but Hyundai says Sonata will be less expensive than Japanese competitors in the compact and mid-size segments. The new Sonata comes only as a 4-door notchback sedan. The new Sonata is less than an inch longer than the old one. Wheelbase, however, has increased two inches to 106.3. Two engines are available, both based on Mitsubishi designs. Mitsubishi owns an equity interest in Hyundai and the two companies share other components and some vehicles. Base engine is a 2.0-liter 4-cylinder that has been substantially revised for 1995 to produce 137 horsepower, nine more than last year. The 4-cylinder is standard on the base model and the GL. On the base, it's available with a standard 5-speed manual or optional 4-speed automatic; on the GL it comes only with the automatic. A 142-horsepower 3.0-liter V-6 is standard on the GLS and optional on the GL and comes only with a new 4-speed automatic transmission. Anti-lock brakes are optional on the GL and GLS models. Hyundai says the new Sonata meets the more stringent side-impact standards for the 1997 model year. The new Sonata is roomier and much more refined than the original, though it doesn't match leaders in the mid-size class such as the Ford Taurus and Honda Accord in overall quality. If, as Hyundai promises, it is priced well below those rivals, it should be worth considering by value-conscious shoppers.

Hyundai Sonata prices not available at time of publication.

HYUNDAI SONATA GLS (Preliminary)

Rating Guide	1	2	3	4	5
Performance					
Acceleration	‖‖‖‖‖‖‖‖‖‖‖‖‖‖‖‖‖‖‖‖‖‖‖‖‖‖‖‖‖‖‖‖‖‖				
Economy	‖‖‖‖‖‖‖‖‖‖‖‖‖‖‖‖				
Driveability	‖‖‖‖‖‖‖‖‖‖‖‖‖‖‖‖‖‖‖‖‖‖‖‖				
Ride	‖‖‖‖‖‖‖‖‖‖‖‖‖‖‖‖‖‖‖‖‖‖‖‖				
Steering/handling	‖‖‖‖‖‖‖‖‖‖‖‖‖‖‖‖‖‖‖‖‖‖‖‖				
Braking	‖‖‖‖‖‖‖‖‖‖‖‖‖‖‖‖‖‖‖‖‖‖‖‖‖‖‖‖‖‖‖‖‖‖				
Noise	‖‖‖‖‖‖‖‖‖‖‖‖‖‖‖‖‖‖‖‖‖‖‖‖				
Accommodations					
Driver seating	‖‖‖‖‖‖‖‖‖‖‖‖‖‖‖‖‖‖‖‖‖‖‖‖				
Instruments/controls	‖‖‖‖‖‖‖‖‖‖‖‖‖‖‖‖‖‖‖‖‖‖‖‖				
Visibility	‖‖‖‖‖‖‖‖‖‖‖‖‖‖‖‖‖‖‖‖‖‖‖‖				
Room/comfort	‖‖‖‖‖‖‖‖‖‖‖‖‖‖‖‖‖‖‖‖‖‖‖‖				
Entry/exit	‖‖‖‖‖‖‖‖‖‖‖‖‖‖‖‖‖‖‖‖‖‖‖‖				
Cargo room	‖‖‖‖‖‖‖‖‖‖‖‖‖‖‖‖‖‖‖‖‖‖‖‖				
Workmanship					
Exterior	‖‖‖‖‖‖‖‖‖‖‖‖‖‖‖‖‖‖‖‖‖‖‖‖				
Interior	‖‖‖‖‖‖‖‖‖‖‖‖‖‖‖‖‖‖‖‖‖‖‖‖				
Value	‖‖‖‖‖‖‖‖‖‖‖‖‖‖‖‖‖‖‖‖‖‖‖‖				

Total Points...60

Specifications

Body type ....4-door notchback	Engine type ....ohc V-6
Wheelbase (in.) 106.3	Engine size (l/cu. in.).........3.0/181
Overall length (in.) 185.0	Horsepower @ rpm ...142 @ 5000
Overall width (in.) 69.7	Torque @ rpm ....168 @ 2500
Overall height (in.) 55.3	Transmission ....auto/4-sp.
Curb weight (lbs.) 3025	Drive wheels ....front
Seating capacity 5	Brakes, F/R ....disc/drum (ABS)
Front head room (in.) 38.5	Tire size 205/60R15
Max. front leg room (in.) 43.3	Fuel tank capacity (gal.) 16.9
Rear head room (in.) ....NA	EPA city/highway mpg 18/24
Min. rear leg room (in.).............NA	Test mileage (mpg) ....NA
Cargo volume (cu. ft.)............13.2	

Warranties The entire car is covered for 3 years/36,000 miles. Major powertrain components are covered for 5 years/60,000 miles. Body perforation rust is covered for 5 years/100,000 miles.

Rating scale 5=Exceptional; 4=Above average; 3=Average; 2=Below average; 1=Poor

INFINITI G20

Built in Japan.

Infiniti G20

PREMIUM SEDAN

A "1993½" version of the front-drive G20 was introduced last spring with standard driver- and passenger-side air bags and was carried over in the fall. The 1994 model of the G20, the least-expensive car in Nissan's luxury-car division, is due in January with minor changes. The only engine is a 140-horsepower 2.0-liter 4-cylinder with dual overhead camshafts. A 5-speed manual transmission is standard and a 4-speed automatic with electronic shift controls is optional. Anti-lock brakes are standard. The addition of dual front air bags as standard equipment makes the G20 much more appealing, though they were accompanied by a price increase of more than $2000. Despite being Infiniti's entry-level car, the G20 is a well-equipped compact sedan with good overall performance. The electronic automatic introduced last spring with the "1993½" model shifts more smoothly than the old one, which tended to shift harshly. The engine is smooth and quiet in low-speed driving but gets loud and rough by about 4000 rpm, and because there's little low-speed torque, you usually have to rev it that high to get brisk performance. The G20 has plenty of room for four adults and ample cargo space for a compact sedan. Most controls are logical and handy, though the climate controls are too low in the dashboard and the power window switches on the center console are hard to find while driving. Though the larger Honda Accord EX is similarly priced, the G20 comes with a longer warranty, roadside assistance, and other benefits that have helped Infiniti score at the top of customer satisfaction ratings.

Infiniti G20 prices are on page 340.

INFINITI G20

Rating Guide	1	2	3	4	5
Performance					
Acceleration	▮▮▮▮▮▮▮▮▮▮▮▮				
Economy	▮▮▮▮▮▮▮▮▮▮▮▮				
Driveability	▮▮▮▮▮▮▮▮▮▮▮▮				
Ride	▮▮▮▮▮▮▮▮▮▮▮▮				
Steering/handling	▮▮▮▮▮▮▮▮▮▮▮▮▮▮▮				
Braking	▮▮▮▮▮▮▮▮▮▮▮▮▮▮▮▮▮▮				
Noise	▮▮▮▮▮▮▮▮▮▮▮▮				
Accommodations					
Driver seating	▮▮▮▮▮▮▮▮▮▮▮▮▮▮▮				
Instruments/controls	▮▮▮▮▮▮▮▮▮▮▮▮▮				
Visibility	▮▮▮▮▮▮▮▮▮▮▮▮▮				
Room/comfort	▮▮▮▮▮▮▮▮▮▮▮▮				
Entry/exit	▮▮▮▮▮▮▮▮▮▮▮▮▮				
Cargo room	▮▮▮▮▮▮▮▮▮▮▮▮				
Workmanship					
Exterior	▮▮▮▮▮▮▮▮▮▮▮▮▮▮				
Interior	▮▮▮▮▮▮▮▮▮▮▮▮▮▮				
Value	▮▮▮▮▮▮▮▮▮▮▮▮▮				

Total Points...58

Specifications

Body type ....4-door notchback
Wheelbase (in.) 100.4
Overall length (in.)...............174.8
Overall width (in.) 66.7
Overall height (in.)..................54.9
Curb weight (lbs.) 2877
Seating capacity...........................5
Front head room (in.) 38.8
Max. front leg room (in.)........42.0
Rear head room (in.) 37.3
Min. rear leg room (in.)..........32.2
Cargo volume (cu. ft.).............14.2

Engine type ....dohc I-4
Engine size (l/cu. in.)..........2.0/122
Horsepower @ rpm ...140 @ 6400
Torque @ rpm ....132 @ 4800
Transmission.................auto/4-sp.
Drive wheels ....front
Brakes, F/R..........disc/disc (ABS)
Tire size 195/65HR14
Fuel tank capacity (gal.) 15.9
EPA city/highway mpg 22/29
Test mileage (mpg) 21.7

Warranties The entire car is covered for 4 years/60,000 miles. Major powertrain components are covered for 6 years/70,000 miles. Body perforation rust is covered for 7 years/unlimited miles.

Rating scale 5=Exceptional; 4=Above average; 3=Average; 2=Below average; 1=Poor

INFINITI J30

Built in Japan.

Infiniti J30t

PREMIUM SEDAN

The J30, a rear-drive 4-door sized and priced between Infiniti's flagship Q45 and entry-level G20 sedans, sees few changes for 1994. Dual air bags and anti-lock brakes have been standard since its introduction as an early 1993 model. The only powertrain available is a 210-horsepower 3.0-liter V-6 (derived from the engine used in the Nissan 300ZX sports car) mated to a 4-speed automatic transmission. Models with the optional Touring Package, designated J30t, come with 4-wheel steering, a firmer suspension, forged alloy wheels, high-performance tires, and a rear spoiler. The J30 comes with a full load of safety and convenience features but lacks the polish and refinement of some competitors such as the less-expensive Lexus ES 300. It's competitive in acceleration among luxury sedans in this price range, but in hard acceleration, the engine is surprisingly loud and even a little coarse. It can be thirsty, too. We reached 24 mpg in highway driving but dropped below 16 mpg in the city. While some Japanese luxury sedans feel soft and cushy, the J30's suspension is firm enough to give the driver plenty of road feel, yet supple enough that the ride is never harsh. The J30 is nearly as long as an Acura Legend but has less passenger and cargo room than the ES 300, which is shorter in wheelbase and overall length. This results in a cozy seating package that's practical only for four adults. With just 10.1 cubic feet of cargo space, the J30 has one of the smallest trunks among luxury sedans. Several good cars can be found in the $30,000 to $40,000 range, so check out the competition before deciding on a J30.

Infiniti J30 prices are on page 341.

CONSUMER GUIDE®

INFINITI J30t

Rating Guide	1	2	3	4	5
Performance					
Acceleration				▓	
Economy		▓			
Driveability				▓	
Ride				▓	
Steering/handling				▓	
Braking					▓
Noise			▓		
Accommodations					
Driver seating				▓	
Instruments/controls				▓	
Visibility			▓		
Room/comfort				▓	
Entry/exit				▓	
Cargo room		▓			
Workmanship					
Exterior					▓
Interior					▓
Value				▓	
Total Points					**59**

Specifications

Body type	4-door notchback	Engine type	dohc V-6
Wheelbase (in.)	108.7	Engine size (l/cu. in.)	3.0/181
Overall length (in.)	191.3	Horsepower @ rpm	210 @ 6400
Overall width (in.)	69.7	Torque @ rpm	193 @ 4800
Overall height (in.)	54.7	Transmission	auto/4-sp.
Curb weight (lbs.)	3527	Drive wheels	rear
Seating capacity	5	Brakes, F/R	disc/disc (ABS)
Front head room (in.)	37.7	Tire size	215/60HR15
Max. front leg room (in.)	41.3	Fuel tank capacity (gal.)	19.0
Rear head room (in.)	36.7	EPA city/highway mpg	18/23
Min. rear leg room (in.)	30.5	Test mileage (mpg)	18.3
Cargo volume (cu. ft.)	10.1		

Warranties The entire car is covered for 4 years/60,000 miles. Major powertrain components are covered for 6 years/70,000 miles. Body perforation rust is covered for 7 years/unlimited miles.

Rating scale 5=Exceptional; 4=Above average; 3=Average; 2=Below average; 1=Poor

INFINITI Q45

Built in Japan.

Infiniti Q45

PREMIUM SEDAN

A passenger-side air bag and a restyled front end with a chrome grille and fog lamps mark the 1994 edition of Infiniti's rear-drive flagship sedan, which went on sale last spring. A driver-side air bag and anti-lock brakes were already standard. The Q45 is powered by a 278-horsepower 4.5-liter V-8 mated to an electronic 4-speed automatic transmission. In addition to the base model, there's the Q45t with the Touring Package, which includes 4-wheel steering, heated front seats, and other amenities, and the Q45a, which includes Full-Active Suspension, traction control, and a CD changer among its features. Full-Active Suspension uses computer-controlled actuators instead of conventional shock absorbers to counteract forces such as body lean, pitch, and dive. Other new features include front seat belt pre-tensioners, a remote keyless entry system, and wood inlays on the center console and doors that add some warmth to the interior, which previously was rather austere. The Q45's natural rival is the Lexus LS 400. Both are excellent cars, with the Infiniti leaning toward the athletic side and the Lexus providing luxurious isolation. The Q45 has a stable highway ride and most bumps are absorbed with little notice. There's more road noise than in the LS 400, but it's not objectionable. Most drivers won't find the handling benefits of the Q45t and Q45a worth the extra cost. There's ample space for four adults in the Q45. Three can fit in the rear seat, but the driveline hump makes the middle position uncomfortable. Besides the LS 400, key alternatives include the Cadillac Seville STS and BMW 540i and 740i.

Infiniti Q45 prices are on page 341.

INFINITI Q45

Rating Guide	1	2	3	4	5
Performance					
Acceleration	▮▮▮				
Economy	▮▮				
Driveability	▮▮▮▮				
Ride	▮▮▮▮				
Steering/handling	▮▮▮▮				
Braking	▮▮▮▮▮				
Noise	▮▮▮				
Accommodations					
Driver seating	▮▮▮				
Instruments/controls	▮▮▮				
Visibility	▮▮▮				
Room/comfort	▮▮▮				
Entry/exit	▮▮▮				
Cargo room	▮▮				
Workmanship					
Exterior	▮▮▮▮▮				
Interior	▮▮▮▮▮				
Value	▮▮▮▮▮				

Total Points...65

Specifications

Body type	4-door notchback	Engine type	dohc V-8
Wheelbase (in.)	113.2	Engine size (l/cu. in.)	4.5/274
Overall length (in.)	199.8	Horsepower @ rpm	278 @ 6000
Overall width (in.)	71.9	Torque @ rpm	292 @ 4000
Overall height (in.)	56.5	Transmission	auto/4-sp.
Curb weight (lbs.)	4039	Drive wheels	rear
Seating capacity	5	Brakes, F/R	disc/disc (ABS)
Front head room (in.)	38.2	Tire size	215/65VR15
Max. front leg room (in.)	43.9	Fuel tank capacity (gal.)	22.5
Rear head room (in.)	36.3	EPA city/highway mpg	17/22
Min. rear leg room (in.)	32.0	Test mileage (mpg)	18.7
Cargo volume (cu. ft.)	14.8		

Warranties The entire car is covered for 4 years/60,000 miles. Major powertrain components are covered for 6 years/70,000 miles. Body perforation rust is covered for 7 years/unlimited miles.

Rating scale 5=Exceptional; 4=Above average; 3=Average; 2=Below average; 1=Poor

ISUZU RODEO

Built in Lafayette, Ind.

Isuzu Rodeo LS

SPORT-UTILITY VEHICLE

Standard equipment revisions are the only major changes for 1994 to the Rodeo, which returns as a 5-door wagon in S and LS form. The base S model has rear-wheel drive, a 120-horsepower 2.6-liter 4-cylinder engine, and a 5-speed manual transmission. A more-expensive S model has a 175-horsepower 3.2-liter V-6, 4-speed automatic transmission, and 4-wheel drive. The top-line LS series comes with the V-6 engine and a choice of transmissions and drive systems. Isuzu's part-time 4WD system is for use only on slick surfaces. It has automatic locking hubs and allows shifting in and out of 4WD High at speeds up to five mph, but the vehicle must be stopped and reversed to disengage 4WD. Anti-lock rear brakes that work only in 2WD are standard. Power steering is standard instead of optional on the base 4-cylinder S this year, while air conditioning is a new standard feature on LS models. Front vent windows have been dropped. Though Rodeo has some good points, a well-equipped 4WD LS is in the same price range as a Ford Explorer or Jeep Grand Cherokee, which are roomier, have full shift-on-the-fly 4WD systems, and 4-wheel anti-lock brakes, The Jeep also comes with a driver-side air bag. Among Rodeo's strong points is an absorbent suspension that provides a comfortable ride and stands up to off-road work. There's also ample head room and leg room, but entry to the back is tight through the narrow doors. While Isuzu's V-6 doesn't have the low-speed muscle of the larger Ford and Jeep sixes, it works well with the automatic transmission. Road noise is prominent enough to interfere with normal conversation at highway speeds.

Isuzu Rodeo prices are on page 342.

ISUZU RODEO LS

Rating Guide	1	2	3	4	5
Performance					
Acceleration					
Economy					
Driveability					
Ride					
Steering/handling					
Braking					
Noise					
Accommodations					
Driver seating					
Instruments/controls					
Visibility					
Room/comfort					
Entry/exit					
Cargo room					
Workmanship					
Exterior					
Interior					
Value					

Total Points..**54**

Specifications

Body type	5-door wagon	Engine type	ohc V-6
Wheelbase (in.)	108.7	Engine size (l/cu. in.)	3.2/193
Overall length (in.)	183.9	Horsepower @ rpm	175 @ 5200
Overall width (in.)	66.5	Torque @ rpm	188 @ 4000
Overall height (in.)	65.4	Transmission	auto/4-sp.
Curb weight (lbs.)	3545	Drive wheels	rear/all
Seating capacity	5	Brakes, F/R	disc/disc (ABS)
Front head room (in.)	38.2	Tire size	225/75R15
Max. front leg room (in.)	42.5	Fuel tank capacity (gal.)	21.9
Rear head room (in.)	37.8	EPA city/highway mpg	15/18
Min. rear leg room (in.)	36.1	Test mileage (mpg)	13.9
Cargo volume (cu. ft.)	74.9		

Warranties The entire vehicle is covered for 3 years/50,000 miles. Major powertrain components are covered for 5 years/60,000 miles. Body perforation rust is covered for 6 years/100,000 miles.

Rating scale 5=Exceptional; 4=Above average; 3=Average; 2=Below average; 1=Poor

ISUZU TROOPER

Built in Japan.

Isuzu Trooper LS

SPORT-UTILITY VEHICLE

Isuzu's top-shelf sport-utility adds a 4-wheel anti-lock brake system (ABS) to more models for 1994 but sees few other changes. Trooper S and LS models have four side doors and unique 70/30 split rear doors. The RS model has two side doors and is 17 inches shorter in wheelbase and overall length. All have a 3.2-liter V-6 engine; it's rated at 175 horsepower on the S model and 190 on the RS and LS. With both engines, a 5-speed manual transmission is standard and a 4-speed electronic automatic is optional. The 4-wheel ABS is now standard on the LS and optional on S and RS. Rear-wheel ABS remains standard on S and RS. Part-time 4-wheel drive (for use only on slick surfaces) is standard on all Troopers. 4WD High can be engaged or disengaged at speeds up to five mph, but returning to 2WD requires stopping and backing up a few feet. Trooper 4-doors are roomy and comfortable. The 2-door RS is smaller than the 4-door yet more expensive than the S. Troopers are competitive in all but one area—their 4WD system. Most rivals have full shift-on-the-fly or permanently engaged 4WD. Acceleration is more than adequate in the LS, though we averaged just 15.8 mpg. The suspension provides a stable yet supple on-road ride in the manner of a large station wagon. The 4-door Troopers boast loads of head room, plus enough rear seat width for three adults to fit without squeezing. Isuzu's trademark 70/30 rear cargo door opens into a tall, long cargo deck. Without full shift-on-the-fly, Trooper takes a back seat to the Ford Explorer and Jeep Grand Cherokee (the latter also has a driver-side air bag).

Isuzu Trooper prices are on page 343.

ISUZU TROOPER LS

Rating Guide	1	2	3	4	5
Performance					
Acceleration					
Economy					
Driveability					
Ride					
Steering/handling					
Braking					
Noise					
Accommodations					
Driver seating					
Instruments/controls					
Visibility					
Room/comfort					
Entry/exit					
Cargo room					
Workmanship					
Exterior					
Interior					
Value					

Total Points...58

Specifications

Body type	4-door wagon	Engine type	dohc V-6
Wheelbase (in.)	108.7	Engine size (l/cu. in.)	3.2/193
Overall length (in.)	183.5	Horsepower @ rpm	190 @ 5600
Overall width (in.)	68.7	Torque @ rpm	195 @ 3800
Overall height (in.)	72.8	Transmission	auto/4-sp.
Curb weight (lbs.)	4210	Drive wheels	rear/all
Seating capacity	5	Brakes, F/R	disc/disc (ABS)
Front head room (in.)	39.8	Tire size	245/70R15
Max. front leg room (in.)	40.8	Fuel tank capacity (gal.)	22.5
Rear head room (in.)	39.8	EPA city/highway mpg	15/18
Min. rear leg room (in.)	39.1	Test mileage (mpg)	15.8
Cargo volume (cu. ft.)	90.0		

Warranties The entire vehicle is covered for 3 years/50,000 miles. Major powertrain components are covered for 5 years/60,000 miles. Body perforation rust is covered for 6 years/100,000 miles.

Rating scale 5=Exceptional; 4=Above average; 3=Average; 2=Below average; 1=Poor

JEEP CHEROKEE — `BUDGET BUY`

Built in Toledo, Ohio.

Jeep Cherokee Country 5-door

SPORT-UTILITY VEHICLE

Side door guard beams and a center high-mounted stoplamp are the main additions to the Jeep Cherokee for 1994. It comes in 3- and 5-door wagon body styles, both available with rear-wheel drive or 4-wheel drive. The base model is called SE this year and it joins the mid-level Sport and top-shelf Country models. Standard on the SE is a 130-horsepower 2.5-liter 4-cylinder engine. It has been available only with a 5-speed manual transmission the past few years, but Jeep says a 3-speed automatic will join the options list later in the model year. Optional on the SE and standard on the Sport and Country is a 190-horsepower 4.0-liter 6-cylinder. The six is available with a standard 5-speed manual or optional 4-speed automatic transmission. Two 4WD systems are available. Command-Trac, a part-time system for use only on slick surfaces, is standard on 4WD models. Selec-Trac, a full-time system that can be used on smooth, dry pavement, is optional on Sport and Country models with the automatic transmission. Four-wheel anti-lock brakes that work in both 2WD and 4WD are optional on models with the 6-cylinder. Cherokee, introduced as a 1984 model, is still among the best choices in a compact 4x4. It carries four adults in comfort and has ample cargo room. The long steering column puts the wheel too close to the driver, however, which makes it hard for some to get comfortable. Most Cherokees are ordered with the strong 6-cylinder engine, which provides good acceleration; the 4-cylinder feels weak by comparison. Despite its age, Cherokee is ahead of some newer rivals in features, and hard to beat for value.

Jeep Cherokee prices are on page 344.

JEEP CHEROKEE COUNTRY

Rating Guide	1	2	3	4	5
Performance					
Acceleration	‖‖‖‖‖‖‖‖‖‖‖‖‖‖‖‖‖‖				
Economy	‖‖‖‖‖‖‖‖‖				
Driveability	‖‖‖‖‖‖‖‖‖‖‖‖‖‖‖‖‖‖				
Ride	‖‖‖‖‖‖‖‖‖‖‖‖‖‖‖				
Steering/handling	‖‖‖‖‖‖‖‖‖‖‖‖‖‖‖				
Braking	‖‖‖‖‖‖‖‖‖‖‖‖‖‖‖‖‖‖‖‖‖‖				
Noise	‖‖‖‖‖‖‖‖‖‖‖‖‖‖‖				
Accommodations					
Driver seating	‖‖‖‖‖‖‖‖‖‖‖‖‖‖‖				
Instruments/controls	‖‖‖‖‖‖‖‖‖‖‖‖‖‖‖				
Visibility	‖‖‖‖‖‖‖‖‖‖‖‖‖‖‖‖‖‖				
Room/comfort	‖‖‖‖‖‖‖‖‖‖‖‖‖‖‖				
Entry/exit	‖‖‖‖‖‖‖‖‖‖‖‖‖‖‖				
Cargo room	‖‖‖‖‖‖‖‖‖‖‖‖‖‖‖				
Workmanship					
Exterior	‖‖‖‖‖‖‖‖‖‖‖‖‖‖‖‖‖‖				
Interior	‖‖‖‖‖‖‖‖‖‖‖‖‖‖‖‖‖‖				
Value	‖‖‖‖‖‖‖‖‖‖‖‖‖‖‖				

Total Points..**57**

Specifications

Body type ....5-door wagon	Engine type ....ohv I-6
Wheelbase (in.) 101.4	Engine size (l/cu. in.).........4.0/242
Overall length (in.)................168.8	Horsepower @ rpm ...190 @ 4750
Overall width (in.) 67.7	Torque @ rpm ....225 @ 4000
Overall height (in.)..................63.9	Transmission.................auto/4-sp.
Curb weight (lbs.) 3090	Drive wheels........................rear/all
Seating capacity.........................5	Brakes, F/R..........disc/disc (ABS)
Front head room (in.) 38.3	Tire size 225/70R15
Max. front leg room (in.) 41.0	Fuel tank capacity (gal.) 20.0
Rear head room (in.) 38.0	EPA city/highway mpg 15/19
Min. rear leg room (in.)...........35.3	Test mileage (mpg) 16.4
Cargo volume (cu. ft.).............71.8	

Warranties Customer's choice of 3-year/36,000-mile warranty or 1-year/12,000-mile basic warranty with 7-year/70,000-mile powertrain warranty. Body perforation rust is covered for 7 years/100,000 miles.

Rating scale 5=Exceptional; 4=Above average; 3=Average; 2=Below average; 1=Poor

JEEP GRAND CHEROKEE

Built in Detroit, Mich.

Jeep Grand Cherokee Limited

SPORT-UTILITY VEHICLE

New safety features and a power sunroof later in the year sum up the major changes to Jeep's upscale sport-utility. The 5-door Grand Cherokee debuted last year with a standard driver-side air bag. Side door guard beams are a new standard feature for its second season and an integrated child safety seat that folds out of the rear seat is supposed to become optional later this year. Grand Cherokee's base model has been renamed SE. Returning are the Laredo and the top-line Limited. Discontinued is the Grand Wagoneer model with its imitation wood exterior trim. A 190-horsepower 4.0-liter 6-cylinder engine is standard on all models and a 220-horsepower V-8 is optional on all. The 6-cylinder comes with either a 5-speed manual or 4-speed automatic transmission and the V-8 only with automatic. The SE and Laredo are offered with 2- or 4-wheel drive and the Limited only with 4WD. Three 4WD systems are available: Command-Trac, a part-time setup for use only on slippery surfaces; Selec-Trac, which can be used on all surfaces; and Quadra-Trac, a permanently engaged 4WD system. Anti-lock brakes that work in both 2WD and 4WD are standard on all. Grand Cherokee is an impressive vehicle that offers several features the rival Ford Explorer lacks. Among them are the air bag, permanent 4WD, and a V-8 engine. However, Jeep's 6-cylinder is all most people will need. Grand Cherokee is roomy inside, though entry/exit to the rear is restricted. Grand Cherokee should be at the top of your shopping list. The Explorer also is a good choice.

Jeep Grand Cherokee prices are on page 347.

JEEP GRAND CHEROKEE

Rating Guide	1	2	3	4	5
Performance					
Acceleration	▓▓▓▓▓▓▓▓				
Economy	▓▓▓				
Driveability	▓▓▓▓▓▓▓▓				
Ride	▓▓▓▓▓▓▓				
Steering/handling	▓▓▓▓▓▓▓▓				
Braking	▓▓▓▓▓▓▓▓▓▓				
Noise	▓▓▓▓▓▓▓▓				
Accommodations					
Driver seating	▓▓▓▓▓▓▓▓				
Instruments/controls	▓▓▓▓▓▓▓▓				
Visibility	▓▓▓▓▓▓▓▓				
Room/comfort	▓▓▓▓▓▓▓▓				
Entry/exit	▓▓▓▓▓▓▓▓				
Cargo room	▓▓▓▓▓▓▓▓				
Workmanship					
Exterior	▓▓▓▓▓▓▓▓				
Interior	▓▓▓▓▓▓▓▓				
Value	▓▓▓▓▓▓▓▓				

Total Points...60

Specifications

Body type	5-door wagon	Engine type	ohv I-6
Wheelbase (in.)	105.9	Engine size (l/cu. in.)	4.0/242
Overall length (in.)	179.0	Horsepower @ rpm	190 @ 4750
Overall width (in.)	70.9	Torque @ rpm	225 @ 4000
Overall height (in.)	64.9	Transmission	auto/4-sp.
Curb weight (lbs.)	3674	Drive wheels	rear/all
Seating capacity	5	Brakes, F/R	disc/disc (ABS)
Front head room (in.)	39.0	Tire size	225/75R15
Max. front leg room (in.)	40.8	Fuel tank capacity (gal.)	23.0
Rear head room (in.)	39.0	EPA city/highway mpg	15/20
Min. rear leg room (in.)	35.7	Test mileage (mpg)	15.2
Cargo volume (cu. ft.)	81.0		

Warranties Customer's choice of 3-year/36,000-mile warranty or 1-year/12,000-mile basic warranty with 7-year/70,000-mile powertrain warranty. Body perforation rust is covered for 7 years/100,000 miles.

Rating scale 5=Exceptional; 4=Above average; 3=Average; 2=Below average; 1=Poor

LEXUS ES 300

Built in Japan.

Lexus ES 300

PREMIUM SEDAN

The front-drive ES 300 gets a passenger-side air bag, a new engine, and several new convenience features for 1994. The entry-level Lexus, a 4-door sedan, shares its design with the Toyota Camry but has different styling and more standard equipment. The new passenger-side air bag joins a driver-side air bag and anti-lock disc brakes as standard safety features. The new engine, a dual-camshaft 3.0-liter V-6, is the same size as last year's but has an aluminum block instead of cast iron and boasts 188 horsepower, three more than last year. Like the old V-6, the new one requires premium gas. The 5-speed manual transmission has been dropped, so a 4-speed electronic automatic is now standard. Other new features are a washer fluid level warning light, outside temperature gauge, headlamps-on indicator, and an audible tone for the standard remote keyless entry system. Like other Lexus models, it also has CFC-free air conditioning. The ES 300 is an impressive car, having many of the attributes of the larger LS 400 sedan at a lower price. The ES 300 accelerates swiftly, smoothly, and quietly, and has more than adequate passing power at highway speeds. On twisting roads the suspension feels soft and allows moderate body roll, but the tires grip well and the steering is precise. The ride is supple and composed on wavy highways. ES 300 has more passenger space inside than its compact-class exterior dimensions imply, though head room for 6-footers is marginal with the optional power moonroof. A loaded Toyota Camry is nearly as nice, but the ES 300 brings the promise of better customer service that comes with buying a Lexus.

Lexus ES 300 prices are on page 350.

LEXUS ES 300

Rating Guide	1	2	3	4	5
Performance					
Acceleration	▓▓▓▓▓▓▓▓				
Economy	▓▓▓▓				
Driveability	▓▓▓▓▓▓▓▓				
Ride	▓▓▓▓▓▓▓▓				
Steering/handling	▓▓▓▓▓▓▓▓				
Braking	▓▓▓▓▓▓▓▓▓▓				
Noise	▓▓▓▓▓▓▓▓				
Accommodations					
Driver seating	▓▓▓▓▓▓▓▓				
Instruments/controls	▓▓▓▓▓▓▓▓				
Visibility	▓▓▓▓▓▓▓▓				
Room/comfort	▓▓▓▓▓▓▓▓				
Entry/exit	▓▓▓▓▓▓▓▓				
Cargo room	▓▓▓▓▓▓				
Workmanship					
Exterior	▓▓▓▓▓▓▓▓▓▓				
Interior	▓▓▓▓▓▓▓▓▓▓				
Value	▓▓▓▓▓▓▓▓				

Total Points...64

Specifications

Body type	4-door notchback	Engine type	dohc V-6
Wheelbase (in.)	103.1	Engine size (l/cu. in.)	3.0/181
Overall length (in.)	187.8	Horsepower @ rpm	188 @ 5200
Overall width (in.)	70.0	Torque @ rpm	203 @ 4400
Overall height (in.)	53.9	Transmission	auto/4-sp.
Curb weight (lbs.)	3374	Drive wheels	front
Seating capacity	5	Brakes, F/R	disc/disc (ABS)
Front head room (in.)	37.8	Tire size	205/65VR15
Max. front leg room (in.)	43.5	Fuel tank capacity (gal.)	18.5
Rear head room (in.)	36.6	EPA city/highway mpg	18/24
Min. rear leg room (in.)	33.1	Test mileage (mpg)	NA
Cargo volume (cu. ft.)	14.3		

Warranties The entire car is covered for 4 years/50,000 miles. Major powertrain components are covered for 6 years/70,000 miles. Body perforation rust is covered for 6 years/unlimited miles.

Rating scale 5=Exceptional; 4=Above average; 3=Average; 2=Below average; 1=Poor

LEXUS GS 300

Built in Japan.

Lexus GS 300

PREMIUM SEDAN

The rear-drive GS 300 arrived last spring as a late 1993 model and carries over unchanged for 1994. Available only as a 4-door sedan, it fits between the flagship LS 400 and entry-level ES 300 in the Lexus lineup. The GS 300 has the same 220-horsepower 3.0-liter inline 6-cylinder engine used in the Lexus SC 300 coupe. In the GS 300, it comes only with an electronic 4-speed automatic transmission. Dual air bags and anti-lock brakes are standard, as is CFC-free air conditioning with automatic temperature control. The GS 300 has virtually all the amenities found on the LS 400 for $10,000 less. However, the GS 300 isn't as swift or quiet as the LS 400 and doesn't ride as comfortably, either. Its 6-cylinder engine is sluggish off the line, but then pulls strongly and smoothly. Passing power is impressive on the open road and the transmission downshifts quickly out of overdrive. The GS 300 handles deftly and has a firmer ride than the LS 400, though it's never harsh. It also lacks the larger sedan's library-quiet highway ride because the suspension and tires make prominent "thumps" over bumps and ruts, though road noise isn't objectionable. The dashboard has a layout similar to the LS 400's. Though there's plenty of leg room all around, there's not much head room for the rear seat with the optional power moonroof. The driveline hump limits practical capacity in back to two people. The GS 300 has lots of features and good quality, but there are plenty of competitors in this price class that also merit consideration, such as the Acura Legend, Cadillac Seville, BMW 5-Series, and Mercedes-Benz E-Class.

Lexus GS 300 prices are on page 350.

LEXUS GS 300

Rating Guide	1	2	3	4	5
Performance					
Acceleration	▓▓▓▓▓▓▓▓				
Economy	▓▓▓▓▓				
Driveability	▓▓▓▓▓▓▓▓				
Ride	▓▓▓▓▓▓▓▓				
Steering/handling	▓▓▓▓▓▓▓▓				
Braking	▓▓▓▓▓▓▓▓▓▓				
Noise	▓▓▓▓▓▓▓▓				
Accommodations					
Driver seating	▓▓▓▓▓▓				
Instruments/controls	▓▓▓▓▓▓				
Visibility	▓▓▓▓▓				
Room/comfort	▓▓▓▓▓				
Entry/exit	▓▓▓▓▓				
Cargo room	▓▓▓▓▓				
Workmanship					
Exterior	▓▓▓▓▓▓▓▓▓▓				
Interior	▓▓▓▓▓▓▓▓▓▓				
Value	▓▓▓▓▓				

Total Points...62

Specifications

Body type	4-door notchback	Engine type	dohc I-6
Wheelbase (in.)	109.4	Engine size (l/cu. in.)	3.0/183
Overall length (in.)	194.9	Horsepower @ rpm	220 @ 5800
Overall width (in.)	70.7	Torque @ rpm	210 @ 4800
Overall height (in.)	55.1	Transmission	auto/4-sp.
Curb weight (lbs.)	3660	Drive wheels	rear
Seating capacity	5	Brakes, F/R	disc/disc (ABS)
Front head room (in.)	36.9	Tire size	215/60VR16
Max. front leg room (in.)	44.0	Fuel tank capacity (gal.)	21.1
Rear head room (in.)	35.6	EPA city/highway mpg	17/23
Min. rear leg room (in.)	33.8	Test mileage (mpg)	17.3
Cargo volume (cu. ft.)	13.0		

Warranties The entire car is covered for 4 years/50,000 miles. Major powertrain components are covered for 6 years/70,000 miles. Body perforation rust is covered for 6 years/unlimited miles.

Rating scale 5=Exceptional; 4=Above average; 3=Average; 2=Below average; 1=Poor

LEXUS LS 400

Built in Japan.

Lexus LS 400

PREMIUM SEDAN

The rear-drive LS 400 sedan, flagship of the Lexus fleet, receives only minor trim changes for 1994. Dual air bags and anti-lock brakes are standard. Traction control is optional. The LS 400 has a 250-horsepower 4.0-liter V-8 and a 4-speed electronic automatic transmission. An electronic air-spring suspension with automatic ride control is available in place of the standard coil-spring suspension. The LS 400 was a great car at a surprisingly low $35,000 when it bowed for 1990. It's still a great car, but the base price has jumped to $49,900—and one packed with options can get near $55,000. As a result, the LS 400 no longer stands out as exceptional value. In addition, competitors from the U.S., Japan, and Europe now match or exceed it in some areas. However, there's still much to recommend this car. The V-8 is strong and incredibly smooth. We timed one at 8.0 seconds to 60 mph, nearly two seconds faster than the company's 6-cylinder sedans. At cruising speed, the V-8 is nearly silent and there's little wind or road noise, making this one of the quietest cars we've tested. The LS 400 is stable at highway speeds and has a supple, surefooted suspension. The dashboard has well-placed controls and a bright, clear gauge cluster. There's generous leg room in the rear seat but little space under the front seats for feet, and the center passenger has to straddle the driveline hump. The LS 400 is softer and more luxurious than the rival Infiniti Q45. Try both before you decide, and also look at the Cadillac Seville STS, BMW 5- and 7-Series, and Mercedes E-Class sedans.

Lexus LS 400 prices are on page 351.

LEXUS LS 400

Rating Guide	1	2	3	4	5
Performance					
Acceleration	▓▓▓▓▓▓▓▓▓▓▓▓▓▓▓▓▓▓▓▓▓▓▓▓▓▓
Economy	▓▓▓▓▓▓▓▓
Driveability	▓▓▓▓▓▓▓▓▓▓▓▓▓▓▓▓▓▓▓▓
Ride	▓▓▓▓▓▓▓▓▓▓▓▓▓▓▓▓▓▓▓▓▓▓▓▓▓▓
Steering/handling	▓▓▓▓▓▓▓▓▓▓▓▓▓▓▓▓▓▓▓▓
Braking	▓▓▓▓▓▓▓▓▓▓▓▓▓▓▓▓▓▓▓▓
Noise	▓▓▓▓▓▓▓▓▓▓▓▓▓▓▓▓▓▓▓▓▓▓▓▓▓▓
Accommodations					
Driver seating	▓▓▓▓▓▓▓▓▓▓▓▓▓▓▓▓▓▓▓▓
Instruments/controls	▓▓▓▓▓▓▓▓▓▓▓▓▓▓▓▓▓▓▓▓
Visibility	▓▓▓▓▓▓▓▓▓▓▓▓▓▓▓▓▓▓▓▓
Room/comfort	▓▓▓▓▓▓▓▓▓▓▓▓▓▓▓▓▓▓▓▓
Entry/exit	▓▓▓▓▓▓▓▓▓▓▓▓▓▓▓▓▓▓▓▓
Cargo room	▓▓▓▓▓▓▓▓▓▓▓▓▓▓▓
Workmanship					
Exterior	▓▓▓▓▓▓▓▓▓▓▓▓▓▓▓▓▓▓▓▓▓▓▓▓▓▓
Interior	▓▓▓▓▓▓▓▓▓▓▓▓▓▓▓▓▓▓▓▓▓▓▓▓▓▓
Value	▓▓▓▓▓▓▓▓▓▓▓▓▓▓▓▓▓▓▓▓

Total Points..68

Specifications

Body type	4-door notchback	Engine type	dohc V-8
Wheelbase (in.)	110.8	Engine size (l/cu. in.)	4.0/242
Overall length (in.)	196.7	Horsepower @ rpm	250 @ 5600
Overall width (in.)	71.7	Torque @ rpm	260 @ 4400
Overall height (in.)	55.3	Transmission	auto/4-sp.
Curb weight (lbs.)	3859	Drive wheels	rear
Seating capacity	5	Brakes, F/R	disc/disc (ABS)
Front head room (in.)	38.6	Tire size	225/60VR16
Max. front leg room (in.)	43.8	Fuel tank capacity (gal.)	22.5
Rear head room (in.)	36.8	EPA city/highway mpg	18/23
Min. rear leg room (in.)	34.3	Test mileage (mpg)	19.6
Cargo volume (cu. ft.)	14.4		

Warranties The entire car is covered for 4 years/50,000 miles. Major powertrain components are covered for 6 years/70,000 miles. Body perforation rust is covered for 6 years/unlimited miles.

Rating scale 5=Exceptional; 4=Above average; 3=Average; 2=Below average; 1=Poor

LEXUS SC 300/400

Built in Japan.

✓ BEST BUY

Lexus SC 400

PREMIUM COUPE

The 1994 versions of the rear-drive Lexus coupes get CFC-free refrigerant for their air conditioning systems but see few other changes. There are two models, the SC 300 and SC 400, and the major mechanical difference between them is their engines. The SC 300 shares its 225-horsepower 3.0-liter inline 6-cylinder with the Lexus GS 300 sedan. The SC 400 has the same 250-horsepower 4.0-liter V-8 engine as the LS 400 sedan. A 5-speed manual transmission is standard on the SC 300 and an electronic 4-speed automatic is optional. The SC 400 comes only with the automatic. Both models have dual air bags and anti-lock brakes. Traction control is optional on models with the automatic transmission. With less weight and a shorter final drive ratio, the SC 400 is a little quicker than the LS 400. We timed one to 60 mph at just 7.3 seconds, versus 8.0 seconds for the sedan. The velvety smooth V-8 provides plenty of power at all speeds. The SC 300, which costs thousands less, isn't far behind. We clocked one with automatic at 8.1 seconds to 60. The SCs have a much firmer ride than the LS 400, yet they're never harsh, and exhibit little body roll in tight turns. Road noise is greater than in the sedan, but wind noise is low and engine noise is subdued. Rear head room is skimpy and leg room vanishes if the front seats are pushed back more than halfway. The dashboard is conveniently laid out and the SC 400's power tilt/telescopic steering wheel is integrated with the memory system for the power driver's seat. The SCs are top-notch luxury coupes, but also check out the Cadillac Eldorado and Lincoln Mark VIII, which offer V-8s for less than the SC 400.

Lexus SC 300/400 prices are on page 352.

CONSUMER GUIDE®

LEXUS SC 400

Rating Guide	1	2	3	4	5

Performance

	Rating
Acceleration	▮▮▮▮▮▮▮▮▮▮ (5)
Economy	▮▮▮ (2)
Driveability	▮▮▮▮▮▮▮▮▮▮ (5)
Ride	▮▮▮▮▮▮▮▮ (4)
Steering/handling	▮▮▮▮▮▮▮▮ (4)
Braking	▮▮▮▮▮▮▮▮▮▮ (5)
Noise	▮▮▮▮▮ (3)

Accommodations

	Rating
Driver seating	▮▮▮▮▮▮▮▮ (4)
Instruments/controls	▮▮▮▮▮▮▮▮ (4)
Visibility	▮▮▮▮▮▮▮▮ (4)
Room/comfort	▮▮▮▮▮ (3)
Entry/exit	▮▮▮▮▮ (3)
Cargo room	▮▮▮▮ (2)

Workmanship

	Rating
Exterior	▮▮▮▮▮▮▮▮▮▮ (5)
Interior	▮▮▮▮▮▮▮▮▮▮ (5)

Value

	Rating
Value	▮▮▮▮▮▮▮▮ (4)

Total Points...60

Specifications

Body type	2-door notchback
Wheelbase (in.)	105.9
Overall length (in.)	191.1
Overall width (in.)	70.5
Overall height (in.)	52.4
Curb weight (lbs.)	3575
Seating capacity	4
Front head room (in.)	38.3
Max. front leg room (in.)	44.1
Rear head room (in.)	36.1
Min. rear leg room (in.)	27.2
Cargo volume (cu. ft.)	9.3
Engine type	dohc V-8
Engine size (l/cu. in.)	4.0/242
Horsepower @ rpm	250 @ 5600
Torque @ rpm	260 @ 4400
Transmission	auto/4-sp.
Drive wheels	rear
Brakes, F/R	disc/disc (ABS)
Tire size	225/55VR16
Fuel tank capacity (gal.)	20.6
EPA city/highway mpg	18/23
Test mileage (mpg)	19.9

Warranties The entire car is covered for 4 years/50,000 miles. Major powertrain components are covered for 6 years/70,000 miles. Body perforation rust is covered for 6 years/unlimited miles.

Rating scale 5=Exceptional; 4=Above average; 3=Average; 2=Below average; 1=Poor

LINCOLN CONTINENTAL

Built in Wixom, Mich.

Lincoln Continental Signature Series

PREMIUM SEDAN

A mildly restyled Continental hit showrooms in May 1993 as an early 1994 model. This front-wheel-drive, 4-door luxury sedan gained a new grille, taillamps, and bodyside moldings, as well as suspension changes designed to improve ride control. A 160-horsepower 3.8-liter V-6 engine, an electronic 4-speed automatic transmission, driver- and passenger-side air bags, and 4-wheel anti-lock disc brakes are standard. Additions this fall include an optional remote keyless entry system that recalls the power driver's seat's pre-set position each time it is activated. Deleted is cloth seat trim, which had been available in place of the standard leather. The automatic-dimming headlamp feature also is killed. Continental will be redesigned for 1995, retaining front drive but gaining the overhead-camshaft 4.6-liter V-8 engine used in the Mark VIII and Town Car. That ought to solve our principle complaint about the current Continental. The 3.8-liter V-6 keeps up with traffic but lacks the strong performance of rivals such as the Cadillac Seville and De Ville, which have V-8s. This is otherwise a pleasant sedan. Road noise is minimal, though wind noise is prominent at highway speeds. The interior has ample room for four adults to stretch and you can squeeze in six. There's plenty of luggage space, with a bumper-height trunk opening to make loading and unloading easier. Though we prefer Cadillac's front-drive rivals, Continental is available at big discounts, whether you're buying or leasing, so don't be scared off by the high retail prices. We urge you to try the rivals at Cadillac before you sign a contract.

Lincoln Continental prices are on page 353.

LINCOLN CONTINENTAL

Rating Guide	1	2	3	4	5
Performance					
Acceleration	▓▓▓▓▓▓▓				
Economy	▓▓▓▓▓				
Driveability	▓▓▓▓▓▓▓▓▓				
Ride	▓▓▓▓▓▓▓▓▓				
Steering/handling	▓▓▓▓▓▓▓▓▓				
Braking	▓▓▓▓▓▓▓▓▓▓▓				
Noise	▓▓▓▓▓▓▓				
Accommodations					
Driver seating	▓▓▓▓▓▓▓▓▓				
Instruments/controls	▓▓▓▓▓▓▓				
Visibility	▓▓▓▓▓▓▓▓▓				
Room/comfort	▓▓▓▓▓▓▓▓▓				
Entry/exit	▓▓▓▓▓▓▓▓▓				
Cargo room	▓▓▓▓▓▓▓▓▓				
Workmanship					
Exterior	▓▓▓▓▓▓▓▓▓				
Interior	▓▓▓▓▓▓▓▓▓				
Value	▓▓▓▓▓▓▓				

Total Points...59

Specifications

Body type	4-door notchback
Wheelbase (in.)	109.0
Overall length (in.)	205.1
Overall width (in.)	72.7
Overall height (in.)	55.5
Curb weight (lbs.)	3628
Seating capacity	6
Front head room (in.)	38.7
Max. front leg room (in.)	41.7
Rear head room (in.)	38.4
Min. rear leg room (in.)	39.2
Cargo volume (cu. ft.)	19.1
Engine type	ohv V-6
Engine size (l/cu. in.)	3.8/232
Horsepower @ rpm	160 @ 4400
Torque @ rpm	225 @ 3000
Transmission	auto/4-sp.
Drive wheels	front
Brakes, F/R	disc/disc (ABS)
Tire size	205/70R15
Fuel tank capacity (gal.)	18.4
EPA city/highway mpg.	18/26
Test mileage (mpg.)	18.5

Warranties The entire car is covered for 4 years/50,000 miles. Body perforation rust is covered for 6 years/100,000 miles.

Rating scale 5=Exceptional; 4=Above average; 3=Average; 2=Below average; 1=Poor

LINCOLN MARK VIII ───

Built in Wixom, Mich.

Lincoln Mark VIII

PREMIUM COUPE

Lincoln redesigned its luxury coupe for 1993 and brings it back this year with only minor revisions. Mark VIII is aimed at premium coupes such as the Lexus SC 300/400 and Cadillac Eldorado. It has rear-wheel drive and standard anti-lock brakes and dual air bags. The Mark VIII has a dual-camshaft version of Ford's 4.6-liter V-8 rated at 280 horsepower and an electronic 4-speed automatic transmission. Traction control is optional. Among the few 1994 changes, the remote keyless entry system is altered to recall the setting of both the power driver's seat and the power outside mirrors. Lincoln says the Mark's standard leather seating surfaces are softer and more aromatic this year, and chrome-plated wheels are a new option in place of the standard aluminum wheels. The Mark VIII provides a pleasant balance of performance and luxury. The engine is silky smooth and delivers strong acceleration, though it uses premium fuel and we averaged just 14.9 mpg. The traction control provides a marked improvement in grip on snow and ice. Mark VIII handles well and though the suspension can be upset by large bumps, it has a softer ride than the Cadillac Eldorado and Lexus SC 400. Instruments are clearly marked and most controls are convenient, though most warning lights are hard to see. Entry/exit to the rear seat is poor and the wide doors require a lot of room to open. There isn't an abundance of interior room. Tall passengers get adequate head and leg room, but rear leg room is limited. This is an impressive car in many areas, but don't buy before testing the Eldorado, SC 400, and Acura Legend Coupe.

Lincoln Mark VIII prices are on page 354.

LINCOLN MARK VIII

Rating Guide	1	2	3	4	5
Performance					
Acceleration	▓▓▓▓▓▓▓▓▓▓▓▓▓▓▓▓▓▓▓▓▓▓▓▓ (5)
Economy	▓▓▓▓ (1)
Driveability	▓▓▓▓▓▓▓▓▓▓▓▓▓▓▓ (3)
Ride	▓▓▓▓▓▓▓▓▓▓▓▓▓▓▓▓ (3)
Steering/handling	▓▓▓▓▓▓▓▓▓▓▓▓▓▓▓▓ (3)
Braking	▓▓▓▓▓▓▓▓▓▓▓▓▓▓▓▓▓▓▓▓ (4)
Noise	▓▓▓▓▓▓▓▓▓▓▓▓▓▓▓▓ (3)
Accommodations					
Driver seating	▓▓▓▓▓▓▓▓▓▓▓▓▓▓▓▓▓▓▓▓ (4)
Instruments/controls	▓▓▓▓▓▓▓▓▓▓▓▓▓▓▓▓▓▓▓▓ (4)
Visibility	▓▓▓▓▓▓▓▓▓▓▓▓▓ (2)
Room/comfort	▓▓▓▓▓▓▓▓▓▓▓▓▓ (2)
Entry/exit	▓▓▓▓▓▓▓▓▓▓▓▓▓ (2)
Cargo room	▓▓▓▓▓▓▓▓▓▓▓▓▓ (2)
Workmanship					
Exterior	▓▓▓▓▓▓▓▓▓▓▓▓▓▓▓▓▓▓▓▓▓▓▓▓ (5)
Interior	▓▓▓▓▓▓▓▓▓▓▓▓▓▓▓▓ (3)
Value	▓▓▓▓▓▓▓▓▓▓▓▓▓▓▓▓ (3)

Total Points..59

Specifications

Body type	2-door notchback	Engine type	dohc V-8
Wheelbase (in.)	113.0	Engine size (l/cu. in.)	4.6/281
Overall length (in.)	206.9	Horsepower @ rpm	280 @ 5500
Overall width (in.)	74.6	Torque @ rpm	285 @ 4500
Overall height (in.)	53.6	Transmission	auto/4-sp.
Curb weight (lbs.)	3768	Drive wheels	rear
Seating capacity	5	Brakes, F/R	disc/disc (ABS)
Front head room (in.)	38.1	Tire size	225/60VR16
Max. front leg room (in.)	42.6	Fuel tank capacity (gal.)	18.0
Rear head room (in.)	37.5	EPA city/highway mpg	18/25
Min. rear leg room (in.)	32.5	Test mileage (mpg).	14.9
Cargo volume (cu. ft.)	14.4		

Warranties The entire car is covered for 4 years/50,000 miles. Body perforation rust is covered for 6 years/100,000 miles.

Rating scale 5=Exceptional; 4=Above average; 3=Average; 2=Below average; 1=Poor

LINCOLN TOWN CAR

Built in Wixom, Mich.

Lincoln Town Car Executive

PREMIUM SEDAN

Town Car's standard V-8 makes more power this year as the main change to this big rear-drive luxury 4-door. All versions use a 4.6-liter overhead-camshaft V-8 that now comes standard with dual exhausts, which had been an $83 option. Horsepower is now 210; with a single exhaust, the engine was rated at 190. Driver- and passenger-side air bags and anti-lock brakes are standard. Traction control is optional. All windows now have standard solar tinted glass and whitewall tires replace blackwalls in the optional Ride Control Package. The Jack Nicklaus Special Edition option group has been dropped. With its pillowy ride, commendable noise isolation, and expansive interior, Town Car delivers all the indulgences a car of its ilk should. The Cadillac Fleetwood, however, matches Town Car in spaciousness and luxury, and adds a 260-horsepower V-8 and standard traction control—all for a lower base price. Still, those who prefer a big rear-drive luxury car won't be disappointed with the Town Car. The interior is big enough for six adults and tall, wide doors make for nearly effortless entry and exit. Town Car has too much heft to sprint away from stoplights but has strong passing power. Road noise is minimal but wind noise is high on the highway. Even with the optional Ride Control Package the ride is cushy and the car bounds and floats over bumps. The power steering is too light and there's lots of body lean in turns. We prefer cars that are more agile and take up less space than the Fleetwood and Town Car. On a value basis, Cadillac has gained the edge in this market segment.

Lincoln Town Car prices are on page 355.

LINCOLN TOWN CAR

Rating Guide	1	2	3	4	5
Performance					
Acceleration	▓▓▓▓▓▓▓▓▓▓▓▓▓ (≈4)				
Economy	▓▓▓▓▓ (≈2)				
Driveability	▓▓▓▓▓▓▓▓▓▓ (≈4)				
Ride	▓▓▓▓▓▓▓▓▓▓▓ (≈4)				
Steering/handling	▓▓▓▓▓▓▓ (≈3)				
Braking	▓▓▓▓▓▓▓▓▓▓▓▓▓ (≈5)				
Noise	▓▓▓▓▓▓▓▓▓▓ (≈4)				
Accommodations					
Driver seating	▓▓▓▓▓▓▓▓▓▓ (≈4)				
Instruments/controls	▓▓▓▓▓▓▓▓▓▓ (≈4)				
Visibility	▓▓▓▓▓▓▓▓ (≈3)				
Room/comfort	▓▓▓▓▓▓▓▓▓▓▓▓▓ (≈5)				
Entry/exit	▓▓▓▓▓▓▓▓▓▓▓▓▓ (≈5)				
Cargo room	▓▓▓▓▓▓▓▓ (≈3)				
Workmanship					
Exterior	▓▓▓▓▓▓▓▓▓▓ (≈4)				
Interior	▓▓▓▓▓▓▓▓▓▓ (≈4)				
Value	▓▓▓▓▓▓▓▓ (≈3)				

Total Points..60

Specifications

Body type ....4-door notchback
Wheelbase (in.) 117.4
Overall length (in.)................218.9
Overall width (in.) 76.9
Overall height (in.)................56.9
Curb weight (lbs.) 4050
Seating capacity 6
Front head room (in.) 39.0
Max. front leg room (in.) 42.6
Rear head room (in.) 38.0
Min. rear leg room (in.) 41.6
Cargo volume (cu. ft.).............22.3

Engine type.......................ohc V-8
Engine size (l/cu. in.)........4.6/281
Horsepower @ rpm ...210 @ 4600
Torque @ rpm ....270 @ 3400
Transmission .... auto/4-sp.
Drive wheels .... rear
Brakes, F/R.......... disc/disc (ABS)
Tire size 215/70R15
Fuel tank capacity (gal.) 20.0
EPA city/highway mpg 18/25
Test mileage (mpg) 19.8

Warranties The entire car is covered for 4 years/50,000 miles. Body perforation rust is covered for 6 years/100,000 miles.

Rating scale 5=Exceptional; 4=Above average; 3=Average; 2=Below average; 1=Poor

MAZDA MIATA

Built in Japan.

Mazda Miata

SPORTS AND GT

This rear-drive 2-seater gets a larger engine and a passenger-side air bag for 1994. A driver-side air bag already was standard. Miata's new engine is a dual-camshaft 1.8-liter 4-cylinder with 128 horsepower. It replaces a 116-horsepower 1.6-liter. A 5-speed manual remains the standard transmission and the optional 4-speed automatic now has electronic shift controls. Four-wheel disc brakes are standard and anti-lock brakes remain optional. Among other changes, additional chassis bracing designed to reduce body flex has been added; the optional alloy wheels are a new 7-spoke design; and the fuel tank grows from 11.9 gallons to 12.7. Miata's major option packages return unchanged and they are to be joined later in the model year by a Package R that includes a new sport suspension. Lively, agile, simple, and fun, Miata has all the requisites for a sports car. The base price is up more than $1300 this year, but Miata remains affordable—as long as you don't go crazy with options. You should be able to buy one for less than full retail price. Miata's new engine has little kick at low speed, though it quickly gets into its power band for brisk acceleration. The firm suspension provides crisp handling, but you feel nearly every bump in the road. Though body flex was never a big problem, the new bracing seems to increase Miata's solidity over bumpy pavement. The cozy cockpit has well-placed gauges and controls and enough room to give tall people adequate working room. Miata remains our favorite sports car and the addition of a passenger-side air bag only makes it better.

Mazda Miata prices are on page 356.

MAZDA MIATA

Rating Guide	1	2	3	4	5
Performance					
Acceleration	▮▮▮▮▮▮▮▮▮▮▮▮▮▮▮▮▮▮▮				
Economy	▮▮▮▮▮▮▮▮▮▮▮▮▮				
Driveability	▮▮▮▮▮▮▮▮▮▮▮▮▮▮▮				
Ride	▮▮▮▮▮▮▮▮▮▮▮▮▮				
Steering/handling	▮▮▮▮▮▮▮▮▮▮▮▮▮▮▮▮▮				
Braking	▮▮▮▮▮▮▮▮▮▮▮▮▮▮▮▮▮▮▮▮▮▮				
Noise	▮▮▮▮▮▮▮▮▮▮				
Accommodations					
Driver seating	▮▮▮▮▮▮▮▮▮▮▮▮▮▮▮▮▮				
Instruments/controls	▮▮▮▮▮▮▮▮▮▮▮▮▮▮▮▮▮				
Visibility	▮▮▮▮▮▮▮▮▮▮▮▮▮▮▮▮▮				
Room/comfort	▮▮▮▮▮▮▮▮▮▮▮▮▮▮				
Entry/exit	▮▮▮▮▮▮▮▮▮▮▮▮▮▮				
Cargo room	▮▮▮▮▮▮				
Workmanship					
Exterior	▮▮▮▮▮▮▮▮▮▮▮▮▮▮▮▮▮				
Interior	▮▮▮▮▮▮▮▮▮▮▮▮▮▮▮▮▮				
Value	▮▮▮▮▮▮▮▮▮▮▮▮▮▮▮▮▮				

Total Points..56

Specifications

Body type ....2-door convertible	Engine type .... dohc I-4
Wheelbase (in.) 89.2	Engine size (l/cu. in.).........1.8/112
Overall length (in.)...............155.4	Horsepower @ rpm ...128 @ 6500
Overall width (in.) 65.9	Torque @ rpm ....110 @ 5000
Overall height (in.).................48.2	Transmission .... manual/5-sp.
Curb weight (lbs.) 2293	Drive wheels .... rear
Seating capacity.........................2	Brakes, F/R..........disc/disc (ABS)
Front head room (in.) 37.1	Tire size 185/60HR14
Max. front leg room (in.) 42.7	Fuel tank capacity (gal.) 12.7
Rear head room (in.) .... —	EPA city/highway mpg 22/27
Min. rear leg room (in.) .... —	Test mileage (mpg) ....NA
Cargo volume (cu. ft.).............. 3.6	

Warranties The entire car is covered for 3 years/50,000 miles. Body perforation rust is covered for 5 years/unlimited miles.

Rating scale 5=Exceptional; 4=Above average; 3=Average; 2=Below average; 1=Poor

MAZDA MPV

Built in Japan.

Mazda MPV

MINIVAN

Mazda's minivan, the MPV (Multi-Purpose Vehicle), gained a driver-side air bag during the 1993 model year and gets additional safety features this year. Additions for 1994 include a center high-mounted stoplamp and side door guard beams. Four-wheel disc brakes also are a new feature, but the standard anti-lock system still operates only on the rear wheels. MPV is available with rear- or 4-wheel drive and is unique among minivans in having a conventional right rear door that swings open instead of sliding. The base engine is a 121-horsepower 2.6-liter 4-cylinder available on 2WD models with five or seven seats. A 155-horsepower 3.0-liter V-6 is available with 2WD or 4WD on models with seven seats. An 8-seat Touring Package is optional on the 2WD V-6 model. A 4-speed automatic is the only transmission. MPV's 4WD system can be used on dry pavement and allows shifting in or out of 4WD below 65 mph. Though it lacks some of the features and roominess of class leaders like the Dodge Caravan and Mercury Villager, MPV is worth considering. It has a flexible passenger package, well-designed dashboard, and a pleasant, car-like driving feel. The 4-cylinder and 4WD models have subpar acceleration because they weigh too much for the available engine torque. The V-6 has adequate pickup but can't match the power of the 3.8-liter V-6s available in the Chrysler minivans and front-drive General Motors minivans. MPV has modest cargo space behind the rear seat on 7- and 8-passenger models. In addition, the MPV is more expensive than Chrysler's minivans.

Mazda MPV prices are on page 357.

MAZDA MPV

Rating Guide	1	2	3	4	5
Performance					
Acceleration	▬▬▬▬▬▬▬▬▬▬▬▬▬▬▬▬▬▬				
Economy	▬▬▬▬▬▬▬				
Driveability	▬▬▬▬▬▬▬▬▬▬▬▬▬▬▬▬▬▬				
Ride	▬▬▬▬▬▬▬▬▬▬▬▬▬▬				
Steering/handling	▬▬▬▬▬▬▬▬▬▬▬▬▬▬▬▬▬▬				
Braking	▬▬▬▬▬▬▬▬▬▬▬▬▬▬▬▬▬▬				
Noise	▬▬▬▬▬▬▬▬▬▬▬▬▬▬▬▬▬▬				
Accommodations					
Driver seating	▬▬▬▬▬▬▬▬▬▬▬▬▬▬▬▬▬▬				
Instruments/controls	▬▬▬▬▬▬▬▬▬▬▬▬▬▬▬▬▬▬				
Visibility	▬▬▬▬▬▬▬▬▬▬▬▬▬▬▬▬▬▬				
Room/comfort	▬▬▬▬▬▬▬▬▬▬▬▬▬▬▬▬▬▬				
Entry/exit	▬▬▬▬▬▬▬▬▬▬▬▬▬▬▬▬▬▬				
Cargo room	▬▬▬▬▬▬▬▬▬▬▬▬▬▬▬▬▬▬				
Workmanship					
Exterior	▬▬▬▬▬▬▬▬▬▬▬▬▬▬▬▬▬▬				
Interior	▬▬▬▬▬▬▬▬▬▬▬▬▬▬▬▬▬▬				
Value	▬▬▬▬▬▬▬▬▬▬▬▬▬▬▬▬▬▬				

Total Points...**57**

Specifications

Body type	4-door van	Engine type	ohc V-6
Wheelbase (in.)	110.4	Engine size (l/cu. in.)	3.0/180
Overall length (in.)	175.8	Horsepower @ rpm	155 @ 5000
Overall width (in.)	71.9	Torque @ rpm	169 @ 4000
Overall height (in.)	68.1	Transmission	auto/4-sp.
Curb weight (lbs.)	3515	Drive wheels	rear
Seating capacity	7	Brakes, F/R	disc/drum (ABS)
Front head room (in.)	40.0	Tire size	215/65R15
Max. front leg room (in.)	40.6	Fuel tank capacity (gal.)	19.8
Rear head room (in.)	39.0	EPA city/highway mpg	16/22
Min. rear leg room (in.)	34.8	Test mileage (mpg)	NA
Cargo volume (cu. ft.)	37.5		

Warranties The entire vehicle is covered for 3 years/50,000 miles. Body perforation rust is covered for 5 years/unlimited miles.

Rating scale 5=Exceptional; 4=Above average; 3=Average; 2=Below average; 1=Poor

MAZDA MX-3

Built in Japan.

Mazda MX-3 GS

SPORTS COUPE

Both versions of this front-drive 3-door hatchback coupe gain standard dual air bags and the base model gets more horsepower. The dual air bags replace motorized front shoulder belts and manual lap belts. Base models again use a 1.6-liter 4-cylinder engine, but horsepower increases from 88 to 105 thanks to two overhead camshafts instead of one and four valves per cylinder instead of two. The GS model retains its 130-horsepower 1.8-liter V-6. On both models, a 5-speed manual transmission is standard and a 4-speed automatic is optional. Anti-lock brakes are now optional on all models except the GS with automatic. The base model gains a standard tilt steering column and, like the GS, is now available with an optional power sunroof. Restyled wheel covers are new to the base MX-3, while the GS gets redesigned alloy wheels. MX-3 has been a slow seller in the highly competitive sports coupe market, so discounts are likely. GS models are pricey, however, making the base MX-3 more attractive for those on a budget. The fortified 4-cylinder engine feels smoother and more robust this year but still can't match the GS's V-6, which produces brisk acceleration. Both engines perform best with manual transmission. One of MX-3's weak points is that road noise is excessive at highway speeds and there's considerable wind noise. Another is that the low, snug driving position makes some drivers feel as if they're sitting in a bathtub. The dashboard puts clearly marked gauges and controls within easy view and reach. The back seat is shaped for two and is better suited for children than adults.

Mazda MX-3 prices are on page 358.

MAZDA MX-3 GS

Rating Guide	1	2	3	4	5
Performance					
Acceleration	▓▓▓▓▓▓▓▓▓▓▓▓▓▓▓▓				
Economy	▓▓▓▓▓▓▓▓▓▓▓▓				
Driveability	▓▓▓▓▓▓▓▓▓▓▓▓▓▓▓▓				
Ride	▓▓▓▓▓▓▓▓▓▓▓				
Steering/handling	▓▓▓▓▓▓▓▓▓▓▓▓▓▓▓▓				
Braking	▓▓▓▓▓▓▓▓▓▓▓▓▓▓▓▓▓▓▓▓				
Noise	▓▓▓▓▓▓▓				
Accommodations					
Driver seating	▓▓▓▓▓▓▓▓▓▓▓▓▓▓▓▓				
Instruments/controls	▓▓▓▓▓▓▓▓▓▓▓▓▓▓▓▓				
Visibility	▓▓▓▓▓▓▓▓▓▓▓				
Room/comfort	▓▓▓▓▓▓▓▓▓▓▓				
Entry/exit	▓▓▓▓▓▓▓▓▓▓▓▓				
Cargo room	▓▓▓▓▓▓▓▓▓▓▓▓▓▓▓▓				
Workmanship					
Exterior	▓▓▓▓▓▓▓▓▓▓▓▓▓▓▓▓				
Interior	▓▓▓▓▓▓▓▓▓▓▓▓▓▓▓▓				
Value	▓▓▓▓▓▓▓▓▓▓▓▓▓▓▓▓				

Total Points..53

Specifications

Body type	3-door hatchback	Engine type	dohc V-6
Wheelbase (in.)	96.3	Engine size (l/cu. in.)	1.8/113
Overall length (in.)	165.7	Horsepower @ rpm	130 @ 6500
Overall width (in.).	66.7	Torque @ rpm	115 @ 4500
Overall height (in.)	51.6	Transmission	manual/5-sp.
Curb weight (lbs.)	2541	Drive wheels	front
Seating capacity	4	Brakes, F/R	disc/disc (ABS)
Front head room (in.)	38.2	Tire size	205/55VR15
Max. front leg room (in.)	42.6	Fuel tank capacity (gal.)	13.2
Rear head room (in.)	33.9	EPA city/highway mpg	23/29
Min. rear leg room (in.)	31.1	Test mileage (mpg).	19.8
Cargo volume (cu. ft.)	36.6		

Warranties The entire car is covered for 3 years/50,000 miles. Body perforation rust is covered for 5 years/unlimited miles.

Rating scale 5=Exceptional; 4=Above average; 3=Average; 2=Below average; 1=Poor

MAZDA RX-7

Built in Japan.

Mazda RX-7

SPORTS AND GT

This 2-seat high-performance sports car gets a passenger-side air bag and a softer suspension for 1994. RX-7 is a rear-drive 3-door hatchback with a turbocharged 255-horsepower 1.3-liter rotary engine. A 5-speed manual transmission is standard and a 4-speed automatic is optional except with the R-2 option package. Anti-lock brakes are standard. The passenger-side air bag joins a driver-side air bag in a revised dashboard. A single model is offered, plus there are three major options packages: a luxury-oriented Touring Package; the performance-oriented R-2 Package; and a new Popular Equipment Package. RX-7's suspension has new settings designed to reduce ride harshness over bumps—particularly on the base and Touring Package models. RX-7 has exhilarating acceleration, though power sometimes is delivered with alarming suddenness. The car's reflexes are razor sharp and its tenacious road grip on dry pavement inspires confidence. Wet roads demand caution because the rear tires can lose traction easily. Even with this year's softer suspension, the ride is still quite stiff and even harsh on rough roads. It's tiring on long drives. Wind noise is low at highway speeds, but the tires and suspension thump and bump loudly on all except glass-smooth surfaces. Though the interior has adequate room for two, the cargo bay is full after just a couple of small suitcases. RX-7 prices are high but still competitive with such rivals as the Toyota Supra Turbo and Nissan 300ZX Turbo. Shopping in this league? If you value high performance over comfort, then put the RX-7 on your list.

Mazda RX-7 prices are on page 360.

CONSUMER GUIDE®

MAZDA RX-7

Rating Guide	1	2	3	4	5
Performance					
Acceleration	▓▓▓▓▓▓▓▓▓▓▓▓▓▓▓▓▓▓▓▓▓▓▓▓▓				
Economy	▓▓▓▓▓				
Driveability	▓▓▓▓▓▓▓▓▓▓▓▓▓▓▓▓▓▓▓				
Ride	▓▓▓▓▓▓▓▓▓▓▓▓▓▓				
Steering/handling	▓▓▓▓▓▓▓▓▓▓▓▓▓▓▓▓▓▓▓▓▓▓▓▓▓				
Braking	▓▓▓▓▓▓▓▓▓▓▓▓▓▓▓▓▓▓▓▓▓▓▓▓▓				
Noise	▓▓▓▓▓▓▓▓▓▓▓▓▓▓				
Accommodations					
Driver seating	▓▓▓▓▓▓▓▓▓▓▓▓▓▓▓▓▓▓▓				
Instruments/controls	▓▓▓▓▓▓▓▓▓▓▓▓▓▓▓▓▓▓▓▓▓▓				
Visibility	▓▓▓▓▓▓▓▓▓▓▓▓▓▓▓▓▓▓▓				
Room/comfort	▓▓▓▓▓▓▓▓▓▓▓▓▓▓▓▓▓▓▓				
Entry/exit	▓▓▓▓▓▓▓▓▓▓▓▓▓▓▓▓▓▓▓				
Cargo room	▓▓▓▓▓▓▓▓▓▓▓▓▓▓				
Workmanship					
Exterior	▓▓▓▓▓▓▓▓▓▓▓▓▓▓▓▓▓▓▓				
Interior	▓▓▓▓▓▓▓▓▓▓▓▓▓▓▓▓▓▓▓				
Value	▓▓▓▓▓▓▓▓▓▓▓▓▓▓▓▓▓▓▓				
Total Points					**53**

Specifications

Body type .... 3-door hatchback	Engine type ....Turbo rotary
Wheelbase (in.) 95.4	Engine size (l/cu. in.)............1.3/81
Overall length (in.) 168.5	Horsepower @ rpm ...255 @ 6500
Overall width (in.) 68.9	Torque @ rpm ....217 @ 5000
Overall height (in.) 48.4	Transmission .... manual/5-sp.
Curb weight (lbs.) 2826	Drive wheels .... rear
Seating capacity 2	Brakes, F/R ....disc/disc (ABS)
Front head room (in.) 37.6	Tire size....................225/50VR16
Max. front leg room (in.) 44.1	Fuel tank capacity (gal.) 20.0
Rear head room (in.) ....—	EPA city/highway mpg 17/25
Min. rear leg room (in.) ....—	Test mileage (mpg) 15.3
Cargo volume (cu. ft.).............17:0	

Warranties The entire car is covered for 3 years/50,000 miles. Body perforation rust is covered for 5 years/unlimited miles.

Rating scale 5=Exceptional; 4=Above average; 3=Average; 2=Below average; 1=Poor

MAZDA 323/PROTEGE

Built in Japan.

Mazda Protege LX

SUBCOMPACT Similar to Ford Escort, Mercury Tracer

A minor front facelift for the Protege sedan is the only change to Mazda's front-drive subcompacts. Carried over unaltered is the 323, a 3-door hatchback that comes only in a base price level with an 82-horsepower 1.6-liter 4-cylinder engine. The Protege 4-door sedan has a 1.8-liter 4-cylinder that makes 103 horsepower in the DX model and 125 in the LX. A 5-speed manual transmission is standard and a 4-speed automatic is optional on all models. The front-drive chassis for the Protege is used for the Ford Escort and Mercury Tracer and the 125-horsepower version of the 1.8-liter engine is used in sporty versions of the Escort and Tracer. Escort and Tracer get a standard driver-side air bag for 1994. The 323 and Protege, however, continue with motorized front shoulder belts. Anti-lock brakes aren't available. Though the 323 has the lowest price, the Protege DX is the best-seller in this line because Americans prefer 4-door notchback sedans to hatchbacks. Protege's DX Convenience Group adds some nice features at modest cost, but if you throw in air conditioning and automatic transmission you're looking at more than $13,000. That's a lot when you can buy a similarly equipped Escort or Tracer for less—and get a standard driver-side air bag. Though Protege is a competent subcompact sedan, it won't match most rivals in safety features until a redesigned 1995 model arrives. Don't overlook the Protege and 323, but be sure to also check out some of their subcompact rivals such as Saturn, Geo Prizm, Honda Civic, and Toyota Tercel. Because the market is so competitive, Mazda dealers should be discounting.

Mazda 323/Protege prices are on page 361.

MAZDA PROTEGE LX

Rating Guide	1	2	3	4	5
Performance					
Acceleration	▓	▓	▓	▓	▓
Economy	▓	▓	▓		
Driveability	▓	▓	▓	▓	
Ride	▓	▓	▓		
Steering/handling	▓	▓	▓	▓	
Braking	▓	▓	▓	▓	
Noise	▓	▓	▓		
Accommodations					
Driver seating	▓	▓	▓	▓	
Instruments/controls	▓	▓	▓	▓	
Visibility	▓	▓	▓	▓	
Room/comfort	▓	▓	▓	▓	
Entry/exit	▓	▓	▓	▓	
Cargo room	▓	▓	▓		
Workmanship					
Exterior	▓	▓	▓	▓	▓
Interior	▓	▓	▓	▓	
Value	▓	▓	▓	▓	

Total Points...55

Specifications

Body type	4-door notchback	Engine type	dohc I-4
Wheelbase (in.)	98.4	Engine size (l/cu. in.)	1.8/112
Overall length (in.)	171.5	Horsepower @ rpm	125 @ 6500
Overall width (in.)	65.9	Torque @ rpm	114 @ 4500
Overall height (in.)	54.1	Transmission	manual/5-sp.
Curb weight (lbs.)	2487	Drive wheels	front
Seating capacity	5	Brakes, F/R	disc/disc
Front head room (in.)	38.6	Tire size	185/60R14
Max. front leg room (in.)	42.2	Fuel tank capacity (gal.)	14.5
Rear head room (in.)	37.1	EPA city/highway mpg	24/30
Min. rear leg room (in.)	34.6	Test mileage (mpg)	NA
Cargo volume (cu. ft.)	12.8		

Warranties The entire car is covered for 3 years/50,000 miles. Body perforation rust is covered for 5 years/unlimited miles.

Rating scale 5=Exceptional; 4=Above average; 3=Average; 2=Below average; 1=Poor

MAZDA 626/MX-6

Built in Flat Rock, Mich.

✓ BEST BUY

Mazda 626 LX

COMPACT (626)/SPORTS COUPE (MX-6)

All versions of the 626 4-door sedan and MX-6 2-door coupe gain a standard passenger-side air bag, plus there's a new 626 model. The passenger-side air bag joins a driver-side air bag that already was standard. These cars share their front-drive platform and the MX-6's engines and basic design also are used for the Ford Probe (see separate report). The 626 DX and LX models have a 118-horsepower 2.0-liter 4-cylinder engine. The ES has a 164-horsepower 2.5-liter V-6. New for 1994 is the LX-V-6, which combines LX equipment with the V-6 engine. The base MX-6 uses the 4-cylinder and the MX-6 LX uses the V-6. On all models, a 5-speed manual transmission is standard and a 4-speed automatic is optional. Anti-lock brakes are now standard on the 626 ES and continue as options on the others. Mazda has given the 626 ES and MX-6 LX more standard equipment for 1994 to justify sharply higher prices, while bringing in the 626 LX V-6 at a price similar to last year's 626 ES. The 626 is a competitive entry in the compact sedan market that deserves strong consideration. One of the principal rivals is the Toyota Camry, which is quieter and more luxurious. The 626 is sportier and has more personality. Despite rather high prices—higher even than similarly equipped Probes—the MX-6 also is a solid entry in its competitive market segment. Though we prefer the V-6 engine in these cars, the 4-cylinder is more economical and should serve most owners well. With either engine, the automatic transmission is slow to downshift for passing and often shifts harshly.

Mazda MX-6 prices are on page 359;
Mazda 626 prices are on page 362.

MAZDA 626 LX

Rating Guide	1	2	3	4	5
Performance					
Acceleration					
Economy					
Driveability					
Ride					
Steering/handling					
Braking					
Noise					
Accommodations					
Driver seating					
Instruments/controls					
Visibility					
Room/comfort					
Entry/exit					
Cargo room					
Workmanship					
Exterior					
Interior					
Value					

Total Points 61

Specifications

Body type	4-door notchback	Engine type	dohc I-4
Wheelbase (in.)	102.8	Engine size (l/cu. in.)	2.0/122
Overall length (in.)	184.4	Horsepower @ rpm	118 @ 5500
Overall width (in.)	68.9	Torque @ rpm	127 @ 4500
Overall height (in.)	51.6	Transmission	manual/5-sp.
Curb weight (lbs.)	2626	Drive wheels	front
Seating capacity	5	Brakes, F/R	disc/disc (ABS)
Front head room (in.)	39.2	Tire size	195/65R14
Max. front leg room (in.)	43.5	Fuel tank capacity (gal.)	15.9
Rear head room (in.)	37.8	EPA city/highway mpg	26/34
Min. rear leg room (in.)	35.8	Test mileage (mpg)	23.9
Cargo volume (cu. ft.)	13.8		

Warranties The entire car is covered for 3 years/50,000 miles. Body perforation rust is covered for 5 years/unlimited miles.

Rating scale 5=Exceptional; 4=Above average; 3=Average; 2=Below average; 1=Poor

MAZDA 929

Built in Japan.

Mazda 929

PREMIUM SEDAN

Minor equipment revisions identify the 1994 edition of Mazda's rear-drive "near-luxury" sedan. The 4-door 929 returns in a single price series with standard driver- and passenger air bags and anti-lock disc brakes. The only engine is a dual-camshaft 3.0-liter V-6, which this year has 193 horsepower, down by two from last year due to emission-related modifications. A 4-speed automatic is the sole transmission. For 1994, a cup holder has been added to the center console, the front shoulder belts are now adjustable for height, and a limited-slip differential is included in the optional Cold Package. Models with the Premium Package again are available with a solar-powered ventilation system that cools the interior when the car is parked in the sun and recharges the battery when ventilation isn't needed. The Premium Package adds a remote keyless entry system this year. There are some things to like about the 929, including dual air bags, but we encourage you to look at some of its competitors. Because there are several good alternatives, Mazda dealers should be heavily discounting their prices. The 929 is attractively styled and has a full complement of safety and convenience features at an attractive price. The 929's V-6 engine delivers more than adequate acceleration (9.4 seconds to 60 mph in our test) but lacks the polish and verve of some competitors. In addition, it's short of interior and trunk space, doesn't offer a tilt steering column or a dashboard glove box, and lags in refinement compared to rivals such as the Acura Legend, Lexus ES 300, and Nissan Maxima.

Mazda 929 prices are on page 363.

MAZDA 929

Rating Guide	1	2	3	4	5
Performance					
Acceleration	▓▓▓▓▓▓▓▓▓				
Economy	▓▓▓▓				
Driveability	▓▓▓▓▓▓				
Ride	▓▓▓▓▓				
Steering/handling	▓▓▓▓▓▓				
Braking	▓▓▓▓▓▓▓▓▓▓				
Noise	▓▓▓▓▓▓				
Accommodations					
Driver seating	▓▓▓▓▓				
Instruments/controls	▓▓▓▓▓				
Visibility	▓▓▓▓▓				
Room/comfort	▓▓▓▓▓▓				
Entry/exit	▓▓▓▓▓▓				
Cargo room	▓▓▓▓▓▓				
Workmanship					
Exterior	▓▓▓▓▓▓▓				
Interior	▓▓▓▓▓▓				
Value	▓▓▓▓▓▓				

Total Points...59

Specifications

Body type	4-door notchback	Engine type	dohc V-6
Wheelbase (in.)	112.2	Engine size (l/cu. in.)	3.0/180
Overall length (in.)	193.7	Horsepower @ rpm	193 @ 5750
Overall width (in.)	70.7	Torque @ rpm	200 @ 3500
Overall height (in.)	54.9	Transmission	auto/4-sp.
Curb weight (lbs.)	3596	Drive wheels	rear
Seating capacity	5	Brakes, F/R	disc/disc (ABS)
Front head room (in.)	37.4	Tire size	205/65R15
Max. front leg room (in.)	43.4	Fuel tank capacity (gal.)	18.5
Rear head room (in.)	37.4	EPA city/highway mpg	19/24
Min. rear leg room (in.)	37.0	Test mileage (mpg)	19.0
Cargo volume (cu. ft.)	12.4		

Warranties The entire car is covered for 3 years/50,000 miles. Body perforation rust is covered for 5 years/unlimited miles.

Rating scale 5=Exceptional; 4=Above average; 3=Average; 2=Below average; 1=Poor

MERCEDES-BENZ C-CLASS —

Built in Germany.

Mercedes-Benz C280

PREMIUM SEDAN

Mercedes-Benz replaces its entry-level 190 series with a new sedan called the C-Class. Like the 190, the C-Class is a rear-wheel-drive 4-door, but it's 2.3 inches longer overall, one inch longer in wheelbase, and 1.2 inches wider. Two models are offered, both wearing Mercedes' new badging. The C220 has a dual-camshaft 147-horsepower 2.2-liter 4-cylinder. The C280 has a dual-cam 2.8-liter inline 6-cylinder with 194 horsepower. A 4-speed automatic is the only transmission. Driver- and passenger-side air bags and anti-lock brakes are standard, and traction control is optional. The C-Class is a better car than the 190 series and debuts at virtually the same base prices. However, rivals priced near the C220 have stronger V-6 engines, while most competitors of the C280 have far more interior space. So, shop such cars as the Acura Legend, Cadillac Seville, BMW 5-Series, and Lexus ES 300 before deciding. Like every Mercedes, the C-Class cars are solid and capable. Both versions suffer leisurely pickup off the line, but have good passing power, especially the C280. Steering response is excellent and handling is balanced. Most bumps can be felt, but the firm suspension easily absorbs the worst of the impacts. Road noise intrudes, however, especially from the rear tires. The driving position is comfortable and the control layout friendly, but tall drivers may not have enough leg or head room. Moving the driver's seat all the way back drastically cuts into rear leg room, which is only adequate in any case. Cargo space is good and an optional rear seatback folds for extra room. Because this car is new, don't expect much in the way of discounts.

Mercedes-Benz C-Class prices are on page 363.

MERCEDES-BENZ C280

Rating Guide	1	2	3	4	5
Performance					
Acceleration				▓	
Economy		▓			
Driveability				▓	
Ride				▓	
Steering/handling				▓	
Braking					▓
Noise				▓	
Accommodations					
Driver seating				▓	
Instruments/controls				▓	
Visibility				▓	
Room/comfort			▓		
Entry/exit			▓		
Cargo room			▓		
Workmanship					
Exterior					▓
Interior					▓
Value			▓		
Total Points					**60**

Specifications

Body type ....4-door notchback
Wheelbase (in.) 105.9
Overall length (in.)................177.4
Overall width (in.) 67.7
Overall height (in.)..................56.1
Curb weight (lbs.) 3173
Seating capacity.........................5
Front head room (in.) 37.2
Max. front leg room (in.) 41.5
Rear head room (in.) 37.0
Min. rear leg room (in.) 32.8
Cargo volume (cu. ft.).............13.7

Engine type ....dohc I-6
Engine size (l/cu. in.)........2.8/173
Horsepower @ rpm ...194 @ 5500
Torque @ rpm ....199 @ 3750
Transmission.................auto/4-sp.
Drive wheels ....rear
Brakes, F/R.........disc/disc (ABS)
Tire size 195/65HR15
Fuel tank capacity (gal.) 16.4
EPA city/highway mpg 20/26
Test mileage (mpg) ....NA

Warranties The entire car (including body perforation rust) is covered for 4 years/50,000 miles.

Rating scale 5=Exceptional; 4=Above average; 3=Average; 2=Below average; 1=Poor

MERCEDES-BENZ E-CLASS —

Built in Germany.

Mercedes-Benz E320

PREMIUM SEDAN/COUPE

This line of rear-drive mid-size cars is mildly restyled and now called the E-Class under Mercedes' new labeling system in which each model wears a numerical suffix to show its metric engine size. Returning body styles include a 4-door sedan, 2-door coupe, 5-door wagon, and 2-door convertible. All have a 4-speed automatic transmission, driver- and passenger-side air bags, and anti-lock brakes. The E320 label is found on all four body styles and draws its name from a 217-horsepower 3.2-liter inline 6-cylinder engine. The E420 sedan has a 275-horsepower 4.2-liter V-8 and the limited-edition E500 sedan has a 315-horsepower 5.0 V-8. The E300 Diesel, with a new naturally aspirated 148-horsepower 3.0-liter diesel engine, is supposed to bow in January as a 1995 model. The 4-wheel-drive 4Matic sedan and wagon are gone, but traction control is standard on the E500 and optional on the others. The grille, hood, trunk lid, and taillamps are restyled on all models. The E-Class is Mercedes' top-selling line and the E320 sedan's 1994 list price is $7400 below last fall's comparable 300E sedan. The wagon is $8200 less than last year and the 4.2-liter V-8 sedan is $5400 less. These still are expensive cars, but they are no longer overpriced compared to the Lexus LS 400, Infiniti Q45, and BMW's 5- and 7-Series V-8 models. The E-Class's 3.2-liter 6-cylinder engine is a willing performer, but you have to move up to the E420 for a V-8 like the Q45 and LS 400. Even then, Mercedes' new price structure makes the E420 competitive with its Japanese rivals. Mercedes is back in the hunt in the premium sedan market.

Mercedes-Benz E-Class prices are on page 365.

MERCEDES-BENZ E320

Rating Guide	1	2	3	4	5
Performance					
Acceleration	▓▓▓▓▓▓▓▓▓▓▓▓▓▓▓▓▓▓▓▓▓▓▓▓				
Economy	▓▓▓▓▓▓▓▓				
Driveability	▓▓▓▓▓▓▓▓▓▓▓▓▓▓▓▓▓				
Ride	▓▓▓▓▓▓▓▓▓▓▓▓▓▓▓				
Steering/handling	▓▓▓▓▓▓▓▓▓▓▓▓▓▓▓▓▓				
Braking	▓▓▓▓▓▓▓▓▓▓▓▓▓▓▓▓▓				
Noise	▓▓▓▓▓▓▓▓▓▓▓▓				
Accommodations					
Driver seating	▓▓▓▓▓▓▓▓▓▓▓▓▓▓▓▓▓▓▓▓				
Instruments/controls	▓▓▓▓▓▓▓▓▓▓▓▓▓▓▓▓▓▓▓▓				
Visibility	▓▓▓▓▓▓▓▓▓▓▓▓▓▓▓				
Room/comfort	▓▓▓▓▓▓▓▓▓▓▓▓▓▓▓				
Entry/exit	▓▓▓▓▓▓▓▓▓▓▓▓▓▓▓▓▓				
Cargo room	▓▓▓▓▓▓▓▓▓▓▓▓▓▓▓▓▓▓▓▓				
Workmanship					
Exterior	▓▓▓▓▓▓▓▓▓▓▓▓▓▓▓▓▓▓▓▓				
Interior	▓▓▓▓▓▓▓▓▓▓▓▓▓▓▓▓▓▓▓▓				
Value	▓▓▓▓▓▓▓▓▓▓▓▓▓▓				
Total Points					**64**

Specifications

Body type	4-door notchback	Engine type	dohc I-6
Wheelbase (in.)	110.2	Engine size (l/cu. in.)	3.2/195
Overall length (in.)	187.2	Horsepower @ rpm	217 @ 5500
Overall width (in.)	68.5	Torque @ rpm	229 @ 3750
Overall height (in.)	56.3	Transmission	auto/4-sp.
Curb weight (lbs.)	3525	Drive wheels	rear
Seating capacity	5	Brakes, F/R	disc/disc (ABS)
Front head room (in.)	36.9	Tire size	195/65R15
Max. front leg room (in.)	41.7	Fuel tank capacity (gal.)	18.5
Rear head room (in.)	36.9	EPA city/highway mpg	19/25
Min. rear leg room (in.)	33.5	Test mileage (mpg)	NA
Cargo volume (cu. ft.)	14.6		

Warranties The entire car (including body perforation rust) is covered for 4 years/50,000 miles.

Rating scale 5=Exceptional; 4=Above average; 3=Average; 2=Below average; 1=Poor

MERCEDES-BENZ S-CLASS —

Built in Germany.

Mercedes-Benz S420

PREMIUM SEDAN/COUPE

Mercedes' largest sedans and coupes are renamed and fuel economy is higher on all seven models, reducing or eliminating the gas-guzzler tax on five. The S-Class roster consists of the S320 and S350 Turbodiesel sedans; the longer S420, S500, and S600 sedans; and the S500 and S600 2-door coupes. The S320 has a 228-horsepower 3.2-liter inline 6-cylinder engine and its $1700 gas tax is eliminated thanks to a more efficient fuel-injection system. The S350 has a 148-horsepower 3.5-liter turbocharged 6-cylinder diesel engine and pays no guzzler tax. The S420 has a 275-horsepower 4.2-liter V-8 and its guzzler tax is reduced by $400 to $1700. The S500 sedan and coupe use a 315-horsepower 5.0-liter V-8, and their guzzler tax drops $900 to $2100. The S600 sedan and coupe have a 389-horsepower 6.0-liter V-12. The guzzler tax on the coupe is reduced by $700 to $3000, but stays at $3700 on the sedan. The S320 has a 5-speed automatic transmission; all other S-Class models use a 4-speed automatic. All these cars have rear-wheel drive, dual air bags, and anti-lock disc brakes. These are impressive cars that, except for S350, use too much gas. Acceleration is tepid on the diesel model, but on the gas models progresses from good to great as the number of cylinders increases. On all models, occupants are well isolated from mechanical, wind, and road noise. The ride is firm but always composed. The S-Class cars are among the world's best, but alternatives ranging from the Lexus LS 400 to the Mercedes' E-Class models offer nearly as much luxury and performance for thousands less.

Mercedes-Benz S-Class prices are on page 366.

MERCEDES-BENZ S420

Rating Guide	1	2	3	4	5
Performance					
Acceleration	▪	▪	▪	▪	
Economy	▪				
Driveability	▪	▪	▪	▪	
Ride	▪	▪	▪	▪	▪
Steering/handling	▪	▪	▪	▪	
Braking	▪	▪	▪	▪	▪
Noise	▪	▪	▪	▪	▪
Accommodations					
Driver seating	▪	▪	▪	▪	
Instruments/controls	▪	▪	▪		
Visibility	▪	▪	▪		
Room/comfort	▪	▪	▪	▪	▪
Entry/exit	▪	▪	▪	▪	▪
Cargo room	▪	▪	▪		
Workmanship					
Exterior	▪	▪	▪	▪	▪
Interior	▪	▪	▪	▪	▪
Value	▪	▪	▪		

Total Points 65

Specifications

Body type ....4-door notchback	Engine type ....dohc V-8
Wheelbase (in.) 123.6	Engine size (l/cu. in.).........4.2/256
Overall length (in.)................205.2	Horsepower @ rpm ...275 @ 5700
Overall width (in.) 74.3	Torque @ rpm ....295 @ 3900
Overall height (in.) 58.9	Transmission ....auto/4-sp.
Curb weight (lbs.) 4760	Drive wheels ....rear
Seating capacity..........................5	Brakes, F/R ....disc/disc (ABS)
Front head room (in.) 38.0	Tire size ......:............235/60HR16
Max. front leg room (in.) 41.3	Fuel tank capacity (gal.) 26.4
Rear head room (in.) 38.5	EPA city/highway mpg 15/20
Min. rear leg room (in.)...........39.6	Test mileage (mpg) ....NA
Cargo volume (cu. ft.).............15.6	

Warranties The entire car (including body perforation rust) is covered for 4 years/50,000 miles.

Rating scale 5=Exceptional; 4=Above average; 3=Average; 2=Below average; 1=Poor

MERCURY CAPRI

Built in Australia.

Mercury Capri XR2

SPORTS COUPE

A passenger-side air bag and a mild facelift are among the changes to this front-drive 4-seat convertible. Capri is based on the platform of the previous-generation Mazda 323 subcompact sedan and is built by Ford in Australia. The base model has a 1.6-liter 4-cylinder engine with 100 horsepower. The XR2 gets a turbocharged version of that engine rated at 132. A 5-speed manual transmission is standard with both engines and a 4-speed automatic is optional on the base model. The passenger-side air bag joins a previously standard driver-side air bag. Four-wheel disc brakes remain standard, but anti-lock brakes still aren't offered. The 1994s wear new bumpers, headlamps, and taillamps, and body-color outside mirrors. Both models get new alloy wheels, while the XR2 gains a standard sport suspension. A hardtop with a glass rear window and a defogger has been dropped from the options list. Mercury cut Capri prices during the 1993 model year and despite minor increases this year, base prices are still below those of a year ago, even with the addition of a second air bag. Mercury doesn't label Capri a sports car, and with good reason. The base model performs much like a front-drive economy car. The XR2 is far more agile and quick, but turbo lag delays its acceleration. With the convertible top up, there are large blind spots to the rear corners. The back seat is so tiny that even small children are uncomfortable. Consider it extra storage space, along with a trunk that holds grocery bags standing up. All convertibles pose some compromises and the Capri has its share. At least now it puts a smaller dent in your bank account.

Mercury Capri prices are on page 368.

MERCURY CAPRI XR2

Rating Guide	1	2	3	4	5
Performance					
Acceleration					
Economy					
Driveability					
Ride					
Steering/handling					
Braking					
Noise					
Accommodations					
Driver seating					
Instruments/controls					
Visibility					
Room/comfort					
Entry/exit					
Cargo room					
Workmanship					
Exterior					
Interior					
Value					

Total Points...52

Specifications

Body type ....2-door convertible	Engine type............Turbo dohc I-4
Wheelbase (in.) 94.7	Engine size (l/cu. in.)...........1.6/97
Overall length (in.)................167.1	Horsepower @ rpm ...132 @ 5000
Overall width (in.) 64.6	Torque @ rpm ....136 @ 3000
Overall height (in.)..................50.4	Transmission ....manual/5-sp.
Curb weight (lbs.) 2423	Drive wheels ....front
Seating capacity 4	Brakes, F/R ....disc/disc
Front head room (in.) 38.1	Tire size.....................195/50VR15
Max. front leg room (in.) 41.2	Fuel tank capacity (gal.) 11.1
Rear head room (in.) 34.4	EPA city/highway mpg 23/28
Min. rear leg room (in.)...........25.8	Test mileage (mpg) ....NA
Cargo volume (cu. ft.)...............8.6	

Warranties The entire car is covered for 3 years/36,000 miles. Body perforation rust is covered for 6 years/100,000 miles.

Rating scale 5=Exceptional; 4=Above average; 3=Average; 2=Below average; 1=Poor

MERCURY VILLAGER— RECOMMENDED

Built in Avon Lake, Ohio.

Mercury Villager LS

MINIVAN Similar to Nissan Quest

A driver-side air bag and a luxury model are new for Villager, which shares its front-drive platform and most interior and mechanical features with the Nissan Quest. These minivans were designed by Nissan and are built at a Ford plant. Villager returns in GS and LS models, and adds a Nautica Special Edition model with luxury trim. Villager uses a 151-horsepower Nissan-made 3.0-liter V-6 and a 4-speed automatic transmission. Motorized front shoulder belts and manual lap belt are retained for the front seats, despite the addition of the driver-side air bag starting with November 1993 production. Anti-lock brakes are standard. Villager and Quest stress passenger comfort over the ability to tow trailers and do heavy-duty work. Acceleration is adequate, but there's not enough power to easily merge into highway traffic with a full load of passengers and cargo. Handling is car-like, though the suspension sometimes bangs over bumps rather than soaking them up. Wind noise is prominent at highway speeds. Room is ample in the front seats, adequate for the middle and rear seats. With all seats in their regular position, there's only a small cargo area at the rear. It's a chore to remove the middle buckets. Once done, you can slide the rear seat forward on tracks in the floor for ample cargo room. Our staff tested a Villager LS for more than 10,000 miles. We averaged 22-23 mpg in highway cruising and dropped as low as 15 mpg in the city. This Villager suffered no major mechanical problems but developed several squeaks and rattles and the transmission had to be serviced to reduce vibration.

Mercury Villager prices are on page 376.

MERCURY VILLAGER LS

Rating Guide	1	2	3	4	5
Performance					
Acceleration					
Economy					
Driveability					
Ride					
Steering/handling					
Braking					
Noise					
Accommodations					
Driver seating					
Instruments/controls					
Visibility					
Room/comfort					
Entry/exit					
Cargo room					
Workmanship					
Exterior					
Interior					
Value					
Total Points **59**					

Specifications

Body type	4-door van	Engine type	ohc V-6
Wheelbase (in.)	112.2	Engine size (l/cu. in.)	3.0/181
Overall length (in.)	189.9	Horsepower @ rpm	151 @ 4800
Overall width (in.)	73.7	Torque @ rpm	174 @ 4400
Overall height (in.)	67.6	Transmission	auto/4-sp.
Curb weight (lbs.)	4015	Drive wheels	front
Seating capacity	7	Brakes, F/R	disc/disc (ABS)
Front head room (in.)	39.4	Tire size	205/75R15
Max. front leg room (in.)	39.9	Fuel tank capacity (gal.)	20.0
Rear head room (in.)	39.7	EPA city/highway mpg	17/23
Min. rear leg room (in.)	34.8	Test mileage (mpg)	19.7
Cargo volume (cu. ft.)	114.8		

Warranties The entire vehicle is covered for 3 years/36,000 miles. Body perforation rust is covered for 6 years/100,000 miles.

Rating scale 5=Exceptional; 4=Above average; 3=Average; 2=Below average; 1=Poor

MITSUBISHI DIAMANTE

Built in Japan and Australia.

Mitsubishi Diamante LS

PREMIUM SEDAN

A standard passenger-side air bag is the major change for Mitsubishi's flagship line in its third season. The Diamante line-up includes ES and LS 4-door sedans built in Japan and a 5-door wagon built in Australia. The wagon, which is priced and equipped similarly to the ES sedan, arrived last winter. Diamante competes in the "near-luxury" market against cars such as the Acura Vigor, Lexus ES 300, Mazda 929, and Nissan Maxima. All Diamante models have front-wheel drive, a 3.0-liter V-6 engine, and an electronic 4-speed automatic transmission. The engine in the ES sedan and wagon has a single overhead camshaft and 175 horsepower. The engine in the LS has dual overhead camshafts and 202 horsepower. Other changes for 1994 include new taillamps for sedans and a 4-spoke steering wheel with remote controls for the stereo. A new 8-speaker Infinity sound system with a graphic equalizer, separate amplifier, and provisions for a CD changer is standard on the LS and optional on the ES and wagon. Also new this year is a remote keyless entry system that's standard on the LS and optional on the ES. Anti-lock brakes (ABS) are again standard on the LS and optional on the ES and wagon. The Euro Handling Package formerly available on the ES has been dropped. Diamante isn't a front-runner in the near-luxury segment, yet it has enough good points to warrant consideration. Performance is good with either engine and both models are well-equipped. An ES model equipped with the optional ABS makes more economic sense than the pricey LS. Slow sales mean big discounts and attractive lease plans should be available.

Mitsubishi Diamante prices are on page 378.

MITSUBISHI DIAMANTE LS

Rating Guide	1	2	3	4	5
Performance					
Acceleration	||||||||||||||||||||||||||||||||||||		
Economy	|||||||||||||||||||||||			
Driveability	||||||||||||||||||||||||||||		
Ride	||||||||||||||||||||||||||		
Steering/handling	||||||||||||||||||||||||||||||		
Braking	||||||||||||||||||||||||||||||||||||||||||	
Noise	||||||||||||||||||||||||			
Accommodations					
Driver seating	||||||||||||||||||||||||||||||		
Instruments/controls	||||||||||||||||||||||||||||||		
Visibility	||||||||||||||||||||||||||		
Room/comfort	||||||||||||||||||||||||||||		
Entry/exit	||||||||||||||||||||||||||||		
Cargo room	||||||||||||||||||||||||			
Workmanship					
Exterior	||||||||||||||||||||||||||||||||||		
Interior	||||||||||||||||||||||||||||||||||		
Value	||||||||||||||||||||||||||		
Total Points					59

Specifications

Body type	4-door notchback
Wheelbase (in.)	107.1
Overall length (in.)	190.2
Overall width (in.)	69.9
Overall height (in.)	52.6
Curb weight (lbs.)	3505
Seating capacity	5
Front head room (in.)	38.6
Max. front leg room (in.)	43.9
Rear head room (in.)	36.9
Min. rear leg room (in.)	34.2
Cargo volume (cu. ft.)	13.6

Engine type	dohc V-6
Engine size (l/cu. in.)	3.0/182
Horsepower @ rpm	202 @ 6000
Torque @ rpm	201 @ 3500
Transmission	auto/4-sp.
Drive wheels	front
Brakes, F/R	disc/disc (ABS)
Tire size	205/65VR15
Fuel tank capacity (gal.)	19.0
EPA city/highway mpg	18/24
Test mileage (mpg)	19.0

Warranties The entire car is covered for 3 years/36,000 miles. Major powertrain components are covered for 5 years/60,000 miles. Body perforation rust is covered for 7 years/100,000 miles.

Rating scale 5=Exceptional; 4=Above average; 3=Average; 2=Below average; 1=Poor

MITSUBISHI ECLIPSE/ ──── EAGLE TALON/ PLYMOUTH LASER

Built in Normal, Ill.

Mitsubishi Eclipse GSX

SPORTS COUPE

This Mitsubishi-designed sports coupe will be eclipsed by a new model that should be unveiled next summer. However, Plymouth isn't expected to get the new model. All three versions of this car are 3-door hatchbacks built in Illinois by Diamond-Star Motors, which is owned by Mitsubishi. In the Eclipse line, the base and GS models have a 1.8-liter 4-cylinder engine with 92 horse-power, while the GS DOHC has a dual-camshaft 2.0-liter engine with 135 horsepower. A 195-horsepower turbocharged 2.0-liter returns in the GS Turbo and the GSX. All models have front-wheel drive except the GSX, which has permanently engaged all-wheel drive (AWD). Anti-lock brakes (ABS) are standard on the GSX and optional on the GS Turbo. Eagle and Plymouth each have four models. The Talon DL and base Laser use the 1.8-liter engine; the Talon ES and Laser RS use the 135-horsepower 2.0-liter engine; and the turbocharged engine powers the Talon TSi and Laser RS Turbo, as well as AWD versions of both. Anti-lock brakes are optional on all Talons and Lasers except the base models. These cars are nearing the end of their life cycle yet they still are accept-able choices among sports coupes. Their biggest fault is that they lack air bags, making do instead with motorized front shoulder belts. Though the AWD models are the most impressive perform-ers, a front-drive version with the 135-horsepower 2.0-liter engine strikes the best balance of performance and value. All three should be available at discounts.

Eagle Talon prices are on page 304; Mitsubishi Eclipse prices are on page 379; and Plymouth Laser prices are on page 406.

MITSUBISHI ECLIPSE GSX

Rating Guide	1	2	3	4	5
Performance					
Acceleration	▮	▮	▮	▮	▮
Economy	▮	▮			
Driveability	▮	▮	▮		
Ride	▮	▮	▮		
Steering/handling	▮	▮	▮	▮	▮
Braking	▮	▮	▮	▮	
Noise	▮	▮	▮		
Accommodations					
Driver seating	▮	▮	▮	▮	
Instruments/controls	▮	▮	▮	▮	
Visibility	▮	▮	▮		
Room/comfort	▮	▮	▮		
Entry/exit	▮	▮	▮		
Cargo room	▮	▮			
Workmanship					
Exterior	▮	▮	▮	▮	
Interior	▮	▮	▮	▮	
Value	▮	▮	▮		
Total Points					**51**

Specifications

Body type	3-door hatchback
Wheelbase (in.)	97.2
Overall length (in.)	172.8
Overall width (in.)	66.7
Overall height (in.)	51.4
Curb weight (lbs.)	3108
Seating capacity	4
Front head room (in.)	37.9
Max. front leg room (in.)	43.9
Rear head room (in.)	34.1
Min. rear leg room (in.)	28.5
Cargo volume (cu. ft.)	10.2
Engine type	Turbo dohc I-4
Engine size (l/cu. in.)	2.0/122
Horsepower @ rpm	195 @ 6000
Torque @ rpm	203 @ 3000
Transmission	manual/5-sp.
Drive wheels	all
Brakes, F/R	disc/disc (ABS)
Tire size	205/55HR16
Fuel tank capacity (gal.)	15.8
EPA city/highway mpg	20/25
Test mileage (mpg)	18.5

Warranties The entire car is covered for 3 years/36,000 miles. Major powertrain components are covered for 5 years/60,000 miles. Body perforation rust is covered for 7 years/100,000 miles.

Rating scale 5=Exceptional; 4=Above average; 3=Average; 2=Below average; 1=Poor

MITSUBISHI EXPO

Built in Japan.

Mitsubishi Expo

COMPACT   Similar to Eagle Summit Wagon, Plymouth Colt Vista

A driver-side air bag is a new standard feature on all versions of the Expo wagon. The air bag is accompanied by a manual, height-adjustable driver-side seat belt. A motorized shoulder belt is still used on the passenger side to meet federal passive-restraint rules. Expo continues in two sizes. The LRV (Light Recreational Vehicle) is a "mini-minivan" with a 99.2-inch wheelbase, two front doors, a sliding right rear door, a rear liftgate, and seats for five. Chrysler Corporation sells similar models as the Eagle Summit Wagon and Plymouth Colt Vista. Regular Expos are 5-door wagons with four swing-out side doors, a liftgate, seats for seven, and a 107-inch wheelbase. The regular Expo is exclusive to Mitsubishi. The Expo line loses its upscale SP models. Base Expos again come in a choice of front-wheel drive or permanent all-wheel drive (AWD). The LRV roster is limited to front-drive base and Sport models. AWD is no longer available on the LRV. A 1.8-liter 4-cylinder engine with 113 horsepower is standard on the base LRV and now comes only with a 5-speed manual transmission. A 2.4-liter 4-cylinder with 136 horsepower is standard on all other models and comes with a 5-speed manual or 4-speed automatic. Anti-lock brakes are optional on all models except the base LRV. Expo and its Chrysler cousins haven't been big sellers partly because they cost as much as a low-end minivan. However, they're roomy, versatile vehicles that work well for those who want more than a sedan or coupe but don't need a minivan. Avoid the 1.8-liter engine because it's too weak for these wagons. All brands should be available at discounts.

MItsubishi Expo prices are on page 380.

MITSUBISHI EXPO

Rating Guide	1	2	3	4	5
Performance					
Acceleration	‖‖‖‖‖‖‖‖‖‖‖‖‖‖‖‖‖‖‖‖‖‖‖				
Economy	‖‖‖‖‖‖‖‖‖‖‖‖‖‖‖‖‖‖‖‖‖‖				
Driveability	‖‖‖‖‖‖‖‖‖‖‖‖‖‖‖‖‖‖‖‖‖‖				
Ride	‖‖‖‖‖‖‖‖‖‖‖‖‖‖‖‖‖‖‖‖‖‖‖‖‖‖‖				
Steering/handling	‖‖‖‖‖‖‖‖‖‖‖‖‖‖‖‖‖‖‖‖‖‖				
Braking	‖‖‖‖‖‖‖‖‖‖‖‖‖‖‖‖‖‖‖‖				
Noise	‖‖‖‖‖‖‖‖‖‖‖‖‖‖‖‖‖‖‖‖‖				
Accommodations					
Driver seating	‖‖‖‖‖‖‖‖‖‖‖‖‖‖‖‖‖‖‖‖‖				
Instruments/controls	‖‖‖‖‖‖‖‖‖‖‖‖‖‖‖‖‖‖‖‖‖				
Visibility	‖‖‖‖‖‖‖‖‖‖‖‖‖‖‖‖‖‖‖‖‖‖‖‖‖‖‖‖‖				
Room/comfort	‖‖‖‖‖‖‖‖‖‖‖‖‖‖‖‖‖‖‖‖‖‖‖‖				
Entry/exit	‖‖‖‖‖‖‖‖‖‖‖‖‖‖‖‖‖‖‖‖‖‖				
Cargo room	‖‖‖‖‖‖‖‖‖‖‖‖‖‖‖‖‖‖‖‖‖‖‖‖				
Workmanship					
Exterior	‖‖‖‖‖‖‖‖‖‖‖‖‖‖‖‖‖‖‖‖‖‖‖				
Interior	‖‖‖‖‖‖‖‖‖‖‖‖‖‖‖‖‖‖‖‖‖‖‖				
Value	‖‖‖‖‖‖‖‖‖‖‖‖‖‖‖‖‖‖‖‖‖‖				
Total Points..**56**					

Specifications

Body type	5-door wagon	Engine type	ohc I-4
Wheelbase (in.)	107.1	Engine size (l/cu. in.)	2.4/144
Overall length (in.)	177.4	Horsepower @ rpm	136 @ 5500
Overall width (in.)	66.7	Torque @ rpm	145 @ 4250
Overall height (in.)	62.6	Transmission	auto/4-sp.
Curb weight (lbs.)	3020	Drive wheels	front
Seating capacity	7	Brakes, F/R	disc/drum
Front head room (in.)	39.3	Tire size	205/70SR14
Max. front leg room (in.)	40.5	Fuel tank capacity (gal.)	15.8
Rear head room (in.)	39.3	EPA city/highway mpg	20/26
Min. rear leg room (in.)	37.7	Test mileage (mpg)	NA
Cargo volume (cu. ft.)	75.0		

Warranties The entire car is covered for 3 years/36,000 miles. Major powertrain components are covered for 5 years/60,000 miles. Body perforation rust is covered for 7 years/100,000 miles.

Rating scale 5=Exceptional; 4=Above average; 3=Average; 2=Below average; 1=Poor

MITSUBISHI GALANT

Built in Normal, Ill.

Mitsubishi Galant ES

COMPACT

The 1994 Galant went on sale last summer as Mitsubishi's new rival for compact and mid-size cars such as the Nissan Altima, Toyota Camry, and Mazda 626. The new Galant comes only as a 4-door notchback sedan with front-wheel drive and standard dual air bags. While the previous Galant was imported from Japan, the new model is built only at Diamond-Star Motors, Mitsubishi's plant in Illinois. The new Galant is 1.3 inches longer in wheelbase and 3.1 inches longer overall. It also is 1.4 inches wider. Interior volume is 109.8 cubic feet, 3.7 cubic feet greater than the old model and just under the EPA's 110 cubic feet minimum for mid-size cars. Four models are available: base S, ES, luxury-oriented LS, and sporty GS. All but the GS have a new 141-horsepower 2.4-liter 4-cylinder. The GS has a 160-horsepower version of the 2.4-liter with dual overhead camshafts instead of one. A 5-speed manual transmission is standard on the S and GS, and not available on the others. A 4-speed automatic is standard on the ES and LS, and optional on the S and GS. Anti-lock brakes are optional on all models except the S. Mitsubishi says a 2.5-liter V-6 engine will be added for the 1995 model year. The Galant is roomy, comfortable, competent on the road, and competitively priced. Aside from lacking a V-6 engine, it stacks up well against other compact sedans. It rides comfortably and takes corners with surefooted confidence. The interior has ample space for four adults, with a rear seat that has generous head and leg room. The roomy trunk has a wide, flat floor and a low liftover for easier loading.

Mitsubishi Galant prices are on page 382.

MITSUBISHI GALANT ES

Rating Guide	1	2	3	4	5
Performance					
Acceleration	▓▓▓▓▓▓▓▓				
Economy	▓▓▓▓▓▓▓				
Driveability	▓▓▓▓▓▓▓				
Ride	▓▓▓▓▓▓▓▓▓▓				
Steering/handling	▓▓▓▓▓▓▓▓				
Braking	▓▓▓▓▓▓▓▓▓▓▓				
Noise	▓▓▓▓▓▓▓				
Accommodations					
Driver seating	▓▓▓▓▓▓▓				
Instruments/controls	▓▓▓▓▓▓▓				
Visibility	▓▓▓▓▓▓▓▓				
Room/comfort	▓▓▓▓▓▓▓▓				
Entry/exit	▓▓▓▓▓▓▓▓▓▓▓				
Cargo room	▓▓▓▓▓▓▓▓				
Workmanship					
Exterior	▓▓▓▓▓▓▓▓				
Interior	▓▓▓▓▓▓▓				
Value	▓▓▓▓▓▓▓				

Total Points **59**

Specifications

Body type	4-door notchback	Engine type	ohc I-4
Wheelbase (in.)	103.7	Engine size (l/cu. in.)	2.4/144
Overall length (in.)	187.0	Horsepower @ rpm	141 @ 5500
Overall width (in.)	68.1	Torque @ rpm	148 @ 3000
Overall height (in.)	53.1	Transmission	auto/4-sp.
Curb weight (lbs.)	2755	Drive wheels	front
Seating capacity	5	Brakes, F/R	disc/disc (ABS)
Front head room (in.)	39.4	Tire size	185/70R14
Max. front leg room (in.)	43.3	Fuel tank capacity (gal.)	16.9
Rear head room (in.)	37.5	EPA city/highway mpg	22/28
Min. rear leg room (in.)	35.0	Test mileage (mpg)	NA
Cargo volume (cu. ft.)	12.5		

Warranties The entire car is covered for 3 years/36,000 miles. Major powertrain components are covered for 5 years/60,000 miles. Body perforation rust is covered for 7 years/100,000 miles.

Rating scale 5=Exceptional; 4=Above average; 3=Average; 2=Below average; 1=Poor

MITSUBISHI MIRAGE

Built in Japan.

Mitsubishi Mirage ES 4-door

SUBCOMPACT Similar to Dodge/Plymouth Colt, Eagle Summit

Though it was redesigned last year, Mitsubishi's subcompact Mirage gets an unusual number of changes for 1994. Heading the list is a standard driver-side air bag and manual seat belt for all models. The 3-point belt replaces a motorized shoulder belt, which is retained on the passenger's side. The front-drive Mirage returns in 4-door sedan and 2-door coupe body styles. This year, the LS coupe gets the 1.8-liter 113-horsepower 4-cylinder engine as standard equipment. Last year, the 1.8-liter engine was standard only on the ES and LS sedans. Other models continue with a 92-horsepower 1.5-liter 4-cylinder. The LS sedan gains as standard a 4-speed automatic transmission. A 5-speed manual remains standard on all other Mirages. A 3-speed automatic is optional on the S 4-door and ES 2-door, and the 4-speed automatic is optional on the ES sedan and LS coupe. Anti-lock brakes, which were optional on the LS sedan last year, have been dropped. Chrysler sells the Mirage in slightly different form under the Dodge/Plymouth Colt and Eagle Summit banners. The new air bag makes these better choices in the crowded small-car field, but they still don't match the best in class—the Honda Civic, Toyota Corolla, and Geo Prizm. Acceleration is lackluster with the 1.5-liter engine and more than adequate with the 1.8-liter. Seating arrangements clearly favor those in front; the rear seat is too crowded for adults to be comfortable. Mirage prices climb quickly as popular options are added, but intense competition in the subcompact market means you won't have to pay full retail.

Mitsubishi Mirage prices are on page 383.

MITSUBISHI MIRAGE ES

Rating Guide	1	2	3	4	5
Performance					
Acceleration	▐▐▐▐▐▐▐▐▐▐▐▐▐▐▐▐				
Economy	▐▐▐▐▐▐▐▐▐▐▐▐▐▐▐▐▐				
Driveability	▐▐▐▐▐▐▐▐▐▐▐▐▐▐				
Ride	▐▐▐▐▐▐▐▐▐▐▐▐▐▐				
Steering/handling	▐▐▐▐▐▐▐▐▐▐▐▐▐▐▐▐▐				
Braking	▐▐▐▐▐▐▐▐▐▐▐▐▐				
Noise	▐▐▐▐▐▐▐▐▐▐▐▐▐▐				
Accommodations					
Driver seating	▐▐▐▐▐▐▐▐▐▐▐▐▐▐▐▐▐				
Instruments/controls	▐▐▐▐▐▐▐▐▐▐▐▐▐▐▐▐▐				
Visibility	▐▐▐▐▐▐▐▐▐▐▐▐▐▐▐▐				
Room/comfort	▐▐▐▐▐▐▐▐▐▐▐▐▐▐				
Entry/exit	▐▐▐▐▐▐▐▐▐▐▐▐▐▐				
Cargo room	▐▐▐▐▐▐▐▐▐▐▐▐▐▐				
Workmanship					
Exterior	▐▐▐▐▐▐▐▐▐▐▐▐▐▐▐▐				
Interior	▐▐▐▐▐▐▐▐▐▐▐▐▐▐▐▐				
Value	▐▐▐▐▐▐▐▐▐▐▐▐▐				

Total Points..54

Specifications

Body type	4-door notchback	Engine type	ohc I-4
Wheelbase (in.)	98.4	Engine size (l/cu. in.)	1.8/112
Overall length (in.)	172.2	Horsepower @ rpm	113 @ 6000
Overall width (in.)	66.5	Torque @ rpm	116 @ 4500
Overall height (in.)	52.2	Transmission	auto/4-sp.
Curb weight (lbs.)	2195	Drive wheels	front
Seating capacity	5	Brakes, F/R	disc/drum (ABS)
Front head room (in.)	38.6	Tire size	185/65R13
Max. front leg room (in.)	42.9	Fuel tank capacity (gal.)	13.2
Rear head room (in.)	36.2	EPA city/highway mpg	26/34
Min. rear leg room (in.)	33.5	Test mileage (mpg)	NA
Cargo volume (cu. ft.)	10.5		

Warranties The entire car is covered for 3 years/36,000 miles. Major powertrain components are covered for 5 years/60,000 miles. Body perforation rust is covered for 7 years/100,000 miles.

Rating scale 5=Exceptional; 4=Above average; 3=Average; 2=Below average; 1=Poor

MITSUBISHI MONTERO ——

Built in Japan.

Mitsubishi Montero SR

SPORT-UTILITY VEHICLE

Mitsubishi's 4-wheel-drive wagon gains a standard driver-side air bag, a more powerful engine, 7-passenger seating, and additional standard equipment. Last year's base and RS models are gone, but the LS and SR return with the air bag in a new 4-spoke steering wheel. The SR has a bigger, more potent engine: a new dual-camshaft 3.5-liter V-6 with 215 horsepower. A 151-horsepower 3.0-liter V-6 with a single camshaft continues in the LS. A 4-speed automatic transmission is standard on the SR and optional on the LS. A 5-speed manual is standard on the LS. Montero has 5-door styling with a side-hinged rear door and standard 4-wheel drive that can be used on smooth, dry pavement. Anti-lock brakes are standard on the SR and optional on the LS. Seating capacity has increased to seven for both models with the addition of a 2-person bench seat at the rear. A leather-wrapped steering wheel and the previously optional power windows, locks and mirrors, and cruise control are now standard. A power driver's seat is now included with the optional Leather and Wood Package, and a new 6-speaker stereo with a graphic equalizer is standard on the SR and optional on the LS. Though Montero is a roomy wagon with several good features, including a convenient 4WD system, it's no bargain compared to the class leaders, the Jeep Grand Cherokee and Ford Explorer. The new 3.5-liter V-6 gives the SR model much stronger acceleration than the LS, which carries too much weight for its 3.0-liter V-6. The SR model, however, starts at more than $31,000. We averaged just 16.5 mpg with a 1993 model and don't expect improvement with either engine this year.

Mitsubishi Montero prices are on page 384.

MITSUBISHI MONTERO SR

Rating Guide	1	2	3	4	5
Performance					
Acceleration			▓		
Economy		▓			
Driveability				▓	
Ride			▓		
Steering/handling			▓		
Braking					▓
Noise			▓		
Accommodations					
Driver seating			▓		
Instruments/controls			▓		
Visibility			▓		
Room/comfort					▓
Entry/exit			▓		
Cargo room					▓
Workmanship					
Exterior			▓		
Interior				▓	
Value			▓		
Total Points					**57**

Specifications

Body type ....5-door wagon
Wheelbase (in.) 107.3
Overall length (in.) 185.2
Overall width (in.) 66.7
Overall height (in.) 73.4
Curb weight (lbs.) 4175
Seating capacity 7
Front head room (in.) 40.9
Max. front leg room (in.) 40.3
Rear head room (in.) 40.0
Min. rear leg room (in.) 37.6
Cargo volume (cu. ft.) 72.7

Engine type ....dohc V-6
Engine size (l/cu. in.) 3.5/213
Horsepower @ rpm ...215 @ 5500
Torque @ rpm ....228 @ 3000
Transmission ....auto/4-sp.
Drive wheels.......................rear/all
Brakes, F/R ....disc/disc (ABS)
Tire size 265/70R15
Fuel tank capacity (gal.) 24.3
EPA city/highway mpg 14/17
Test mileage (mpg) ....NA

Warranties The entire vehicle is covered for 3 years/36,000 miles. Major powertrain components are covered for 5 years/60,000 miles. Body perforation rust is covered for 7 years/100,000 miles.

Rating scale 5=Exceptional; 4=Above average; 3=Average; 2=Below average; 1=Poor

MITSUBISHI 3000GT/ ─────
DODGE STEALTH
Built in Japan.

Mitsubishi 3000GT VR-4

SPORTS AND GT

This Mitsubishi sports car returns for its fifth model year with a passenger-side air bag as a new standard feature, 30 more horsepower and a new transmission for the turbocharged models, and a mild facelift. A driver-side air bag has been standard since the 3000GT and Stealth were introduced as 1990 models. The twin-turbo 3.0-liter V-6 in the all-wheel drive 3000GT VR-4 and Stealth R/T Turbo has 320 horsepower this year and 315 pounds/feet of torque (eight more than last year). The VR-4 and R/T Turbo again come only with a manual, but now it's a 6-speed transmission instead of a 5-speed. In the 3000GT line, the front-drive base and SL models retain a naturally aspirated 3.0-liter V-6 with 222 horsepower. In the Stealth line, there also are two front-drive models: The base Stealth has a 164-horsepower 3.0-liter V-6 and the R/T has the 222-horsepower engine. A 5-speed manual transmission is standard and a 4-speed automatic is optional on the front-drive models. All models wear a reshaped nose with four exposed headlamps (replacing dual hidden headlamps) and integral fog lamps, new wheels, restyled side scoops, and styling tweaks at the rear. We were highly impressed by the performance of the VR-4 we tested, though we tired of the stiff suspension on bumpy pavements and wished there was less noise. A 3000GT SL or Stealth R/T with the 222-horsepower engine is more comfortable yet packs enough performance to satisfy most drivers. They're also considerably less expensive than the turbo models.

Dodge Stealth prices are on page 301;
Mitsubishi 3000GT prices are on page 385.

MITSUBISHI 3000GT VR-4

Rating Guide	1	2	3	4	5
Performance					
Acceleration	||||||||||||||||||||||||||||||||||||||||||||||||||||||||||
Economy	||||||||||||||||||||
Driveability	||||||||||||||||||||||||||||||
Ride	||||||||||||||||||||||||||||||
Steering/handling	||||||||||||||||||||||||||||||||||||||||||||||
Braking	||||||||||||||||||||||||||||||||||||||||||||||
Noise	||||||||||||||||||||||||||||||
Accommodations					
Driver seating	||||||||||||||||||||||||||||||||||||||||
Instruments/controls	||||||||||||||||||||||||||||||||||||||||
Visibility	||||||||||||||||||||||||||||||
Room/comfort	||||||||||||||||||||||||||||||
Entry/exit	||||||||||||||||||||||||||||||
Cargo room	||||||||||||||||||||||||||||||
Workmanship					
Exterior	||||||||||||||||||||||||||||||||||||||||
Interior	||||||||||||||||||||||||||||||||||||
Value	||||||||||||||||||||||||||||||||||||

Total Points...49

Specifications

Body type ....3-door hatchback	Engine type ....Turbo dohc V-6
Wheelbase (in.) 97.2	Engine size (l/cu. in.)........3.0/181
Overall length (in.)................179.7	Horsepower @ rpm ...320 @ 6000
Overall width (in.) 72.4	Torque @ rpm ....315 @ 2500
Overall height (in.).................49.1	Transmission ....manual/6-sp.
Curb weight (lbs.) 3803	Drive wheels ....all
Seating capacity............................4	Brakes, F/R..........disc/disc (ABS)
Front head room (in.) 37.1	Tire size......................245/45ZR17
Max. front leg room (in.) 44.2	Fuel tank capacity (gal.) 19.8
Rear head room (in.) 34.1	EPA city/highway mpg 18/24
Min. rear leg room (in.)..........28.5	Test mileage (mpg) ....NA
Cargo volume (cu. ft.).............11.1	

Warranties The entire car is covered for 3 years/36,000 miles. Major powertrain components are covered for 5 years/60,000 miles. Body perforation rust is covered for 7 years/100,000 miles.

Rating scale 5=Exceptional; 4=Above average; 3=Average; 2=Below average; 1=Poor

NISSAN ALTIMA ——— RECOMMENDED

Built in Smyrna, Tenn.

Nissan Altima GXE

COMPACT

A passenger-side air bag and 3-point manual front seat belts are the major new features this year on Altima, which was introduced last year and became a sales hit for Nissan. In 1993, Altima, a front-drive compact sedan, was Nissan's second best selling U.S. model behind the Sentra. Last year, Altima had a driver-side air bag and motorized front shoulder belts. This year, there also is a standard passenger-side air bag and the motorized belts have been replaced by conventional manual lap/shoulder belts. The only engine is a 150-horsepower 2.4-liter 4-cylinder. A 5-speed manual transmission is standard on the base XE, the GXE, and sporty SE models. A 4-speed automatic is standard on the luxury GLE model and optional on the others. Anti-lock brakes are optional on all models. Though it's not the roomiest or most refined compact sedan, Altima has above-average acceleration and handling ability, and it comes well-equipped at competitive prices. We've tested a GXE (the most popular model) with automatic transmission for more than 10,000 miles without any mechanical problems. We've averaged slightly more than 20 mpg from mostly urban driving. Acceleration is lively from a standing start (9.4 seconds to 60 mph) and passing response spirited, though the engine is loud and rough at higher speeds. The transmission on our test car changes gears sluggishly, even in full-throttle acceleration, and there's a pronounced flare in engine speed as the transmission slowly shifts from first to second. Overall, however, we rate Nissan's compact sedan highly and encourage you to give it a close look.

Nissan Altima prices are on page 386.

CONSUMER GUIDE®

NISSAN ALTIMA GXE

Rating Guide	1	2	3	4	5
Performance					
Acceleration				▓▓▓▓	
Economy			▓▓▓		
Driveability				▓▓▓▓	
Ride				▓▓▓▓	
Steering/handling				▓▓▓▓	
Braking					▓▓▓▓▓
Noise			▓▓▓		
Accommodations					
Driver seating				▓▓▓▓	
Instruments/controls				▓▓▓▓	
Visibility			▓▓▓		
Room/comfort				▓▓▓▓	
Entry/exit				▓▓▓▓	
Cargo room				▓▓▓▓	
Workmanship					
Exterior				▓▓▓▓	
Interior				▓▓▓▓	
Value				▓▓▓▓	
Total Points					**58**

Specifications

Body type	4-door notchback
Wheelbase (in.)	103.1
Overall length (in.)	180.5
Overall width (in.)	67.1
Overall height (in.)	55.9
Curb weight (lbs.)	2829
Seating capacity	5
Front head room (in.)	39.3
Max. front leg room (in.)	42.6
Rear head room (in.)	37.6
Min. rear leg room (in.)	34.7
Cargo volume (cu. ft.)	14.0
Engine type	dohc I-4
Engine size (l/cu. in.)	2.4/146
Horsepower @ rpm	150 @ 5600
Torque @ rpm	154 @ 4400
Transmission	auto/4-sp.
Drive wheels	front
Brakes, F/R	disc/disc (ABS)
Tire size	205/60R15
Fuel tank capacity (gal.)	15.9
EPA city/highway mpg	21/29
Test mileage (mpg)	20.2

Warranties The entire car is covered for 3 years/36,000 miles. Major powertrain components are covered for 5 years/ 60,000 miles. Body perforation rust is covered for 5 years/unlimited miles.

Rating scale 5=Exceptional; 4=Above average; 3=Average; 2=Below average; 1=Poor

NISSAN MAXIMA

Built in Japan.

Nissan Maxima GXE

PREMIUM SEDAN

Maxima is nearing the end of the road in its present form, so there are few changes for 1994. The current design, which debuted for the 1989 model year, will be replaced by next summer. The next Maxima also will be a front-drive sedan but is expected to be larger and have more powerful V-6 engines. The key change for 1994 is that anti-lock brakes, which previously were a stand-alone option on the SE, now are available only with the optional power sunroof. The anti-lock feature remains a stand-alone option on the GXE model. The SE's tires now have an all-season tread design; the size is unchanged at 205/65VR15. Both models are powered by 3.0-liter V-6 engines. On the GXE, it has a single overhead camshaft and 160 horsepower. On the SE, it has dual overhead camshafts and 190 horsepower. A 5-speed manual transmission is standard on the SE and a 4-speed automatic is optional. The GXE comes only with the automatic. A driver-side air bag is standard on both models, which also have motorized front shoulder belts. Despite being five years old, the Maxima is still a good choice in a "near-luxury" sedan. The SE is a potent, sporty performer that matches up well to higher-priced models. The GXE, which is just as refined and stresses luxury over sporty qualities, also is well worth considering. Maxima has a well-organized dashboard and comfortable driving position, impressive solidity (which Chrysler targeted for its new LH sedans), a comfortable ride, and poised front-drive handling. Nissan has been offering $1000 rebates on the GXE and discounted leases that make the Maxima more affordable.

Nissan Maxima prices are on page 387.

CONSUMER GUIDE®

NISSAN MAXIMA GXE

Rating Guide	1	2	3	4	5
Performance					
Acceleration					
Economy					
Driveability					
Ride					
Steering/handling					
Braking					
Noise					
Accommodations					
Driver seating					
Instruments/controls					
Visibility					
Room/comfort					
Entry/exit					
Cargo room					
Workmanship					
Exterior					
Interior					
Value					
Total Points **63**					

Specifications

Body type ....4-door notchback	Engine type ....ohc V-6
Wheelbase (in.) 104.3	Engine size (l/cu. in.).........3.0/181
Overall length (in.)................187.6	Horsepower @ rpm ...160 @ 5200
Overall width (in.) 69.3	Torque @ rpm ....182 @ 2800
Overall height (in.)..................55.1	Transmission.................auto/4-sp.
Curb weight (lbs.) 3129	Drive wheels ....front
Seating capacity...........................5	Brakes, F/R...........disc/disc (ABS)
Front head room (in.) 39.5	Tire size 205/65R15
Max. front leg room (in.) 43.7	Fuel tank capacity (gal.) 18.5
Rear head room (in.) 36.9	EPA city/highway mpg 19/26
Min. rear leg room (in.)...........33.2	Test mileage (mpg) ....NA
Cargo volume (cu. ft.).............14.5	

Warranties The entire car is covered for 3 years/36,000 miles. Major powertrain components are covered for 5 years/60,000 miles. Body perforation rust is covered for 5 years/unlimited miles.

Rating scale 5=Exceptional; 4=Above average; 3=Average; 2=Below average; 1=Poor

NISSAN PATHFINDER

Built in Japan.

Nissan Pathfinder SE

SPORT-UTILITY VEHICLE

Nissan tries to cash in on growing demand for luxury sport-utility vehicles with a new top-shelf LE model for its Pathfinder line. Standard equipment on the LE includes leather upholstery, heated front seats, luggage rack, semi-automatic air conditioning, a CD player, and other features that are either optional or not available on less-expensive versions. Pathfinder comes only as a 5-door wagon. In addition to the LE, there are base XE and sportier SE price levels. The XE is available with rear-wheel drive or 4-wheel drive. The others come only with 4WD, a part-time system for use on slick surfaces. It allows shifting into 4WD High at speeds up to 25 mph, but the vehicle must be stopped and driven in reverse to disengage 4WD. All models have a 153-horsepower 3.0-liter V-6 engine. A 5-speed manual transmission is standard and a 4-speed automatic is optional on all models except the LE, which comes only with the automatic. Anti-lock rear brakes that work only in 2WD are standard on all models. A new instrument panel replaces an upright, angular design with a more modern, flowing design. Pathfinder is well down the sales chart among sport-utility vehicles because of its high prices and truck-like demeanor compared to the Ford Explorer and Jeep Grand Cherokee, the class leaders. Though off-the-line acceleration is decent, Pathfinder is shy of low-end torque for strong pull up steep hills, especially with heavy loads. Fuel economy was dismal in our last test: 14.7 mpg with automatic. The 4WD is another minus. Without full shift-on-the-fly, it's far less convenient than most competitors' systems.

Nissan Pathfinder prices are on page 388.

NISSAN PATHFINDER SE

Rating Guide	1	2	3	4	5
Performance					
Acceleration					
Economy					
Driveability					
Ride					
Steering/handling					
Braking					
Noise					
Accommodations					
Driver seating					
Instruments/controls					
Visibility					
Room/comfort					
Entry/exit					
Cargo room					
Workmanship					
Exterior					
Interior					
Value					

Total Points...**53**

Specifications

Body type	5-door wagon	Engine type	ohc V-6
Wheelbase (in.)	104.3	Engine size (l/cu. in.)	3.0/181
Overall length (in.)	171.9	Horsepower @ rpm	153 @ 4800
Overall width (in.)	66.5	Torque @ rpm	180 @ 4000
Overall height (in.)	65.7	Transmission	auto/4-sp.
Curb weight (lbs.)	3890	Drive wheels	rear/all
Seating capacity	5	Brakes, F/R	disc/disc (ABS)
Front head room (in.)	39.3	Tire size	235/75R15
Max. front leg room (in.)	42.6	Fuel tank capacity (gal.)	20.4
Rear head room (in.)	36.8	EPA city/highway mpg	15/18
Min. rear leg room (in.)	33.1	Test mileage (mpg)	14.7
Cargo volume (cu. ft.)	80.2		

Warranties The entire vehicle is covered for 3 years/36,000 miles. Major powertrain components are covered for 5 years/60,000 miles. Body perforation rust is covered for 5 years/unlimited miles.

Rating scale 5=Exceptional; 4=Above average; 3=Average; 2=Below average; 1=Poor

NISSAN QUEST — RECOMMENDED

Built in Avon Lake, Ohio.

Nissan Quest GXE

MINIVAN Similar to Mercury Villager

Nissan's front-drive minivan gets a standard driver-side air bag as its major addition for 1994. Quest is built from the same design as the Mercury Villager (see separate report), which also gets the air bag. Both vehicles were designed by Nissan but are built at a Ford plant in Ohio. Installation of air bags didn't begin until late November, so early 1994 Quests didn't have them. The 1993 Quest and Villager met all passenger-car safety standards with motorized front shoulder belts as the passive restraint system. The motorized belts are retained this year. Anti-lock brakes were optional on both the base XE and more-expensive GXE models last year. This year, they're standard on the GXE. Other changes include a standard heavy-duty radiator and 3500-pound towing capacity (up from 2000 pounds last year). Quest has a 151-horsepower 3.0-liter V-6 engine and a 4-speed electronic automatic transmission. Both are made by Nissan and also used in the Villager. Seats for seven are standard, with two front buckets, a 2-place middle bench, and a 3-place rear bench. The middle seat is removable and the rear seat slides up to the middle position on floor-mounted tracks. Like the Villager, Quest is a roomy family vehicle that's easy to drive and has flexible seating and cargo accommodations. The engine is smooth and powerful enough for most situations, though more power wouldn't hurt. We've tested Nissan and Mercury versions of this minivan and the Quests have had a more comfortable ride. Quest and Villager deserve a close look, especially if you value family-car finesse over maximum cargo space and towing ability.

Nissan Quest prices are on page 389.

NISSAN QUEST GXE

Rating Guide	1	2	3	4	5
Performance					
Acceleration	||||||||||||||||||||||||||||||||||			
Economy	|||||||||||||||||||||||				
Driveability	|||||||||||||||||||||||||||||||||||			
Ride	||||||||||||||||||||||||||||||||||||||||		
Steering/handling	||||||||||||||||||||||||||||||||||			
Braking	||||||||||||||||||||||||||||||||||||||||||||||
Noise	|||||||||||||||||||||||||||||||||			
Accommodations					
Driver seating	||||||||||||||||||||||||||||||||||			
Instruments/controls	||||||||||||||||||||||||||||||||||			
Visibility	||||||||||||||||||||||||||||||||||||		
Room/comfort	||||||||||||||||||||||||||||||||||||||||		
Entry/exit	||||||||||||||||||||||||||||||||||			
Cargo room	||||||||||||||||||||||||||||||||||||||||		
Workmanship					
Exterior	||||||||||||||||||||||||||||||||||			
Interior	||||||||||||||||||||||||||||||||||			
Value	||||||||||||||||||||||||||||||||||			
Total Points...**61**					

Specifications

Body type ....4-door van	Engine type ....ohc V-6
Wheelbase (in.) 112.2	Engine size (l/cu. in.).........3.0/181
Overall length (in.) 189.9	Horsepower @ rpm ...151 @ 4800
Overall width (in.) 73.7	Torque @ rpm ....174 @ 4400
Overall height (in.) 65.6	Transmission ....auto/4-sp.
Curb weight (lbs.) 3782	Drive wheels ....front
Seating capacity 7	Brakes, F/R ....disc/disc (ABS)
Front head room (in.) 39.4	Tire size 205/75R15
Max. front leg room (in.) 39.9	Fuel tank capacity (gal.) 20.0
Rear head room (in.) 39.7	EPA city/highway mpg 17/23
Min. rear leg room (in.) 34.8	Test mileage (mpg) 18.5
Cargo volume (cu. ft.)...........114.8	

Warranties The entire vehicle is covered for 3 years/36,000 miles. Major powertrain components are covered for 5 years/60,000 miles. Body perforation rust is covered for 5 years/unlimited miles.

Rating scale 5=Exceptional; 4=Above average; 3=Average; 2=Below average; 1=Poor

NISSAN SENTRA

Built in Smyrna, Tenn., and Japan.

Nissan Sentra GXE

SUBCOMPACT

The XE model has more standard equipment this year as the big change for Sentra, a front-drive subcompact. Additional standard equipment on the XE includes air conditioning, a stereo with cassette player, and cruise control, all of which were in last year's Value Option Package. The 2-door Sentra comes in E, XE, SE, and SE-R models, and the 4-door comes in E, XE, and GXE models. All except the SE-R have a 110-horsepower 1.6-liter 4-cylinder engine. The sporty SE-R has a 140-horsepower 2.0-liter 4-cylinder. A 5-speed manual transmission is standard and a 4-speed automatic is optional on all models. A driver-side air bag is standard on the GXE and optional on other Sentras. The 2-door models meet the federal requirement for passive restraints with door-mounted automatic front seat belts. The 4-door models have motorized front shoulder belts. The passive belts are retained on models with the air bag. Anti-lock brakes are optional on the GXE and SE-R. Sentra offers good gas mileage, top-notch assembly, and a driver-side air bag—though it's optional on all except the most expensive model. Both the 2- and 4-doors have generous room in the front seats, though there's too little leg room for adults in the back seat. With the 1.6-liter engine and 5-speed manual, acceleration is decent and mileage great. With the automatic transmission, you have to floor the throttle for brisk acceleration. Sentra's prices have risen considerably. The least-expensive version is over $10,000 and if you want automatic transmission the starting price is nearly $12,000. Nissan dealers should be willing to bargain on price, however.

Nissan Sentra prices are on page 390.

NISSAN SENTRA GXE

Rating Guide	1	2	3	4	5
Performance					
Acceleration	▮▮▮▮▮▮▮				
Economy	▮▮▮▮▮▮▮▮				
Driveability	▮▮▮▮▮▮				
Ride	▮▮▮▮▮▮				
Steering/handling	▮▮▮▮▮▮▮▮				
Braking	▮▮▮▮▮▮▮▮▮				
Noise	▮▮▮▮▮				
Accommodations					
Driver seating	▮▮▮▮▮▮				
Instruments/controls	▮▮▮▮▮▮				
Visibility	▮▮▮▮▮▮▮▮▮				
Room/comfort	▮▮▮▮▮▮▮				
Entry/exit	▮▮▮▮▮▮▮				
Cargo room	▮▮▮▮▮▮				
Workmanship					
Exterior	▮▮▮▮▮▮				
Interior	▮▮▮▮▮▮				
Value	▮▮▮▮▮▮▮▮▮				

Total Points 57

Specifications

Body type ....4-door notchback	Engine type ....dohc I-4
Wheelbase (in.) 95.7	Engine size (l/cu. in.)...........1.6/97
Overall length (in.) 170.3	Horsepower @ rpm ...110 @ 6000
Overall width (in.) 65.6	Torque @ rpm ....108 @ 4000
Overall height (in.) 53.9	Transmission.................auto/4-sp.
Curb weight (lbs.) 2359	Drive wheels ....front
Seating capacity.........................5	Brakes, F/R..........disc/disc (ABS)
Front head room (in.) 38.5	Tire size 175/70R13
Max. front leg room (in.) 41.9	Fuel tank capacity (gal.) 13.2
Rear head room (in.) 36.6	EPA city/highway mpg 26/35
Min. rear leg room (in.)...........30.9	Test mileage (mpg) 25.9
Cargo volume (cu. ft.).............11.7	

Warranties The entire car is covered for 3 years/36,000 miles. Major powertrain components are covered for 5 years/60,000. Body perforation rust is covered for 5 years/unlimited miles.

Rating scale 5=Exceptional; 4=Above average; 3=Average; 2=Below average; 1=Poor

NISSAN 240SX

Built in Japan.

Nissan 240SX LE convertible

SPORTS COUPE

The 240SX comes only as a convertible for the 1994 model year. A redesigned coupe is scheduled to arrive next spring as an early 1995 model with rear-wheel drive, same as the current models. Nissan has dropped its front-drive NX 1600/2000 coupes, which were derived from the Sentra subcompact, leaving the 240SX as the company's only sports coupe. The 1994 model has a 155-horsepower 2.4-liter 4-cylinder engine and comes only in an LE price level with a 4-speed automatic transmission. The convertible's body is derived from a 2-door coupe and a portion of the center roof pillars is retained to serve as the upper anchor point for the front seat belts. The belts can be left buckled to automatically deploy when the doors are closed. The convertible, which also has a power top and power windows and locks, is unchanged from last year except that "cherry red pearl" is a new color choice. The 240SX is okay as far as convertibles go, but there's nothing special here to recommend it over competitors such as the Chrysler LeBaron, Mercury Capri, Chevrolet Cavalier, Pontiac Sunbird, or the 2-seat Mazda Miata. In fact, with neither a driver-side air bag nor anti-lock brakes available even as options, the 240SX slides further down our shopping list this year. The main attraction here besides the fun of open-air motoring is sharp handling from the 240SX's rear-drive chassis. As is typical of small convertibles, the 240SX has adequate space for the front seats and little for the rear. With a base price of nearly $24,000, the 240SX is no bargain, either. That's thousands more than a Miata or a Capri.

Nissan 240SX prices are on page 391.

NISSAN 240SX LE CONVERTIBLE

Rating Guide	1	2	3	4	5
Performance					
Acceleration			▓		
Economy			▓		
Driveability			▓		
Ride			▓		
Steering/handling					▓
Braking				▓	
Noise		▓			
Accommodations					
Driver seating			▓		
Instruments/controls				▓	
Visibility			▓		
Room/comfort			▓		
Entry/exit			▓		
Cargo room			▓		
Workmanship					
Exterior				▓	
Interior				▓	
Value			▓		
Total Points					48

Specifications

Body type	2-door convertible	Engine type	dohc I-4
Wheelbase (in.)	97.4	Engine size (l/cu. in.)	2.4/146
Overall length (in.)	178.0	Horsepower @ rpm	155 @ 5600
Overall width (in.)	66.5	Torque @ rpm	160 @ 4400
Overall height (in.)	50.8	Transmission	auto/4-sp.
Curb weight (lbs.)	2870	Drive wheels	rear
Seating capacity	4	Brakes, F/R	disc/disc
Front head room (in.)	38.3	Tire size	195/60R15
Max. front leg room (in.)	41.0	Fuel tank capacity (gal.)	15.9
Rear head room (in.)	35.5	EPA city/highway mpg	21/26
Min. rear leg room (in.)	25.4	Test mileage (mpg)	21.8
Cargo volume (cu. ft.)	5.1		

Warranties The entire car is covered for 3 years/36,000 miles. Major powertrain components are covered for 5 years/60,000 miles. Body perforation rust is covered for 5 years/unlimited miles.

Rating scale 5=Exceptional; 4=Above average; 3=Average; 2=Below average; 1=Poor

OLDSMOBILE ACHIEVA

Built in Lansing, Mich.

Oldsmobile Achieva S 2-door

COMPACT Similar to Buick Skylark, Pontiac Grand Am

A driver-side air bag is a new standard feature and a 3.1-liter V-6 engine and 4-speed automatic transmission are new options for Achieva, Oldsmobile's front-drive compact. Achieva previously met the federal requirement for passive restraints with automatic front seat belts, which are retained for 1994. The 160-horsepower 3.1-liter V-6 replaces a 3.3-liter V-6, which also had 160 horsepower. The V-6 comes only with an electronic 4-speed automatic transmission, a new option for Achieva. Base engine is a 115-horsepower 2.3-liter 4-cylinder that's available with a 5-speed manual transmission or 3- or 4-speed automatics. Two dual-camshaft 2.3-liter engines, called Quad 4, are available: A 170-horsepower version comes with the 5-speed manual transmission and a 155-horsepower version comes with the 4-speed automatic. This year's lineup has a 2-door coupe and 4-door sedan in a base S price level, plus a sporty SC 2-door and an upscale SL 4-door. Achieva also comes in one-price Special Edition models that start at $13,995. In addition, there are specially priced California models. Achieva is built from the same design as the Buick Skylark and Pontiac Grand Am, which also get the standard air bag this year. Anti-lock brakes are standard on all three. The Skylark and Grand Am have different styling and engines. With a standard air bag, Achieva is more attractive from a safety standpoint. The Special Edition and California models make it more attractive from a price standpoint. These fully-equipped models are priced hundreds—even thousands—below Japanese rivals such as the Toyota Camry and Mazda 626.

Oldsmobile Achieva prices are on page 392.

OLDSMOBILE ACHIEVA S

Rating Guide	1	2	3	4	5
Performance					
Acceleration	▓▓▓▓▓▓				
Economy	▓▓▓▓▓▓				
Driveability	▓▓▓▓▓▓				
Ride	▓▓▓▓▓▓				
Steering/handling	▓▓▓▓▓▓▓				
Braking	▓▓▓▓▓▓▓▓▓▓				
Noise	▓▓▓▓				
Accommodations					
Driver seating	▓▓▓▓▓▓▓				
Instruments/controls	▓▓▓▓▓▓▓				
Visibility	▓▓▓▓▓▓▓				
Room/comfort	▓▓▓▓▓▓				
Entry/exit	▓▓▓▓▓▓				
Cargo room	▓▓▓▓▓▓				
Workmanship					
Exterior	▓▓▓▓▓▓▓				
Interior	▓▓▓▓▓▓▓				
Value	▓▓▓▓▓▓▓▓				

Total Points 55

Specifications

Body type	2-door notchback	Engine type	ohc I-4
Wheelbase (in.)	103.4	Engine size (l/cu. in.)	2.3/138
Overall length (in.)	187.9	Horsepower @ rpm	115 @ 5200
Overall width (in.)	67.5	Torque @ rpm	140 @ 3200
Overall height (in.)	53.4	Transmission	auto/3-sp.
Curb weight (lbs.)	2738	Drive wheels	front
Seating capacity	5	Brakes, F/R	disc/drum (ABS)
Front head room (in.)	37.8	Tire size	185/75R14
Max. front leg room (in.)	43.3	Fuel tank capacity (gal.)	15.2
Rear head room (in.)	37.0	EPA city/highway mpg	22/32
Min. rear leg room (in.)	33.5	Test mileage (mpg)	21.3
Cargo volume (cu. ft.)	14.0		

Warranties The entire car is covered for 3 years/36,000 miles. Body perforation rust is covered for 6 years/100,000 miles.

Rating scale 5=Exceptional; 4=Above average; 3=Average; 2=Below average; 1=Poor

OLDSMOBILE AURORA

Built in Orion, Mich.

Oldsmobile Aurora

PREMIUM SEDAN

Aurora is a 1995 model scheduled to go on sale next spring as the first product of a new philosophy at Oldsmobile for designing, building, and selling cars. In designing the Aurora, Oldsmobile chose the Lexus LS 400 as its benchmark competitor. Aurora is built on a new front-drive chassis that will be shared with the 1995 Buick Riviera coupe. Aurora will come only as a 4-door sedan with seats for five instead of Oldsmobile's usual 6-passenger capacity. The only components shared with other Oldsmobiles are the radios. Even the Oldsmobile name will be downplayed in marketing—and may not appear on production models. The car will be sold as the "Aurora by Oldsmobile." Aurora's only engine is a 250-horsepower 4.0-liter V-8 with dual overhead camshafts. It is derived from the Cadillac 4.6-liter Northstar V-8 and teams with an electronic 4-speed automatic transmission. There will be just one model with a base price of $31,995. Standard equipment includes dual air bags, anti-lock 4-wheel disc brakes, and traction control that can be turned off by an interior switch. So far we've driven only hand-built prototypes of the Aurora and we're highly impressed. Though the engine doesn't snap your head back in hard acceleration, it delivers brisk acceleration and ample passing power. The transmission shifts so smoothly you seldom notice it. Aurora has commendable ride control at high speeds and though it's firmer than the Lexus LS 400, it is never harsh or stiff. Though some of our assessments may change when we drive production models, we think Oldsmobile is on target with the Aurora.

Oldsmobile Aurora standard equipment is on page 394.

OLDSMOBILE AURORA (Preliminary)

Rating Guide	1	2	3	4	5
Performance					
Acceleration	▓▓▓▓▓▓▓▓▓▓▓▓				
Economy	▓▓▓▓▓▓				
Driveability	▓▓▓▓▓▓▓▓▓▓▓▓▓▓▓				
Ride	▓▓▓▓▓▓▓▓▓▓▓				
Steering/handling	▓▓▓▓▓▓▓▓▓▓▓▓				
Braking	▓▓▓▓▓▓▓▓▓▓▓▓▓▓▓				
Noise	▓▓▓▓▓▓▓▓▓				
Accommodations					
Driver seating	▓▓▓▓▓▓▓▓▓▓▓▓				
Instruments/controls	▓▓▓▓▓▓▓▓▓▓▓▓				
Visibility	▓▓▓▓▓▓▓▓▓▓▓				
Room/comfort	▓▓▓▓▓▓▓▓▓▓▓				
Entry/exit	▓▓▓▓▓▓▓▓▓▓▓▓				
Cargo room	▓▓▓▓▓▓▓▓▓▓▓▓				
Workmanship					
Exterior	▓▓▓▓▓▓▓▓▓▓▓▓				
Interior	▓▓▓▓▓▓▓▓▓▓▓▓				
Value	▓▓▓▓▓▓▓▓▓▓▓▓				
Total Points					**60**

Specifications

Body type	4-door notchback	Engine type	dohc V-8
Wheelbase (in.)	113.8	Engine size (l/cu. in.)	4.0/244
Overall length (in.)	205.4	Horsepower @ rpm	250 @ 5600
Overall width (in.)	74.4	Torque @ rpm	260 @ 4400
Overall height (in.)	55.4	Transmission	auto/4-sp.
Curb weight (lbs.)	4000	Drive wheels	front
Seating capacity	5	Brakes, F/R	disc/disc (ABS)
Front head room (in.)	38.4	Tire size	235/60R16
Max. front leg room (in.)	42.6	Fuel tank capacity (gal.)	20.0
Rear head room (in.)	36.9	EPA city/highway mpg	16/25
Min. rear leg room (in.)	38.4	Test mileage (mpg)	NA
Cargo volume (cu. ft.)	16.1		

Warranties Not available.

Rating scale 5=Exceptional; 4=Above average; 3=Average; 2=Below average; 1=Poor

OLDSMOBILE CUTLASS SUPREME

Built in Doraville, Ga.

Oldsmobile Cutlass Supreme convertible

MID-SIZE Similar to Buick Regal, Chevrolet Lumina, Pontiac Grand Prix

Oldsmobile adds a driver-side air bag and makes anti-lock brakes standard on all versions of the front-drive Cutlass Supreme this year. In addition, there is a more powerful base engine and a standard electronic 4-speed automatic transmission for all models. Cutlass Supreme previously met the federal requirement for passive restraints with door-mounted automatic front seat belts, which are retained on the 1994 models. The International Series is gone, leaving an S price level for the 2-door coupe and 4-door sedan. In addition, there is a 2-door convertible with more standard equipment, including the Sport Luxury (SL) Package. The SL Package is optional on the S models. The bulk of Cutlass Supreme sales, however, are expected to be one-price Special Edition versions of the coupe and sedan that start at $16,995, including the $525 destination charge. There also are specially equipped California models. Standard engine this year is a 160-horsepower 3.1-liter V-6, which replaces a 140-horsepower engine of the same size. Optional for all models is a 210-horsepower 3.4-liter V-6. The Cutlass Supreme is built from the same design as the Buick Regal, Chevrolet Lumina, and Pontiac Grand Prix. Though the Cutlass Supreme isn't one of our favorite mid-size cars, it has improved in our eyes this year with the addition of a driver-side air bag, which was overdue. However, key rivals such as the Ford Taurus, Mercury Sable, and Honda Accord have standard dual air bags.

Oldsmobile Cutlass Supreme prices are on page 397.

OLDSMOBILE CUTLASS SUPREME CONVERTIBLE

Rating Guide	1	2	3	4	5
Performance					
Acceleration	▓▓▓▓▓▓▓▓▓▓▓▓				
Economy	▓▓▓▓▓▓				
Driveability	▓▓▓▓▓▓▓▓▓▓▓▓				
Ride	▓▓▓▓▓▓▓▓▓▓				
Steering/handling	▓▓▓▓▓▓▓▓▓▓				
Braking	▓▓▓▓▓▓▓▓▓▓▓▓▓▓				
Noise	▓▓▓▓▓▓▓▓▓▓				
Accommodations					
Driver seating	▓▓▓▓▓▓▓▓▓▓▓▓				
Instruments/controls	▓▓▓▓▓▓▓▓▓▓				
Visibility	▓▓▓▓▓▓▓▓				
Room/comfort	▓▓▓▓▓▓▓▓				
Entry/exit	▓▓▓▓▓▓▓▓				
Cargo room	▓▓▓▓▓▓▓▓				
Workmanship					
Exterior	▓▓▓▓▓▓▓▓▓▓				
Interior	▓▓▓▓▓▓▓▓▓▓				
Value	▓▓▓▓▓▓▓▓▓▓				
Total Points					**53**

Specifications

Body type	2-door convertible
Wheelbase (in.)	107.5
Overall length (in.)	193.9
Overall width (in.)	71.0
Overall height (in.)	54.3
Curb weight (lbs.)	3651
Seating capacity	5
Front head room (in.)	38.7
Max. front leg room (in.)	42.4
Rear head room (in.)	38.0
Min. rear leg room (in.)	34.8
Cargo volume (cu. ft.)	12.1
Engine type	dohc V-6
Engine size (l/cu. in.)	3.4/207
Horsepower @ rpm	210 @ 5200
Torque @ rpm	215 @ 4000
Transmission	auto/4-sp.
Drive wheels	front
Brakes, F/R	disc/disc (ABS)
Tire size	225/60R16
Fuel tank capacity (gal.)	16.5
EPA city/highway mpg	17/26
Test mileage (mpg)	17.2

Warranties The entire car is covered for 3 years/36,000 miles. Body perforation rust is covered for 6 years/100,000 miles.

Rating scale 5=Exceptional; 4=Above average; 3=Average; 2=Below average; 1=Poor

PLYMOUTH SUNDANCE/ DODGE SHADOW

Built in Sterling Heights, Mich.

Plymouth Sundance Duster 3-door

SUBCOMPACT

For 1994, the front-drive Sundance and Shadow gain a motorized shoulder belt for the front passenger. Both come as 3- and 5-door hatchbacks with a standard driver-side air bag and optional anti-lock brakes (with automatic transmission only). Production of the 5-door versions stops in January when the new Dodge/Plymouth Neon 4-door sedan debuts. The 3-door versions will survive through the end of the model year. The Shadow convertible was dropped at the end of the 1993 model run. Sundance comes in base and sportier Duster trim, and Shadow in base and ES versions. On base models, a 2.2-liter 4-cylinder engine with 93 horsepower is standard and a 2.5-liter 4-cylinder with 100 is optional. The 2.5-liter is standard on the Shadow ES. A 141-horsepower 3.0-liter V-6 is standard on the Duster and optional on the ES. A 5-speed manual transmission is standard on all models. A 3-speed automatic is optional with the 4-cylinder engines and a 4-speed is optional with the V-6. The 2.2-liter is stronger than most economy car engines but noisy and rough. The 2.5-liter is smoother and more responsive yet just as noisy. The V-6 provides strong acceleration, and the ES and Duster, with their wider tires and firmer suspension have above-average handling ability. There's ample room for the front seats, but rear leg and head room are skimpy. Though these cars are unrefined, they don't feel as lightweight as some other entry-level offerings, and the air bag, available anti-lock brakes, and V-6 are attractive features.

Dodge Shadow prices are on page 298;
Plymouth Sundance prices are on page 408.

PLYMOUTH SUNDANCE DUSTER

Rating Guide	1	2	3	4	5
Performance					
Acceleration	▓▓▓▓▓▓▓▓▓▓▓▓▓▓▓▓▓▓▓				
Economy	▓▓▓▓▓▓▓▓▓▓▓▓▓				
Driveability	▓▓▓▓▓▓▓▓▓▓▓▓▓				
Ride	▓▓▓▓▓▓				
Steering/handling	▓▓▓▓▓▓▓▓▓▓▓▓▓▓▓▓▓				
Braking	▓▓▓▓▓▓▓▓▓▓▓▓▓				
Noise	▓▓▓▓▓▓▓▓▓▓				
Accommodations					
Driver seating	▓▓▓▓▓▓▓▓▓▓▓▓▓				
Instruments/controls	▓▓▓▓▓▓▓▓▓▓▓▓▓				
Visibility	▓▓▓▓▓▓▓▓▓▓▓▓				
Room/comfort	▓▓▓▓▓▓▓▓▓▓▓▓▓				
Entry/exit	▓▓▓▓▓▓▓▓▓▓				
Cargo room	▓▓▓▓▓▓▓▓▓▓▓▓▓▓▓▓▓				
Workmanship					
Exterior	▓▓▓▓▓▓▓▓▓▓▓▓▓				
Interior	▓▓▓▓▓▓▓▓▓▓▓▓▓				
Value	▓▓▓▓▓▓▓▓▓▓▓▓▓▓▓▓▓▓▓▓				

Total Points...51

Specifications

Body type	3-door hatchback	Engine type	ohc V-6
Wheelbase (in.)	97.2	Engine size (l/cu. in.)	3.0/181
Overall length (in.)	171.9	Horsepower @ rpm	141 @ 5000
Overall width (in.)	67.3	Torque @ rpm	171 @ 2400
Overall height (in.)	53.1	Transmission	auto/4-sp.
Curb weight (lbs.)	2613	Drive wheels	front
Seating capacity	5	Brakes, F/R	disc/drum
Front head room (in.)	38.4	Tire size	195/60R15
Max. front leg room (in.)	41.5	Fuel tank capacity (gal.)	14.0
Rear head room (in.)	37.4	EPA city/highway mpg	19/24
Min. rear leg room (in.)	34.0	Test mileage (mpg)	23.6
Cargo volume (cu. ft.)	33.3		

Warranties Customer's choice of 3-year/36,000-mile warranty or 1-year/12,000-mile basic warranty with 7-year/70,000-mile powertrain warranty. Body perforation rust is covered for 7 years/100,000 miles.

Rating scale 5=Exceptional; 4=Above average; 3=Average; 2=Below average; 1=Poor

PONTIAC BONNEVILLE

RECOMMENDED

Built in Orion, Mich.

Pontiac Bonneville SE

FULL-SIZE Similar to Buick LeSabre, Oldsmobile Eighty Eight

Pontiac's full-size front-drive sedan gets a standard passenger-side air bag, a revised model lineup, and a more powerful optional supercharged engine for 1994. Bonneville now comes in base SE and upscale SSE models. Californians can also get an SLE model that includes the Sport Luxury Edition option package at a reduced price. The SSEi model has been dropped and most of its features are included in a new SSEi Supercharger Package that includes the supercharged 3.8-liter V-6, which is rated at 225 horsepower this year, 20 more than last year. A 170-horsepower 3.8-liter V-6 is standard on both models, as are anti-lock brakes. Though it's similar to the Buick LeSabre and Oldsmobile Eighty Eight, Bonneville is the only one to offer the supercharged engine. GM's Computer Command Ride (CCR) suspension is a new option for SSE models with traction control (also an option). It automatically adjusts the suspension firmness based on vehicle speed. Bonneville is much sportier than the similar LeSabre or Eighty Eight, but be warned that models with the 16-inch tires sacrifice ride comfort to improve handling ability. The supercharged engine provides robust acceleration but drinks too much premium gas. The base engine is more than enough for most needs and the automatic transmission shifts promptly and smoothly. Though the dashboard is well laid out, the radio is a long reach and some drivers don't like Pontiac's red instrument lighting. Bonneville has a spacious interior and trunk. Overall, it's one of the best choices in a big American sedan.

Pontiac Bonneville prices are on page 415.

PONTIAC BONNEVILLE SE

Rating Guide	1	2	3	4	5

Performance

Acceleration					
Economy					
Driveability					
Ride					
Steering/handling					
Braking					
Noise					

Accommodations

Driver seating					
Instruments/controls					
Visibility					
Room/comfort					
Entry/exit					
Cargo room					

Workmanship

Exterior					
Interior					
Value					

Total Points...61

Specifications

Body type ....4-door notchback
Wheelbase (in.) 110.8
Overall length (in.) 199.5
Overall width (in.) 74.5
Overall height (in.) 55.7
Curb weight (lbs.) 3446
Seating capacity...........................5
Front head room (in.) 39.2
Max. front leg room (in.) 43.0
Rear head room (in.) 38.3
Min. rear leg room (in.) 38.6
Cargo volume (cu. ft.).............18.0

Engine type.......................ohv V-6
Engine size (l/cu. in.).........3.8/231
Horsepower @ rpm ...170 @ 4800
Torque @ rpm ....225 @ 3200
Transmission.................auto/4-sp.
Drive wheels ....front
Brakes, F/R ....disc/drum (ABS)
Tire size 225/60R16
Fuel tank capacity (gal.).........18.0
EPA city/highway mpg 19/28
Test mileage (mpg) 17.6

Warranties The entire car is covered for 3 years/36,000 miles. Body perforation rust is covered for 6 years/100,000 miles.

Rating scale 5=Exceptional; 4=Above average; 3=Average; 2=Below average; 1=Poor

PONTIAC GRAND AM/ ⸻
BUICK SKYLARK

Built in Lansing, Mich.

Pontiac Grand Am SE 4-door

COMPACT Similar to Oldsmobile Achieva

These front-drive 2- and 4-door compacts gain a standard driver-side air bag, a new V-6 engine, and a new automatic transmission for 1994. Anti-lock brakes are standard on all models. The Grand Am comes in base SE and sporty GT trim. Skylark comes in Custom and Gran Sport in both body styles, and as a Limited sedan. The Grand Am SE and Skylark Custom and Limited come with a 115-horsepower 2.3-liter 4-cylinder engine. A 5-speed manual transmission is standard, with 3- and 4-speed automatics optional. The Grand Am GT comes with a dual-camshaft version of this engine called the Quad 4. It's rated at 155 horsepower with a 4-speed automatic transmission (a new feature this year) and 175 with the 5-speed manual. Optional on all models is a new 155-horsepower 3.1-liter V-6, which replaces a 3.3-liter V-6 and comes only with the 4-speed automatic. We recommend the V-6 engine over any of the 4-cylinders. It teams with the smooth-shifting 4-speed automatic for a pleasing combination of power and refinement. Grand Am GT and Skylark Gran Sport models have a tauter suspension that may make the ride too stiff for some tastes. There's adequate leg and head room front and rear for average-size adults. Entry to the rear on sedan models is tight because the doors are narrow at the bottom. The Grand Am has a more ergonomic dashboard than the Skylark, which spreads some gauges out so far they're hard to see. These cars are price competitive, and California customers are being offered discounted one-price models.

Buick Skylark prices are on page 261;
Pontiac Grand Am prices are on page 420.

PONTIAC GRAND AM SE

Rating Guide	1	2	3	4	5
Performance					
Acceleration					
Economy					
Driveability					
Ride					
Steering/handling					
Braking					
Noise					
Accommodations					
Driver seating					
Instruments/controls					
Visibility					
Room/comfort					
Entry/exit					
Cargo room					
Workmanship					
Exterior					
Interior					
Value					

Total Points..**57**

Specifications

Body type ....4-door notchback		Engine type ....ohv V-6	
Wheelbase (in.) 103.4		Engine size (l/cu. in.).........3.1/191	
Overall length (in.) 186.9		Horsepower @ rpm ...155 @ 5200	
Overall width (in.) 67.5		Torque @ rpm ....185 @ 4000	
Overall height (in.) 53.2		Transmission ....auto/4-sp.	
Curb weight (lbs.) 2793		Drive wheels ....front	
Seating capacity..........................5		Brakes, F/R ....disc/drum (ABS)	
Front head room (in.) 37.8		Tire size 205/55R16	
Max. front leg room (in.) 43.3		Fuel tank capacity (gal.) 15.2	
Rear head room (in.) 37.0		EPA city/highway mpg 20/29	
Min. rear leg room (in.) 34.9		Test mileage (mpg) ....NA	
Cargo volume (cu. ft.).............13.2			

Warranties The entire car is covered for 3 years/36,000 miles. Body perforation rust is covered for 6 years/100,000 miles.

Rating scale 5=Exceptional; 4=Above average; 3=Average; 2=Below average; 1=Poor

PONTIAC GRAND PRIX

Built in Kansas City, Kan.

Pontiac Grand Prix SE 2-door

MID-SIZE Similar to Buick Regal, Chevrolet Lumina, Oldsmobile Cutlass Supreme

The front-drive Grand Prix gets dual air bags in a redesigned interior, a simplified lineup, and a stronger base engine for 1994. Its GM siblings at Buick and Oldsmobile get only a driver-side air bag, while the Lumina will get dual air bags next spring. Grand Prix comes as a 2-door coupe and 4-door sedan, both in a single SE price series, though there also are one-price California models. Front safety belts on sedans are now anchored to the roof pillars; on coupes, they remain anchored to the doors. Anti-lock brakes are optional on all models. The base engine remains a 3.1-liter V-6, but it's now rated at 160 horsepower, up by 20 over last year. Optional is a dual-camshaft 3.4-liter V-6 rated at 210 horsepower, 10 more than last year. A 4-speed automatic is the only transmission available. Coupes gain a host of new standard features, including 5-spoke 16-inch alloy wheels, cruise control, and a new leather-wrapped steering wheel with integral radio controls. Grand Prix's 1994 updates are long overdue and finally bring it within hailing distance of the leading Ford Taurus. Most of the credit goes to the dual air bags and the redesigned interior. Coupe or sedan, Grand Prix's cabin has ample room for four adults. The revised 3.1-liter engine is smoother and livelier than last year's, and should be strong enough for most needs. The 3.4-liter engine is more powerful but also an expensive option. This year's prices are highly competitive considering all that's standard.

Pontiac Grand Prix prices are on page 422.

PONTIAC GRAND PRIX SE

Rating Guide	1	2	3	4	5
Performance					
Acceleration	▓	▓	▓		
Economy	▓	▓	▓		
Driveability	▓	▓	▓	▓	
Ride	▓	▓	▓		
Steering/handling	▓	▓	▓	▓	
Braking	▓	▓	▓	▓	▓
Noise	▓	▓	▓		
Accommodations					
Driver seating	▓	▓	▓	▓	
Instruments/controls	▓	▓	▓	▓	
Visibility	▓	▓	▓	▓	
Room/comfort	▓	▓	▓		
Entry/exit	▓	▓	▓		
Cargo room	▓	▓	▓		
Workmanship					
Exterior	▓	▓	▓	▓	
Interior	▓	▓	▓	▓	
Value	▓	▓	▓		

Total Points...**57**

Specifications

Body type	2-door notchback	Engine type	ohv V-6
Wheelbase (in.)	107.5	Engine size (l/cu. in.)	3.1/191
Overall length (in.)	194.8	Horsepower @ rpm	160 @ 5200
Overall width (in.)	71.9	Torque @ rpm	185 @ 4000
Overall height (in.)	52.8	Transmission	auto/4-sp.
Curb weight (lbs.)	3275	Drive wheels	front
Seating capacity	5	Brakes, F/R	disc/disc (ABS)
Front head room (in.)	37.8	Tire size	215/60R16
Max. front leg room (in.)	42.3	Fuel tank capacity (gal.)	16.5
Rear head room (in.)	36.6	EPA city/highway mpg	19/29
Min. rear leg room (in.)	34.8	Test mileage (mpg)	NA
Cargo volume (cu. ft.)	14.9		

Warranties The entire car is covered for 3 years/36,000 miles. Body perforation rust is covered for 6 years/100,000 miles.

Rating scale 5=Exceptional; 4=Above average; 3=Average; 2=Below average; 1=Poor

SAAB 900

Built in Sweden.

Saab 900S 5-door

PREMIUM SEDAN

The redesigned 900 is the first Saab available with a V-6 engine and the first to be built with help from General Motors, which owns 50 percent of Saab's car business. It retains front-wheel-drive but grows 3.3 inches in wheelbase and two inches overall. Saab initially offers only a 5-door hatchback body style. A 3-door hatchback and 2-door convertible are due in the spring. Meanwhile, Saab dealers are selling off leftover convertibles from the previous generation. The 900S has a 150-horsepower 2.3-liter 4-cylinder engine. The 900SE has a 170-horsepower 2.5-liter V-6 that, like the new 900's basic platform, is derived from one used by GM's European Vauxhall and Opel brands. A 5-speed manual transmission is standard. The optional 4-speed automatic has Sport, Economy, and Winter settings. Traction control is standard on the 900SE and not available on the 900S. Dual air bags and anti-lock brakes are standard on both. Integrated rear child booster seats are due to become optional later in the year. The new 900 has generous head and leg room and enormous cargo space for a compact-sized car, but this quirky design probably won't appeal to mainstream buyers. The 4-cylinder 900S has adequate power with manual transmission but feels weak with automatic. The V-6 feels strong and smooth and works particularly well with the automatic. These cars have sporty handling and the taut suspension provides excellent control. However, it also has a choppy ride on bad pavement. The new 900S is competitively priced. At $20,990 to start, the 900S deserves a look by those who value function over form.

Saab 900 prices are on page 428.

SAAB 900S (Preliminary)

Rating Guide	1	2	3	4	5
Performance					
Acceleration	▮▮▮▮▮▮▮▮				
Economy	▮▮▮▮▮▮▮▮				
Driveability	▮▮▮▮▮▮▮▮▮▮				
Ride	▮▮▮▮▮▮▮▮				
Steering/handling	▮▮▮▮▮▮▮▮▮				
Braking	▮▮▮▮▮▮▮▮▮▮▮▮				
Noise	▮▮▮▮▮▮▮▮				
Accommodations					
Driver seating	▮▮▮▮▮▮▮				
Instruments/controls	▮▮▮▮▮▮▮				
Visibility	▮▮▮▮▮▮				
Room/comfort	▮▮▮▮▮▮				
Entry/exit	▮▮▮▮▮▮				
Cargo room	▮▮▮▮▮▮				
Workmanship					
Exterior	▮▮▮▮▮▮▮				
Interior	▮▮▮▮▮▮▮				
Value	▮▮▮▮▮▮▮				
Total Points **60**					

Specifications

Body type	5-door hatchback	Engine type	dohc I-4
Wheelbase (in.)	102.5	Engine size (l/cu. in.)	2.3/140
Overall length (in.)	182.6	Horsepower @ rpm	150 @ 5700
Overall width (in.)	67.4	Torque @ rpm	155 @ 4300
Overall height (in.)	58.5	Transmission	auto/4-sp.
Curb weight (lbs.)	2950	Drive wheels	front
Seating capacity	5	Brakes, F/R	disc/disc (ABS)
Front head room (in.)	38.0	Tire size	195/60VR15
Max. front leg room (in.)	42.3	Fuel tank capacity (gal.)	18.0
Rear head room (in.)	37.6	EPA city/highway mpg	19/26
Min. rear leg room (in.)	36.0	Test mileage (mpg)	NA
Cargo volume (cu. ft.)	24.0		

Warranties The entire car is covered for 3 years/40,000 miles. Major powertrain components are covered for 6 years/80,000 miles. Body perforation rust is covered for 6 years/unlimited miles.

Rating scale 5=Exceptional; 4=Above average; 3=Average; 2=Below average; 1=Poor

SAAB 9000

Built in Sweden.

Saab 9000CSE

PREMIUM SEDAN

A passenger-side air bag joins a driver-side air bag as the major new feature for this front-drive car. The 9000 comes as a 5-door hatchback in CS, CSE, and Aero price levels. Gone is the CD 4-door notchback sedan, leaving only a CDE 4-door. CS and CSE models have with a 146-horsepower 2.3-liter 4-cylinder engine. Available on the CS and CSE and standard on the CDE is a turbocharged 2.3-liter rated at 200 horsepower. The Aero has a 225-horsepower version of the turbo with the 5-speed manual transmission and the 200-horsepower version with the optional 4-speed automatic. Anti-lock brakes are standard on all models. Among other changes: Heat-reducing solar-control glass is now standard; the Aero has new alloy wheels; CS models get front and rear fog lights; and traction control is deleted from turbocharged models. Saab is revising the traction control so it can be turned off. These Saabs have capable handling, generous cargo space, and huge, comfortable interiors. They compete with rivals powered by 6-cylinder and V-8 engines, and that counts for a lot when list prices begin at nearly $29,000. The base 9000 engine provides adequate acceleration. Turbos have outstanding power, but don't deliver it with the refinement of the engines in rivals such as the Acura Legend, Cadillac Seville, and Lexus ES 300. The worst ergonomic feature is the standard automatic climate system, which assumes a different setting virtually each time the ignition is turned on. Saab dealers should be offering hefty discounts because buyers know there are many good alternatives to the 9000 in this price range.

Saab 9000 prices are on page 429.

SAAB 9000CSE Turbo

Rating Guide	1	2	3	4	5
Performance					
Acceleration	▮▮▮▮▮▮▮▮▮▮▮▮▮▮▮▮				
Economy	▮▮▮▮▮▮▮▮▮▮▮				
Driveability	▮▮▮▮▮▮▮▮▮▮▮▮▮▮▮▮▮				
Ride	▮▮▮▮▮▮▮▮▮▮▮▮▮▮				
Steering/handling	▮▮▮▮▮▮▮▮▮▮▮▮▮▮▮▮▮				
Braking	▮▮▮▮▮▮▮▮▮▮▮▮▮▮▮▮▮▮				
Noise	▮▮▮▮▮▮▮▮▮▮▮▮				
Accommodations					
Driver seating	▮▮▮▮▮▮▮▮▮▮▮▮▮▮				
Instruments/controls	▮▮▮▮▮▮▮▮▮▮▮▮▮▮▮▮				
Visibility	▮▮▮▮▮▮▮▮▮▮▮▮▮▮				
Room/comfort	▮▮▮▮▮▮▮▮▮▮▮▮▮▮▮▮▮				
Entry/exit	▮▮▮▮▮▮▮▮▮▮▮▮▮▮				
Cargo room	▮▮▮▮▮▮▮▮▮▮▮▮▮▮▮▮▮				
Workmanship					
Exterior	▮▮▮▮▮▮▮▮▮▮▮▮▮▮▮▮				
Interior	▮▮▮▮▮▮▮▮▮▮▮▮▮▮▮▮				
Value	▮▮▮▮▮▮▮▮▮▮▮▮				

Total Points...60

Specifications

Body type ....5-door hatchback
Wheelbase (in.) 105.2
Overall length (in.) 187.4
Overall width (in.) 69.4
Overall height (in.) 55.9
Curb weight (lbs.) 3110
Seating capacity...........................5
Front head room (in.) 38.5
Max. front leg room (in.) 41.5
Rear head room (in.) 37.4
Min. rear leg room (in.) 38.7
Cargo volume (cu. ft.).............56.5

Engine type ....Turbo dohc I-4
Engine size (l/cu. in.).........2.3/140
Horsepower @ rpm ...200 @ 5500
Torque @ rpm ....238 @ 1800
Transmission.................auto/4-sp.
Drive wheels ....front
Brakes, F/R...........disc/disc (ABS)
Tire size....................195/65VR15
Fuel tank capacity (gal.) 17.4
EPA city/highway mpg 18/26
Test mileage (mpg) 21.3

Warranties The entire car is covered for 3 years/40,000 miles. Major powertrain components are covered for 6 years/80,000 miles. Body perforation rust is covered for 6 years/unlimited miles.

Rating scale 5=Exceptional; 4=Above average; 3=Average; 2=Below average; 1=Poor

SATURN SC1/SC2 — `BUDGET BUY`

Built in Spring Hill, Tenn.

Saturn SC1

SPORTS COUPE

Saturn's front-drive SC1 and SC2 sports coupes get revised power door locks for 1994. A driver-side air bag is standard and anti-lock brakes (ABS) are optional. Traction control is included when ABS is ordered with the automatic transmission. Like Saturn's sedans, the coupes have plastic lower-body panels that resist rust and minor dings. The SC1 continues with an 85-horse-power single-cam 1.9-liter 4-cylinder engine, while the upscale SC2 has a 124-horsepower dual-camshaft variant. With both engines, a 5-speed manual transmission is standard and a 4-speed automatic is optional. The optional power door locks gain a new feature this year: One turn of the key unlocks the driver's door and a second turn unlocks the passenger's door. The SC1 offers most of the virtues of the SC2 at lower cost. It performs adequate-ly with the smooth-shifting 5-speed manual transmission, but acceleration is tepid with automatic. The SC2 is a strong performer with either transmission. Like most sport coupes, these two suffer from limited rear seat room, though there's plenty of space in front even for tall drivers. Large windows and thin roof pillars give the interior an airy feel and allow a clear view in all directions. Gauges are clearly marked, and most controls are easy to reach. Though the SC1 and SC2 are noisy and somewhat unrefined compared to Japanese rivals, they have compiled impressive records for quali-ty and customer satisfaction. Furthermore, Saturn's no-haggle price policy means that the buying experience is relatively pain-less. Though you'll pay full sticker price, the prices are reasonable.

Saturn SC1/SC2 prices are on page 430.

SATURN SC1

Rating Guide	1	2	3	4	5
Performance					
Acceleration	‖‖‖‖‖‖‖‖‖‖‖‖‖‖				
Economy	‖‖‖‖‖‖‖‖‖‖‖‖‖‖‖‖‖‖‖‖‖‖				
Driveability	‖‖‖‖‖‖‖‖‖‖‖‖‖‖‖‖‖‖‖‖				
Ride	‖‖‖‖‖‖‖‖‖‖‖‖‖‖‖‖‖‖				
Steering/handling	‖‖‖‖‖‖‖‖‖‖‖‖‖‖				
Braking	‖‖‖‖‖‖‖‖‖‖‖‖‖‖‖‖‖‖‖‖‖‖				
Noise	‖‖‖‖‖‖‖‖‖‖‖‖‖				
Accommodations					
Driver seating	‖‖‖‖‖‖‖‖‖‖‖‖‖‖				
Instruments/controls	‖‖‖‖‖‖‖‖‖‖‖‖‖‖‖‖‖‖				
Visibility	‖‖‖‖‖‖‖‖‖‖‖‖‖‖‖‖				
Room/comfort	‖‖‖‖‖‖‖‖‖‖‖				
Entry/exit	‖‖‖‖‖‖‖‖‖‖‖				
Cargo room	‖‖‖‖‖‖‖‖‖‖‖‖‖‖				
Workmanship					
Exterior	‖‖‖‖‖‖‖‖‖‖‖‖‖‖‖‖‖‖				
Interior	‖‖‖‖‖‖‖‖‖‖‖‖‖‖‖‖‖‖				
Value	‖‖‖‖‖‖‖‖‖‖‖‖‖‖‖‖‖‖‖‖				

Total Points..55

Specifications

Body type	2-door notchback	Engine type	ohc I-4
Wheelbase (in.)	99.2	Engine size (l/cu. in.)	1.9/116
Overall length (in.)	173.2	Horsepower @ rpm	85 @ 5000
Overall width (in.)	67.5	Torque @ rpm	107 @ 2400
Overall height (in.)	50.6	Transmission	manual/5-sp.
Curb weight (lbs.)	2280	Drive wheels	front
Seating capacity	4	Brakes, F/R	disc/disc (ABS)
Front head room (in.)	37.6	Tire size	175/70R14
Max. front leg room (in.)	42.6	Fuel tank capacity (gal.)	12.8
Rear head room (in.)	35.0	EPA city/highway mpg	28/37
Min. rear leg room (in.)	26.4	Test mileage (mpg)	32.0
Cargo volume (cu. ft.)	10.9		

Warranties The entire car is covered for 3 years/36,000 miles. Body perforation rust is covered for 6 years/100,000 miles.

Rating scale 5=Exceptional; 4=Above average; 3=Average; 2=Below average; 1=Poor

SATURN SEDAN/ WAGON

Built in Spring Hill, Tenn.

Saturn SL2

SUBCOMPACT

A central unlocking feature for the optional power door locks is the main change for Saturn's front-drive sedans and wagons. A driver-side air bag is standard and anti-lock brakes are optional on all models. Four-door sedans come in SL, SL1, and SL2 form. The 5-door wagon comes in SW1 and SW2 models. All have a 1.9-liter 4-cylinder engine. In the SL, SL1, and SW1, the engine has a single overhead camshaft and 85 horsepower. The SL2 and SW2 have dual overhead cams and 124 horsepower. A 5-speed manual transmission is standard and a 4-speed electronic automatic is optional. When anti-lock brakes are ordered with the automatic transmission, traction control is included—an unusual feature in this class. The new central unlocking feature adds some convenience: One turn of the key unlocks the driver's door and a second turn unlocks the others. The single-cam engine in the SL, SL1, and SW1 gives adequate acceleration with the manual transmission, but it becomes anemic with the automatic. The dual-cam engine provides lively acceleration with either transmission. Both engines are loud and harsh, and road and wind noise join the fray at highway speeds. There's ample head room in front, though leg room may be tight for taller drivers. In back, there's just as much head room but less leg room, though two adults can fit. The dashboard has a convenient design with gauges that are easy to read and controls that are easy to reach. Good assembly quality, competent performance, an impressive list of safety features, and reasonable prices make these cars well worth considering, though you'll likely pay full sticker price.

Saturn Sedan/Wagon prices are on page 431.

SATURN SL2

Rating Guide	1	2	3	4	5
Performance					
Acceleration	▮▮▮▮▮▮▮▮▮				
Economy	▮▮▮▮▮▮▮▮▮				
Driveability	▮▮▮▮▮▮▮▮▮				
Ride	▮▮▮▮▮▮▮▮▮				
Steering/handling	▮▮▮▮▮▮▮▮▮▮▮				
Braking	▮▮▮▮▮▮▮▮▮▮▮▮▮▮				
Noise	▮▮▮▮▮				
Accommodations					
Driver seating	▮▮▮▮▮▮▮▮▮▮				
Instruments/controls	▮▮▮▮▮▮▮▮▮▮▮				
Visibility	▮▮▮▮▮▮▮▮▮▮				
Room/comfort	▮▮▮▮▮▮▮▮▮▮				
Entry/exit	▮▮▮▮▮▮▮▮▮▮				
Cargo room	▮▮▮▮▮▮▮▮▮▮				
Workmanship					
Exterior	▮▮▮▮▮▮▮▮▮▮▮				
Interior	▮▮▮▮▮▮▮▮▮▮▮				
Value	▮▮▮▮▮▮▮▮▮▮▮				
Total Points					**56**

Specifications

Body type	4-door notchback	Engine type	dohc I-4
Wheelbase (in.)	102.4	Engine size (l/cu. in.)	1.9/116
Overall length (in.)	176.3	Horsepower @ rpm	124 @ 5600
Overall width (in.)	67.6	Torque @ rpm	122 @ 4800
Overall height (in.)	52.5	Transmission	auto/4-sp.
Curb weight (lbs.)	2313	Drive wheels	front
Seating capacity	5	Brakes, F/R	disc/disc (ABS)
Front head room (in.)	38.5	Tire size	195/60R15
Max. front leg room (in.)	42.5	Fuel tank capacity (gal.)	12.8
Rear head room (in.)	36.3	EPA city/highway mpg	23/32
Min. rear leg room (in.)	32.6	Test mileage (mpg)	27.8
Cargo volume (cu. ft.)	11.9		

Warranties The entire car is covered for 3 years/36,000 miles. Body perforation rust is covered for 6 years/100,000 miles.

Rating scale 5=Exceptional; 4=Above average; 3=Average; 2=Below average; 1=Poor

SUBARU IMPREZA

Built in Japan.

Subaru Impreza LS 4-door

SUBCOMPACT

Introduced last spring, the Impreza adds a standard passenger-side air bag for 1994 and expands the availability of the optional anti-lock brakes. A driver-side air bag already was standard. Impreza comes as a 4-door sedan in base, L, and LS models and as a 5-door wagon in L and LS trim. The only engine is a 110-horsepower 1.8-liter 4-cylinder. The base sedan comes only with front-wheel drive and a 5-speed manual transmission. The L and top-shelf LS models come in both body styles and are available with front-wheel drive or permanently engaged all-wheel drive (AWD). A 5-speed manual transmission is standard and a 4-speed automatic is optional on the L models. The LS comes only with the automatic. Anti-lock brakes are now standard on the LS and optional on the L models. Also new this year is a power sunroof; it's optional on the L models and standard on the LS. A 1993 AWD wagon we tested with the 5-speed felt sluggish off the line and an AWD sedan with the automatic was downright slow. Nevertheless, we averaged 24.7 with the sedan and 24.8 mpg overall with the wagon, reaching 30 mpg on the highway—quite good for an AWD car. Impreza has ample head room and adequate rear leg room. The dashboard is logically laid out, with controls grouped around the gauge cluster where they're easy to find and operate. Despite its strengths, Impreza is just another small car in a crowded field and it doesn't rate as high in performance or value as the Honda Civic and Geo Prizm. Available all-wheel drive is the only feature that sets it apart. Subaru dealers should be willing to bargain.

Subaru Impreza prices are on page 432.

SUBARU IMPREZA AWD SEDAN

Rating Guide	1	2	3	4	5
Performance					
Acceleration	▓▓▓				
Economy	▓▓▓				
Driveability	▓▓▓				
Ride	▓▓▓				
Steering/handling	▓▓▓▓				
Braking	▓▓▓▓▓				
Noise	▓▓▓				
Accommodations					
Driver seating	▓▓▓▓				
Instruments/controls	▓▓▓▓				
Visibility	▓▓▓				
Room/comfort	▓▓▓				
Entry/exit	▓▓▓				
Cargo room	▓▓▓				
Workmanship					
Exterior	▓▓▓▓				
Interior	▓▓▓▓				
Value	▓▓▓				

Total Points...55

Specifications

Body type	4-door notchback	Engine type	ohc flat-4
Wheelbase (in.)	99.2	Engine size (l/cu. in.)	1.8/109
Overall length (in.)	171.0	Horsepower @ rpm	110 @ 5600
Overall width (in.)	67.1	Torque @ rpm	110 @ 4400
Overall height (in.)	55.5	Transmission	auto/4-sp.
Curb weight (lbs.)	2325	Drive wheels	all
Seating capacity	5	Brakes, F/R	disc/disc (ABS)
Front head room (in.)	39.2	Tire size	175/70R14
Max. front leg room (in.)	43.1	Fuel tank capacity (gal.)	13.2
Rear head room (in.)	36.7	EPA city/highway mpg	22/28
Min. rear leg room (in.)	32.5	Test mileage (mpg)	24.7
Cargo volume (cu. ft.)	11.1		

Warranties The entire car is covered for 3 years/36,000 miles. Major powertrain components are covered for 5 years/60,000 miles. Body perforation rust is covered for 5 years/unlimited miles.

Rating scale 5=Exceptional; 4=Above average; 3=Average; 2=Below average; 1=Poor

SUBARU LEGACY

Built in Lafayette, Ind., and Japan.

Subaru Legacy L wagon

COMPACT

Legacy's big news for 1994 is the addition of four new "active lifestyle" wagons that are keyed to particular themes. The compact Legacy continues in 4-door sedan and 5-door wagon body styles, each available with front-wheel drive or permanently engaged all-wheel-drive (AWD). The 4-door comes as L, LS, LSi, and Sport Sedan models, and the wagon as L, LS, LSi, and Touring Wagon models, plus the four new "lifestyle" models. A 2.2-liter 4-cylinder produces 130 horsepower in all models except the Sport Sedan and Touring Wagon, where, with the help of a turbocharger, it produces 160 horsepower. Both engines team with either a 5-speed manual transmission or a 4-speed automatic, depending on the model. L and LS models are available with either front-wheel drive or AWD; all other models come only with AWD. A driver-side air bag is standard on all Legacys. Anti-lock brakes are optional on L models and standard on all others. All of the new lifestyle models are based on the Legacy L wagon and have unique interior fabrics, exterior trim, and alloy wheels. Only the Sun Sport has front-wheel drive; the Alpine Sport, Outdoor, and GT variants are AWD. Legacy has plenty of room for four adults, plus ample cargo space in both the sedan and wagon. The turbocharged Sport Sedan and Touring Wagon are strong performers: 8.7 seconds to 60 mph in our tests. Other Legacys deliver decent acceleration with either transmission. Like other Subarus, the Legacy's biggest advantage is its available AWD, which provides excellent foul-weather traction without any input from the driver. Slow sales mean big discounts should be available on Legacy.

Subaru Legacy prices are on page 433.

SUBARU LEGACY 4WD WAGON

Rating Guide	1	2	3	4	5
Performance					
Acceleration	▓▓▓▓▓				
Economy	▓▓▓▓				
Driveability	▓▓▓▓▓				
Ride	▓▓▓▓▓				
Steering/handling	▓▓▓▓▓▓▓				
Braking	▓▓▓▓▓▓▓▓▓▓				
Noise	▓▓▓▓▓				
Accommodations					
Driver seating	▓▓▓▓▓				
Instruments/controls	▓▓▓▓▓▓▓				
Visibility	▓▓▓▓▓▓▓				
Room/comfort	▓▓▓▓▓▓▓				
Entry/exit	▓▓▓▓▓▓▓				
Cargo room	▓▓▓▓▓▓▓				
Workmanship					
Exterior	▓▓▓▓▓▓▓				
Interior	▓▓▓▓▓▓				
Value	▓▓▓▓▓▓				
Total Points **57**					

Specifications

Body type	5-door wagon	Engine type	ohc flat-4
Wheelbase (in.)	101.6	Engine size (l/cu. in.)	2.2/135
Overall length (in.)	181.9	Horsepower @ rpm	130 @ 5600
Overall width (in.)	66.5	Torque @ rpm	137 @ 4400
Overall height (in.)	54.7	Transmission	auto/4-sp.
Curb weight (lbs.)	3155	Drive wheels	all
Seating capacity	5	Brakes, F/R	disc/disc (ABS)
Front head room (in.)	38.4	Tire size	185/70HR14
Max. front leg room (in.)	43.1	Fuel tank capacity (gal.)	15.9
Rear head room (in.)	37.8	EPA city/highway mpg	21/27
Min. rear leg room (in.)	35.6	Test mileage (mpg)	19.0
Cargo volume (cu. ft.)	71.0		

Warranties The entire car is covered for 3 years/36,000 miles. Major powertrain components are covered for 5 years/60,000 miles. Body perforation rust is covered for 5 years/unlimited miles.

Rating scale 5=Exceptional; 4=Above average; 3=Average; 2=Below average; 1=Poor

TOYOTA CAMRY

Built in Georgetown, Ky., and Japan.

Toyota Camry LE 4-door

COMPACT

A standard passenger-side air bag, a 2-door coupe, and a more muscular V-6 engine join the front-drive Camry line for 1994. A driver-side air bag has been standard since 1992. Anti-lock brakes remain optional on all Camrys. Model choices for the new coupe include DX, LE, and SE. The sedan comes in DX, LE, XLE, and SE price levels, while the wagon comes in the DX and LE price levels. Base engine is a 130-horsepower 2.2-liter 4-cylinder. Available on all models except the DX is a new aluminum-block 3.0-liter V-6 with 188 horsepower, three more than last year's iron-block version. A 5-speed manual transmission is standard on the DX coupe and sedan. A 4-speed automatic is optional on those two and standard on all other models. Camry, which is built from the same design as the Lexus ES 300, is the leader in refinement among mid-size and compact family cars. The 4-cylinder engine is smooth and responsive, and provides adequate acceleration and passing power with the automatic transmission. The new V-6 feels even smoother and stronger than the old one, which was potent and extremely smooth itself. Camry has a soft, absorbent ride and corners with confidence. The front-drive design and all-season tires give it good traction on wet roads. Camry's interior is as roomy as some mid-size cars', though the rear seatback is stiff and too reclined, making it uncomfortable for some people. The dashboard has a modern, convenient design and all controls are easy to see and reach. Camry leads the league in most key categories, but cars this good don't come cheaply. An LE sedan, for example, starts at more than $19,000.

Toyota Camry prices are on page 435.

TOYOTA CAMRY LE

Rating Guide	1	2	3	4	5
Performance					
Acceleration	▓▓▓▓▓▓▓				
Economy	▓▓▓▓▓▓▓				
Driveability	▓▓▓▓▓▓▓▓▓				
Ride	▓▓▓▓▓▓▓▓▓				
Steering/handling	▓▓▓▓▓▓▓▓▓				
Braking	▓▓▓▓▓▓▓▓▓▓▓				
Noise	▓▓▓▓▓▓▓▓				
Accommodations					
Driver seating	▓▓▓▓▓▓▓▓				
Instruments/controls	▓▓▓▓▓▓▓▓				
Visibility	▓▓▓▓▓▓▓				
Room/comfort	▓▓▓▓▓▓▓				
Entry/exit	▓▓▓▓▓▓▓				
Cargo room	▓▓▓▓▓▓				
Workmanship					
Exterior	▓▓▓▓▓▓▓▓▓▓▓				
Interior	▓▓▓▓▓▓▓▓▓▓▓				
Value	▓▓▓▓▓▓▓▓▓▓				
Total Points **63**					

Specifications

Body type ....4-door notchback	Engine type ....dohc I-4
Wheelbase (in.) 103.1	Engine size (l/cu. in.)..........2.2/132
Overall length (in.)................187.8	Horsepower @ rpm ...130 @ 5400
Overall width (in.) 69.7	Torque @ rpm ....145 @ 4400
Overall height (in.)..................55.1	Transmission.................auto/4-sp.
Curb weight (lbs.) 2932	Drive wheels ....front
Seating capacity...........................5	Brakes, F/R...........disc/disc (ABS)
Front head room (in.) 38.4	Tire size 205/65HR15
Max. front leg room (in.) 43.5	Fuel tank capacity (gal.) 18.5
Rear head room (in.) 37.1	EPA city/highway mpg 21/28
Min. rear leg room (in.) 35.0	Test mileage (mpg) 22.9
Cargo volume (cu. ft.).............14.9	

Warranties The entire car is covered for 3 years/36,000 miles. Major powertrain components are covered for 5 years/60,000 miles. Body perforation rust is covered for 5 years/unlimited miles.

Rating scale 5=Exceptional; 4=Above average; 3=Average; 2=Below average; 1=Poor

TOYOTA CELICA

Built in Japan.

Toyota Celica GT 2-door

SPORTS COUPE

The front-drive Celica has been redesigned for 1994. The new version comes as a 2-door notchback and 3-door hatchback (called "Liftback" by Toyota). Both are offered in base ST and more-expensive GT trim. Driver- and passenger-side air bags are standard and anti-lock brakes are optional on all Celicas. The GT-S, All-Trac Turbo, and convertible are history, though a new ragtop is scheduled to arrive during 1994. A new Leather Sport Package is optional on the GT 3-door. Wheelbase and overall length are up by less than an inch, though the new car is some two inches wider. STs have a 1.8-liter 4-cylinder engine with 110 horsepower (which replaces a 103-horsepower 1.6-liter). GTs retain a 135-horsepower 2.2-liter 4-cylinder. A 5-speed manual transmission is standard and a 4-speed automatic is optional with both. Though we've had only brief test drives so far, the new Celicas seem better than the old in nearly every way except engine noise. Though the ST's new 1.8-liter engine is lively and smooth, it has little low-end torque and feels lazy with automatic. The GT's 2.2-liter engine is discernibly stronger but roars and throbs in hard driving. All the 1994s suffer too much tire noise but also feel more solid than previous Celicas. They ride with surprising suppleness and handling is better than ever. The rear seat is tight for adults, and with the optional sunroof, there's marginal head clearance in front for 6-footers. The instrument and control layout is great. Overall, though it's a more pleasing car, the new Celica lacks the value and performance of the Ford Probe and Mazda MX-6.

Toyota Celica prices are on page 437.

TOYOTA CELICA GT

Rating Guide	1	2	3	4	5
Performance					
Acceleration	▓▓▓▓▓▓▓				
Economy	▓▓▓▓▓				
Driveability	▓▓▓▓▓				
Ride	▓▓▓▓▓▓▓▓				
Steering/handling	▓▓▓▓▓▓▓▓				
Braking	▓▓▓▓▓▓▓▓▓				
Noise	▓▓▓▓				
Accommodations					
Driver seating	▓▓▓▓▓▓				
Instruments/controls	▓▓▓▓▓▓				
Visibility	▓▓▓▓▓▓				
Room/comfort	▓▓▓▓				
Entry/exit	▓▓▓▓				
Cargo room	▓▓▓▓▓▓				
Workmanship					
Exterior	▓▓▓▓▓▓▓▓▓				
Interior	▓▓▓▓▓▓▓▓				
Value	▓▓▓▓▓▓				

Total Points **54**

Specifications

Body type ....2-door notchback	Engine type ....dohc I-4
Wheelbase (in.) 99.9	Engine size (l/cu. in.).........2.2/132
Overall length (in.) 177.0	Horsepower @ rpm ...135 @ 5400
Overall width (in.) 68.9	Torque @ rpm ....145 @ 4400
Overall height (in.) 51.0	Transmission.................auto/4-sp.
Curb weight (lbs.) 2560	Drive wheels ....front
Seating capacity..........................4	Brakes, F/R ....disc/disc (ABS)
Front head room (in.) 38.3	Tire size....................205/55VR15
Max. front leg room (in.) 43.1	Fuel tank capacity (gal.) 15.9
Rear head room (in.) 34.9	EPA city/highway mpg 23/30
Min. rear leg room (in.)...........26.6	Test mileage (mpg) ....NA
Cargo volume (cu. ft.)..............10.6	

Warranties The entire car is covered for 3 years/36,000 miles. Major powertrain components are covered for 5 years/60,000 miles. Body perforation rust is covered for 5 years/unlimited miles.

Rating scale 5=Exceptional; 4=Above average; 3=Average; 2=Below average; 1=Poor

TOYOTA COROLLA

Built in Fremont, Calif., Canada, and Japan.

Toyota Corolla LE

SUBCOMPACT   Similar to Geo Prizm

Corolla's major change for 1994 is the addition of a standard passenger-side air bag, which joins a driver-side bag that arrived last year when this front-drive car was redesigned. Anti-lock brakes remain optional. Offerings include a 4-door notchback sedan in base, DX, and luxury LE price levels, and a DX 5-door wagon. The base 4-door continues with a 105-horsepower 1.6-liter 4-cylinder engine, while other models retain a 1.8-liter 4-cylinder with 115 horsepower. A 5-speed manual transmission is standard on the base and DX models. A 3-speed automatic is optional on the base and a 4-speed automatic is optional on the DX and standard on the LE. Most Corolla sedans are built in California, along with the similar Geo Prizm, at a plant Toyota shares with General Motors. Others are built in Canada and Japan, and all wagons are built in Japan. Corolla sets the standard for refinement among sub-compacts. It's quieter, roomier, and rides more comfortably than most rivals, and has commendable assembly quality. The 1.8-liter engine is noticeably stronger than the base sedan's 1.6-liter and also quieter. The automatic generally works well with the 1.8-liter engine, but it's slow to downshift for passing. Corolla's suspension feels stable and absorbs bumps better than some larger cars. Road, wind, and engine noise are as well suppressed as in some more-expensive vehicles. Sedans have a sizeable trunk with a lid that opens nearly at bumper level. We like Corolla a lot, but prices were high last year and are even higher this year. Competition, including from the similar Prizm, mean Toyota dealers have to bargain.

Toyota Corolla prices are on page 438.

TOYOTA COROLLA LE

Rating Guide	1	2	3	4	5
Performance					
Acceleration	▓▓▓▓▓▓				
Economy	▓▓▓▓▓▓▓▓▓▓▓				
Driveability	▓▓▓▓▓▓				
Ride	▓▓▓▓▓▓				
Steering/handling	▓▓▓▓▓▓				
Braking	▓▓▓▓▓▓▓▓▓				
Noise	▓▓▓▓▓▓▓				
Accommodations					
Driver seating	▓▓▓▓▓▓				
Instruments/controls	▓▓▓▓▓▓				
Visibility	▓▓▓▓▓▓				
Room/comfort	▓▓▓▓▓▓				
Entry/exit	▓▓▓▓▓▓				
Cargo room	▓▓▓▓▓▓				
Workmanship					
Exterior	▓▓▓▓▓▓▓▓				
Interior	▓▓▓▓▓▓▓▓				
Value	▓▓▓▓▓▓▓▓				

Total Points 59

Specifications

Body type	4-door notchback	Engine type	dohc I-4
Wheelbase (in.)	97.4	Engine size (l/cu. in.)	1.8/110
Overall length (in.)	172.0	Horsepower @ rpm	115 @ 5600
Overall width (in.)	66.3	Torque @ rpm	115 @ 4800
Overall height (in.)	53.5	Transmission	auto/4-sp.
Curb weight (lbs.)	2447	Drive wheels	front
Seating capacity	5	Brakes, F/R	disc/disc (ABS)
Front head room (in.)	38.8	Tire size	185/65R14
Max. front leg room (in.)	42.4	Fuel tank capacity (gal.)	13.2
Rear head room (in.)	37.1	EPA city/highway mpg	26/32
Min. rear leg room (in.)	33.0	Test mileage (mpg)	30.1
Cargo volume (cu. ft.)	12.7		

Warranties The entire car is covered for 3 years/36,000 miles. Major powertrain components are covered for 5 years/60,000 miles. Body perforation rust is covered for 5 years/unlimited miles.

Rating scale 5=Exceptional; 4=Above average; 3=Average; 2=Below average; 1=Poor

TOYOTA LAND CRUISER

Built in Japan.

Toyota Land Cruiser

SPORT-UTILITY VEHICLE

Toyota's luxury sport-utility wagon is a virtual rerun this year. The only changes involve nine instead of five speakers for the standard audio system and adoption of safety belts with an automatic locking retractor feature for all passenger positions. Land Cruiser continues as a 5-door wagon with a 212-horsepower 4.5-liter inline 6-cylinder engine, a 4-speed overdrive automatic transmission, and permanently engaged 4-wheel drive. Anti-lock brakes are available as a separate option and in an option package that includes front and rear differential locks for severe low-speed off-road conditions. Five-passenger seating is standard and an optional 3-place third seat increases capacity to eight. Land Cruiser is an enormously capable sport-utility vehicle that has the excellent assembly quality typical of Toyota products. The price is enormous, too, when compared to the Ford Explorer and Jeep Grand Cherokee, which offer similar mechanical features at lower cost. With dual overhead cams and four valves per cylinder, Land Cruiser's 4.5-liter engine is somewhat exotic for this class. It gets the job done by bringing enough power and torque to move this rig's considerable weight, though fuel economy is abysmal (13 mpg in our last test). Land Cruiser has a firm, almost stiff ride that is appropriate for its tough, truck-like character, though it can be uncomfortable on a long drive. There's loads of space in the surprisingly car-like interior. The permanent 4-wheel drive is nice, but anti-lock brakes also should be standard in a $34,000 vehicle. Toyota sells every Land Cruiser it imports, so dealers aren't inclined to discount.

Toyota Land Cruiser prices are on page 440.

TOYOTA LAND CRUISER

Rating Guide	1	2	3	4	5
Performance					
Acceleration	▓▓▓▓▓▓▓▓▓▓▓▓▓▓▓▓▓▓				
Economy	▓▓▓▓▓				
Driveability	▓▓▓▓▓▓▓▓▓▓▓▓▓▓				
Ride	▓▓▓▓▓▓▓▓▓▓▓				
Steering/handling	▓▓▓▓▓▓▓▓▓▓▓				
Braking	▓▓▓▓▓▓▓▓▓▓▓▓▓▓▓				
Noise	▓▓▓▓▓▓▓▓▓▓▓				
Accommodations					
Driver seating	▓▓▓▓▓▓▓▓▓▓▓▓▓▓				
Instruments/controls	▓▓▓▓▓▓▓▓▓▓▓▓▓				
Visibility	▓▓▓▓▓▓▓▓▓▓▓▓▓				
Room/comfort	▓▓▓▓▓▓▓▓▓▓▓▓▓▓▓▓				
Entry/exit	▓▓▓▓▓▓▓▓▓▓▓▓				
Cargo room	▓▓▓▓▓▓▓▓▓▓▓▓▓▓▓▓▓▓				
Workmanship					
Exterior	▓▓▓▓▓▓▓▓▓▓▓▓▓				
Interior	▓▓▓▓▓▓▓▓▓▓▓▓▓				
Value	▓▓▓▓▓▓▓▓▓▓▓▓▓				
Total Points					**58**

Specifications

Body type	5-door wagon	Engine type	dohc I-6
Wheelbase (in.)	112.2	Engine size (l/cu. in.)	4.5/275
Overall length (in.)	188.2	Horsepower @ rpm	212 @ 4600
Overall width (in.)	76.0	Torque @ rpm	275 @ 3200
Overall height (in.)	73.2	Transmission	auto/4-sp.
Curb weight (lbs.)	4762	Drive wheels	all
Seating capacity	8	Brakes, F/R	disc/disc (ABS)
Front head room (in.)	40.7	Tire size	275/70R16
Max. front leg room (in.)	42.2	Fuel tank capacity (gal.)	25.1
Rear head room (in.)	40.0	EPA city/highway mpg	12/15
Min. rear leg room (in.)	33.6	Test mileage (mpg)	NA
Cargo volume (cu. ft.)	91.1		

Warranties The entire vehicle is covered for 3 years/36,000 miles. Major powertrain components are covered for 5 years/60,000 miles. Body perforation rust is covered for 5 years/unlimited miles.

Rating scale 5=Exceptional; 4=Above average; 3=Average; 2=Below average; 1=Poor

TOYOTA MR2

Built in Japan.

Toyota MR2 Turbo

SPORTS AND GT

The 1994 MR2 is scheduled to arrive early this year bearing a new passenger-side air bag to go along with its driver-side air bag. This rear-drive sports car has a transverse-mounted engine behind its 2-seat cockpit. The base model has a 2.2-liter 4-cylinder engine with 135 horsepower. The Turbo model uses a 2.0-liter 4-cylinder with 200 horsepower. A 5-speed manual transmission is standard on both models. A 4-speed automatic is optional only on the base model. Anti-lock brakes are optional on both versions. A T-bar roof with removable panels remains standard on the Turbo and optional on the base model, where a pop-up/removable sun-roof is also available. For 1994, both models also get revised tail-lamps and minor tweaks to the suspension. In addition, the normally aspirated base model gains standard air conditioning (now CFC-free) and the rear spoiler previously reserved for its Turbo companion. MR2 is a great performer, but it now starts at nearly $20,000 and the turbocharged model, at around $25,000, is out of reach for most buyers. Yet no one else offers a 2-seat, mid-engine sports car for less, and you don't need the turbocharged version to enjoy an MR2. With the engine right behind your ears, you'll hear lots of mechanical noise along with plenty of road noise. With the firm suspension and wide tires, you'll feel most bumps and endure some harshness on washboard surfaces, but you'll be able to scoot around corners like a go-cart. Cargo space is limited, so you have to travel light. The MR2 has been a slow seller since it was redesigned nearly four years ago, so dealers should be willing to bargain.

Toyota MR2 prices are on page 440.

TOYOTA MR2 TURBO

Rating Guide	1	2	3	4	5
Performance					
Acceleration	▓▓▓▓▓▓▓▓▓▓▓▓▓▓▓▓▓▓▓▓▓▓▓▓▓ (5)				
Economy	▓▓▓▓▓▓▓▓▓▓ (2)				
Driveability	▓▓▓▓▓▓▓▓▓▓▓▓▓▓▓▓▓▓▓▓ (4)				
Ride	▓▓▓▓▓▓▓▓▓▓▓▓▓▓▓ (3)				
Steering/handling	▓▓▓▓▓▓▓▓▓▓▓▓▓▓▓▓▓▓▓▓▓▓▓▓▓ (5)				
Braking	▓▓▓▓▓▓▓▓▓▓▓▓▓▓▓▓▓▓▓▓ (4)				
Noise	▓▓▓▓▓▓▓▓▓▓▓▓▓▓▓ (3)				
Accommodations					
Driver seating	▓▓▓▓▓▓▓▓▓▓▓▓▓▓▓▓▓▓▓▓ (4)				
Instruments/controls	▓▓▓▓▓▓▓▓▓▓▓▓▓▓▓▓▓▓▓▓▓▓▓▓▓ (5)				
Visibility	▓▓▓▓▓▓▓▓▓▓▓▓▓▓▓▓▓▓▓▓ (4)				
Room/comfort	▓▓▓▓▓▓▓▓▓▓▓▓▓▓▓▓▓▓▓▓ (4)				
Entry/exit	▓▓▓▓▓▓▓▓▓▓▓▓▓▓▓ (3)				
Cargo room	▓▓▓▓▓▓▓▓▓▓ (2)				
Workmanship					
Exterior	▓▓▓▓▓▓▓▓▓▓▓▓▓▓▓▓▓▓▓▓ (4)				
Interior	▓▓▓▓▓▓▓▓▓▓▓▓▓▓▓▓▓▓▓▓ (4)				
Value	▓▓▓▓▓▓▓▓▓▓▓▓▓▓▓▓▓▓▓▓ (4)				
Total Points					**50**

Specifications

Body type	2-door notchback	Engine type	Turbo dohc I-4
Wheelbase (in.)	94.5	Engine size (l/cu. in.)	2.0/122
Overall length (in.)	164.2	Horsepower @ rpm	200 @ 6000
Overall width (in.)	66.9	Torque @ rpm	200 @ 3200
Overall height (in.)	48.6	Transmission	manual/5-sp.
Curb weight (lbs.)	2822	Drive wheels	rear
Seating capacity	2	Brakes, F/R	disc/disc
Front head room (in.)	37.5	Tire size	225/50VR15
Max. front leg room (in.)	43.4	Fuel tank capacity (gal.)	14.3
Rear head room (in.)	—	EPA city/highway mpg	20/27
Min. rear leg room (in.)	—	Test mileage (mpg)	19.6
Cargo volume (cu. ft.)	6.6		

Warranties The entire car is covered for 3 years/36,000 miles. Major powertrain components are covered for 5 years/60,000 miles. Body perforation rust is covered for 5 years/unlimited miles.

Rating scale 5=Exceptional; 4=Above average; 3=Average; 2=Below average; 1=Poor

TOYOTA PASEO

Built in Japan.

Toyota Paseo

SPORTS COUPE

Toyota's entry-level sports coupe switches to a CFC-free refrigerant for its optional air conditioning and adds automatic locking retractors to the passengers' seat belts. The automatic retractors cinch the belts tight to make them easier to use with child safety seats. A driver-side air bag remains standard and anti-lock brakes remain optional on the front-drive Paseo. The driver's seat has a conventional manual 3-point seat belt, while the front passenger's seat has a door-mounted shoulder belt that can be left buckled to automatically deploy when the door is closed. A separate lap belt buckles manually. Paseo shares its front-drive chassis with the Tercel but has its own 2-door notchback styling and a more powerful 1.5-liter 4-cylinder engine. In the Paseo, the engine has dual overhead camshafts instead of one and 100 horsepower instead of 82. It teams with a standard 5-speed manual or optional 4-speed automatic transmission. Toyota positions Paseo below the Celica sports coupe in size and price. Its strong points include good gas mileage, a standard driver-side air bag, and optional anti-lock brakes. Like most sports coupes, Paseo is a 2+2—which means it has a back seat that's too small for adults. Though the engine doesn't produce much power at low speeds, it has enough for adequate acceleration and highway passing. Unfortunately, it runs roughly and is loud when worked hard. There's also too much tire noise on coarse pavement. Though some rivals offer better performance and sexier styling, few match Toyota's reputation for durability and traditionally high resale value.

Toyota Paseo prices are on page 442

TOYOTA PASEO

Rating Guide	1	2	3	4	5
Performance					
Acceleration					
Economy					
Driveability					
Ride					
Steering/handling					
Braking					
Noise					
Accommodations					
Driver seating					
Instruments/controls					
Visibility					
Room/comfort					
Entry/exit					
Cargo room					
Workmanship					
Exterior					
Interior					
Value					
Total Points					53

Specifications

Body type	2-door notchback	Engine type	dohc I-4
Wheelbase (in.)	93.7	Engine size (l/cu. in.)	1.5/90
Overall length (in.)	163.2	Horsepower @ rpm	100 @ 6400
Overall width (in.)	65.2	Torque @ rpm	91 @ 3200
Overall height (in.)	50.2	Transmission	manual/5-sp.
Curb weight (lbs.)	2070	Drive wheels	front
Seating capacity	4	Brakes, F/R	disc/drum
Front head room (in.)	37.7	Tire size	185/60R14
Max. front leg room (in.)	41.1	Fuel tank capacity (gal.)	11.9
Rear head room (in.)	32.0	EPA city/highway mpg	28/34
Min. rear leg room (in.)	30.0	Test mileage (mpg)	31.7
Cargo volume (cu. ft.)	7.7		

Warranties The entire car is covered for 3 years/36,000 miles. Major powertrain components are covered for 5 years/60,000 miles. Body perforation rust is covered for 5 years/unlimited miles.

Rating scale 5=Exceptional; 4=Above average; 3=Average; 2=Below average; 1=Poor

TOYOTA PREVIA

Built in Japan.

Toyota Previa LE

MINIVAN

Toyota's minivan gains a standard passenger-side air bag, an available supercharged engine, and CFC-free air conditioning for 1994. Previa is available in DX and LE models with rear-wheel drive or permanently engaged 4-wheel drive, which Toyota calls All-Trac. Currently, the only engine is a 138-horsepower 2.4-liter 4-cylinder mounted below the driver's seat. A supercharged version of the 2.4-liter engine with 161 horsepower is due to arrive in March in the LE S/C and LE S/C All-Trac models. The 5-speed manual transmission previously standard on the DX has been dropped, so all Previas come with a 4-speed automatic. Anti-lock brakes are optional across the board. Seats for seven are standard on all models. The center seat is removable and the rear seat is split so that both halves can be folded outward, against the sides of the vehicle. Acceleration with the base 4-cylinder is fairly brisk from low speeds, but there's not enough torque for brisk passing and the engine feels coarse during hard acceleration. A prototype LE S/C we tested was raspy but more responsive off the line and much more capable in passing situations. Previa has a roomy interior that's easy to get into and out of. The fold-up rear bench is a clever alternative to removable seats, but when folded up it blocks the driver's view over the right shoulder. The unusual-looking dashboard puts most controls within easy reach, though the climate controls are poorly marked. Though Previa has commendable assembly quality, it is too expensive to match the value of competitors like the Chrysler minivans.

Toyota Previa prices are on page 442.

TOYOTA PREVIA LE

Rating Guide	1	2	3	4	5
Performance					
Acceleration	▋▋▋▋▋▋				
Economy	▋▋▋▋▋				
Driveability	▋▋▋▋▋▋				
Ride	▋▋▋▋▋▋▋				
Steering/handling	▋▋▋▋▋▋				
Braking	▋▋▋▋▋▋				
Noise	▋▋▋▋▋▋				
Accommodations					
Driver seating	▋▋▋▋▋▋▋				
Instruments/controls	▋▋▋▋▋▋▋				
Visibility	▋▋▋▋▋▋▋				
Room/comfort	▋▋▋▋▋▋▋▋▋				
Entry/exit	▋▋▋▋▋▋▋				
Cargo room	▋▋▋▋▋▋▋▋▋				
Workmanship					
Exterior	▋▋▋▋▋▋▋				
Interior	▋▋▋▋▋▋▋				
Value	▋▋▋▋▋▋▋				
Total Points					**57**

Specifications

Body type	4-door van	Engine type	dohc I-4
Wheelbase (in.)	112.8	Engine size (l/cu. in.)	2.4/149
Overall length (in.)	187.0	Horsepower @ rpm	138 @ 5000
Overall width (in.)	70.8	Torque @ rpm	154 @ 4000
Overall height (in.)	68.7	Transmission	auto/4-sp.
Curb weight (lbs.)	3580	Drive wheels	rear
Seating capacity	7	Brakes, F/R	disc/disc
Front head room (in.)	39.4	Tire size	215/65R15
Max. front leg room (in.)	40.1	Fuel tank capacity (gal.)	19.8
Rear head room (in.)	38.5	EPA city/highway mpg	17/22
Min. rear leg room (in.)	36.6	Test mileage (mpg)	18.5
Cargo volume (cu. ft.)	157.8		

Warranties The entire car is covered for 3 years/36,000 miles. Major powertrain components are covered for 5 years/60,000 miles. Body perforation rust is covered for 5 years/unlimited miles.

Rating scale 5=Exceptional; 4=Above average; 3=Average; 2=Below average; 1=Poor

TOYOTA SUPRA

Built in Japan.

Toyota Supra Turbo

SPORTS AND GT

A redesigned Supra was introduced last summer and the 1994 version gets one minor change: a lower final-drive ratio for the base model to give it quicker acceleration. Supra is a 3-door hatchback coupe that comes in base and Turbo versions, both available with a fixed roof or removable roof panels (called Sport Roof). Dual air bags, anti-lock brakes, and a limited-slip differential are standard on all models. The Turbo also has traction control. Power comes from a dual-camshaft 3.0-liter inline 6-cylinder engine. In the base model it's rated at 220 horsepower; twin turbochargers give the Turbo model 320 horsepower. Base models come with a standard 5-speed manual transmission and Turbos with a 6-speed manual. A 4-speed automatic is optional on both. We tested a Turbo with automatic and despite the lofty power rating, around-town driving can be exasperating. Put your foot down and there's little response at first, but then the car bolts ahead as the turbos spool up. On the highway, power comes on immediately. Handling is top-notch and though the suspension soaks up bumps fairly well, the low-profile tires transmit every little ripple into the cockpit. The driver and front passenger are treated to ample head and leg room, but the rear seat is much too cramped for adults. Gauges and controls are generally easy to see and reach, though the radio is mounted too low. Visibility is good to the front, fair to the sides, and lousy to the rear. Supra's lofty performance envelope and high level of fit and finish make it a must-see in the over-$30,000 sports-car arena.

Toyota Supra prices are on page 443.

TOYOTA SUPRA TURBO

Rating Guide	1	2	3	4	5
Performance					
Acceleration	▮▮▮▮▮▮▮▮▮▮▮▮▮▮▮▮▮▮▮▮▮▮▮▮▮
Economy	▮▮▮▮▮▮▮▮▮▮
Driveability	▮▮▮▮▮▮▮▮▮▮▮▮▮▮▮▮▮▮▮
Ride	▮▮▮▮▮▮▮▮▮▮▮▮▮▮▮
Steering/handling	▮▮▮▮▮▮▮▮▮▮▮▮▮▮▮▮▮▮▮▮▮▮▮▮▮
Braking	▮▮▮▮▮▮▮▮▮▮▮▮▮▮▮▮▮▮▮▮▮▮▮▮▮
Noise	▮▮▮▮▮▮▮▮▮▮
Accommodations					
Driver seating	▮▮▮▮▮▮▮▮▮▮▮▮▮▮▮▮▮▮▮▮▮▮
Instruments/controls	▮▮▮▮▮▮▮▮▮▮▮▮▮▮▮▮▮▮▮▮▮▮
Visibility	▮▮▮▮▮▮▮▮▮▮▮▮▮▮▮
Room/comfort	▮▮▮▮▮▮▮▮▮▮▮▮▮▮▮
Entry/exit	▮▮▮▮▮▮▮▮▮▮▮▮▮▮▮
Cargo room	▮▮▮▮▮▮▮▮▮▮▮▮▮▮▮
Workmanship					
Exterior	▮▮▮▮▮▮▮▮▮▮▮▮▮▮▮▮▮▮▮▮▮
Interior	▮▮▮▮▮▮▮▮▮▮▮▮▮▮▮▮▮▮▮▮▮
Value	▮▮▮▮▮▮▮▮▮▮▮▮▮▮▮▮

Total Points...52

Specifications

Body type	3-door hatchback	Engine type	Turbo dohc I-6
Wheelbase (in.)	100.4	Engine size (l/cu. in.)	3.0/183
Overall length (in.)	177.7	Horsepower @ rpm	320 @ 5600
Overall width (in.)	71.3	Torque @ rpm	315 @ 4000
Overall height (in.)	50.2	Transmission	auto/4-sp.
Curb weight (lbs.)	3215	Drive wheels	rear
Seating capacity	4	Brakes, F/R	disc/disc (ABS)
Front head room (in.)	37.5	Tire size	255/40ZR17
Max. front leg room (in.)	42.2	Fuel tank capacity (gal.)	18.5
Rear head room (in.)	32.9	EPA city/highway mpg	19/23
Min. rear leg room (in.)	23.8	Test mileage (mpg)	NA
Cargo volume (cu. ft.)	10.1		

Warranties The entire car is covered for 3 years/36,000 miles. Major powertrain components are covered for 5 years/60,000 miles. Body perforation rust is covered for 5 years/unlimited miles.

Rating scale 5=Exceptional; 4=Above average; 3=Average; 2=Below average; 1=Poor

TOYOTA TERCEL

Built in Japan.

Toyota Tercel DX 2-door

SUBCOMPACT

Toyota's entry-level front-drive subcompact gets CFC-free refrigerant for the optional air conditioning and automatic locking retractors for passengers' seat belts this year. The new automatic locking retractors are designed to make the belts easier to use with child safety seats. A driver-side air bag is standard. The driver also has a manual seat belt, while the front passenger has a door-mounted belt that can be left buckled to automatically deploy when the door is opened. Anti-lock brakes are optional. Tercel comes as a 2-door notchback sedan in Standard and DX price levels and as a 4-door sedan in the DX price level. All models are powered by an 82-horsepower 1.5-liter 4-cylinder engine. The Standard 2-door comes only with a 4-speed manual transmission. On the DX models, a 5-speed manual is standard and a 3-speed automatic is optional. Tercel's engine doesn't have much power for sprinting from stop lights or passing on the highway, so you have to plan your moves carefully. Tercel also has a choppy, harsh ride, plus there's too much road noise and suspension thumping on anything but smooth roads. Front-seat passengers have ample head room and adequate leg room, but rear-seat passengers will be cramped if they're taller than about 5-foot-10, and leg room gets tight if the front seats are moved very far back. Unlike the larger Corolla, which sets the standard for refinement among small cars, Tercel is a noisy "econocar" with no outstanding qualities. However, it's an economical, well-made subcompact that promises to uphold Toyota's reputation for reliability and have good resale value.

Toyota Tercel prices are on page 444.

TOYOTA TERCEL DELUXE

Rating Guide	1	2	3	4	5

Performance

Acceleration	▬▬▬▬▬▬▬▬▬▬ (≈3.5)				
Economy	▬▬▬▬▬▬▬▬▬▬▬▬ (≈4)				
Driveability	▬▬▬▬▬▬▬▬▬▬▬▬ (≈4)				
Ride	▬▬▬▬▬▬▬▬ (≈3)				
Steering/handling	▬▬▬▬▬▬▬▬▬▬ (≈3.5)				
Braking	▬▬▬▬▬▬▬▬▬▬ (≈3.5)				
Noise	▬▬▬▬▬▬▬▬ (≈3)				

Accommodations

Driver seating	▬▬▬▬▬▬▬▬▬▬ (≈3.5)				
Instruments/controls	▬▬▬▬▬▬▬▬▬▬▬▬ (≈4)				
Visibility	▬▬▬▬▬▬▬▬▬▬▬▬▬▬▬▬ (≈5)				
Room/comfort	▬▬▬▬▬▬▬▬ (≈3)				
Entry/exit	▬▬▬▬▬▬▬▬▬▬ (≈3.5)				
Cargo room	▬▬▬▬▬▬▬▬▬▬ (≈3.5)				

Workmanship

Exterior	▬▬▬▬▬▬▬▬▬▬ (≈3.5)				
Interior	▬▬▬▬▬▬▬▬▬▬ (≈3.5)				
Value	▬▬▬▬▬▬▬▬▬▬ (≈3.5)				

Total Points 55

Specifications

Body type ....2-door notchback	Engine type ....ohc I-4
Wheelbase (in.) 93.7	Engine size (l/cu. in.)...........1.5/90
Overall length (in.)...............161.8	Horsepower @ rpm .....82 @ 5200
Overall width (in.) 64.8	Torque @ rpm ....89 @ 4400
Overall height (in.) 53.2	Transmission.................auto/3-sp.
Curb weight (lbs.) 2025	Drive wheels ....front
Seating capacity...........................5	Brakes, F/R....................disc/drum
Front head room (in.) 38.7	Tire size.....................155/80SR13
Max. front leg room (in.) 41.2	Fuel tank capacity (gal.).........11.9
Rear head room (in.) 36.7	EPA city/highway mpg 26/29
Min. rear leg room (in.)..........31.9	Test mileage (mpg) 26.3
Cargo volume (cu. ft.).............10.7	

Warranties The entire car is covered for 3 years/36,000 miles. Major powertrain components are covered for 5 years/60,000 miles. Body perforation rust is covered for 5 years/unlimited miles.

Rating scale 5=Exceptional; 4=Above average; 3=Average; 2=Below average; 1=Poor

TOYOTA 4RUNNER

Built in Japan.

Toyota 4Runner V6

SPORT-UTILITY

Four-wheel anti-lock brakes are a new option and a center high-mounted stoplamp and side door guard beams are new standard features on 4Runner for 1994. The 4-wheel anti-lock feature, which is available only with the V-6 engine, costs an additional $660. The 4Runner returns as a 5-door wagon available in four flavors. The base 4WD model has a 2.4-liter 4-cylinder engine with 116 horsepower and is sold only with a 5-speed manual transmission. The rear anti-lock feature is optional on the 4-cylinder model. There's a rear-drive V-6 model with a standard 4-speed automatic transmission and a 4WD V-6 model with a choice of either the manual or automatic transmission. The V-6 is a 3.0-liter engine with 150 horsepower. The 4WD system is Toyota's 4WDemand, which is for use only on slick surfaces but allows shifting between 2WD and 4WD High at speeds up to 50 mph. The 4Runner's chief attractions are tight, thorough assembly quality and a commendable reputation for reliability. It also scores highly in customer satisfaction surveys. However, 4Runner is far more compact inside than the top-selling Ford Explorer and Jeep Grand Cherokee, with barely adequate space for four. Entry/exit is hurt by a high stance. Fuel economy is mediocre at best and acceleration is nothing special either. We averaged just 13.8 mpg with a V-6 model, which struggled to 60 mph in 13 seconds. The 4-cylinder is even slower. High prices are another problem. Dress up a 4Runner with a few appearance and convenience options and the price is pushing $25,000. The Explorer and Grand Cherokee have more room and better performance for less.

Toyota 4Runner prices are on page 445.

TOYOTA 4RUNNER

Rating Guide	1	2	3	4	5
Performance					
Acceleration	▓▓▓▓▓▓▓				
Economy	▓▓▓				
Driveability	▓▓▓▓▓▓▓▓				
Ride	▓▓▓▓▓▓▓▓				
Steering/handling	▓▓▓▓▓▓▓▓				
Braking	▓▓▓▓▓▓▓▓				
Noise	▓▓▓▓▓▓▓				
Accommodations					
Driver seating	▓▓▓▓▓▓				
Instruments/controls	▓▓▓▓▓▓▓▓				
Visibility	▓▓▓▓▓▓▓				
Room/comfort	▓▓▓▓▓▓▓▓				
Entry/exit	▓▓▓▓▓▓				
Cargo room	▓▓▓▓▓▓▓▓▓▓				
Workmanship					
Exterior	▓▓▓▓▓▓▓▓				
Interior	▓▓▓▓▓▓▓▓				
Value	▓▓▓▓▓▓▓				

Total Points...**53**

Specifications

Body type	5-door wagon	Engine type	ohc V-6
Wheelbase (in.)	103.3	Engine size (l/cu. in.)	3.0/180
Overall length (in.)	176.6	Horsepower @ rpm	150 @ 4800
Overall width (in.)	66.5	Torque @ rpm	180 @ 3400
Overall height (in.)	66.1	Transmission	auto/4-sp.
Curb weight (lbs.)	4105	Drive wheels	rear/all
Seating capacity	5	Brakes, F/R	disc/drum (ABS)
Front head room (in.)	38.7	Tire size	31x10.5R15
Max. front leg room (in.)	41.5	Fuel tank capacity (gal.)	17.2
Rear head room (in.)	38.3	EPA city/highway mpg	14/16
Min. rear leg room (in.)	31.6	Test mileage (mpg)	13.8
Cargo volume (cu. ft.)	78.3		

Warranties The entire vehicle is covered for 3 years/36,000 miles. Major powertrain components are covered for 5 years/60,000 miles. Body perforation rust is covered for 5 years/unlimited miles.

Rating scale 5=Exceptional; 4=Above average; 3=Average; 2=Below average; 1=Poor

VOLKSWAGEN GOLF/JETTA –

Built in Mexico.

Volkswagen Jetta GL

SUBCOMPACT

Redesigned versions of the Golf and Jetta debuted last May as late 1993 offerings, but sales were confined to Southern California. Their official names are Golf III and Jetta III, denoting that they are the third generation of this front-drive subcompact. Golf GL 5-door hatchbacks and Jetta GL 4-door notchbacks were the first to arrive. Other models are being phased in as 1994s. All except the earliest 1994 models have standard dual air bags. The 1993s and early 1994 models had door-mounted automatic front shoulder belts. An upscale Jetta GLS is supposed to be on sale by now and a performance-oriented Jetta GLX is due in February. Anti-lock brakes are standard or optional on all Jettas. A Golf 3-door hatchback also is supposed to join the fold in February, followed in March by a sporty GTI version. GL and GLS models have a 115-horsepower 2.0-liter 4-cylinder engine. The GTI and GLX have a 178-horsepower 2.8-liter V-6. A 5-speed manual transmission is standard on all and a new 4-speed electronic automatic is optional except on the GTI. A convertible is scheduled to arrive this spring. In most ways, the new Golf and Jetta are evolutionary rather than revolutionary. Acceleration with the automatic transmission is much improved, both from a stop and in highway passing. Road and exhaust noise are still prominent at highway speeds, however. As with the previous generation, these cars have sporty handling. The dashboard has a functional design with easy-to-reach controls and there's adequate room for four adults in all models. In general, if you liked the old Golf and Jetta, you'll love the new ones.

Volkswagen Golf/Jetta prices are on page 447.

VOLKSWAGEN JETTA GL

Rating Guide	1	2	3	4	5
Performance					
Acceleration	▓▓▓▓▓▓▓▓▓▓▓▓▓▓▓▓▓				
Economy	▓▓▓▓▓▓▓▓▓▓▓▓▓				
Driveability	▓▓▓▓▓▓▓▓▓▓▓▓▓▓▓▓▓				
Ride	▓▓▓▓▓▓▓▓▓▓▓▓▓				
Steering/handling	▓▓▓▓▓▓▓▓▓▓▓▓▓▓▓▓▓				
Braking	▓▓▓▓▓▓▓▓▓▓▓▓▓				
Noise	▓▓▓▓▓▓▓▓▓▓▓▓▓				
Accommodations					
Driver seating	▓▓▓▓▓▓▓▓▓▓▓▓▓				
Instruments/controls	▓▓▓▓▓▓▓▓▓▓▓▓▓▓▓▓▓				
Visibility	▓▓▓▓▓▓▓▓▓▓▓▓▓				
Room/comfort	▓▓▓▓▓▓▓▓▓▓▓▓▓				
Entry/exit	▓▓▓▓▓▓▓▓▓▓▓▓▓				
Cargo room	▓▓▓▓▓▓▓▓▓▓▓▓▓▓▓▓▓				
Workmanship					
Exterior	▓▓▓▓▓▓▓▓▓▓▓▓▓				
Interior	▓▓▓▓▓▓▓▓▓▓▓▓▓				
Value	▓▓▓▓▓▓▓▓▓▓▓▓▓				
Total Points					**56**

Specifications

Body type	4-door notchback	Engine type	ohc I-4
Wheelbase (in.)	97.4	Engine size (l/cu. in.)	2.0/115
Overall length (in.)	113.4	Horsepower @ rpm	115 @ 5400
Overall width (in.)	66.7	Torque @ rpm	122 @ 3200
Overall height (in.)	56.2	Transmission	auto/4-sp.
Curb weight (lbs.)	2735	Drive wheels	front
Seating capacity	5	Brakes, F/R	disc/drum
Front head room (in.)	39.2	Tire size	195/60R14
Max. front leg room (in.)	42.3	Fuel tank capacity (gal.)	14.5
Rear head room (in.)	37.3	EPA city/highway mpg	21/27
Min. rear leg room (in.)	31.6	Test mileage (mpg)	NA
Cargo volume (cu. ft.)	15.0		

Warranties The entire car is covered for 2 years/24,000 miles. Major powertrain components are covered for 10 years/100,000 miles. Body perforation rust is covered for 6 years/unlimited miles.

Rating scale 5=Exceptional; 4=Above average; 3=Average; 2=Below average; 1=Poor

VOLVO 850

Built in Sweden.

Volvo 850 4-door

PREMIUM SEDAN

Volvo's front-wheel-drive line gains a 5-door wagon and an optional turbocharged engine. Like all Volvos, the 850 models have dual air bags and anti-lock brakes as standard equipment. The new wagon seats five and comes with a folding rear seat that has a built-in booster seat for children between 50 and 80 pounds. The booster seat is a dealer-installed option on the sedan. A rear-facing third seat is optional on the wagon. Base engine for all models is a 168-horsepower 2.4-liter 5-cylinder. A 5-speed manual transmission is standard and a 4-speed electronic automatic is optional. The new turbocharged 5-cylinder displaces 2.3 liters, has 222 horsepower, and comes only with the automatic. Traction control is optional on all 850s. A new base-level sedan has been created by dropping the alloy wheels and sunroof, and replacing automatic temperature control with manual air conditioning. Level II features, which are standard on the wagon and optional on the sedan, include a power sunroof, power driver's seat, and remote keyless entry. The 850 Turbo sedan and wagon have the Level II equipment plus additional luxury touches. We haven't driven an 850 Turbo, but the standard engine doesn't have enough low-speed torque to accelerate quickly from a stop. The suspension is firm enough to provide a stable highway ride and athletic cornering ability, yet absorbent enough to soak up most bumps without breaking stride. There's plenty of head and leg room for four adults, but the interior isn't wide enough to fit three people in back. Though we're not overwhelmed by the 850, it has more safety features and more value than some rivals in the same price range.

Volvo 850 prices are on page 448.

VOLVO 850 LEVEL II

Rating Guide	1	2	3	4	5
Performance					
Acceleration			▮		
Economy			▮		
Driveability			▮		
Ride			▮		
Steering/handling				▮	
Braking					▮
Noise			▮		
Accommodations					
Driver seating			▮		
Instruments/controls			▮		
Visibility			▮		
Room/comfort			▮		
Entry/exit			▮		
Cargo room				▮	
Workmanship					
Exterior				▮	
Interior				▮	
Value			▮		
Total Points					**60**

Specifications

Body type	4-door notchback	Engine type	dohc I-5
Wheelbase (in.)	104.9	Engine size (l/cu. in.)	2.4/149
Overall length (in.)	183.5	Horsepower @ rpm	168 @ 6200
Overall width (in.)	69.3	Torque @ rpm	162 @ 3300
Overall height (in.)	55.7	Transmission	auto/4-sp.
Curb weight (lbs.)	3190	Drive wheels	front
Seating capacity	5	Brakes, F/R	disc/disc (ABS)
Front head room (in.)	38.0	Tire size	195/60R15
Max. front leg room (in.)	41.4	Fuel tank capacity (gal.)	19.3
Rear head room (in.)	37.3	EPA city/highway mpg	20/27
Min. rear leg room (in.)	35.3	Test mileage (mpg)	21.8
Cargo volume (cu. ft.)	14.7		

Warranties The entire car is covered for 4 years/50,000 miles. Body perforation rust is covered for 5 years/unlimited miles and structural rust is covered for 8 years/unlimited miles.

Rating scale 5=Exceptional; 4=Above average; 3=Average; 2=Below average; 1=Poor

PRICES

ACURA

Acura Integra	Retail Price	Dealer Invoice	Fair Price
RS 3-door hatchback, 5-speed	$14820	$12723	$14320
RS 3-door hatchback, automatic	15570	13367	15070
LS 3-door hatchback, 5-speed	17450	14981	16950
LS 3-door hatchback, automatic	18200	15625	17700
GS-R 3-door hatchback, 5-speed	19650	16870	19150
RS 4-door notchback, 5-speed	15580	13375	15080
RS 4-door notchback, automatic	16330	14019	15830
LS 4-door notchback, 5-speed	17450	14981	16950
LS 4-door notchback, automatic	18200	15626	17700
GS-R 4-door notchback, 5-speed	19980	17153	19480
Destination charge	365	365	365

Standard Equipment:

RS: 1.8-liter DOHC 4-cylinder engine, 5-speed manual or 4-speed automatic transmission, 4-wheel disc brakes, driver- and passenger-side air bags, variable-assist power steering, cloth reclining front bucket seats with driver-side lumbar support adjustment, center console with armrest, 50/50 split folding rear seat (hatchback), one piece folding rear seat (notchback), power windows and mirrors, power door locks (notchbacks), AM/FM cassette player with four speakers, power antenna, tinted glass, remote fuel door and decklid/hatch releases, fog lamps, rear defogger, rear wiper/washer (hatchback), tachometer, coolant temperature gauge, tilt steering column, intermittent wipers, door pockets, cargo cover (hatchback), 195/60HR14 tires. **LS** adds: anti-lock brakes, air conditioning, power door locks, power moonroof (hatchback), cruise control, map lights (hatchback), 195/60HR14 all-season tires. **GS-R** adds: 1.8-liter DOHC VTEC engine, rear spoiler, AM/FM cassette with six speakers, power moonroof, 195/55VR15 all-season tires, alloy wheels.

Options are available as dealer-installed accessories.

Acura Legend	Retail Price	Dealer Invoice	Fair Price
L 4-door notchback, 5-speed	$33800	$28335	$31096
L 4-door notchback, automatic	34600	29005	31832
L 4-door w/leather interior, 5-speed	35300	29592	32476
L 4-door w/leather interior, automatic	36100	30263	33212
LS 4-door notchback, automatic	38600	32358	35512

	Retail Price	Dealer Invoice	Fair Price
GS 4-door notchback, 6-speed	$40700	$34119	$37444
GS 4-door notchback, automatic	40700	34119	37444
L 2-door coupe, 6-speed	—	—	—
L 2-door coupe, automatic	—	—	—
LS 2-door coupe, 6-speed	—	—	—
LS 2-door coupe, automatic	—	—	—
Destination charge	385	385	385

Coupe prices not available at time of publication.

Standard Equipment:

L: 3.2-liter V-6, 5-speed manual or 4-speed automatic transmission, anti-lock 4-wheel disc brakes, driver- and passenger-side air bags, variable-assist power steering, air conditioning, front bucket seats, 8-way power driver's seat, 4-way power passenger seat, power windows and locks, cruise control, telescopic steering column, steering wheel memory system, power moonroof with sunshade, tinted glass, heated power mirrors, Acura/Bose music system, steering wheel mounted radio controls, theft-deterrent system, intermittent wipers, bodyside moldings, rear defogger, remote fuel door and decklid releases, lighted visor mirrors, front door pockets, center console with armrest, digital clock, 205/60VR15 tires, alloy wheels. **L Coupe** adds: 6-speed manual transmission, leather upholstery, leather-wrapped steering wheel, rear headrests. **LS** adds: leather upholstery and leather-wrapped steering wheel (sedan), walnut interior trim, heated front seats, automatic climate control, AM/FM cassette with diversity antenna and anti-theft feature, illuminated entry system. **LS Coupe** adds: traction control, 215/55VR16 tires. **GS** adds to LS sedan: 6-speed manual or 4-speed automatic transmission, traction control, sport suspension, body-color grille, 215/55VR16 tires.

Options are available as dealer-installed accessories.

Acura Vigor

	Retail Price	Dealer Invoice	Fair Price
LS 4-door notchback, 5-speed	$26350	$22355	$23155
LS 4-door notchback, automatic	27100	22992	23792
GS 4-door notchback, 5-speed	28350	24052	24852
GS 4-door notchback, automatic	29100	24688	25488
Destination charge	385	385	385

Standard Equipment:

LS: 2.5-liter 5-cylinder engine, 5-speed manual or 4-speed automatic transmission, anti-lock 4-wheel disc brakes, power steering, driver- and passenger-side air bags, air conditioning, tinted glass, power windows, door locks and mirrors, cruise control, theft-deterrent system, leather-wrapped steering wheel, lighted visor mirror, rear reading lights, fog lamps, remote fuel and decklid releases, variable intermittent wipers, tachometer, digital clock, cloth upholstery, tilt steering column, rear window defogger, 8-speaker AM/FM cassette, power antenna, alloy wheels, 205/60HR15 all-season tires. **GS** adds: leather upholstery, CD player, power moonroof, rear map pockets, 4-way power driver's seat.

Options are available as dealer-installed accessories.

AUDI

1993 Audi 90	Retail Price	Dealer Invoice	Fair Price
S 4-door notchback	$26650	$22631	$23431
CS 4-door notchback	29500	25025	25825
CS Quattro Sport, 4-door notchback	33050	28007	28807
Destination charge	450	450	450

Standard Equipment:

S: 2.8-liter V-6 engine, 5-speed manual transmission, driver-side air bag, anti-lock 4-wheel disc brakes, air conditioning, power steering, leather-wrapped steering wheel, AM/FM cassette, dual diversity antenna, velour upholstery, power windows and locks, childproof rear door locks, cruise control, tinted glass, headlight washers, retained accessory power, alarm system, fog lights, rear window defroster, front and rear fold-down armrests, digital clock, center console, remote trunk and fuel door releases, heated power mirrors, front seatback map pockets, bodyside moldings, reclining front seats with height adjustment, split-folding rear seat, intermittent wipers, tachometer, carpeted floor mats, 195/65HR15 all-season tires, alloy wheels. **CS** adds: automatic climate control, wood trim, remote locking system, power sunroof, 8-way power driver's seat, leather upholstery. **CS Quattro Sport** adds: all-wheel drive, sport bucket seats, rear spoiler, sport suspension, 205/60VR15 performance tires, 10-spoke alloy wheels.

Optional Equipment:

4-speed automatic transmission (NA Quattro)	800	750	720
All-Weather Package, S	420	336	378
CS, CS Quattro	320	256	288
Includes heated front door locks (S), heated front seats, heated windshield washer nozzles.			
Pearlescent paint	500	400	450

	Retail Price	Dealer Invoice	Fair Price
Power sunroof, S	$910	$728	$819
Expandable ski/storage sack, CS Quattro	150	120	135
195/65HR15 all-season tires, CS Quattro	NC	NC	NC

1993 Audi 100/S4	Retail Price	Dealer Invoice	Fair Price
4-door notchback	$31300	$26224	$27224
S 4-door notchback	34150	28590	29590
CS 4-door notchback	38650	32325	33325
CS Quattro 4-door notchback	41850	34981	35981
CS Quattro 5-door wagon	45150	37720	38720
S4 4-door notchback	47750	39878	—
Destination charge	450	450	450

S4 fair price not available at time of publication.

Standard Equipment:

100: 2.8-liter V-6 engine, 5-speed manual transmission, anti-lock 4-wheel disc brakes, power steering, driver- and passenger-side air bags, tilt and telescoping steering column, velour reclining front bucket seats with height and lumbar adjustments, front and rear folding armrests, air conditioning, tachometer, oil temperature and pressure gauges, voltmeter, coolant temperature gauge, trip odometer, Auto Check System, power windows and locks, cruise control, heated power mirrors, power sunroof, AM/FM cassette with diversity antenna, wood trim, seatback pockets, leather-wrapped steering wheel, reading lamps, lighted visor mirrors, anti-theft alarm, tinted glass, rear defogger, intermittent wipers, analog clock, rear fog lights, remote decklid release, floormats, 195/65HR15 tires. **S** adds: variable-assist power steering, 8-way power front bucket seats, ski/storage sack, alloy wheels. **CS** adds: front fog lights, trip computer with outside temperature gauge, automatic climate control, remote locking system, driver-seat memory system, power glass moonroof, Bose music system. **Quattro sedan** adds: permanently engaged 4-wheel drive. **Quattro wagon** adds: 4-speed automatic transmission, leather upholstery, heated front seats, third seat, rear wiper/washer, headlight washers, roof rack. **S4** adds to Quattro sedan: 2.2-liter turbocharged 5-cylinder engine, engine oil cooler, 5-speed manual transmission, voice-activated cellular telephone, carbon fiber interior trim, 225/50ZR16 tires.

Optional Equipment:

4-speed automatic transmission (std. wagon)	800	750	720
Leather seats, S and CS (std. wagon)	1385	1150	1247
Pearlescent metallic paint, S, CS, and S4	500	400	450

Prices are accurate at time of publication; subject to manufacturer's change.

	Retail Price	Dealer Invoice	Fair Price
All-Weather Pkg., S	$470	$376	$423
CS (std. wagon)	370	296	333
Heated front seats and windshield washer nozzles, heated front door locks (S), headlight washers.			
Voice-activated telephone, CS	990	792	891
10-disc CD changer, CS 4-doors	790	632	711
All-weather 215/60VR15 tires, S4	NC	NC	NC

BMW

BMW 3-Series	Retail Price	Dealer Invoice	Fair Price
318i 4-door notchback	$24675	$20680	$22948
318is 2-door notchback	25800	21625	23994
325i 4-door notchback	30850	25855	28691
325is 2-door notchback	32200	26985	29946
325iC 2-door convertible	38800	32520	36084
Destination charge	450	450	450

Standard Equipment:

318i/318is: 1.8-liter DOHC 4-cylinder engine, 5-speed manual transmission, speed-sensitive variable-assist power steering, anti-lock 4-wheel disc brakes, driver- and passenger-side air bags, dual control air conditioning, cloth or leatherette reclining bucket seats with height/tilt adjustments, split folding rear seat (318is), power windows and locks, power mirrors, power sunroof, AM/FM cassette, power diversity antenna, tachometer, trip odometer, digital clock, outside temperature display, tinted glass, intermittent wipers, rear defogger, Service Interval Indicator, Active Check Control system, toolkit, 185/65HR15 tires (318i), 205/60HR15 tires (318is), full-size spare tire. **325 models** add: 2.5-liter DOHC 6-cylinder engine, cruise control, fog lights, 8-way power front seats, premium sound system, 205/60HR15 tires. **325is and 325iC** add: leather upholstery, split folding rear seat (325is).

Optional Equipment:

4-speed automatic transmission	900	740	819
Limited-slip differential	530	530	482
Cruise control, 318i and 318is	695	570	632
Split folding rear seat, 318i and 325i	275	225	250

	Retail Price	Dealer Invoice	Fair Price
Leather upholstery, 325i	$1150	$940	$1047
Rollover Protection System, 325iC	1390	1140	1265
All-season traction (ASC+T), 325i, 325is, and 325iC	995	815	905
Sport Pkg. 1, 325i and 325is	875	720	796
Sport seats, sport suspension, cross-spoke wheels.			
Sport Pkg. 2, 325i convertible	600	495	546
Sport seats, cross-spoke wheels.			
Heated front seats and heated mirrors	450	370	410
On-board computer, 325i, 325is, and 325iC	430	355	391
Metallic paint	475	390	432

BMW 5-Series

	Retail Price	Dealer Invoice	Fair Price
525i 4-door notchback	$38425	$32200	$35735
525i Touring 5-door wagon	40600	34025	37758
530i 4-door notchback	41500	33780	38595
530i Touring 5-door wagon	45800	38385	42594
540i 4-door notchback	47500	39805	44175
Destination charge	450	450	450
Gas Guzzler Tax, 530i with manual transmission and 540i	1000	1000	1000

Standard Equipment:

525i: 2.5-liter DOHC 6-cylinder engine, 5-speed manual transmission, variable-assist power steering, anti-lock 4-wheel disc brakes, driver- and passenger-side air bags, cruise control, air conditioning with dual climate controls, 10-way power front seats, leather seats, leather-wrapped steering wheel, wood interior trim, folding center armrests, anti-theft AM/FM stereo cassette, telescopic steering column, power windows and locks, heated power mirrors, fog lights, tinted glass, tachometer, map lights, intermittent wipers, heated windshield-washer jets, heated driver-side door lock, rear defogger, seatback pockets, trip odometer, power sunroof, Service Interval Indicator, Active Check Control system, fuel economy indicator, lighted visor mirrors, toolkit, 205/60HR15 tires, alloy wheels. **525i Touring** adds: 4-speed automatic transmission, split folding rear seat, cargo area cover, 225/60VR15 tires. **530i** adds to 525i: 3.0-liter DOHC V-8 engine, outside temperature display, 225/60ZR15 tires. **530i Touring** adds to 525i Touring: 3.0-liter DOHC V-8 engine, 5-speed automatic transmission, ASC+T traction control, 225/60ZR15 tires. **540i** adds to 530i: 4.0-liter DOHC V-8 engine, 5-speed automatic transmission, on board computer.

BMW

Optional Equipment:

	Retail Price	Dealer Invoice	Fair Price
4-speed automatic transmission, 525i............	$900	$740	$820
5-speed automatic transmission, 530i............	1100	900	1000
ASC+T traction control, 525i and			
525i Touring	995	815	905
530i and 540i	1350	1110	1230
Power sunroof, 530i Touring	1325	1090	1208
Heated front seats	370	305	338
On Board Computer (std. 540i)	430	355	393
Luggage net, Touring	260	215	238

BMW 7-Series

	Retail Price	Dealer Invoice	Fair Price
740i 4-door notchback	$55950	$45745	$50745
740iL 4-door notchback	59950	49015	54015
750iL 4-door notchback	83950	68640	73640
Destination charge	450	450	450
Gas Guzzler Tax, 740i, 740iL	1000	1000	1000
750iL	3000	3000	3000

Standard Equipment:

740i/740iL: 4.0-liter DOHC V-8 engine, 5-speed automatic transmission, anti-lock 4-wheel disc brakes, variable-assist power steering, driver- and passenger-side air bags, automatic climate control system with dual controls, 10-way power front seats with driver-side memory system, driver-seat lumbar support adjustment, power tilt/telescopic steering wheel with memory, leather and walnut interior trim, door pockets, power windows and locks, heated power mirrors with 3-position memory, intermittent wipers, heated windshield-washer jets, heated driver-side door lock, cruise control, rear head restraints, rear armrest with storage, automatic dimming mirror, front and rear reading lamps, tinted glass, lighted visor mirrors, Service Interval Indicator, Active Check Control system, on board computer, rear defogger, power sunroof, fog lamps, AM/FM cassette, luggage net, toolkit, 225/60ZR15 tires, alloy wheels, full-size spare tire. **750iL** adds: 5.0-liter V-12 engine, 4-speed automatic transmission, ASC+T traction control, heated front seats, cellular telephone, 6-disc CD changer, power rear sunshade, ski sack.

Optional Equipment:

EDC (Electronic Damping Control)	1500	1200	1395
Heated front seats, 740i, 740iL	370	305	344
Power rear sunshade, 740iL	465	370	432

CONSUMER GUIDE®

	Retail Price	Dealer Invoice	Fair Price
ASC+T traction control, 740i and 740iL	$1350	$1110	$1256
Ski sack, 740i and 740iL	190	155	177

BUICK

Buick Century	Retail Price	Dealer Invoice	Fair Price
Special 4-door notchback	$15495	$13868	$14368
Special 5-door wagon	16345	14629	15129
Special 5-door wagon (California)...................	15995	—	—
Custom 4-door notchback	16695	14608	15108
Destination charge	525	525	525

California wagon dealer invoice and fair price not available at time of publication. California wagon price includes destination charge.

Standard Equipment:

Special: 2.2-liter 4-cylinder engine, 3-speed automatic transmission, anti-lock brakes, driver-side air bag, door-mounted automatic front seatbelts, power steering, air conditioning, automatic power door locks, tilt steering wheel, intermittent wipers, left remote and right manual mirrors, tinted glass, trip odometer, map lights, 55/45 cloth seats with armrest, power front seatback recliners, AM/FM radio with digital clock and seek and scan, body-color bodyside molding, 185/75R14 tires. **Wagon** has: remote tailgate release, split-folding rear seatback, cargo area light, cargo area storage compartments, black bodyside molding. **California wagon** adds: cruise control, power windows, rear defogger, rear-facing third seat, front storage armrest, roof luggage carrier, air deflector, cargo area cover, visor mirrors, 185/75R14 whitewall tires. **Custom** adds: front storage armrest, cup holders, covered visor mirrors, bright wheel opening moldings, door courtesy lights, whitewall tires.

Optional Equipment:

3.1-liter V-6 engine	610	525	555
4-speed automatic transmission	200	172	182
Requires 3.1-liter V-6 engine.			
Luxury Pkg. SD, Special 4-door	582	501	530
Special wagon	737	634	671
Cruise control, rear defogger, covered visor mirrors, front storage armrest, 185/75R14 whitewall tires, front and rear floormats. Wagon also includes roof luggage carrier, and air deflector.			
Prestige Pkg. SE, Special 4-door	1244	1070	1132

Prices are accurate at time of publication; subject to manufacturer's change.

BUICK

	Retail Price	Dealer Invoice	Fair Price
Special wagon	$1593	$1370	$1450

Pkg. SD plus power windows and mirrors, remote trunk release, cassette player, mirror reading lights, trunk net. Wagon also includes rear-facing third seat and swing-out vent window, cargo area security cover.

	Retail Price	Dealer Invoice	Fair Price
Luxury Pkg. SD, Custom 4-door	1254	1078	1141

Includes cruise control, rear defogger, power windows and mirrors, cassette player, automatic power antenna, remote trunk release, mirror reading lights, trunk net, front and rear floormats, accent stripes, 195/75R14 whitewall tires.

	Retail Price	Dealer Invoice	Fair Price
Prestige Pkg. SE, Custom 4-door	1856	1596	1689

Custom 4-door Pkg. SD plus 6-way power driver's seat, remote keyless entry, lighted visor mirrors, premium speaker system.

	Retail Price	Dealer Invoice	Fair Price
Remote keyless entry	135	116	123
Decklid luggage rack, notchbacks	115	99	105
Cassette player, Special and Special w/Pkg. SD	140	120	127
CD player, Special and Special w/Pkg. SD	414	356	377
Special w/Pkg. SE, Custom w/ Pkg. SD/SE	274	236	249
Premium speakers, notchbacks	70	60	64
Wagon	35	30	32
Power antenna, Special	85	73	77
Requires power windows.			
Power windows, Special	330	284	300
6-way power driver's seat, Custom, Custom w/Pkg. SD, (NA wagon)	305	262	300
Bodyside stripes, Special	45	39	41
Bodyside woodgrain trim, wagon	350	301	318
Leather and vinyl 55/45 seat w/storage armrest, notchbacks	500	430	455
Rear wiper, wagon	85	73	77
Lighted visor mirrors, Special	92	79	84
Requires mirror reading lights.			
Mirror reading lights, Special	6	5	5
Remote decklid release, notchbacks	60	52	55
Door edge guards	25	22	23
Heavy duty engine and transmission cooling	40	34	36
Requires 3.1-liter V-6 engine.			
Locking wire wheel covers	240	206	218
Styled steel wheels, Special	115	99	105
Alloy wheels	295	254	268
185/75R14 whitewall tires, Special	68	58	62

	Retail Price	Dealer Invoice	Fair Price
195/75R14 tires, Special	$40	$34	$36
195/75R14 whitewall tires, Special	108	93	98
Special w/Pkg. SD/SE	40	34	36

Buick LeSabre	Retail Price	Dealer Invoice	Fair Price
Custom 4-door notchback	$20860	$18253	$18853
Custom 4-door notchback (California)	19995	—	—
Limited 4-door notchback	24420	21368	21968
Destination charge	575	575	575

California model dealer invoice and fair price not available at time of publication. California model includes destination charge.

Standard Equipment:

Custom: 3.8-liter V-6, 4-speed automatic transmission, anti-lock brakes, driver- and passenger-side air bags, power steering, air conditioning, power door locks, power windows with driver-side express down and passenger lockout, AM/FM radio with clock, tilt steering wheel, intermittent wipers, Pass-Key theft-deterrent system, body-color left remote and right manual mirrors, tinted glass, instrument panel courtesy lights, trip odometer, 55/45 cloth seats with armrest, manual front seatback recliners, 205/70R15 all-season tires, wheel covers. **California model** adds: 6-way power driver's seat, storage armrest, power mirrors, rear defogger, AM/FM cassette player, trunk net, striping, floormats, alloy wheels. **Limited** adds to Custom: variable-assist power steering, cruise control, rear defogger, remote keyless entry, remote decklid release, 6-way power driver's seat, front storage armrest with cup holders, cassette player, power mirrors, power antenna, passenger-side lighted visor mirror, front and rear door courtesy lights, front and rear reading lights, floormats, trunk net, 205/70R15 all-season whitewall tires, alloy wheels.

Optional Equipment:

Traction control system, Limited	175	151	159
Luxury Pkg. SD, Custom	1106	951	1006

Includes cruise control, rear defogger, cassette player, front seat storage armrest, trunk net, floormats, striping, 205/70R15 all-season whitewall tires, alloy wheels.

Prestige Pkg. SE, Custom	1852	1593	1685

Pkg. SD plus remote keyless entry system, power mirrors, remote decklid release, 6-way power driver's seat, power antenna, passenger-side lighted visor mirror, door edge guards.

Prestige Pkg. SE, Limited	670	576	610

Prices are accurate at time of publication; subject to manufacturer's change.

BUICK

	Retail Price	Dealer Invoice	Fair Price
Includes 6-way power passenger seat, dual control air conditioning with rear seat climate controls, AM stereo, cornering lamps.			
Gran Touring Pkg., Custom w/Pkg. SE, and Limited	$399	$343	$363
Includes Gran Touring Suspension, 3:06 axle ratio, automatic level control, leather-wrapped steering wheel, 215/60R16 touring tires, alloy wheels.			
Trailer Towing Pkg., w/o Gran Touring Pkg.	325	280	296
w/Gran Touring Pkg.	150	129	137
Engine and transmission oil coolers, automatic level control.			
Leather/vinyl 55/45 seat, Limited	500	430	455
Gauges and tachometer, Limited	163	140	148
6-way power driver's seat, Custom w/Pkg. SD	305	262	278
Requires Power mirrors.			
Power mirrors, Custom w/Pkg. SD	78	67	71
U1L audio system, Custom w/SE, and Limited w/SD	120	103	109
Includes cassette player, AM stereo, Concert Sound II speakers.			
UM3 audio system, Custom w/Pkg. SE, and Limited	364	313	331
Limited w/Pkg. SE	244	210	222
Includes CD player, AM stereo, Concert Sound II speakers.			
Alloy wheels, Custom	325	280	296
Locking wire wheel covers, Custom w/Pkg. SD/SE, and Limited	NC	NC	NC
205/70R15 whitewall tires, Custom	76	65	69

Buick Park Avenue	Retail Price	Dealer Invoice	Fair Price
4-door notchback	$26999	$23354	$24054
Ultra 4-door notchback	31699	27420	28620
Destination charge	625	625	625

Standard Equipment:

3.8-liter V-6 engine, 4-speed automatic transmission, anti-lock brakes, variable-assist power steering, driver- and passenger-side air bags, air conditioning, 55/45 cloth reclining front seat with storage armrest and cup holders, 6-way power driver's seat, automatic level control, power windows with driver-side express down and passenger lockout, power door locks, power mirrors, overhead console, cruise control, rear defogger, tilt steering wheel, AM/FM cassette player, solar-control tinted glass, Pass-Key theft-deterrent system, remote decklid and fuel door releases, front and rear reading and courtesy lights, passenger-side lighted visor mirror, intermittent wipers, trip odometer, 205/70R15 tires, alloy wheels. **Ultra** adds: supercharged 3.8-liter V-6 engine, automatic climate control with dual temperature controls, rear seat climate controls, 6-way power front seats with power recliners, leather upholstery, leather-wrapped steering wheel, rear head restraints, remote keyless entry system, illuminated entry system with retained accessory power, Twilight Sentinel headlamp control, analog gauge cluster with tachometer, trip odometer, coolant temperature and oil pressure gauges, power antenna, power decklid pulldown, automatic programmable power door locks, Reminder Pkg. (includes low washer fluid, low coolant, and door ajar indicators), theft-deterrent system with starter interrupt, trunk net, cornering lamps, automatic day/night inside rearview mirror, Concert Sound II speakers, lighted driver-side visor mirror, trunk net, 4-note horn, 215/70R15 all-season tires.

Optional Equipment:	Retail Price	Dealer Invoice	Fair Price
Luxury Pkg. SD, base	$1821	$1566	$1657

Includes power passenger seat with power recliner, illuminated entry with retained accessory power, remote keyless entry, dual air conditioning controls, theft-deterrent system with starter interrupt, automatic programmable door locks, power decklid pulldown, power antenna, automatic day/night inside rearview mirror, driver-side visor mirror, analog gauge cluster, lamp monitors, Twilight Sentinel headlamp control, Concert Sound II speakers, cornering lamps, Reminder Pkg. (includes low washer fluid, low coolant, and door ajar indicators), door edge guards, trunk net, 4-note horn, 215/70R15 whitewall tires.

Prestige Pkg. SE, base	2496	2147	2271

Pkg. SD plus AM stereo with music search, steering wheel radio controls, heated outside mirrors with automatic left day/night mirror, memory driver's seat and mirrors, rear seat climate controls, self-sealing tires, trunk mat.

Luxury Pkg. SD, Ultra	730	628	664

Includes automatic ride control, traction control system, AM stereo with music search, steering wheel radio and temperature controls.

Prestige Pkg. SE, Ultra	1245	1071	1133

Pkg. SD plus heated outside mirrors with automatic left day/night mirror, heated driver's seat, memory driver's seat and mirrors, self-sealing tires, trunk mat.

AM/FM cassette, base w/SD, Ultra	50	43	46

Includes AM stereo with music search and Concert Sound II speakers.

Delco-Bose music system with AM stereo,			
Ultra	723	622	658
Ultra w/SD/SE	673	579	612
CD player with AM stereo, base	364	313	331

Prices are accurate at time of publication; subject to manufacturer's change.

BUICK

	Retail Price	Dealer Invoice	Fair Price
Base w/SD, and Ultra	$294	$253	$268
Base w/SE, and Ultra w/SD/SE	244	210	222
Astroroof, base w/SE	918	789	835
Ultra w/SD/SE	802	690	730
Deletes lamp monitors and rear vanity mirrors.			
Trailering Pkg.	150	129	137
w/Gran Touring Pkg.	123	106	112
Includes auxiliary transmission oil and engine oil cooling, Gran Touring suspension and 3:06 axle ratio.			
Gran Touring Pkg., base	224	193	204
Includes Gran Touring suspension, 215/60R16 touring tires, 3:06 axle ratio, alloy wheels, leather-wrapped steering wheel.			
Automatic level control, base w/SE	380	327	346
Traction control system, base w/SD/SE	175	151	159
Leather/vinyl 55/45 seat w/storage armrest, base	500	430	455
Heated driver's seat, base w/SE	105	90	96
Ultra w/SD	60	52	55
Self-sealing tires, base and Ultra w/o SE	150	129	137
205/70R15 whitewall tires, base	76	65	69
Wire wheel covers	NC	NC	NC

Buick Regal

	Retail Price	Dealer Invoice	Fair Price
Custom 2-door notchback	$17999	$15749	$16249
Custom 3800 4-door notchback (California)	18695	—	—
Custom 4-door notchback	18299	16012	16512
Custom V-6 4-door notchback (California)	19495	—	—
Custom V-6 leather 4-door notchback (California)	18995	—	—
Limited 4-door notchback	19799	17324	17824
Gran Sport 2-door notchback	19999	17499	17999
Gran Sport 2-door notchback (California)	18995	—	—
Gran Sport 4-door notchback	20299	17761	18261
Destination charge	525	525	525

California models' dealer invoice and fair price not available at time of publication. California models include destination charge.

Standard Equipment:

Custom: 3.1-liter V-6 engine, 4-speed automatic transmission, driver-side air bag, anti-lock 4-wheel disc brakes, power steering, air conditioning, door-mounted automatic front seatbelts, automatic power door locks, power windows with driver-side express down and passenger lockout, tilt steering wheel, cloth reclining 55/45 front seat with storage armrest and cup holders, front seatback recliners, tinted glass, intermittent wipers, Pass-Key theft-deterrent system, left remote and right manual mirrors, visor mirrors, AM/FM radio with clock, 205/70R15 tires, wheel covers. **California Custom 3800 and Custom V-6** add: 3.8-liter V-6 engine, cruise control, bucket seats, 6-way power driver's seat, leather upholstery (Custom 3800), rear defogger (Custom 3800), dual climate controls, remote keyless entry ststem, remote decklid release, AM/FM cassette player, Concert Sound speakers, power antenna, power mirrors, overhead reading/courtesy lights, trunk net, floormats, alloy wheels. **California Custom V-6 leather** adds to Custom V-6: leather upholstery, rear defogger. **Limited** adds to Custom: 3.8-liter V-6 engine, 4-way manual driver's seat and 2-way manual passenger's seat, seatback map pockets, front overhead courtesy/reading lights. **Gran Sport** adds: Gran Touring suspension, leather-wrapped steering wheel, cloth reclining bucket seats, console with armrest, storage, and cup holders, fog lamps (2-door), body-color grille, 225/60R16 all-season tires, alloy wheels. **California Gran Sport 2-door** adds: cruise control, dual climate controls, remote keyless entry system, 6-way power driver's seat, rear defogger, power mirrors, AM/FM cassette player, Concert Sound speakers, power antenna, remote decklid release, reading/ courtesy lights, trunk net, floormats.

Optional Equipment:

	Retail Price	Dealer Invoice	Fair Price
3.8-liter V-6	$395	$340	$359
Luxury Pkg. SD, Custom	848	729	772

Power mirrors, power antenna, cruise control, rear defogger, remote decklid release, cassette tape player, trunk net, floormats.

Prestige Pkg. SE, Custom 2-door	1432	1232	1303
Custom 4-door	1443	1241	1313

Pkg. SD plus remote keyless entry, front and rear courtesy/reading lights, 6-way power driver's seat, Concert Sound II speakers, trunk net.

Luxury Pkg. SD, Limited 4-door	918	789	835

Power mirrors, power antenna, cruise control, rear defogger, remote decklid release, cassette player, dual climate controls, Concert Sound II speakers, floormats.

Prestige Pkg. SE, Limited 4-door	1640	1410	1492

Pkg. SD plus 6-way power driver's seat, remote keyless entry, steering-wheel radio and temperature controls, lighted visor mirrors, door courtesy lights, trunk net.

BUICK

	Retail Price	Dealer Invoice	Fair Price
Luxury Pkg. SD, Gran Sport	$918	$789	$835
Power mirrors, power antenna, cruise control, rear defogger, remote decklid release, dual climate controls, cassette player, Concert Sound II speakers, floormats.			
Prestige Pkg. SE, Gran Sport 2-door	1570	1350	1429
4-door	1640	1410	1492
Pkg. SD plus 6-way power driver's seat, remote keyless entry, steering wheel radio and temperature controls, lighted visor mirrors, trunk net. 4-door includes door courtesy lights.			
Gran Touring Pkg., Custom and Limited	675	581	614
Gran Touring suspension, leather-wrapped steering wheel, 225/60R16 tires, alloy wheels.			
UX1 audio system, Custom w/SD/SE, Limited w/SD/SE, Gran Sport w/SD/SE	150	129	137
Includes AM stereo, search and repeat, and equalizer.			
CD player, Custom w/SD/SE, Limited w/SD/SE, Gran Sport w/SD/SE	274	236	249
Steering wheel radio and temperature controls, Custom w/SD/SE	125	108	114
Concert Sound II speakers, Custom w/SD	70	60	64
Power antenna, Custom	85	73	77
Remote keyless entry, Limited w/SD, Gran Sport w/SD	135	116	123
Power sunroof, Custom w/SE, Limited w/SE, Gran Sport w/SE	695	598	632
Gran Sport also requires 6-way power driver's seat.			
6-way power driver's seat, Custom w/SD	305	262	278
Limited w/SD, Gran Sport w/SD	270	232	246
Dual 6-way power front seats, Limited w/SE, Gran Sport w/SE	305	262	278
Leather/vinyl 55/45 front seat, Limited	500	430	455
Leather/vinyl bucket seats, Limited and Gran Sport	500	430	455
Lighted visor mirrors, Custom w/SE	92	79	84
Rear defogger delete, (credit)	(170)	(146)	(146)
Heavy duty cooling	150	129	137
Includes engine oil cooler. Requires 3.8-liter V-6 engine.			
Decklid luggage rack	115	99	105
Chrome bodyside/fascia molding, Custom 2-door w/SE	150	129	137

	Retail Price	Dealer Invoice	Fair Price
Door edge guards, Limited w/SE	$25	$22	$23
Engine block heater	18	15	16
Wire wheel covers, Custom and Limited	240	206	218
15-inch alloy wheels, Custom and Limited	325	280	296

Buick Roadmaster	Retail Price	Dealer Invoice	Fair Price
4-door notchback	$23999	$20999	$21599
4-door notchback (California)	22995	—	—
Estate 5-door wagon	25599	22399	22999
Limited 4-door notchback	26399	23099	23699
Destination charge	575	575	575

California model dealer invoice and fair price not available at time of publication. California model includes destination charge.

Standard Equipment:

5.7-liter V-8 engine, 4-speed automatic transmission, anti-lock brakes, driver- and passenger-side air bags, power steering, air conditioning, power windows with driver-side express down and passenger lockout, power door locks, Pass-Key theft-deterrent system with starter interrupt, AM/FM radio, cloth 55/45 seats with storage armrest and manual seatback recliners, front seatback map pockets, tilt steering wheel, remote decklid release, inside day/night mirror with reading lights, left remote and right manual mirrors, delayed illuminated entry, tinted glass, rear defogger, intermittent wipers, analog gauge cluster with coolant temperature and oil pressure gauges, trip odometer, low fuel warning light, windshield washer fluid, oil, voltage, and coolant level indicators, oil life monitor, visor mirrors, 4-note horn, trunk net, floormats, 235/70R15 all-season whitewall tires, wheel covers. **California model** adds: 6-way power driver's seat, leather upholstery, climate control, remote keyless entry, automatic door locks, power mirrors, Concert sound speakers, illuminated entry system, door courtesy/warning lights. **Estate Wagon** adds: variable-assist steering, luggage rack, solar-control windshield, rear window wiper/washer, vista roof, woodgrain exterior trim, 225/75R15 tires, alloy wheels. **Limited** adds to base: variable-assist steering, automatic climate control, power antenna, remote keyless entry, automatic door locks, front door courtesy and warning lights, automatic day/night rearview mirror, lighted visor mirrors, cassette player, 6-way power front seats with power recliners.

Optional Equipment:

Luxury Pkg. SD, base sedan	858	738	755

6-way power driver's seat, power heated mirrrors, automatic climate control, power antenna, cassette player, Concert Sound speakers.

Luxury Pkg. SD, wagon	1467	1262	1291

Prices are accurate at time of publication; subject to manufacturer's change.

BUICK

6-way power driver's seat, cruise control, automatic climate control, automatic day/night rearview mirror, power heated mirrors, power antenna, storage armrest, front door courtesy and warning lights, cassette player, cargo area security cover, vista shade, floormats.

	Retail Price	Dealer Invoice	Fair Price
Prestige Pkg. SE, base sedan	$1565	$1346	$1377

Pkg. SD plus power passenger seat, automatic power door locks, remote keyless entry, door courtesy and warning lights, automatic day/night rearview mirror, lighted visor mirrors.

Prestige Pkg. SE, Limited	350	301	308

Power decklid pull-down, Twilight Sentinel headlamp control, cornering lamps, self-sealing tires.

Prestige Pkg. SE, wagon	2144	1844	1887

Pkg. SD plus 6-way power passenger seat, remote keyless entry, automatic door locks, Twilight Sentinel headlamp control, lighted visor mirrors, cornering lamps.

Trailer Towing Pkg., wagon	325	280	286
Base sedan, Limited w/SD	375	323	330
Limited w/SE	225	194	198

2.93 axle ratio, heavy duty engine and transmission cooling, automatic level control, engine oil cooler; sedans add heavy duty suspension and solar-control windshield.

Limited-slip differential	100	86	88
Heavy-duty cooling, wagon	150	129	132
Base sedan w/SD/SE, Limited	200	172	176

Sedans include solar-control windshield.

Automatic level control	175	151	154

Requires SD or SE Pkg.

Leather 55/45 seats, base 4-door,

Limited	760	654	669
wagon	540	464	475

AM/FM cassette player, wagon

w/SD/SE	185	159	163
Base sedan w/SD/ SE, Limited	150	129	132

Includes equalizer, AM stereo, clock and premium speakers.

AM/FM CD player, wagon w/SD/SE	429	369	378
Base sedan w/SD/SE, Limited	394	339	347

Includes equalizer, AM stereo, clock and premium speakers.

Programmable door locks	25	22	22

Requires SD Pkg. and remote keyless entry.

Remote keyless entry	135	116	119

Requires SD Pkg. and automatic door locks.

Lower accent paint, sedans w/SD/SE	150	129	132
Third seat delete (credit), wagon	(215)	(185)	(185)
Vinyl landau roof, sedans w/SD/SE	695	598	612

	Retail Price	Dealer Invoice	Fair Price
Alloy wheels, sedans	$325	$280	$286
Self-sealing 235/70R15 tires, base sedan, wagon, Limited w/SD	150	129	132
Full-size spare tire, sedans	65	56	57
Full-size spare tire with alloy wheel, sedans	115	99	101

Buick Skylark

	Retail Price	Dealer Invoice	Fair Price
Custom 2-door notchback	$13599	$12715	$13115
Custom 2-door notchback (California Pkg. 1)..................................	13995	—	—
Custom 2-door notchback (California Pkg. 2)..................................	14995	—	—
Custom V-6 2-door notchback (California)..	15795	—	—
Custom 4-door notchback	13599	12715	13115
Custom 4-door notchback (California Pkg. 1)..................................	13995	—	—
Custom 4-door notchback (California Pkg. 2)..................................	14995	—	—
Limited 4-door notchback	16199	14660	15060
Gran Sport (GS) 2-door notchback	18299	16561	16961
Gran Sport (GS) 4-door notchback	18299	16561	16961
Destination charge	485	485	485

California models' dealer invoice and fair price not available at time of publication. California models include destination charge.

Standard Equipment:

Custom: 2.3-liter 4-cylinder engine, 3-speed automatic transmission, driver-side air bag, anti-lock brakes, door-mounted automatic front seatbelts, power steering, tilt steering wheel, cloth 55/45 split bench seat with seat-back recliners, trip odometer, AM/FM radio, tinted glass, automatic power locks, remote fuel door and decklid releases, left remote and right manual mirrors, overhead console with courtesy lights, rear courtesy/reading lights, bright grille, 185/75R14 tires, wheel covers. **California Pkg. 1 models** add: air conditioning, cruise control, 4-way manual driver's seat (4-door), rear defogger, intermittent wipers, armrest with storage, tilt steering wheel, floormats. **California Pkg. 2** adds to Pkg. 1: 4-speed automatic transmission, 195/65R15 touring tires, deluxe wheel covers. **California Custom V-6 2-door** adds to Custom 2-door: 3.1-liter V-6 engine, 4-speed automatic transmission, air conditioning, cruise control, rear defogger, intermittent wipers, AM/FM cassette player, bucket seats, 4-way manual driver's seat,

BUICK

tachometer, oil pressure and coolant temperature gauges, voltmeter, trip odometer, floormats, 195/65R15 touring tires. **Limited** adds to Custom: air conditioning, cruise control, tachometer, oil pressure and coolant temperature gauges, power windows, intermittent wipers, 4-way manual driver's seat, front storage armrest, visor mirrors. **GS** adds: 3.1-liter V-6 engine, 4-speed automatic transmission, Gran Touring suspension, reclining leather/cloth bucket seats, split folding rear seatback, leather-wrapped steering wheel and shift handle, body-color grille, lower accent paint, trunk net, floormats, 205/55R16 tires, alloy wheels.

Optional Equipment:

	Retail Price	Dealer Invoice	Fair Price
3.1-liter V-6 engine (std. GS)	$410	$353	$373
4-speed automatic transmission (std. GS)	200	172	182
Air conditioning, Custom	830	714	755
Luxury Pkg. SD, Custom	1623	1396	1477

Air conditioning, rear defogger, cruise control, tilt steering wheel, intermittent wipers, 4-way driver's seat, front seat storage armrest, floormats.

	Retail Price	Dealer Invoice	Fair Price
Prestige Pkg. SE, Custom 2-door	2087	1795	1899
Custom 4-door	2152	1851	1958

Pkg. SD plus cassette player, power windows, covered visor mirrors.

	Retail Price	Dealer Invoice	Fair Price
Prestige Pkg. SE, Limited	1013	871	922

6-way power driver's seat, rear defogger, power mirrors, cassette player, power antenna, Concert Sound speakers, lighted visor mirrors, reading lights, floormats, trunk net.

	Retail Price	Dealer Invoice	Fair Price
Prestige Pkg. SE, GS	1083	931	986

6-way power driver's seat, rear defogger, power mirrors, remote keyless entry, cassette player, power antenna, Concert Sound speakers, lighted visor mirrors, reading lights.

	Retail Price	Dealer Invoice	Fair Price
6-way power driver's seat, Custom w/SD/SE, Limited w/SD, GS w/SD	270	232	246
Bucket seats and full console, Custom w/SE and Limited w/SE	160	138	146
Split folding rear seat, Limited w/SE	150	129	137
Analog gauge cluster, Custom w/SD/SE	126	108	115

Includes tachometer, trip odometer, voltmeter, oil pressure and coolant temperature gauges.

	Retail Price	Dealer Invoice	Fair Price
Power mirrors, Custom w/SD/SE, Limited w/SE, GS w/SE	78	67	71
Remote keyless entry system, Limited w/SE	135	116	123
Gran Touring suspension, Limited w/SE	27	23	25

Requires 3.1-liter engine.

	Retail Price	Dealer Invoice	Fair Price
Power antenna	$85	$73	$77
Cassette player	165	142	150
CD player, Limited w/SE and Gran Sport w/SE	394	339	359
Alloy wheels with 205/55R16 touring blackwall tires, Limited w/SE	575	495	523
Styled polycast wheels, Custom and Limited	115	99	105
195/65R15 blackwall touring tires, Custom and Limited	131	113	119
Requires styled steel wheel covers.			
Styled steel wheel covers, Custom and Limited	28	24	25
Requires 195/65R15 blackwall tires.			
185/75R14 whitewall tires, Custom and Limited	68	58	62

CADILLAC

Cadillac De Ville/Concours	Retail Price	Dealer Invoice	Fair Price
Sedan de Ville 4-door notchback	$32990	$30186	—
Concours 4-door notchback	36950	33480	—
Destination charge	625	625	625

Fair price not available at time of publication.

Standard Equipment:

De Ville: 4.9-liter V-8 engine, 4-speed automatic transmission, anti-lock 4-wheel disc brakes, driver- and passenger-side air bags, variable-assist power steering, reclining power front seats with storage armrest, automatic climate control, outside temperature readout, power windows, automatic power locks, remote keyless entry system, heated power mirrors, cruise control, AM/FM cassette with equalizer, power antenna, automatic parking brake release, Twilight Sentinel, tinted glass, automatic level control, intermittent wipers, Driver Information Center, trip odometer, tilt steering wheel, leather-wrapped steering wheel, power decklid release, remote fuel door release, rear defogger, Pass-Key II anti-theft system, automatic day/night inside rear view mirror, Speed Sensitive Suspension, cornering lamps, floormats, 215/70R15 whitewall tires, alloy wheels. **Concours** adds: 4.6-liter DOHC V-8 engine, traction control, Road-Sensing Suspension, leather seats, Zebrano wood trim, power front seat recliners, driver's seat power

CADILLAC

lumbar support with memory, Active Audio System with cassette and 11 speakers, automatic day/night driver side mirror, power decklid pull-down, trunk mat and cargo net, front and rear lighted visor mirrors and map lights, 225/60HR16 blackwall tires.

Optional Equipment:

	Retail Price	Dealer Invoice	Fair Price
Traction control, De Ville	$175	$149	$158
Option Pkg. 1SB, De Ville	428	364	385
Automatic day/night driver side mirror, lighted visor mirrors, power decklid pull-down, trunk mat and cargo net.			
Heated windshield system	309	263	275
De Ville requires Option Pkg. 1SB.			
Heated front seats, De Ville	310	264	276
Concours	120	102	107
De Ville requires Option Pkg. 1SB and leather seats and includes power recliners.			
Astroroof	1550	1318	1380
Theft-deterrent system	295	251	263
Active Audio System with cassette player, De Ville	274	233	244
with cassette and CD player, De Ville	670	570	596
with cassette and CD player, Concours	396	337	352
Chrome wheels	1195	1016	1064
Alloy wheels, De Ville	NC	NC	NC
White diamond paint	500	425	445
Accent striping	75	64	67

Cadillac Eldorado	Retail Price	Dealer Invoice	Fair Price
2-door notchback	$37290	$32245	$33045
Touring Coupe 2-door notchback	40590	35110	35910
Destination charge	625	625	625

Standard Equipment:

4.6-liter DOHC V-8 engine, 4-speed automatic transmission, anti-lock 4-wheel disc brakes, driver- and passenger-side air bags, speed-sensitive power steering, automatic parking brake release, road-sensing suspension, automatic level control, traction control, automatic climate control, cloth power front bucket seats with power recliners, center console with armrest and storage bins, overhead console, power windows, automatic power locks, remote keyless entry system, cruise control, heated power mirrors, rear defogger, solar-control tinted glass, automatic day/night rearview mirror, Active Audio AM/FM cassette, power antenna, remote fuel door release, power decklid release and pull-down, trip odometer, Driver Information Center, Zebrano wood trim, intermittent wipers, leather-wrapped steering wheel, tilt steering wheel, Pass-Key II anti-theft system, Twilight Sentinel, cornering lamps, reading lights, lighted visor mirrors, floormats, trunk mat and cargo net, 225/60R16 tires, alloy wheels. **Touring Coupe** adds: high-output 4.6-liter V-8 engine, power lumbar adjusters, leather seats, automatic day/night driver-side mirror, theft-deterrent system, fog lamps, 225/60ZR16 tires.

Optional Equipment:

	Retail Price	Dealer Invoice	Fair Price
Sport Appearance Pkg., base	$146	$124	$131
Analog instrumentation, floor console with leather-wrapped shift knob, Touring Coupe alloy wheels.			
Astroroof	1550	1318	1395
Heated windshield system	309	263	278
Leather upholstery, base	650	553	585
Heated front seats	120	102	108
Base requires leather upholstery.			
Power lumbar support, base	292	248	263
Requires leather upholstery.			
Automatic day/night			
rearview mirror, base	110	94	99
Theft-deterrent system, base	295	251	266
Delco/Bose audio system with cassette			
and CD player	972	826	875
White diamond paint	500	425	450
225/60R16 whitewall tires, base	76	65	68
Chrome wheels	1195	1016	1076

Cadillac Fleetwood	Retail Price	Dealer Invoice	Fair Price
4-door notchback	$33990	$31101	$31901
Destination charge	625	625	625

Standard Equipment:

5.7-liter V-8, 4-speed automatic transmission, anti-lock brakes, driver- and passenger-side air bags, variable-assist power steering, traction control, power 55/45 front seat with power recliners and storage armrest, automatic climate control, outside temperature readout, power windows and locks, illuminated entry, cruise control, heated power mirrors, lighted vanity mirrors, Pass-Key II anti-theft deterrent system, AM/FM cassette with equalizer, power antenna, automatic level control, leather-wrapped tilt steering wheel, trip odometer, cornering lamps, automatic parking brake release, tinted glass, intermittent wipers, rear defogger, floormats, door edge guards, Twilight Sentinel, power decklid pulldown and release, trunk mat and cargo net, 235/70R15 whitewall tires, alloy wheels.

Optional Equipment:

	Retail Price	Dealer Invoice	Fair Price
Security Pkg.	$545	$463	$491

Automatic power door locks, remote keyless entry system, remote fuel door release, theft-deterrent system.

Trailer Towing Pkg.	70	60	63
Performance axle ratio, base	NC	NC	NC
Astroroof	1550	1318	1395
Fleetwood Brougham Pkg.			
with cloth trim	1680	1428	1512
with leather trim	2250	1913	2025

Heated front seats, 2-position driver's seat memory feature, power lumbar adjustment, articulating front headrests, rear seat storage armrest with cup holders, rear lighted vanity mirrors, full padded roof, unique trim and alloy wheels, 2.93:1 rear axle ratio.

Leather upholstery, base	570	485	513
Automatic day/night rearview mirror	110	93	99
Compact disc and cassette players	396	337	356
Full padded vinyl roof delete, Brougham	NC	NC	NC
Full padded vinyl roof, base	925	787	833
Chrome wheels	1195	1016	1076
Full size spare tire	95	80	85

Cadillac Seville

	Retail Price	Dealer Invoice	Fair Price
SLS 4-door notchback	$40990	$35456	$36456
STS 4-door notchback	44890	38830	39830
Destination charge	625	625	625

Standard Equipment:

SLS: 4.6-liter DOHC V-8 engine, 4-speed automatic transmission, anti-lock 4-wheel disc brakes, driver- and passenger-side air bags, speed-sensitive power steering, Road-Sensing Suspension, traction control, automatic level control, cloth power front seats with power recliners, center console with armrest and storage bins, overhead console, dual zone automatic climate control with outside temperature display, Zebrano wood trim, power windows, automatic power door locks, cruise control, heated power mirrors, automatic day/night rearview mirror, AM/FM cassette, power antenna, remote fuel door and decklid releases, power decklid pull-down, Driver Information Center, Pass-Key II theft-deterrent system, remote keyless entry, leather-wrapped tilt steering wheel, intermittent wipers, rear defogger, solar-control tinted glass, floormats, decklid liner, trunk mat and cargo net, Twilight Sentinel, cornering lamps, reading lights, lighted visor mirrors, trip odometer, automatic parking brake release, 225/60R16 tires, alloy wheels. **STS** adds: High-output 4.6-liter V-8 engine, touring suspension, leather upholstery, front seat power lumbar adjustment, analog instruments with tachometer, anti-theft alarm, full console, driver-side automatic day/night outside mirror, fog lamps, 225/60ZR16 tires.

Optional Equipment:

	Retail Price	Dealer Invoice	Fair Price
Sport Interior Pkg., SLS.................................	$146	$124	$131
Analog instruments, full center console, leather-wrapped shift knob.			
Astroroof	1550	1318	1395
Anti-theft alarm, SLS.....................................	295	251	266
Heated windshield	309	263	278
Leather upholstery, SLS.................................	650	553	585
Heated front seats	120	102	108
SLS requires leather upholstery.			
Power lumbar adjustment, SLS	292	248	263
Requires leather upholstery.			
Driver-side automatic day/night outside mirror, SLS...................................	110	94	99
Delco/Bose audio system w/cassette and CD players	972	826	875
White diamond paint	500	425	450
Chrome wheels	1195	1016	1076

CHEVROLET

Chevrolet Beretta	Retail Price	Dealer Invoice	Fair Price
2-door notchback	$12415	$11236	$11436
2-door notchback (California Pkg. 1)	12295	—	—
2-door notchback (California Pkg. 2)	12995	—	—
Z26 2-door notchback	15310	13856	14056
Z26 2-door notchback (California)	15995	—	—
Destination charge	485	485	485

California models' dealer invoice and fair price not available at time of publication. California models include destination charge.

Standard Equipment:

2.2-liter 4-cylinder engine, 5-speed manual transmission, anti-lock brakes, driver-side air bag, power steering, air conditioning, automatic door locks, cloth reclining front bucket seats with 4-way manual driver's seat, center shift console with armrest and storage compartment, cup holders, dual

CHEVROLET

remote mirrors, door map pockets, passenger-side visor mirror, tinted glass, AM/FM radio, door pockets, 185/75R14 tires, wheel covers. **California Pkg. 1** adds: 3-speed automatic transmission, rear defogger, intermittent wipers, reading lights, driver-side visor mirror, floormats. **California Pkg. 2** adds to Pkg. 1: 3.1-liter V-6 engine, 4-speed automatic transmission, AM/FM cassette player, tilt steering wheel, trunk net. **Z26** adds: 2.3-liter DOHC 4-cylinder engine, Level II Sport suspension, 4-way manual passenger seat, front seat lumbar supports, body-color grille and mirrors, front lower and rear spoilers, fog lamps, intermittent wipers, Gauge Pkg. with tachometer and trip odometer, cassette player, day/night rearview mirror with reading lamps, trunk net, 205/60R15 tires. **California Z26** adds: 3.1-liter V-6 engine, 4-speed automatic transmission, cruise control, rear defogger, intermittent wipers, tilt steering wheel, power windows, remote decklid release, alloy wheels, floormats.

Optional Equipment:	Retail Price	Dealer Invoice	Fair Price
3.1-liter V-6 engine, base	$1275	$1097	$1122
Z26	525	452	462
Includes 4-speed automatic transmission.			
3-speed automatic transmission,			
base	555	477	488
Preferred Equipment Group 1, base	165	142	145
w/cassette player, add	140	120	123
w/AM stereo and CD player, add	396	341	348
Intermittent wipers, day/night rearview mirror with reading lamps, visor mirrors, trunk net, floormats.			
Preferred Group 2, base	745	641	656
w/cassette player, add	140	120	123
w/AM stereo and CD player, add	396	341	348
Group 1 plus cruise control, tilt-steering wheel, power decklid release, split folding rear seat.			
Preferred Equipment Group 1, Z26	463	398	407
w/AM stereo and CD player, add	256	220	225
Cruise control, tilt steering wheel, power decklid release, floormats.			
Cassette player (std. Z26)	140	120	123
CD player, base	396	341	348
Z26	256	220	225
Rear defogger	170	146	150
Gauge Pkg., base	111	95	98
Includes tachometer, coolant temperature and oil pressure gauges, voltmeter, trip odometer.			
Rear spoiler, base	110	95	97
Removable sunroof	350	301	308
Power windows	275	237	242
Engine block heater	20	17	18

	Retail Price	Dealer Invoice	Fair Price
195/70R14 tires, base	$93	$80	$82
205/60R15 tires (std. Z26)	175	151	154
205/55R16 tires	372	320	327

Chevrolet Camaro

	Retail Price	Dealer Invoice	Fair Price
3-door hatchback	$13399	$12260	—
Convertible	18745	17152	—
Z28 3-door hatchback	16779	15353	—
Z28 convertible	22075	20199	—
Destination charge	490	490	490

Fair price not available at time of publication.

Standard Equipment:

3.4-liter V-6 engine, 5-speed manual transmission, anti-lock brakes, driver- and passenger-side air bags, power steering, reclining front bucket seats with 4-way adjustable driver's seat, center console with cup holders and lighted storage compartment, folding rear seatback, solar-control tinted glass, left remote and right manual black sport mirrors, tilt steering wheel, intermittent wipers, AM/FM cassette, day/night rearview mirror with dual reading lights, Pass-Key theft-deterrent system, tachometer, voltmeter, oil pressure and temperature gauges, trip odometer, low oil level indicator system, covered visor mirrors, door map pockets, rear spoiler, front floormats, 215/60R16 all-season tires. **Z28** adds: 5.7-liter V-8 engine, 6-speed manual transmission, 4-wheel anti-lock disc brakes, limited-slip differential, performance ride and handling suspension, low coolant indicator system, 235/55R16 all-season tires, alloy wheels. **Base and Z28 convertibles** add: rear defogger, power folding top, 3-piece hard boot with storage bag.

Optional Equipment:

4-speed automatic transmission	595	512	—
Air conditioning	895	770	—
Base Preferred Equipment Group 1	1240	1066	—
Air conditioning, cruise control, remote hatch release, fog lamps.			
Base Preferred Equipment Group 2	2036	1751	—
Group 1 plus power windows with driver-side express down, power locks and mirrors, remote illuminated entry and hatch release, leather-wrapped steering wheel, transmission shifter and parking brake release.			
Z28 Preferred Equipment Group 1	1350	1161	—
w/4-speed automatic transmission	1240	1066	—
Air conditioning, cruise control, remote hatch release, fog lamps, engine oil cooler (6-speed manual transmission).			
Z28 Preferred Equipment Group 2	2146	1846	—
w/4-speed automatic transmission	2036	1751	—

Prices are accurate at time of publication, subject to manufacturer's change.

CHEVROLET

	Retail Price	Dealer Invoice	Fair Price

Group 1 plus power windows with driver-side express down, power locks and mirrors, remote illuminated entry and hatch release, leather-wrapped steering wheel, transmission shifter and parking brake release.

Performance Pkg., Z28	310	267	—

Engine oil cooler, Special Handling Suspension System (includes larger stabilizer bars, stiffer shock absorbers and bushings). Requires 6-speed manual transmission and 245/50ZR16 tires. Not available with Groups 1 and 2, power driver's seat or removable roof panels.

6-way power driver's seat	270	232	—
Performance axle ratio	110	95	—

Includes engine oil cooler. Requires 6-speed manual transmission and 245/50ZR16 tires.

Rear defogger	170	146	—
Power locks	220	189	—

Requires Preferred Group 1.

Removable roof panels	895	770	—

Includes locks and storage provisions.

Delco/Bose AM/FM cassette player	275	237	—
Delco/Bose AM/FM CD player	531	457	—
Color-keyed bodyside moldings	60	52	—
235/55R16 all-season tires, base	132	114	—

Requires alloy wheels.

245/50ZR16 tires, Z28	144	124	—
Alloy wheels, base..	275	237	—

Chevrolet Caprice

	Retail Price	Dealer Invoice	Fair Price
Classic 4-door notchback	$18995	$16620	$17020
Classic 4-door notchback (California)	17995	—	—
Classic LS 4-door notchback	21435	18756	19156
Classic LS 4-door notchback (California)........	19995	—	—
5-door wagon	20855	18248	18648
Destination charge	575	575	575

California models' dealer invoice and fair price not available at time of publication. California models include destination charge.

Standard Equipment:

Classic: 4.3-liter V-8 engine, 4-speed automatic transmission, anti-lock brakes, driver- and passenger-side air bags, power steering, air conditioning, cloth bench seat with center armrest, tilt steering wheel, AM/FM radio, Pass-Key theft-deterrent system, tinted glass, trip odometer, oil change monitor, intermittent wipers, door pockets, left remote and right manual mirrors, passenger-side visor mirror, cup holders, floormats, 215/75R15 tires, full wheel covers. **Wagon** has rear-facing third seat, cassette player, luggage rack, 2-way tailgate, rear wiper/washer, power tailgate window release, 225/75R15 whitewall tires. **California model** adds to Classic: cruise control, rear defogger, AM/FM cassette player, power windows with driver-side express down, power mirrors, door locks and decklid release, cloth 55/45 seats, 215/75R15 whitewall tires, full size spare tire, deluxe wheel covers. **Classic LS** adds to Classic: cruise control, power door locks and decklid release, power windows with driver-side express down, power mirrors, power driver's seat, Custom 55/45 cloth seats with recliners and seat-back pockets, front and rear armrests, front and rear reading/courtesy lights, cassette player, driver-side visor mirror, lighted passenger-side visor mirror, trunk net, low fluid level warning lights, cornering lamps, gold grille and striping, alloy wheels. **Classic LS California model** adds to LS: leather 55/45 front seat, rear defogger, 215/75R15 whitewall tires.

Optional Equipment:

	Retail Price	Dealer Invoice	Fair Price
5.7-liter V-8 engine, Classic w/Group 1 or 2, Classic LS, and wagon	$325	$280	$289
Classic and Classic LS requires Sport suspension.			
Preferred Equipment Group 1, Classic	953	820	848
Cruise control, power windows with driver-side express down, power door locks, mirrors, and decklid release.			
w/cassette player, add	175	151	154
w/CD player, add	431	371	379
Preferred Equipment Group 2, Classic	1607	1382	1430
Group 1 plus 6-way power driver's seat, cassette player, power antenna, passenger-side lighted visor mirror, front and rear reading lamps.			
w/CD player, add	256	220	225
Preferred Equipment Group 1, Classic LS	860	740	765
6-way power passenger's seat, remote keyless entry, remote decklid release, rear defogger, heated mirrors, power antenna, automatic day/night rearview mirror.			
w/CD player, add	256	220	225
Preferred Equipment Group 1, wagon	1273	1095	1133
Cruise control, power windows with driver-side express down, power door/tailgate locks, power mirrors.			
w/CD player, add	256	220	225
Preferred Equipment Group 2, wagon	2146	1846	1910
6-way power passenger's seat, rear defogger, heated mirrors, power antenna, automatic day/night rearview mirror, passenger-side lighted visor mirror, rear reading lights, deluxe rear compartment decor, rear compartment security cover.			
w/CD player, add	256	220	225

Prices are accurate at time of publication; subject to manufacturer's change.

CHEVROLET

	Retail Price	Dealer Invoice	Fair Price
Cruise control	$225	$194	$198
Power door locks, Classic	250	215	223
Wagon	325	280	289
Wagon includes tailgate lock.			
Rear defogger	170	146	151
w/heated mirrors	205	176	182
Cloth 55/45 seat, Classic and wagon	223	192	198
NA wagon Group 2.			
Custom cloth 55/45 seat, wagon w/Group 2	342	294	304
Leather 55/45 front seat, Classic LS w/Group 1	645	555	574
Limited-slip differential, notchbacks	250	215	223
wagon	100	86	89
Sport suspension, notchbacks	508	437	452
Increased capacity front and rear shock absorbers, heavy duty front and rear springs, front and rear stabilizer bars.			
Automatic leveling suspension, wagon	175	151	156
Ride/Handling suspension, notchbacks	49	42	44
Trailering Pkg., notchbacks	21	18	19
Includes heavy duty cooling.			
Cassette player	175	151	156
Includes AM/FM radio with seek and scan, auto reverse, digital clock.			
CD player, Classic	431	371	384
Classic LS and wagon	256	220	228
Includes AM/FM radio with seek and scan.			
Woodgrain exterior trim, wagon	595	512	530
2-tone paint	141	121	125
Pinstriping, Classic and wagon	61	52	54
Cargo net	30	26	27
Wire wheel covers, Classic and wagon	215	185	191
Deluxe wheel covers, Classic and wagon	70	60	62
225/75R15 all-season whitewall tires (std. wagon)	(NC)	(NC)	(NC)
215/70R15 all-season whitewall tires	176	151	157
215/75R15 all-season whitewall tires	80	69	71
235/70R15 all-season whitewall tires	90	77	80
Above tires with full-size spare tire	115	99	102
with full-size spare tire and wire wheel covers	65	56	58
235/70R15 all-season tires	(NC)	(NC)	(NC)

	Retail Price	Dealer Invoice	Fair Price
with full-size spare tire	$110	$95	$98
with full-size spare tire and wire wheel covers	60	52	53

Chevrolet Cavalier

	Retail Price	Dealer Invoice	Fair Price
VL 2-door notchback	$8845	$8359	$8559
VL 4-door notchback	8995	8500	8700
VL 2-door notchback (Calif.)	9995	—	—
RS 2-door notchback	10715	10019	10219
RS 4-door notchback	11315	10580	10780
RS 2-door convertible	16995	15890	16390
5-door wagon	11465	10720	10920
Z24 2-door notchback	13995	12665	12865
Z24 2-door convertible	19995	18095	18595
Destination charge	475	475	475

California VL 2-door dealer invoice and fair price not available at time of publication. California VL 2-door price includes destination charge.

Standard Equipment:

VL: 2.2-liter 4-cylinder engine, 5-speed manual transmission, anti-lock brakes, door-mounted automatic front seatbelts, power steering, tinted glass, cloth reclining front bucket seats, automatic power locks, floor console with armrest, left remote and right manual mirrors, 185/75R14 tires, wheel covers. **California VL 2-door** adds: air conditioning, AM/FM cassette player, rear defogger, intermittent wipers, remote decklid release, visor mirrors, floormats. **RS** adds: 3-speed automatic transmission (4-door), air conditioning, AM/FM radio, intermittent wipers, dome/reading light, visor mirrors, easy entry passenger seat (2-door), mechanical decklid release, body-side moldings, striping; **convertible** has 3-speed automatic transmission, power windows with driver-side express down, map light, trunk net, power top. **Wagon** adds to RS 2-door: 3-speed automatic transmission, power tailgate release, split folding rear seat. **Z24** adds: 3.1-liter V-6, 5-speed manual transmission, Level III sport suspension, 4-way manual driver's seat, cassette player, Gauge Package with tachometer, trip odometer, tilt steering wheel, body-color fascias, rear spoiler, 205/60R15 tires, alloy wheels; **convertible** has power windows with driver-side express down, map light, trunk net, power top.

Optional Equipment:

3.1-liter V-6 (NA VL)	834	717	734

Includes Performance Handling Pkg., Level III sport suspension, Gauge Pkg., 195/70R14 tires.

Prices are accurate at time of publication; subject to manufacturer's change.

CHEVROLET

	Retail Price	Dealer Invoice	Fair Price
3-speed automatic transmission (std. wagon and RS 4-door and convertible)	$495	$426	$436
Air conditioning	785	675	691
Preferred Equipment Group 1, VL 2- and 4-door	173	149	152
Remote decklid release, intermittent wipers, visor mirrors, bodyside moldings, floormats.			
Preferred Equipment Group 2, VL 2- and 4-door	543	467	478
Group 1 plus cruise control, tilt steering wheel.			
Preferred Equipment Group 1, wagon	435	374	383
Cruise control, intermittent wipers, tilt steering wheel.			
Preferred Equipment Group 1, RS 2- and 4-door, RS convertible	370	318	326
Cruise control, tilt steering wheel.			
Preferred Equipment Group 1, Z24 2-door......	670	576	590
Cruise control, power windows with driver-side express down, split-folding rear seat, trunk net.			
Roof luggage carrier, wagon w/Group 1	115	99	101
Rear spoiler, RS 2-door	110	95	97
Rear defogger	170	146	150
Split folding rear seat, RS 2- and 4-door	180	155	158
Includes trunk net.			
Vinyl bucket seats, convertibles	75	65	66
Removable sunroof, Z24 2-door	350	301	308
Power windows (NA VL), 2-doors	265	228	233
4-doors and wagons	330	284	290
AM/FM radio, VL	332	286	292
AM/FM cassette, VL	472	406	415
Wagon and RS	140	120	123
AM/FM CD player, VL	728	626	641
Wagon and RS	396	341	348
Z24	256	220	225
Engine block heater	20	17	18
205/60R15 white outline letter tires, Z24	98	84	86

Chevrolet Corsica

	Retail Price	Dealer Invoice	Fair Price
4-door notchback	$13145	$11896	$12196
4-door notchback (California Pkg. 1)	12495	—	—
4-door notchback (California Pkg. 2)	13495	—	—
Destination charge	485	485	485

Dealer invoice and fair price for California models not available at time of publication. California models include destination charge.

Standard Equipment:

2.2-liter 4-cylinder engine, 3-speed automatic transmission, anti-lock brakes, driver-side air bag, door-mounted automatic front seatbelts, power steering, air conditioning, automatic power door locks, cloth reclining front bucket seats, 4-way manual driver's seat, center console with cup holders and storage, AM/FM radio, remote manual mirrors, tinted glass, passenger-side visor mirror, front door pockets, 185/75R14 tires, full wheel covers. **California Pkg. 1** adds: rear defogger, intermittent wipers, reading lights, driver-side visor mirror, trunk net, floormats. **California Pkg. 2** adds to Pkg. 1: 3.1-liter V-6 engine, 4-speed automatic transmission, AM/FM cassette player, tilt steering wheel.

Optional Equipment:	Retail Price	Dealer Invoice	Fair Price
3.1-liter V-6	$720	$619	$634
Includes 4-speed automatic transmission.			
Preferred Equipment Group 1	165	142	145
Intermittent wipers, day/night rearview mirror with reading lights, driver- and passenger-side covered visor mirrors, trunk net, floormats.			
Preferred Equipment Group 2	745	641	656
Group 1 plus cruise control, tilt steering wheel, power decklid release, split folding rear seat with armrest.			
Power windows	340	292	299
Rear defogger	170	146	150
AM/FM cassette player	140	120	123
AM/FM CD player	396	341	348
Styled steel wheels	56	48	49
185/75R14 whitewall tires	68	58	60
Engine block heater	20	17	18

Chevrolet Corvette	Retail Price	Dealer Invoice	Fair Price
3-door hatchback	$36185	$30938	$31938
2-door convertible	42960	36731	38231
Destination charge	550	550	550

Standard Equipment:

5.7-liter V-8, 6-speed manual or 4-speed automatic transmission, anti-lock 4-wheel disc brakes, driver- and passenger-side air bags, power steering, Acceleration Slip Regulation, Pass-Key theft-deterrent system, automatic keyless entry with remote hatch release, air conditioning, liquid-crystal gauges with analog and digital display, AM/FM cassette, power antenna, cruise control, rear defogger, reclining leather bucket seats, center console with coin tray and cassette/CD storage, armrest with lockable storage compartment, leather-wrapped tilt steering wheel, solar-control tint-

Prices are accurate at time of publication; subject to manufacturer's change.

ed glass, heated power mirrors, power windows with driver-side express down, power door locks, intermittent wipers, removable roof panel (hatchback), day/night rearview mirror with reading lights, fog lamps, lighted visor mirrors, Goodyear Eagle GS-C tires (255/45ZR17 front, 285/40ZR17 rear), alloy wheels. **Convertible** adds: manual folding top.

Optional Equipment:

	Retail Price	Dealer Invoice	Fair Price
ZR-1 Special Performance Pkg.	$31258	$26257	—
5.7-liter DOHC V-8, Selective Ride and Handling Pkg., heavy-duty brake system, 6-way power driver's and passenger's seats, leather adjustable sport bucket seats, automatic climate control, low-tire-pressure warning, Delco/Bose Gold audio system with CD and cassette players, 275/40ZR17 front and 315/35ZR17 rear tires, 5-spoke alloy wheels.			
Preferred Equipment Group 1	1333	1120	1186
Automatic climate control, Delco/Bose audio system, 6-way power driver's seat.			
ZO7 Adjustable Performance Handling Pkg.	2045	1718	1820
Selective Ride and Handling Pkg., Bilstein Adjustable Ride Control System, stiffer springs, stabilizer bars, and bushings, heavy-duty brakes, 275/40ZR17 tires. Requires power seats; 4-speed automatic transmission requires performance axle ratio.			
FX3 Selective Ride and Handling Pkg.	1695	1424	1509
Bilstein Adjustable Ride Control System. Requires power seats.			
Leather adjustable sport bucket seats	625	525	556
Requires driver's and passenger's 6-way power seats.			
6-way power seats, each	305	256	271
Delco/Bose system with cassette and CD player with Group 1	396	333	352
Performance axle ratio	50	42	45
Low tire pressure warning indicator	325	273	289
Transparent blue or bronze tint single removable roof panel	650	546	579
Dual transparent blue or bronze tint removable roof panels	950	798	846
Removable hardtop, convertible	1995	1676	1776

Chevrolet Lumina

	Retail Price	Dealer Invoice	Fair Price
4-door notchback	$15305	$13392	$13642
Euro 2-door notchback	16875	14766	15016
Euro 4-door notchback	16515	14451	14701
Euro 4-door notchback (California)	15995	—	—
Z34 2-door notchback	19310	16896	17146
Destination charge	525	525	525

California Euro dealer invoice and fair price not available at time of publication. California Euro includes destination charge.

Standard Equipment:

3.1-liter V-6 engine, 4-speed automatic transmission, 4-wheel disc brakes, power steering, door-mounted automatic front seatbelts, air conditioning, automatic power locks, 60/40 cloth reclining front seat with center armrest and 4-way manual driver-side adjustment, tilt steering wheel, AM/FM radio, visor mirrors, tinted glass, left remote and right manual mirrors, day/night rearview mirror with reading lights, intermittent wipers, floormats, 195/75R14 tires, wheel covers. **Euro** adds: anti-lock brakes, firmer suspension, cassette player, power windows (2-door), rear spoiler, upgraded upholstery, front storage armrest, 205/70R15 tires, alloy wheels. **California Euro** adds: cruise control, cloth bucket or 60/40 split bench seats with 6-way power driver's seat, Delco/Bose Audio System with cassette player, rear defogger, power windows and decklid release, remote mirrors, Gauge Pkg. with tachometer, trunk net. **Z34** adds: 3.4-liter DOHC V-6 engine, cruise control, power windows, reclining cloth bucket seats with 4-way driver-side manual seat adjustment, full floor console, remote mirrors, rear spoiler, Gauge Package with tachometer, power decklid release, trunk net, 225/60R16 tires, alloy wheels.

Optional Equipment:

	Retail Price	Dealer Invoice	Fair Price
Anti-lock brakes, base	$450	$387	$398
Cruise control	225	194	199
Preferred Equipment Group 1, base	790	679	699
Cruise control, power windows and decklid release, remote mirrors, trunk net, decklid luggage rack.			
Group 1 w/o decklid luggage rack	675	581	597
Preferred Equipment Group 1, Euro 2-door	445	383	394
Euro 4-door	775	667	686
Cruise control, power windows (std. 2-door), power decklid release, remote mirrors, Gauge Pkg. with tachometer, trunk net.			
Preferred Equipment Group 1, Euro with BYP Sedan Pkg.	775	667	686
Cruise control, power windows and decklid release, remote mirrors, Gauge Pkg. with tachometer, trunk net.			
Euro 3.4 Sedan Pkg.	1376	1183	1218
3.4-liter DOHC V-6 engine, dual exhaust outlets, sport suspension, reclining cloth bucket seats with full floor console, 4-way manual driver-side seat adjustment, Gauge Pkg. with tachometer, monochromatic color exterior treatment, 225/60R16 tires, alloy wheels.			
Cloth 60/40 front seat with storage armrest	90	77	80
Cloth bucket seats with console, Euro	50	43	44
6-way power driver's seat (NA 2-doors)	270	232	239

Prices are accurate at time of publication; subject to manufacturer's change.

CHEVROLET

	Retail Price	Dealer Invoice	Fair Price
Cassette player	$140	$120	$124
Delco/Bose audio system, base	475	409	420
Euro and Z34	335	288	296
CD player, base	396	341	350
Euro and Z34	256	220	227
Rear defogger	170	146	150
Rear spoiler delete, Euro (credit)	(128)	(110)	(110)
Decklid luggage rack	115	99	102
Cellular telephone provision	45	39	40
195/75R14 whitewall tires, base	72	62	64
215/60R16 tires, Euro	112	96	99

Chevrolet Lumina Minivan	Retail Price	Dealer Invoice	Fair Price
4-door van	$16815	$15218	$15718
4-door van (California)	17495	—	—
Destination charge	530	530	530

California model dealer invoice and fair price not available at time of publication. California model includes destination charge.

Standard Equipment:

3.1-liter V-6, 3-speed automatic transmission, anti-lock brakes, driver-side air bag, power steering, reclining front bucket seats, 4-way manual driver's seat, 3-passenger middle seat, tinted glass with solar-control windshield, lockable center console with cup holders, front and rear reading lights, rear auxiliary power outlet, left remote and right manual mirrors, AM/FM radio, intermittent wipers, rear wiper/washer, 205/70R15 tires, wheel covers. **California** model adds: front air conditioning, cruise control, tilt steering wheel, AM/FM cassette player, rear defogger, power windows, door locks and mirrors, remote keyless entry system, deep-tinted glass, 7-passenger seating with reclining front bucket seats, child safety seats, cargo area net, 205/70R15 touring tires, alloy wheels.

Optional Equipment:

	Retail Price	Dealer Invoice	Fair Price
3.8-liter V-6	$619	$532	$551

Requires 4-speed automatic transmission and air conditioning.

4-speed automatic transmission	200	172	178

Requires 3.8-liter V-6 engine.

Front air conditioning	830	714	739
Front and rear air conditioning	1280	1101	1139

Requires 3.8-liter V-6 engine and Preferred Equipment Group 2 or 3.

Preferred Equipment Group 1	778	669	692

Front air conditioning, cruise control, tilt steering wheel, power door/tailgate locks with side door delay, power mirrors.

	Retail Price	Dealer Invoice	Fair Price
Preferred Equipment Group 2	$2323	$1998	$2067
Group 1 plus cassette player, power windows with driver-side express down, rear defogger, remote keyless entry, deep-tinted glass, 7-passenger seating, cargo area net.			
Preferred Equipment Group 3	2843	2445	2530
Group 2 plus LS Trim Pkg. (includes body-color bumpers and rocker panels, upgraded cloth upholstery) and 6-way power driver's seat.			
7-passenger seating	660	568	587
Two front bucket seats and five modular rear seats.			
Trailering Pkg.	320	275	285
Includes load leveling suspension. Requires 3.8-liter V-6 engine and Preferred Equipment Group 2 or 3.			
Traction Control	350	301	312
Requires Group 3.			
Manual sunroof (NA base or with Group 1) ..	300	258	267
Luggage rack (NA base)	145	125	129
Rear defogger	170	146	151
Deep-tinted glass	245	211	218
Power door/tailgate locks	300	258	267
Power windows (NA base)	275	237	245
Includes driver-side express down.			
Power mirrors	78	67	69
6-way power driver's seat			
(NA base or with Group 1)	270	232	240
Child safety seats	225	194	200
Requires 7-passenger seating.			
Power sliding side door	295	254	263
Requires Group 3.			
Remote keyless entry	125	108	111
Load leveling suspension			
(NA base or with Group 1)	170	146	151
Requires 205/70R15 tires (3.1-liter); 205/70R15 tires and Trailering Pkg. (3.8-liter).			
Cruise control	225	194	200
Tilt steering wheel	145	125	129
Cassette player	140	120	125
CD player	396	341	352
w/Group 2 and 3	256	220	228
Custom 2-tone paint	148	127	132
Cargo area net	30	26	27
205/70R15 touring tires	35	30	31
205/70R15 self-sealing tires	150	129	134
Alloy wheels	275	237	245
Engine block heater	20	17	18

Prices are accurate at time of publication; subject to manufacturer's change.

CHEVROLET

Chevrolet S10 Blazer

	Retail Price	Dealer Invoice	Fair Price
3-door wagon, 2WD	$15438	$13971	$14171
3-door wagon, 4WD	17234	15597	15797
5-door wagon, 2WD	16728	15139	15589
5-door wagon, 4WD	18962	17161	17611
Destination charge	475	475	475

Standard Equipment:

3-door: 4.3-liter V-6, 5-speed manual transmission, anti-lock brakes, power steering, solar-control tinted glass, coolant temperature and oil pressure gauges, voltmeter, AM radio, tow hooks (4WD), dual outside mirrors, front armrests, trip odometer, highback vinyl front reclining bucket seats with folding seatbacks, door map pockets, intermittent wipers, day/night rearview mirror, 205/75R15 tires, full-size spare tire. **5-door** adds: 60/40 reclining cloth front bench seat with storage armrest and cup holders, folding rear bench seat (4WD), Tahoe trim (includes reading lights and illuminated entry, lighted visor mirrors, chrome bumpers and grille, bright bodyside and wheel opening moldings, bright wheel trim rings [4WD], floormats, upgraded interior trim). 4WD models have Insta-Trac part-time 4WD.

Optional Equipment:

RY8 Enhanced Powertrain Pkg.	1160	998	1032

High output 4.3-liter V-6, 4-speed automatic transmission, engine and transmission oil coolers.

Optional axle ratio	(NC)	(NC)	(NC)
Locking differential	252	217	224
Electronic shift transfer case, 4WD	123	106	109
Air conditioning	780	671	694
Tahoe Equipment Group 2,			
2WD 3-door	1378	1185	1226
4WD 3-door	1346	1158	1198

Chrome bumpers and grille, bright bodyside and wheel opening moldings, bright wheel trim rings (4WD), upgraded interior trim, seat separator console, reading lights, lighted visor mirrors, cargo net, tilt steering wheel, cruise control, AM/FM radio, cloth reclining bucket seats with manual lumbar adjustment, folding rear seat, deep-tinted side glass with light-tinted rear window, 205/75R15 white-letter tires.

Tahoe Equipment Group 2,			
2WD 5-door	651	560	579
4WD 5-door	190	163	169

Cruise control, tilt steering wheel, cloth reclining bucket seats with manual lumbar support, folding rear seat (std. 4WD), AM/FM radio, deep-tinted side glass with light-tinted rear window, 205/75R15 white letter tires.

Tahoe Equipment Group 3, 2WD 3-door	2943	2531	2619

	Retail Price	Dealer Invoice	Fair Price
4WD 3-door	$2943	$2531	$2619
2WD 5-door	2365	2034	2105
4WD 5-door	1962	1687	1746

Group 2 plus air conditioning, cassette player, Driver Convenience Pkg. ZM8 (remote tailgate release and rear defogger), Operating Convenience Pkg. (power door locks and windows), rear wiper/washer, luggage carrier, alloy wheels.

Tahoe LT Preferred Equipment Group,

	Retail Price	Dealer Invoice	Fair Price
2WD 3-door	4245	3651	3778
4WD 3-door	4410	3793	3925
2WD 5-door	3776	3247	3361
4WD 5-door	3538	3043	3149

LT trim adds to Tahoe trim reclining leather bucket seats with power lumbar adjustment, 6-way power driver's seat, overhead console, remote keyless entry system, 205/75R15 white letter tires (2WD), 235/75R15 white letter tires (4WD), 2-tone paint, air conditioning, tilt steering wheel, cruise control, power tailgate release, rear defogger, cassette player, deep-tinted glass with light-tinted rear window, rear wiper/washer.

Folding cloth rear seat (std. 4WD 5-door)	435	374	387
with vinyl trim	409	352	364
Deluxe cloth 60/40 reclining bench seat, 5-door	(NC)	(NC)	(NC)
5-door with Tahoe Group 2 or 3 (credit)	(237)	(203)	(203)

Credit when 60/40 reclining cloth bench seat replaces standard reclining cloth bucket seats.

Custom highback vinyl bucket seats (NA 5-doors)	(NC)	(NC)	(NC)
Deluxe cloth highback reclining bucket seats with manual lumbar adjustment,			
3-door	221	190	197
5-door	211	181	188
Deluxe cloth highback reclining bucket seats with power lumbar adjustment and 6-way power driver's seat, 3-door	366	315	326
5-door	501	431	446
3- and 5-door with Tahoe Group 2 or 3	290	249	258
3- and 5-door with Tahoe LT Group (credit)	(650)	(559)	(559)

Requires Operating Convenience Pkg.

Operating Convenience Pkg., 3-door	367	316	327
5-door	542	466	482

Includes power windows with driver-side express down and automatic power door locks.

CHEVROLET

	Retail Price	Dealer Invoice	Fair Price
Driver Convenience Pkg. ZQ3	$383	$329	$341
Includes cruise control and tilt steering wheel.			
Driver Convenience Pkg. ZM8	197	169	175
Includes rear defogger and remote tailgate release.			
Remote keyless entry system	135	116	120
Electronic instrumentation	195	168	174
Air dam with fog lamps	115	99	102
Power mirrors	83	71	74
Heavy duty shock absorbers	40	34	36
Heavy duty front springs	63	54	56
Includes heavy duty shock absorbers.			
Heavy duty battery	56	48	50
Heavy duty cooling system,			
with 5-speed manual transmission	135	116	120
Spare wheel and tire carrier	159	137	142
Cold Climate Pkg., 5-door	109	94	97
3-door	179	154	159
Front console	145	125	129
Overhead console	83	71	74
Luggage carrier, base and Tahoe Group 2 ...	126	108	112
Deep-tinted glass	225	194	200
Tahoe Group 2 and 3, Tahoe LT	81	70	72
with light-tinted rear window			
(std. Tahoe LT)	144	124	128
Rear wiper/washer	125	108	111
Requires Driver Convenience Pkg. ZM8.			
Sliding side window, 3-door	257	221	229
Requires deep-tint glass.			
Radio delete (credit)	(95)	(82)	(82)
AM/FM radio	131	113	117
AM/FM cassette	253	218	225
with Tahoe Group 2	122	105	109
AM/FM cassette with equalizer	403	347	359
with Tahoe Group 2	272	234	242
with Tahoe Group 3 and Tahoe LT	150	129	134
AM/FM CD player	537	462	478
with Tahoe Group 2	406	349	361
with Tahoe Group 3 and Tahoe LT	284	244	253
Shield Pkg. (NA 2WD)	75	65	67
Includes transfer case, front differential skid plates, fuel tank and steering linkage shield.			
Off-road suspension	182	157	162
with Tahoe Group 2 or 3	122	105	109
Trailering Special Equipment (heavy duty)			

	Retail Price	Dealer Invoice	Fair Price
with Enhanced Powertrain Pkg.	$210	$181	$187
with 5-speed manual transmission	345	297	307
Trailering Special Equipment (light duty),			
with Enhanced Powertrain Pkg.	109	94	97
with 5-speed manual transmission	300	258	267
Special 2-tone paint	227	195	202
Custom 2-tone (std. Tahoe LT)	275	237	245
Wheel opening moldings, 3-door	43	37	38
5-door	13	11	12
Rally wheels, 3-door	92	79	82
Alloy wheels	340	292	303
5-door or Tahoe Group 2	248	213	221
Special alloy wheels, 5-door or			
with Tahoe Group 2	280	241	249
205/75R15 on/off-road			
white letter tires	170	146	151
with Tahoe Group 2 or 3	49	42	44
205/75R15 all-season			
white letter tires	121	104	108
235/75R15 all-season			
white letter tires	286	246	255
with Tahoe Group 2 or 3	165	142	147
235/75R15 on/off road white			
letter tires (NA 2WD)	345	297	307
with Tahoe Group 2 or 3	224	193	199

CHRYSLER

Chrysler Concorde	Retail Price	Dealer Invoice	Fair Price
4-door notchback w/Pkg. 22A	$19896	$17427	$18427
Destination charge	525	525	525

Standard Equipment:

Pkg. 22A: 3.3-liter V-6 engine, 4-speed automatic transmission, 4-wheel anti-lock disc brakes, driver- and passenger-side air bags, touring suspension, power steering, air conditioning, tinted glass with solar control front and rear windows, cloth front bucket seats, lumbar adjustment, front console with armrest, tachometer, trip odometer, coolant temperature gauge, AM/FM cassette radio, rear defogger, intermittent wipers, heated power mirrors, tilt steering wheel, cruise control, remote decklid release, visor mirrors, reading lights, trunk cargo net, floormats, 205/70R15 tires.

Prices are accurate at time of publication; subject to manufacturer's change.

CHRYSLER

Optional Equipment:	Retail Price	Dealer Invoice	Fair Price
Pkg. 22B	$596	$506	$566
Power windows and locks, lighted visor mirrors.			
Pkg. 22C/26C	1226	1042	1165
Pkg. 22B plus automatic temperature control, power driver's seat, illuminated/remote entry systems. Pkg. 26C requires 3.5-liter engine.			
Pkg. 22D/26D	2350	1997	2233
Pkg. 26C plus speed-sensitive power steering, Infinity cassette system, overhead console, security alarm, automatic day/night rearview mirror. Pkg. 26D requires 3.5-liter engine.			
3.5-liter V-6 engine	725	616	689
Requires Pkg. 26C or 26D.			
Traction control,			
w/Pkg. 22C, 26C, 22D, or 26D	175	149	166
Integrated child seat	100	85	95
Cloth 50/50 front bench seat	NC	NC	NC
Power driver's seat, w/Pkg. 22B	377	320	358
Power driver's and front passenger's seats,			
w/Pkg. 22B	754	641	716
w/Pkg. 22C, 26C, 22D, or 26D	377	320	358
Leather seats, w/Pkg. 22C,			
26C, 26D	1069	909	1016
Includes power front seats, leather-wrapped steering wheel and shift knob. Not available with integrated child seat.			
Power moonroof, w/Pkg. 22C or 26C	1094	930	1039
w/Pkg. 22D or 26D	716	609	680
Remote/Illuminated Entry System,			
w/Pkg. 22B	221	188	210
Security alarm, w/Pkg. 22C or 26C	149	127	142
Full overhead console, w/Pkg. 22C or 26C	378	321	359
Includes trip computer, compass, outside temperature readout, lighted visor mirrors.			
Chrysler/Infinity cassette system,			
w/Pkg. 22C or 26C	708	602	673
Includes equalizer, 11 speakers, amplifier, power antenna.			
Chrysler/Infinity CD system,			
w/Pkg. 22C or 26C	877	745	833
w/Pkg. 22D or 26D	169	144	161
Includes equalizer, 11 speakers, amplifier, power antenna.			
16-inch Wheel and Handling Group,			
w/Pkg. 22B, 22C, or 26C	628	534	597
w/Pkg. 22D or 26D	524	445	498
Variable-assist power steering, 225/60R16 touring tires, alloy wheels.			
Conventional spare tire	95	81	90
Extra cost paint	97	82	92

Chrysler LeBaron Convertible	Retail Price	Dealer Invoice	Fair Price
GTC 2-door convertible w/Pkg. 26A	$16999	$15939	$16439
Destination charge	530	530	530

Standard Equipment:

Pkg. 26A: 3.0-liter V-6 engine, 4-speed automatic transmission, driver- and passenger-side air bags, power steering, power convertible top, air conditioning, cloth reclining front bucket seats, center console with armrest, rear defogger, tinted glass, tachometer, coolant temperature and oil pressure gauges, voltmeter, trip odometer, dual remote mirrors, AM/FM cassette radio, power windows, intermittent wipers, reading lights, 205/60R15 tires, wheel covers.

Optional Equipment:

Pkg. 26T	1000	850	870
Deluxe Convenience Group, Power Convenience Group, power driver's seat, remote decklid release, floormats.			
Pkg. 26W	2000	1700	1740
Pkg. 26T plus leather seats, leather-wrapped steering wheel, Light Group, alloy wheels.			
Anti-lock disc brakes	699	594	608
Deluxe Convenience Group	372	316	324
Cruise control, tilt steering wheel.			
Power Convenience Group	338	287	294
Automatic power locks, heated power mirrors.			
Bright LX Decor Group	50	43	44
Bright grille, decklid and taillamp moldings, bodyside moldings, exterior badges.			
Light Group, w/Pkg. 26T	196	167	171
Includes illuminated entry system and lighted vanity mirrors.			
Vinyl seats, w/Pkg. 26T	102	87	89
Leather seats, w/Pkg. 26T	668	568	581
Includes 6-way power driver's seat.			
Premium leather seats, w/Pkg. 26T	1092	928	950
w/Pkg. 26W	424	360	369
Includes 12-way power driver's seat.			
Trip computer, w/Pkg. 26T or 26W	93	79	81
Security alarm, w/Pkg. 26T or 26W	149	127	130
AM/FM cassette with equalizer and Infinity speakers, w/Pkg. 26T or 26W	524	445	456
CD player with equalizer and Infinity speakers, w/Pkg. 26T or 26W	694	590	604
Extra cost paint	97	82	84

Prices are accurate at time of publication; subject to manufacturer's change.

CHRYSLER

	Retail Price	Dealer Invoice	Fair Price
16-inch Alloy Wheel/Performance Group, w/Pkg. 26T	$516	$439	$449
w/Pkg. 26W	188	160	164
Performance Handling Suspension, 205/55R16 performance tires, alloy wheels.			
15-inch alloy wheels, w/Pkg. 26T	328	279	285

Chrysler LeBaron Sedan	Retail Price	Dealer Invoice	Fair Price
LE 4-door notchback	$16551	$14869	$15169
Landau 4-door notchback	17933	16072	16372
Destination charge	505	505	505

Standard Equipment:

LE: 3.0-liter V-6 engine, 3-speed automatic transmission, driver-side air bag, motorized front passenger shoulder belt, power steering, air conditioning, cloth 50/50 front seat, split folding rear seat, tachometer, trip odometer, coolant temperature and oil pressure gauges, voltmeter, tilt steering wheel, cruise control, power windows and locks, AM/FM radio, tinted glass, rear defogger, heated power mirrors, intermittent wipers, visor mirrors, map lights, remote decklid release, floormats, striping, 195/70R14 tires, wheel covers. **Landau** adds to base: 4-speed automatic transmission, cassette player, landau vinyl roof, whitewall tires.

Optional Equipment:

LE Pkg. 28U	173	147	151
4-speed automatic transmission.			
LE Pkg. 28X	639	543	559
Handling Suspension, cassette player, 205/60R15 tires, alloy wheels. Requires 4-speed automatic transmission.			
Landau Pkg. 28L	760	646	665
Interior Illumination Group, overhead console, leather-wrapped steering wheel, wire wheel covers.			
Anti-lock 4-wheel disc brakes	699	594	612
Interior Illumination Group, LE	195	166	171
Illuminated entry, lighted visor mirrors.			
Electronic Display Group, Landau w/Pkg. 28L	317	269	277
Electronic instruments, trip computer.			
Power driver's seat, LE w/Pkg. 28U or 28X, Landau	306	260	268
Cassette player, LE	170	145	149

	Retail Price	Dealer Invoice	Fair Price
Cassette with equalizer and			
Infinity speakers, LE w/Pkg. 28U	$520	$442	$455
LE w/Pkg. 28X or Landau	350	298	306
Wire wheel covers, Landau	240	204	210
Leather seats, Landau	974	828	852
Includes power driver's seat, leather-wrapped steering wheel.			
195/70R14 whitewall tires,			
LE w/Pkg. 26 U or 28U	73	62	64
Conventional spare tire,			
LE w/Pkg. 26U or 28U, Landau	95	81	83

Chrysler New Yorker/LHS	Retail Price	Dealer Invoice	Fair Price
New Yorker 4-door notchback	$25541	$22380	$23541
LHS 4-door notchback	30283	26491	28283
Destination charge	585	585	585

Standard Equipment:

New Yorker: 3.5-liter V-6 engine, 4-speed automatic transmission, anti-lock 4-wheel disc brakes, driver- and passenger-side air bags, variable-assist power steering, air conditioning, 50/50 cloth front seat with center armrests, 8-way power driver's seat with manual lumbar adjustment, tilt steering wheel, cruise control, power windows and locks, heated power mirrors, speed-sensitive intermittent wipers, rear defogger, solar control tinted glass, tachometer, trip odometer, coolant temperature gauge, AM/FM cassette, power decklid release, lighted visor mirrors, reading lights, floormats, trunk cargo net, 225/60R16 tires, wheel covers. **LHS** adds: traction control, touring suspension, automatic temperature control, leather upholstery, 8-way power passenger seat, power front seat recliners, center console with cup holders and storage bin, overhead console with compass and thermometer, trip computer, leather-wrapped steering wheel and shift knob, power antenna, automatic day/night rearview mirror, remote keyless illuminated entry system, time-delay headlamp system, power moonroof, Chrysler/Infinity cassette system with equalizer and 11 speakers, theft security alarm, fog lamps, 225/60HR16 touring tires, alloy wheels, conventional spare tire.

Optional Equipment:

New Yorker Pkg. 26B	1338	1137	1271

Automatic temperature control, mini overhead console with compass and outside temperature readout, trip computer, Remote/Illuminated Entry Group, Chrysler/Infinity AM/FM cassette system with equalizer and 11 speakers, power antenna, automatic day/night rearview mirror, time-delay headlamp system, security alarm, lighted visor mirrors.

Prices are accurate at time of publication; subject to manufacturer's change.

CHRYSLER

	Retail Price	Dealer Invoice	Fair Price
New Yorker Pkg. 26C	$2633	$2238	$2501

Pkg. 26B plus 8-way power passenger seat, leather upholstery, leather-wrapped steering wheel, alloy wheels, conventional spare tire.

	Retail Price	Dealer Invoice	Fair Price
8-way power front passenger seat, New Yorker	377	320	358
Leather seats, New Yorker	1075	914	1021

Includes power front passenger seat and leather-wrapped steering wheel.

	Retail Price	Dealer Invoice	Fair Price
Traction control, New Yorker	175	149	166
Power moonroof, New Yorker w/Pkg. 26B or 26C	792	673	752
Chrysler/Infinity CD System, New Yorker w/Pkg. 26B or 26C, LHS	169	144	161

Includes equalizer, power antenna, and 11 speakers.

	Retail Price	Dealer Invoice	Fair Price
Extra cost paint	97	82	92
Bright platinum metallic paint	200	170	190
Alloy wheels, New Yorker	328	279	312
Conventional spare tire, New Yorker	95	81	90

Chrysler Town & Country

	Retail Price	Dealer Invoice	Fair Price
4-door van with Pkg. 29X	$27284	$24700	$25600
AWD 4-door van with Pkg. 29X	29380	26544	27444
Destination charge	560	560	560

Standard Equipment:

Pkg. 29X: 3.8-liter V-6, 4-speed automatic transmission, anti-lock brakes, power steering, driver- and passenger-side air bags, front and rear air conditioning, 7-passenger seating (bucket seats in front and middle rows and 3-passenger rear bench seat), power driver's seat, cloth and leather upholstery, power front door and rear quarter vent windows, programmable power locks, forward storage console, overhead console (with compass, outside temperature readout, and front and rear reading lights), rear defogger, intermittent wipers, rear wiper/washer, cruise control, leather-wrapped tilt steering wheel, illuminated remote keyless entry system, remote fuel door and decklid releases, tinted windshield and front door glass, sunscreen glass (other windows), electronic instruments (tachometer, coolant temperature and oil pressure gauges, trip odometer), floormats, luggage rack, heated power mirrors, lighted visor mirrors, AM/FM cassette with six Infinity speakers, imitation woodgrain exterior trim, fog lamps, 205/70R15 tires, alloy wheels. **AWD** has permanent all-wheel drive.

Optional Equipment:

Leather seat trim	NC	NC	NC

	Retail Price	Dealer Invoice	Fair Price
Pkg. 29Y	NC	NC	NC
Substitutes gold stripe and gold painted alloy wheels for woodgrain exterior trim.			
7-passenger bench seating	NC	NC	NC
Front bucket seats, reclining 2-passenger middle and folding 3-passenger rear bench seats. Includes integrated child seats.			
Trailer Towing Group	$270	$230	$236
AWD	201	171	176
CD player with equalizer and six Infinity speakers	170	145	149
Extra cost paint	97	82	85
Whitewall tires, with Pkg. 29X	69	59	60
Alloy wheels, gold painted, with Pkg. 29X	NC	NC	NC
Alloy wheels, white painted, with Pkg. 29Y	NC	NC	NC

DODGE

Dodge Caravan	Retail Price	Dealer Invoice	Fair Price
Base SWB	$14919	$13629	$14329
Base Grand	18178	16522	17222
SE SWB	18139	16462	17162
Grand SE	19304	17513	18413
Grand SE AWD	21982	19869	20769
LE SWB	21963	19827	20727
Grand LE	22883	20662	21562
Grand LE AWD	25560	23017	23917
ES SWB	22472	20275	21175
Grand ES	23392	21110	22010
Grand ES AWD	26069	23466	24366
Destination charge	560	560	560

SWB denotes standard wheelbase; AWD denotes All-Wheel Drive.

Standard Equipment:

Base: 2.5-liter 4-cylinder engine, 5-speed manual transmission, driver- and passenger-side air bags, power steering, cloth front bucket seats, 3-passenger middle bench seat, tinted glass, trip odometer, coolant temperature gauge, dual outside mirrors, visor mirrors, AM/FM radio, intermittent wipers, rear wiper/washer, 195/75R14 tires, wheel covers. **Base Grand** adds: 3.0-liter V-6 engine, 3-speed automatic transmission, 7-passenger seating (front buckets

DODGE

and 2-place middle and 3-place rear bench seats), rear trim panel storage and cup holders, 205/70R15 tires. **SE** adds to Base: 3.0-liter V-6 engine, 3-speed automatic transmission, cruise control, power mirrors, cassette player, power remote tailgate release, tilt steering wheel, front passenger lockable underseat storage drawer, striping, dual note horn. **Grand SE** adds to Base Grand: 3.3-liter V-6 engine, 4-speed automatic transmission, cruise control, power mirrors, cassette player, power remote tailgate release, tilt steering wheel, front passenger lockable underseat storage drawer, striping, dual note horn. **LE** adds to SE: front air conditioning, front storage console, overhead console with trip computer, rear defogger, power rear quarter vent windows, power door locks, remote keyless entry system, tachometer, oil pressure gauge, voltmeter, heated power mirrors, lighted visor mirrors, illuminated entry system, headlamp time delay, floormats, 205/70R15 tires. **Grand LE** adds to Grand SE: front air conditioning, front storage console, overhead console with trip computer, rear defogger, power rear quarter vent windows, power door locks, remote keyless entry system, tachometer, oil pressure gauge, voltmeter, heated power mirrors, lighted visor mirrors, illuminated entry system, headlamp time delay, floormats. **ES** adds to LE and Grand LE: ES Decor Group. **AWD** models have permanently engaged all-wheel drive.

Quick Order Packages:

	Retail Price	Dealer Invoice	Fair Price
Pkgs. 21T, 22T, 24T Base SWB and 26T Base SWB, Base Grand	$213	$181	$196

Front air conditioning, map and cargo lights, power remote liftgate release, front passenger underseat lockable storage drawer, bodyside molding, dual horns. Pkg. 22T requires 3-speed automatic transmission; Pkg. 24T requires 3.0-liter engine and 3-speed automatic transmission; Pkg. 26T requires 3.0-liter engine and 4-speed transmission.

Pkg. 26B SE SWB and Pkg. 28B SE SWB, Grand SE, Grand SE AWD	213	181	196

Pkgs. 24-28B add to SE standard equipment front air conditioning, map and cargo lights, rear defogger. SE SWB Pkg. 24B requires 4-speed automatic transmission; SE SWB Pkg. 28B requires 3.3-liter engine and 4-speed automatic transmission.

Pkg. 26D SE SWB, and Pkg. 28D SE SWB, Grand SE, Grand SE AWD	1159	985	1066

Pkgs. 26-28D add to Pkgs. 26-28B forward and overhead consoles, oil pressure and voltage gauges, tachometer, lighted visor mirrors, Light Group, power door locks and rear quarter vent windows, floormats, deluxe insulation. SE SWB Pkg. 26D requires 4-speed automatic transmission; SE SWB Pkg. 28D requires 3.3-liter engine and 4-speed automatic transmission.

Pkg. 26K LE SWB, and Pkg. 28K LE SWB, Grand LE, Grand LE AWD and Pkg. 29K Grand LE, Grand LE AWD	306	260	282

	Retail Price	Dealer Invoice	Fair Price

Pkgs. 26K-29K add to LE standard equipment: power driver's seat, power windows, AM/FM radio with cassette player, equalizer and six Infinity speakers, sunscreen glass. LE SWB Pkg. 26K requires 4-speed automatic transmission; LE SWB Pkg. 28K requires 3.3-liter engine and 4-speed automatic transmission; Grand LE and Grand LE AWD require 3.8-liter engine.

Pkg. 28L and 29L Grand LE, Grand LE AWD	$962	$818	$885

Pkgs. 28L-29L add to 28K-29K: Woodgrain Decor Group (woodgrain trim and moldings, front and rear body-color fascias, luggage rack, whitewall tires, alloy wheels). Requires 3.8-liter engine.

Pkg. 26M and ES SWB, and Pkg. 28M ES SWB, Grand ES and Pkg. 29M, Grand ES	431	366	397
Pkg. 28 and 29M, Grand ES AWD	306	260	282

Pkgs. 26M-29M add to 26K-29K, ES SWB, Grand ES SWB: ES Decor Group (body-color fascia, cladding, and grille, fog lamps, alloy wheels), Sport Handling Group (heavy duty brakes, firmer front and rear sway bars, upgraded front struts and rear shocks, 205/70R15 tires, alloy wheels). Pkgs. 28M-29M add to 28K-29K Grand ES AWD: ES Decor Pkg. with Sport Handling Suspension, 205/70R15 tires, alloy wheels. (Sport Handling Group not available with AWD); deletes 2-tone paint. ES SWB Pkg. 26M requires 4-speed automatic transmission; ES SWB Pkg. 28M requires 3.3-liter engine and 4-speed automatic transmission; Grand ES and Grand ES AWD require 3.8-liter engine.

Individual Options:

3.0-liter V-6, Base SWB	767	652	706
Requires 3-speed automatic transmission.			
3.3-liter V-6, SE, LE, and ES SWB	102	87	94
Requires 4-speed automatic transmission.			
3.8-liter V-6, Grand LE, ES	302	257	278
Includes 4-speed transmission.			
3-speed automatic transmission, Base SWB	601	511	553
4-speed automatic transmission, SE, LE ES, SWB and Base Grand	198	168	182
Anti-lock brakes: SE SWB with Pkgs. 26-28B or 26-28D	687	584	632
SE SWB with Pkgs. 26-28B or 26-28D and alloy wheels, Trailer Tow, Sport Handling, Gold Special Edition, or Sport Wagon Groups; Grand SE with Pkgs. 28B or 28D	599	509	551

Prices are accurate at time of publication; subject to manufacturer's change.

DODGE

	Retail Price	Dealer Invoice	Fair Price
LE SWB with Pkgs. 26-28K or 26-28M; Grand LE with Pkgs. 26-28K, 26-28L, or 26-28M	$599	$509	$551
Front air conditioning, Base SWB and Base Grand	857	728	788
Front air conditioning with sunscreen glass, Base SWB with Pkg. 26T, SE SWB with Pkg. 26-28B and 26-28D, Base Grand with Pkg. 26T and SE Grand with Pkg. 28B and 28D	414	352	381
Not available with Sport Wagon Decor Group.			
Sunscreen glass, Grand SE AWD with Pkg. 28B and 28D	414	352	381
Rear air conditioning with rear heater and sunscreen glass, Base Grand with Pkg. 26T, Grand SE with Pkg. 28B, Grand SE AWD with Pkg. 28B	988	840	909
Grand SE and Grand SE AWD with Pkg. 28B and Sport Wagon Decor Group....	574	488	528
with Trailer Towing Group	925	786	851
with Sport Wagon Decor Group and Trailer Towing Group	511	434	470
Grand SE and Grand SE AWD with Pkg. 28D	880	748	810
with Sport Wagon Decor Group	466	396	429
with Trailer Towing Group	818	695	753
with Sport Wagon Decor Group and Trailer Towing Group	404	343	372
Grand LE and Grand LE AWD with Pkgs. 28-29K, 28-29L, or 28-29M	466	396	429
with Trailer Towing Group	404	343	372
Requires rear defogger.			
Rear bench seat, Base SWB	346	294	318
7-passenger seating with integrated child seat, Base SWB	570	485	524
SE, LE and ES SWB, Grand, Grand AWD .	225	191	207
Quad Command Seating, SE, LE, and ES	597	507	549
Two front and two middle bucket seats, 3-passenger rear bench seat.			
Converta-Bed 7-passenger seating, SE, LE, and ES	553	470	509
Leather trim, ES	865	735	796
Not available with integrated child seat.			
Heavy Duty Trailer Towing Group, SE SWB with Pkgs. 26-28B and 26-28D	556	473	512

	Retail Price	Dealer Invoice	Fair Price
with Gold Special Edition Group	$442	$376	$407
LE SWB with Pkgs. 26-28K, Grand SE with Pkgs. 28B and 28D and Grand LE with Pkgs. 28-29K and 28-29L	442	376	407
SE SWB with Pkgs. 26-28B and 26-28D, LE SWB with Pkgs. 26-28K, ES SWB with Pkgs. 26-28M, Grand SE with Pkgs. 28B and 28D, Grand LE with Pkgs. 28-29K and 28-29L, Grand ES with Pkgs. 26-28M .	410	349	377
Grand SE AWD with Pkgs. 28B and 28D, Grand LE AWD with Pkgs. 28-29K, 28-29L, and 28-29M	373	317	343

Heavy duty brakes, battery, load suspension and radiator, trailer towing wiring harness, 205/70R15 all-season tires, conventional spare tire.

Sport Handling Group, SWB SE with Pkg. 26-28B and 26-28D	239	203	220
Grand SE with Pkg. 28B and 28D, Grand LE with Pkg. 28-29L	125	106	115

Heavy duty brakes, front and rear sway bars, 205/70R15 tires. Not available with Sport Wagon Decor Pkg.

LE SWB with Pkg. 26-28K and Grand LE with Pkg. 28-29K	488	415	449

Heavy duty brakes, front and rear sway bars, 205/70R15 tires, alloy wheels.

Convenience Group I, Base SWB and Base Grand	372	316	342

Cruise control, tilt steering wheel.

Convenience Group II, Base SWB and Base Grand	694	590	638
SE SWB with Pkg. 26-28B and Grand SE with Pkg. 28B.............................	265	225	244

Convenience Group I plus power mirrors and door locks.

Convenience Group III, SE SWB with Pkg. 26-28B and Grand SE with Pkg. 28B	673	572	619
SE SWB with Pkg. 26-28D and Grand SE with Pkg. 28D	408	347	375

Convenience Group II plus power windows and remote keyless entry system.

AWD Convenience Group I, Grand SE AWD with Pkg. 28B	265	225	244

Power mirrors and door locks.

AWD Convenience Group II, Grand SE AWD with Pkg. 28B	673	572	619

DODGE

	Retail Price	Dealer Invoice	Fair Price
with Pkg. 28D	$408	$347	$375
AWD Convenience Group I plus power windows and remote keyless entry system.			
Gold Special Edition Group, SE	250	213	230
Gold striping, moldings and badging, 205/70R15 tires, gold-color alloy wheels.			
Sport Wagon Decor Group, SE	750	638	690
Sunscreen glass, front and rear fascias, leather-wrapped steering wheel, fog lamps, Sport Handling Group, alloy wheels.			
Rear defogger	168	143	155
Power door locks	265	225	244
Luggage rack	143	122	132
Cassette player	170	145	156
AM and FM stereo with CD player, equalizer and six Infinity speakers SE SWB with Pkg. 26-28D, Grand SE with Pkg. 28D, Grand SE AWD with Pkg. 28D	501	426	461
LE SWB with Pkg. 26-28K and 26-28L, Grand LE with Pkg. 28-29K, 28-29L, 28-29M, Grand LE AWD with Pkg. 28-29K, 28-29L, 28-29M	170	145	156
Infinity speaker system, SE	202	172	186
Firm Ride Heavy Load Suspension, 2WD	178	151	163
with Sport Handling Group	146	124	134
Includes conventional spare tire.			
205/70R14 whitewall tires, Base SWB and SE SWB	143	122	132
205/70R15 whitewall tires, SWB SE, SWB LE, Base Grand, Grand SE, Grand LE, Grand SE AWD, Grand LE AWD	69	59	63
Not available with Sport Handling, Gold Special Edition, Sport Wagon Groups.			
Conventional spare tire	109	93	100
15-inch alloy wheels, LE SWB with Pkg. 26-28K, Grand LE with Pkg. 28-29K, Grand LE AWD with Pkg. 28-29K	363	309	334
Extra-cost paint	97	82	89

Dodge/Plymouth Colt

	Retail Price	Dealer Invoice	Fair Price
Base 2-door notchback	$9120	$8714	$8914
ES/GL 2-door notchback	10060	9571	9771
Base 4-door notchback	11428	10844	11044
ES/GL 4-door notchback	12181	11472	11672

	Retail Price	Dealer Invoice	Fair Price
Destination charge	$430	$430	$430

Dodge and Plymouth Colts are identical. Dodge's higher-priced models are called ES and Plymouth's are called GL.

Standard Equipment:

Base 2-door: 1.5-liter 4-cylinder engine, 5-speed manual transmission, driver-side air bag, motorized front passenger shoulder belt. cloth reclining front bucket seats, front console with armrest, engine temperature gauge, left remote mirror, automatic day/night rearview mirror, 145/80R13 tires. **Base 4-door adds:** 1.8-liter 4-cylinder engine, power steering, split folding rear seat, dual outside mirrors, trip odometer, body-colored bumpers, rear spolier, 175/70R13 tires, wheel covers. **ES/GL 2-door** adds to base 2-door: dual remote mirrors, trip odometer, body-colored bumpers, 155/80R13 tires, wheel covers. **ES/GL 4-door** adds: upgraded interior trim, tachometer (5-speed), intermittent wipers, remote fuel door and decklid releases, 185/65R14 tires.

Optional Equipment:

Pkg. 21C, base 2-door	419	360	369
Rear defogger, tinted glass, AM/FM radio, dual outside mirrors.			
Pkg. 21D, base 2-door	1229	1057	1082
Pkg. 21C plus air conditioning.			
Pkg. 21G/22G, ES/GL 2-door	100	86	88
Rear defogger, tinted glass, AM/FM radio. Pkg. 22G requires 3-speed automatic transmission.			
Pkg. 21H/22H, ES/GL 2-door	1386	1192	1220
Pkg. 21G plus power steering, air conditioning, cassette player, split folding rear seat, intermittent wipers, remote fuel door and decklid releases. Pkg. 22H requires 3-speed automatic transmission.			
Pkg. 23K/24K, ES/GL 2-door	1834	1577	1614
Pkg. 21H plus 1.8-liter engine, touring suspension, tachometer (5-speed), 185/65R14 tires, alloy wheels. Pkg. 24K requires 4-speed automatic transmission.			
Pkg. 23C/24C, base 4-door	580	499	510
Tinted glass, rear defogger, AM/FM radio, bodyside moldings, floormats, intermittent wipers, dual remote mirrors, remote fuel door and decklid releases. Pkg. 24C requires 4-speed automatic transmission.			
Pkg. 23D/24D, base 4-door	1390	1195	1223
Pkg. 23C plus air conditioning. Pkg. 24D requires 4-speed automatic transmission.			
Pkg. 23K/24K, ES/GL 4-door	1213	1043	1067
Air conditioning, tinted glass, rear defogger, AM/FM cassette, floormats, variable-intermittent wipers, tilt steering column, cruise control, power mirrors. Pkg. 24K requires 4-speed automatic transmission.			

Prices are accurate at time of publication; subject to manufacturer's change.

DODGE

	Retail Price	Dealer Invoice	Fair Price
Pkg. 23L/24L, ES/GL 4-door	$1996	$1717	$1756
Pkg. 23L plus power windows and locks, alloy wheels. Pkg. 24L requires 4-speed automatic transmission.			
3-speed automatic transmission	518	445	456
Requires 1.5-liter engine.			
4-speed automatic transmission	641	551	564
Requires 1.8-liter engine.			
Anti-lock disc brakes, ES/GL 4-door	699	601	615
Air conditioning	810	697	713
Rear defogger	66	57	58
AM/FM radio with four-speakers, base 4-door	271	233	238
AM/FM cassette w/clock and four-speakers	181	156	159
Requires Option Pkg.			
Bodyside moldings, base with any Option Pkg.	54	46	48

Dodge Intrepid	Retail Price	Dealer Invoice	Fair Price
4-door notchback	$17690	$15537	$16537
ES 4-door notchback	19630	17186	18186
Destination charge	525	525	525

Standard Equipment:

3.3-liter V-6 engine, 4-speed automatic transmission, driver- and passenger-side air bags, power steering, air conditioning, cloth front bucket seats, console with armrest and cupholders, solar control glass, dual remote mirrors, rear defogger, tilt steering wheel, intermittent wipers, tachometer, coolant temperature gauge, headlamp shut-off delay, trip odometer, AM/FM radio, reading lights, visor mirrors, touring suspension, 205/70R15 tires, wheel covers. **ES** adds: 4-wheel disc brakes, variable-assist power steering, cruise control, premium cloth front bucket seats with lumbar support adjustment, cassette player, remote decklid release, fog lamps, Message Center, floormats, trunk cargo net, 225/60R16 touring tires, alloy wheels.

Optional Equipment:

Pkg. 22C, base	891	757	846
Power windows and locks, cruise control, cassette player, floormats.			
Pkg. 22D/26D, base	1653	1405	1570
Pkg. 22C plus 4-wheel disc brakes, power driver's seat, heated power mirrors, remote decklid release, Message Center, lighted visor mirrors. Pkg. 26D requires 3.5-liter engine.			

	Retail Price	Dealer Invoice	Fair Price
Pkg. 22L/26L, ES	$1268	$1078	$1205

Power driver's seat, power windows and locks, Remote/Illuminated Entry Group, heated power mirrors, leather-wrapped steering wheel, lighted visor mirrors. Pkg. 26L requires 3.5-liter engine.

Pkg. 26M, ES	3016	2563	2865

Pkg. 22L plus anti-lock brakes, automatic temperature control, overhead console with compass and thermometer, automatic day/night rearview mirror, Chrysler/Infinity cassette system, security alarm, conventional spare tire. Requires 3.5-liter engine.

3.5-liter V-6 engine	725	616	689
Anti-lock 4-wheel disc brakes, base	624	530	593
ES, Base w/Pkgs. 22D, 26D	599	509	569
Traction control, ES w/Pkgs. 22L, 26L, 26M	175	149	166

Requires anti-lock brakes.

Automatic temperature control, ES w/Pkgs. 22L, 26L.................	152	129	144
Overhead console, base w/Pkgs. 22D, 26D	296	252	281
ES w/Pkgs. 22L, 26L	378	321	359

Compass/temperature/traveler displays, front and rear reading lamps, storage compartment. Base requires bucket seats.

AM/FM cassette, base	200	170	190
Chrysler/Infinity Spatial Imaging Cassette Sound System, base w/Pkgs. 22D, 26D, ES w/Pkgs. 22L, 26L	708	602	673

AM/FM cassette with equalizer, amplifier, 11 Infinity speakers, power antenna.

Chrysler/Infinity Spatial Imaging Compact Disc Sound System, base w/Pkgs. 22D, 26D, ES w/Pkgs. 22L, 26L	877	745	833
ES w/Pkg. 26M	169	144	161

AM/FM stereo, compact disc player, equalizer, amplifier, power antenna.

Power moonroof, base w/Pkgs. 22D, 26D	1012	860	961
ES w/Pkgs. 22L, 26L	1094	930	1039
ES w/Pkg. 26M	716	609	680
Power door locks, base	250	213	238
Power decklid release, base w/Pkg. 22C	61	52	58
Power Convenience Group, ES	684	581	650

Power windows and locks, heated power mirrors.

Integrated child seat	100	85	95

Not available with leather seats.

DODGE

	Retail Price	Dealer Invoice	Fair Price
Cloth 50/50 front bench seat, base	NC	NC	NC
Power driver's and passenger's seats, ES w/Pkgs. 22L, 26L	$377	$320	$358
Leather front bucket seats, ES w/Pkgs. 22L, 22L, 26M	1009	858	959
Includes power front seats, leather-wrapped shift knob.			
Cruise control, base	224	190	213
Remote/ Illuminated Entry Group, base w/Pkgs. 22D, 26D	221	188	210
Keyless remote and illuminated entry systems.			
Security alarm, ES w/Pkgs. 22L, 26L	149	127	142
Requires automatic temperature control, Power Convenience Group.			
Performance Handling Group, ES w/Pkgs. 22L, 26L	217	184	206
Performance suspension, 225/60R16 performance tires. Requires anti-lock brakes, traction control, conventional spare tire.			
16-inch Wheel and Handling Group, base w/Pkgs. 22C, 22D, 26D	404	343	384
Variable-assist power steering, 16-inch polycast wheels 225/60R16, touring tires.			
Conventional spare tire	95	81	90
Extra cost paint	97	82	92

Dodge Shadow	Retail Price	Dealer Invoice	Fair Price
3-door hatchback	$8806	$8263	$8453
5-door hatchback	9206	8631	8821
ES 3-door hatchback	10252	9532	9722
ES 5-door hatchback	10652	9892	10082
Destination charge	505	505	505

Standard Equipment:

2.2-liter 4-cylinder engine, 5-speed manual transmission, power steering, driver-side air bag, motorized front passenger shoulder belt, cloth/vinyl reclining front bucket seats, mini console with storage, trip odometer, coolant temperature gauge, voltmeter, left remote mirror, tinted rear window, removable shelf panel, 185/70R14 tires. **ES** adds: 2.5-liter 4-cylinder engine, dual remote mirrors, AM/FM radio, color-keyed bumpers, rear spoiler, striping, sport suspension, 195/60HR15 tires, wheel covers.

Optional Equipment:

3-speed automatic transmission.....................	557	473	482
3.0-liter engine, ES..	794	675	687

	Retail Price	Dealer Invoice	Fair Price
2.5-liter engine, base	$286	$243	$247
Pkgs. 21Y/22Y/23Y/24Y, base	1545	1313	1336

Air conditioning, tinted glass, rear defogger, dual remote mirrors, AM/FM radio, visor mirrors, intermittent wipers, Light Group, floormats, wheel covers, body-color fascias, color-keyed instrument panel bezels, body-side moldings, striping. Pkg. 22Y requires 3-speed automatic transmission; Pkg. 23Y requires 2.5-liter engine; Pkg. 24Y requires 2.5-liter engine and 3-speed automatic transmission.

Pkg. 28G, ES	1424	1211	1232

Adds 3.0-liter engine and 4-speed automatic transmission.

Pkg. 23H, 24H, 27H, 28H, ES	978	831	846

Air conditioning, tinted glass, rear defogger, cassette player, remote hatch release, Light Group, tachometer, intermittent wipers, console with storage armrest and cup holders, fog lamps, floormats, visor mirrors.

4-speed automatic transmission, ES	730	621	631

Requires 3.0-liter engine.

Anti-lock brakes	699	594	605

Requires automatic transmission

Air conditioning and tinted glass	900	765	779
Light Group	77	65	67
Overhead console, ES w/Pkgs. 23-28H	265	225	229

Includes thermometer and compass. Requires power windows and locks, power mirrors.

Rear defogger	173	147	150
Power locks, 3-door	199	169	172
5-door	240	204	208

Base requires Option Pkg.

Dual remote mirrors, base	69	59	60
Power mirrors, ES w/Pkgs. 23-28H	57	48	49

Requires power door locks.

Power driver's seat, ES w/Pkgs. 23-28H.........	306	260	265

Requires power windows, locks, and mirrors.

Power windows, ES 3-door

w/Pkgs. 23-28H	265	225	229
ES 5-door w/Pkgs. 23-28H	331	281	286

Requires power locks and mirrors.

AM/FM radio, base	284	241	246
AM/FM cassette, base w/Pkgs. 21-24W	504	428	436
Base w/Pkgs. 21-24Y	170	145	147
ES	220	187	190
AM/FM cassette with Infinity speakers			
and equalizer, ES w/Pkgs. 23-28G	520	442	450
ES w/Pkgs. 23-28H	300	255	260

Requires power door locks, intermittent wipers.

DODGE

	Retail Price	Dealer Invoice	Fair Price
Intermittent wipers	$66	$56	$57
AM/FM CD with Infinity speakers and			
equalizer, ES w/Pkg. 23G-28G	690	587	597
ES w/Pkg. 23-28H	470	400	407
Cruise control	224	190	194
Requires tilt steering wheel.			
Sunroof	379	322	328
Tilt steering wheel	148	126	128
Requires intermittent wipers.			
Remote liftgate release, base			
w/Pkgs. 21-24Y	24	20	21
Conventional spare tire	85	72	74
ES with alloy wheel	213	181	184
205/60R14 tires, ES (credit)	(107)	(91)	(91)
Requires 14-inch alloy wheels.			
14-inch alloy wheels, base			
w/Pkgs. 21-24W	376	320	325
Base w/Pkgs. 21-24Y, ES	328	279	284
15-inch alloy wheels, ES	328	279	284
Floormats	46	39	40
Extra-cost paint	97	82	84

Dodge Spirit	Retail Price	Dealer Invoice	Fair Price
4-door notchback	$12470	$11339	$11539
Destination charge	505	505	505

Standard Equipment:

2.5-liter 4-cylinder engine, 5-speed manual transmission, power steering, driver-side air bag, motorized front passenger shoulder belt, cloth reclining front bucket seats, coolant temperature gauge, voltmeter, trip odometer, center console, tinted glass, dual remote mirrors, visor mirrors, bodyside moldings, AM/FM radio with two speakers, intermittent wipers, floormats, striping, 185/70R14 tires, wheel covers.

Optional Equipment:

Pkg. 22D/24D/26D	1179	1038	1069

3-speed automatic transmission, air conditioning, 50/50 split front bench seat, rear defogger, tilt steering wheel, cruise control, floormats. Pkg. 24D requires 2.5-liter flexible fuel engine. Pkg. 26D requires 3.0-liter V-6 engine.

Pkg. 24E/28E	2062	1788	1815

	Retail Price	Dealer Invoice	Fair Price
Pkg. 22D plus 2.5-liter flexible fuel engine, power windows and locks, heated power mirrors, split folding rear seat, remote decklid release. Pkg. 28E requires 3.0-liter V-6 engine and 4-speed automatic transmission.			
2.5-liter flexible fuel 4-cylinder engine	NC	NC	NC
3.0-liter V-6 engine, w/Pkgs. 26D, 28E	$798	$678	$702
Includes 195/70R14 tires.			
4-speed automatic transmission, w/Pkg. 28E	173	147	152
Anti-lock 4-wheel disc brakes	699	594	615
Not available with Pkg. 26D.			
Argent Special Equipment Group	200	170	176
Luggage rack, 195/70R14 tires, alloy wheels. (NA w/5-speed manual transmission.)			
Gold Decor Special Equipment Group	200	170	176
Luggage rack, gold badging and molding inserts, 195/70R14 tires. Requires Option Pkg.			
Rear defogger	173	147	152
Cassette player and four speakers	170	145	150
Requires Option Pkg.			
Power driver's seat, w/Pkgs. 24E, 28E	306	260	269
Split folding rear seat, w/Pkgs. 24E, 28E	NC	NC	NC
Power locks, w/Pkgs. 22D, 24D, 26D	250	213	220
Mini trip computer/Message Center	93	79	82
Requires Option Pkg.			
195/70R14 whitewall tires, w/Pkgs. 22D, 24D, 24E	104	88	92
w/Pkgs. 26D, 28E	73	62	64
Requires Option Pkg.			
Extra-cost paint	97	82	85

Dodge Stealth

	Retail Price	Dealer Invoice	Fair Price
3-door hatchback	$20935	$19038	$19538
R/T 3-door hatchback	23680	21453	22453
R/T Turbo 3-door hatchback	37512	33626	35126
Destination charge	430	430	430

Standard Equipment:

3.0-liter V-6 engine, 5-speed manual transmission, 4-wheel disc brakes, power steering, driver- and passenger-side air bags, cloth/vinyl reclining front bucket seats, driver's seat lumbar and height adjustment, split folding rear seat, console with armrest, tachometer, coolant temperature and oil

DODGE

pressure gauges, trip odometer, tinted glass, rear defogger, intermittent wipers, remote fuel door and hatch releases, power mirrors, AM/FM radio, tilt steering column, leather-wrapped steering wheel, visor mirrors, 205/65HR15 tires, wheel covers. **R/T** adds: 3.0-liter DOHC V-6 engine, 225/55VR16 tires, alloy wheels. **R/T Turbo** adds: turbocharged engine, 6-speed manual transmission, permanent 4-wheel drive, anti-lock brakes, 4-wheel steering, Electronic Variable Damping Suspension, automatic climate control, turbo boost gauge, heated power mirrors, power windows and locks, power driver's seat with power lumbar adjustment, AM/FM cassette with equalizer, power antenna, cruise control, remote keyless entry system, security alarm, lighted visor mirrors, rear spoiler, rear wiper/washer, floormats, 245/45ZR17 tires.

Optional Equipment:

	Retail Price	Dealer Invoice	Fair Price
Pkg. 21C/22C, base and Pkg. 23H/24H, RT ...	$2294	$1973	$2065
Air conditioning, power windows and locks, cruise control, remote keyless entry system, cassette player with equalizer, rear wiper/washer, rear spoiler, floormats. Pkgs. 22C and 24H require automatic transmission.			
Pkg. 23M/24M, R/T	3197	2749	2877
Pkg. 23H plus trunk-mounted CD changer, eight Infinity speakers. Pkg. 24M requires automatic transmission.			
Pkg. 23P/24P, R/T	7928	6818	7135
Pkg. 23M plus Luxury Equipment Group (Electronic Variable Damping Suspension, power driver's seat, heated power mirrors, steering wheel radio controls, power antenna), sunroof. Pkg. 24P requires automatic transmission.			
Pkg. 25W, R/T Turbo AWD	903	777	813
Trunk-mounted CD changer, eight Infinity speakers.			
Pkg. 25Y, R/T Turbo AWD	1264	1087	1138
Pkg. 25W plus sunroof.			
4-speed automatic transmission, base, R/T	863	742	777
Leather seats, R/T	843	724	759
Security Pkg.	1225	1054	1103
Base w/Pkgs. 21C, 22C	960	826	864
R/T w/Pkgs. 23H, 24H, 23M, 24M	960	826	864
Anti-lock brakes, security alarm, remote keyless entry system, power locks.			
Trunk-mounted CD changer	542	466	488
Requires Option Pkg.			
Sunroof	361	310	325
Requires Option Pkg.			
Chrome wheels, R/T Turbo AWD	482	415	434
Extra cost paint	181	156	163

EAGLE

Eagle Summit	Retail Price	Dealer Invoice	Fair Price
DL 2-door notchback	$9120	$8714	$8914
ES 2-door notchback	10060	9571	9771
LX 4-door	11428	10844	11044
ES 4-door notchback	12181	11472	11672
Destination charge	430	430	430

Standard Equipment:

DL 2-door: 1.5-liter 4-cylinder engine, 5-speed manual transmission, driver-side air bag, motorized front shoulder belts, cloth/vinyl reclining front bucket seats, center console with armrest, engine temperature gauge, left manual mirror, 145/80R13 tires; **ES 2-door** adds: cloth seats, dual remote mirrors, color-keyed bumpers and bodyside moldings, rear spolier, 155/80R13 tires, wheel covers. **LX 4-door** adds to DL 2-door: 1.8-liter 4-cylinder engine, power steering, cloth seats, touring suspension, dual manual mirrors, trip odometer, color-keyed bumpers, 175/70R13 tires, wheel covers. **ES 4-door** adds: split folding rear seat with armrest, tachometer (5-speed), dual remote mirrors, intermittent wipers, remote fuel door release, visor mirrors, color-keyed bodyside moldings, 185/65R14 tires.

Optional Equipment:

Pkg. 21C, DL	419	360	369
Tinted glass, rear defogger, dual manual mirrors, AM/FM radio.			
Pkg. 21D, DL	1229	1057	1082
Pkg. 21C plus air conditioning.			
Pkg. 21G/22G, ES 2-door	100	86	88
Tinted glass, rear defogger, AM/FM radio. Pkg. 22G requires 3-speed automatic transmission.			
Pkg. 21H/22H, ES 2-door	1386	1192	1220
Pkg. 21G plus air conditioning, cassette player, power steering, split folding rear seat, remote fuel door and decklid releases, intermittent wipers. Pkg. 22H requires 3-speed automatic transmission.			
Pkg. 23K/24K, ES 2-door	1834	1577	1614
Pkg. 21H plus 1.8-liter 4-cylinder engine and ESi Pkg. (touring suspension, 185/65R14 tires, alloy wheels). 5-speed adds tachometer. Pkg. 24K requires 4-speed automatic transmission.			
Pkg. 23C/24C, LX	580	499	510
Tinted glass, rear defogger, AM/FM radio, bodyside moldings, floormats, dual remote mirrors, remote fuel door and decklid releases, intermittent wipers, passenger visor mirror. Pkg. 24C requires 4-speed automatic transmission.			

Prices are accurate at time of publication; subject to manufacturer's change.

EAGLE

	Retail Price	Dealer Invoice	Fair Price
Pkg. 23D/24D, LX	$1390	$1195	$1223
Pkg. 23C plus air conditioning. Pkg. 24D requires 4-speed automatic transmission.			
Pkg. 23K/24K, ES 4-door	1213	1043	1067
Air conditioning, tinted glass, rear defogger, AM/FM cassette, floormats, tilt steering column, cruise control, variable-intermittent wipers, power mirrors. Pkg. 24K requires 4-speed automatic transmission.			
Pkg. 23L/24L, ES 4-door	1996	1717	1756
Pkg. 23K plus power windows and locks, ESi Pkg. (alloy wheels). Pkg. 24L requires 4-speed automatic transmission.			
3-speed automatic transmission, 2-door	518	445	456
Requires 1.5-liter engine.			
4-speed automatic transmission	641	551	564
Requires 1.8-liter engine.			
Anti-lock disc brakes, ES 4-door	699	601	615
Air conditioning	810	697	713
Rear defogger	66	57	58
AM/FM radio, LX	271	233	238
AM/FM cassette	181	156	159
Bodyside moldings, DL, LX	54	46	48

Eagle Talon	Retail Price	Dealer Invoice	Fair Price
DL 3-door hatchback	$11892	$11083	$11383
ES 3-door hatchback	14362	13331	13731
TSi 3-door hatchback	15885	14717	15217
TSi AWD 3-door hatchback	17978	16620	17120
Destination charge	430	430	430

Standard Equipment:

DL: 1.8-liter 4-cylinder engine, 5-speed manual transmission, 4-wheel disc brakes, motorized front shoulder belts, cloth reclining front bucket seats, split folding rear seat, front console, tinted glass, tachometer, coolant temperature and oil pressure gauges, trip odometer, map lights, dual remote mirrors, visor mirrors, AM/FM radio, remote fuel door and hatch releases, tilt steering column, intermittent wipers, rear spoiler, 185/70R14 tires, wheel covers. **ES** adds: 2.0-liter 4-cylinder engine, power steering, driver's seat lumbar support adjustment, console with storage and armrest, power mirrors, AM/FM cassette, rear defogger, floormats, tonneau cover, fog lamps, 205/55R16 tires. **TSi** adds: turbocharged engine, performance seats, turbo boost gauge, leather-wrapped steering wheel, 205/55VR16 tires. **TSi AWD** adds: permanent 4-wheel drive, limited-slip differential, firmer suspension, alloy wheels.

Optional Equipment:	Retail Price	Dealer Invoice	Fair Price
Pkg. 21T/22T, DL	$1099	$934	$967
Air conditioning, power steering. Pkg. 22T requires automatic transmission.			
Pkg. 21L/22L, DL	515	438	453
Power steering, rear defogger, cupholder console, cargo area cover, front floormats. Pkg. 22L requires automatic transmission.			
Pkg. 21M/22M, DL	1758	1494	1547
Pkg. 21L plus air conditioning, cruise control, cassette player. Pkg. 22M requires automatic transmission.			
Pkg. 23B/24B, ES	1045	888	920
Air conditioning, cruise control. Pkg. 24B requires automatic transmission.			
Pkg. 23C/24C, ES	1646	1399	1448
Pkg. 23B plus power windows and locks, rear wiper/washer. Pkg. 24C requires automatic transmission.			
Pkg. 23D/24D, ES	2164	1839	1904
Pkg. 23C plus cassette player with equalizer, alloy wheels. Pkg. 24D requires automatic transmission.			
Pkg. 25G/26G, TSi	2164	1839	1904
Air conditioning, cruise control, rear wiper/washer, power windows and locks, cassette player with equalizer, alloy wheels. Pkg. 26G requires automatic transmission.			
Pkg. 25J/26J, TSi AWD	1862	1583	1639
Air conditioning, cruise control, rear wiper/washer, power windows and locks, cassette player with equalizer. Pkg. 26J requires automatic transmission.			
4-speed automatic transmission, base and ES	716	609	630
TSi and TSi AWD...	857	728	754
Anti-lock brakes, ES and TSi	699	594	615
Rear defogger, DL	130	111	114
AM/FM cassette with CD player, ES and TSi	517	439	455
AM/FM cassette, DL	198	168	174
Removable sunroof	373	317	328
Leather seats, TSi	444	377	391
Alloy wheels, ES w/Pkg. 23C/24C	302	257	266

Eagle Vision	Retail Price	Dealer Invoice	Fair Price
ESi 4-door notchback	$19747	$17300	$18300
TSi 4-door notchback	23212	20280	21280
Destination charge	525	525	525

Standard Equipment:

ESi: 3.3-liter V-6 engine, 4-speed automatic transmission, 4-wheel disc brakes, driver- and passenger-side air bags, variable-assist power steering, air conditioning, reclining front bucket seats with lumbar support adjustment, console with armrest and cup holders, remote decklid release, rear defogger, tinted glass, intermittent wipers, tachometer, trip odometer, coolant temperature gauge, power windows and locks, dual power mirrors, AM/FM cassette, tilt steering wheel, cruise control, touring suspension, dual visor mirrors, reading lights, floormats, 205/70R15 tires, wheel covers. **TSi** adds: 3.5-liter V-6 engine, anti-lock brakes, automatic temperature control, power driver's seat, overhead console with compass and thermometer, illuminated/remote keyless entry system, trip computer, leather-wrapped steering wheel, lighted visor mirrors, trunk cargo net, 2-tone front and rear fascias, fog lamps, 225/60R16 tires, alloy wheels.

Optional Equipment:

	Retail Price	Dealer Invoice	Fair Price
Pkg. 22C, ESi	$601	$511	$571
Power driver's seat, illuminated/remote keyless entry sytem, lighted visor mirrors.			
Pkg. 22D, ESi	1767	1502	1679
Pkg. 22C plus automatic temperature control, automatic day/night rearview mirror, Chrysler/Infinity cassette system, security alarm, overhead console with compass and thermometer, trip computer.			
Pkg. 26L, TSi	980	833	931
Power front passenger's seat, automatic day/night rearview mirror, Chrysler/Infinity cassette system.			
Pkg. 26M, TSi	1706	1450	1621
Pkg. 26L plus leather seats, security alarm, conventional spare tire.			
Anti-lock brakes, ESi	599	509	569
Traction control, TSi w/Pkg. 26L	175	149	166
Power passenger seat, TSi	377	320	358
Power driver's seat, ESi	377	320	358
Integrated child seat	100	85	95
Not available with leather seats.			
Leather seats, TSi w/Pkg. 26L	620	527	589
Performance Handling Group,			
TSi w/Pkgs. 26L, 26M	217	184	206
Performance suspension, 225/60VR16 tires. Requires traction control and conventional spare tire.			
Chrysler/Infinity cassette system	708	602	673
Includes equalizer, 11 speakers, power antenna.			
Chrysler/Infinity CD system, ESi w/Pkg. 22D,			
TSi w/Pkgs. 26L, 26M	169	144	161
Includes equalizer, 11 speakers, power antenna.			
Security alarm, TSi w/Pkg. 26L	149	127	142
Alloy wheel group	374	318	355
225/60R16 tires, alloy wheels.			
Conventional spare tire	95	81	90

FORD

Ford Aerostar

	Retail Price	Dealer Invoice	Fair Price
XL regular length, 2WD	$14980	$13342	$13642
XL extended, 2WD	16425	14614	14914
XL regular length, 4WD	18450	16397	16697
XL extended, 4WD	19345	17183	17483
XL Plus regular, 2WD	16515	14693	14993
XL Plus extended, 2WD	17555	15609	15909
XL Plus regular, 4WD	19525	17342	17642
XL Plus extended, 4WD	20350	18068	18368
XLT regular length, 2WD	20420	18130	18430
XLT extended, 2WD	20900	18552	18852
XLT regular length, 4WD	21975	19498	19798
XLT extended, 4WD	22840	20259	20559
Eddie Bauer regular length, 2WD	23300	20664	20964
Eddie Bauer extended, 2WD	24100	21368	21668
Eddie Bauer regular length, 4WD	25210	22345	22645
Eddie Bauer extended, 4WD	26120	23146	23446
Destination charge	535	535	535

Standard Equipment:

XL: 3.0-liter V-6 with 5-speed manual transmission 2WD (4WD models have 4.0-liter V-6 with 4-speed automatic transmission, permanent 4WD), anti-lock rear brakes, driver-side air bag, power steering, cloth and vinyl front bucket seats, 3-passenger fold-down bench seat, tinted glass, dual outside mirrors, right visor mirror, rear wiper/washer, intermittent wipers, remote fuel door release, AM/FM radio, 215/70R14 tires. **XL Plus** adds: Dual captain's chairs, 2-passenger middle and 3-passenger rear bench seats, cloth upholstery, storage bin under right front seat. **XLT** adds: 4-speed automatic transmission, dual captain's with power lumbar support, front air conditioning, cruise control, tilt steering wheel, underseat storage bin, door and seatback map pockets, dual-note horn, 2-tone paint, liftgate convenience net, Light Group, leather-wrapped steering wheel. **Eddie Bauer** adds: 4.0-liter V-6 engine (ex. regular-length 2WD), front and rear air conditioning with auxiliary heater, Electronics Group, Power Convenience Group, luggage rack, mini console, AM/FM cassette, rear defogger, rear seat/bed, upgraded upholstery, 2-tone paint, floormats, forged alloy wheels.

Optional Equipment:

4.0-liter V-6, Ext. 2WD	$300	$255	$262
4-speed automatic transmission, XL 2WD	750	637	656

Prices are accurate at time of publication; subject to manufacturer's change.

FORD

	Retail Price	Dealer Invoice	Fair Price
Limited-slip axle	$252	$215	$220
Optional axle ratio	38	32	33
Base Preferred Equipment			
Pkg. 400A, XL Base	37	31	32
Air conditioning, right underseat storage bin.			
XL Preferred Equipment			
Pkg. 401A, XL Plus	734	623	642
Deluxe paint stripe, air conditioning, privacy glass, cruise control, tilt steering wheel.			
XLT Preferred Equipment Pkg. 403A, XLT	315	267	275
Privacy glass, rear defogger, power windows and locks, power mirrors, cassette player.			
Eddie Bauer Pkg. 405A	338	287	295
Privacy glass, floor console with storage and cup holders.			
Dual captain's chairs, XL Base	644	547	563
7-passenger seating: with front captain's chairs,			
XL Base	1043	886	912
with Pkg. 401A or 403A	552	470	483
with four captain's chairs, XLT	598	508	523
Four captain's chairs and seat/bed, XLT	622	528	544
Eddie Bauer	NC	NC	NC
with leather upholstery	848	720	742
Child safety seats	224	191	196
Front air conditioning, XL	857	729	749
High-capacity front air conditioning			
with rear heater	576	489	504
Floor console with storage and cup holders	174	147	152
Floor console delete (credit)	(61)	(52)	(52)
Rear defogger	168	142	147
Electronics Group, with Pkg. 403A	813	691	711
Electronic instruments, AM/FM stereo cassette with equalizer and clock, trip computer, autolamp and electrochromatic mirror.			
Exterior Appearance Group,			
with Pkg. 400A	576	522	504
with Pkg. 401A	174	147	152
with Pkg. 403A	94	79	82
XLT without privacy glass and			
Power Convenience Group	513	436	448
Styled wheel covers, privacy glass, 2-tone paint, swing-lock outside mirrors.			
Light Group	159	135	139
Underhood, glove box and instrument panel lights, illuminated entry system.			
Luggage rack (std. Eddie Bauer)	143	121	125
Swing-lock mirrors (NA XLT			
and Eddie Bauer)	52	45	45

	Retail Price	Dealer Invoice	Fair Price
with Exterior Appearance Group and Power Convenience Group	NC	NC	NC
Bodyside molding	$63	$53	$55
Power Convenience Group	538	457	470
with Exterior Appearance Pkg.	485	413	424
Power windows and locks, power mirrors.			
Cruise control and tilt steering wheel	371	315	324
Sport Appearance Pkg.	733	623	641
High-gloss silver metallic treatment, color-keyed headlight frames and grille, striping, full wheel covers.			
Trailer Towing Pkg.	282	239	246
Class I wiring harness, heavy duty turn signal flasher, limited-slip axle with axle ratio upgrade.			
XL Plus Convenience Group, with Pkg. 401A	827	703	723
Privacy glass, cruise control, tilt steering wheel, deluxe paint stripe.			
XLT Convenience Group, with Pkg. 403A	901	766	788
with Exterior Appearance Group	849	721	742
Power Convenience Group, AM/FM cassette, rear defogger.			
Deluxe paint stripe	43	36	37
Delete for credit, XL Plus	(29)	(25)	(25)
Underseat storage bin	37	31	32
with captain's chairs	NC	NC	NC
Privacy glass	413	351	361
AM/FM cassette	195	165	170
Includes headphones.			
Forged alloy wheels	363	309	317
Engine block heater	33	28	28
215/70R14SL whitewall all-season tires	84	72	73

Ford Crown Victoria	Retail Price	Dealer Invoice	Fair Price
4-door notchback	$19300	$17743	$18243
Special Value 4-door notchback	19180	17690	—
LX 4-door notchback	20715	19096	19596
LX Special Value 4-door (w/Pkg. 113A)	20995	19404	—
LX Special Value 4-door (w/Pkg. 114A)	23585	21697	—
Destination charge	575	575	575

Special Value fair prices not available at time of publication. Special Value prices include destination charge.

Standard Equipment:

4.6-liter V-8, 4-speed automatic transmission, 4-wheel disc brakes, vari-

FORD

able-assist power steering, driver- and passenger-side air bags, air conditioning, cloth reclining split bench seat, map pockets, digital clock, power windows and mirrors, coolant temperature gauge, trip odometer, tilt steering wheel, tinted glass, automatic parking brake release, intermittent wipers, AM/FM radio, 215/70R15 all-season tires. **Special Value** adds Preferred Equipment Pkg. 111A. **LX** adds: Upgraded interior trim, remote fuel door release, power driver's seat, carpeted spare tire cover. **LX Special Value** adds Preferred Equipment Pkg. 113A or 114A.

Optional Equipment:

	Retail Price	Dealer Invoice	Fair Price
Anti-lock brakes with Traction Assist	$665	$592	$599
Preferred Equipment Pkg. 111A, base	445	406	408
Group 1 plus illuminated entry system, front and rear floormats.			
Preferred Equipment Pkg. 113A, LX	845	767	770
Pkg. 111A plus Group 2 and 3, leather-wrapped steering wheel, Light/Decor Group, power driver's seat.			
Pkg. 114A, LX	3435	3060	3091
Pkg. 113A plus Group 4.			
Group 1, base	770	685	693
LX	670	596	603
Includes rear defogger, power door locks, remote fuel door and decklid releases, cruise control, cargo net, spare tire cover.			
Group 2, LX	245	218	220
AM/FM cassette player and power antenna.			
Group 3, LX	485	432	436
Alloy wheels and cornering lamps.			
Group 4, LX	2720	2421	2448
with Group 2	2555	2274	2299
Anti-lock brakes with Traction-Assist, high level audio system, automatic air conditioning, trip computer, outside temperature indicator, heavy duty battery, electronic digital instruments, automatic day/night rearview mirror, rear air suspension, remote keyless entry system, power front seats. Requires Light/Decor Group.			
Cellular telephone, LX	745	663	670
Includes storage armrest.			
Leather upholstery, LX	625	557	562
with power passenger seat	530	472	477
Leather-wrapped steering wheel, LX	90	80	81
Illuminated entry system	80	71	72
Keyless entry, LX	215	191	193
Rear air suspension, LX	270	240	243
Power driver's seat, base	290	258	261
Power front passenger seat, LX	480	427	432
Includes power lumbar support and recliners for both front seats.			
Heavy Duty Trailer Towing Pkg.	690	614	621

	Retail Price	Dealer Invoice	Fair Price
with Pkg. 114A	$395	$352	$355

Includes rear air spring suspension, heavy-duty battery, flasher system and U-joint, extra cooling, dual exhaust, wiring harness, power steering and transmission oil coolers, full-size spare tire, Traction-Lok axle (except with anti-lock brakes). Not available with Handling and Performance Package.

	Retail Price	Dealer Invoice	Fair Price
Light/Decor Group	225	201	202

Includes illuminated visor mirrors, map and dome lights, engine compartment lights, bodyside paint stripes, secondary visors.

	Retail Price	Dealer Invoice	Fair Price
Handling and Performance Pkg., LX	1765	1571	1588
with Group 3	1345	1197	1210
with Group 4	830	739	747
with Pkg. 114A	410	365	369

Includes performance springs, shocks and stabilizer bars, alloy wheels, anti-lock brakes with Traction-Assist, dual exhaust, 3.27 axle ratio, power steering cooler, rear air suspension, 225/60R15 tires.

	Retail Price	Dealer Invoice	Fair Price
AM/FM cassette	165	147	148
High level audio system	480	427	432
with Group 2 or Pkg. 113A , 114A	315	280	283

AM/FM cassette, upgraded amplifier and speakers.

	Retail Price	Dealer Invoice	Fair Price
JBL audio system, LX	500	445	448
Trunk mounted CD changer	785	699	706
215/70R15 whitewall tires	80	71	72
Full-size spare tire	80	71	72
with Handling and Performance Pkg.	198	168	178
Floormats, front	25	23	25
Floormats, rear	20	18	20
Engine block heater	25	23	25

Ford Escort

	Retail Price	Dealer Invoice	Fair Price
Std. 3-door hatchback	$9035	$8322	$8522
LX 3-door hatchback	9890	9100	9300
LX 4-door notchback	10550	9701	9901
LX 5-door hatchback	10325	9496	9696
LX 5-door wagon	10880	10000	10200
GT 3-door hatchback	12300	11293	11493
Destination charge	375	375	375

Standard Equipment:

Std.: 1.9-liter 4-cylinder engine, 5-speed manual transmission, driver-side air bag, motorized front passenger belt, cloth and vinyl reclining bucket seats, one-piece folding rear seatback, center console with cup holders, tinted glass, trip odometer, variable intermittent wipers, flip-out quarter window (3-

door), cargo cover, door pockets, right visor mirror, 175/70R13 all-season tires. **LX** adds: upgraded upholstery and door trim panels, 60/40 split rear seatback, AM/FM radio, digital clock, bodyside molding, full wheel covers. **Wagon** adds 175/65R14 all-season tires: **4-door** adds: tachometer, variable-intermittent wipers. **GT** adds: 1.8-liter DOHC engine, power steering, 4-wheel disc brakes, sport suspension, tachometer, cloth sport seats, leather-wrapped steering wheel, AM/FM cassette, Light Group, lighted visor mirrors, removable cup holder tray, remote fuel door and decklid releases, power mirrors, lighted visor mirrors, fog lamps, rear spoiler, rocker panel cladding, 185/60HR15 all-season tires, alloy wheels.

Optional Equipment:

	Retail Price	Dealer Invoice	Fair Price
4-speed automatic transmission	$790	$703	$771
LX requires power steering.			
Anti-lock brakes, GT	565	503	509
Air conditioning, LX and GT	725	646	653
LX requires power steering.			
Power steering, LX	250	223	225
Comfort Group, Std.	800	712	720
Air conditioning, power steering.			
Preferred Pkg. 320A, LX	235	211	212
Power steering, Light/Convenience Group, rear defogger.			
Preferred Pkg. 330A, GT	530	472	477
Rear defogger, air conditioning, tilt steering column, cruise control.			
One Price Pkg. 321A (5-speed) and 322A			
(automatic): LX 3-door, 5-speed	1130	1008	—
LX 3-door, automatic	1920	1711	—
LX 4-door, 5-speed	470	420	—
LX 4-door, automatic	1260	1123	—
LX 5-door, 5-speed	695	621	—
LX 5-door, automatic	1485	1324	—
LX wagon, 5-speed	140	126	—
LX wagon, automatic	930	829	—
Air conditioning, power steering, cassette player, Light/Convenience Group, rear defogger. Pkg 322A includes 4-speed automatic transmission. Wagon adds Wagon Group.			
Sunrise Red Decor Group, GT	350	312	315
Sunrise red exterior, color-keyed wheels, gray cloth upholstery, front floormats with "GT" embroidered in red.			
Sport Appearance Group, LX 3-door	720	641	648
Alloy wheels, tachometer, liftgate spoiler, rear cladding.			
Rear defogger	160	143	144
Light/Convenience Group, LX	300	268	270
Light Group, power mirrors, remote fuel door and hatch releases, removable cup holder tray.			

	Retail Price	Dealer Invoice	Fair Price
Light Group, LX	$110	$98	$99

Removable cup holder tray, dual map, cargo area, underhood and ignition key lights, headlights-on warning chime, illuminated visor mirrors.

	Retail Price	Dealer Invoice	Fair Price
Luxury Convenience Group,			
LX (except 4-door)	410	365	369
LX 4-door and GT	355	316	320

Tilt steering column, cruise control, tachometer.

	Retail Price	Dealer Invoice	Fair Price
Power Equipment Group, 4-door, 5-door hatchback and wagon with			
Luxury Convenience Group	520	463	468
Wagon without Luxury Convenience Group	575	512	518
3-door LX with Luxury Convenience Group and GT	460	410	414
3-door LX without Luxury Convenience Group	515	459	464

Power windows and locks, tachometer.

	Retail Price	Dealer Invoice	Fair Price
Power mirrors, LX	95	85	86
Power moonroof, LX and GT (NA wagon)	525	468	473

LX requires Light/Convenience Group, power steering.

	Retail Price	Dealer Invoice	Fair Price
Remote fuel door/liftgate releases, LX	95	85	86
AM/FM radio, Std.	300	267	270
AM/FM cassette, Std.	465	414	419
LX	165	147	149
CD player, Std.	740	658	666
LX	445	396	401
GT	280	249	252
Premium sound system	130	116	117

Requires AM/FM cassette.

	Retail Price	Dealer Invoice	Fair Price
Radio delete (credit), LX	(300)	(267)	(267)
GT (credit)	(465)	(414)	(414)
Wagon Group	240	213	216

Luggage rack, rear wiper/washer. Requires Light/Convenience Group.

	Retail Price	Dealer Invoice	Fair Price
Clearcoat paint	85	76	77
Engine block heater	20	18	19

Ford Explorer	Retail Price	Dealer Invoice	Fair Price
XL 3-door wagon, 2WD	$17240	$15361	$15861
XL 3-door wagon, 4WD	18990	16902	17402
Sport 3-door wagon, 2WD	18290	16286	16786
Sport 3-door wagon, 4WD	20000	17790	18290
Eddie Bauer 3-door wagon, 2WD	21250	18891	19391
Eddie Bauer 3-door wagon, 4WD	22950	20387	20887

Prices are accurate at time of publication; subject to manufacturer's change.

FORD

	Retail Price	Dealer Invoice	Fair Price
XL 5-door wagon, 2WD	$18130	$16145	$16845
XL 5-door wagon, 4WD	19900	17702	18402
XLT 5-door wagon, 2WD	20610	18327	19027
XLT 5-door wagon, 4WD	22410	19911	20611
Eddie Bauer 5-door wagon, 2WD	23400	20782	21482
Eddie Bauer 5-door wagon, 4WD	25205	22370	23070
Limited 5-door wagon, 2WD	26735	23717	24617
Limited 5-door wagon, 4WD	28535	25301	26201
Destination charge	485	485	485

Standard Equipment:

XL: 4.0-liter V-6, 5-speed manual transmission, anti-lock brakes, power steering, knitted vinyl front bucket seats, split folding rear seat, tinted glass, Light Group, intermittent wipers, dual outside mirrors, carpet, load floor tiedown hooks, rear seat heat duct, tachometer, coolant temperature gauge, tachometer, trip odometer, AM/FM radio, digital clock, 225/70R15 all-season tires, full-size spare tire. **Sport** adds: rear quarter and rear window privacy glass, rear wiper/washer, rear defogger, map light, load floor tiedown net, cargo area cover, leather-wrapped steering wheel, lighted visor mirrors, alloy wheels. **XLT** adds: cloth captain's chairs, floor console, power mirrors, upgraded door panels with pockets, power windows and locks, cruise control, tilt steering wheel, privacy glass rear door, rear quarter and liftgate, map pockets, floormats. **Eddie Bauer** adds to Sport: power driver's seat with lumbar support, power passenger seat (5-door), duffle and garment bags, luggage rack, privacy glass on rear quarter and liftgate windows (5-door includes rear door windows), 235/75R15 OWL tires. **Limited** adds: air conditioning, power luxury leather bucket seats with 3-position driver's-side memory, matching split/folding rear seat, floor console, color-keyed overhead console with compass, temperature gauge, reading lamps and storage compartment, Electronic Group (remote keyless entry with theft-deterrent system, and electrochromic mirror with autolamp), color-keyed front bumper, front fascia with fog lamps, grille, bodyside moldings, striping, color-keyed leather-wrapped steering wheel, and spoke interior trim, heated mirrors, spoke alloy wheels. 4WD models have Touch Drive part-time 4WD.

Optional Equipment:

4-speed automatic transmission	890	757	845
Limited-slip rear axle	255	217	242
Optional axle ratio (upgrade)	45	38	42
Optional axle ratio (upgrade) with trailer tow	360	306	342
Air conditioning	780	663	741
with manual transmission	NC	NC	NC

	Retail Price	Dealer Invoice	Fair Price
Preferred Pkg. 931A, Sport 3-door	NC	NC	NC
Air conditioning, Power Equipment Group, cloth captain's chairs with console, 235/75R15 outlined white letter tires.			
Preferred Pkg. 932A,			
Eddie Bauer 3-door	$100	$85	$95
Air conditioning, JBL audio system with cassette, leather seats.			
Preferred Pkg. 941A, XLT with automatic	445	378	422
XLT with 5-speed	NC	NC	NC
Air conditioning, striping, premium cassette player.			
Preferred Pkg. 942A,			
Eddie Bauer 5-door	251	214	238
Air conditioning, premium cassette player, leather seats.			
Preferred Pkg. 943A, Limited	395	336	375
JBL Audio System with cassette, running boards (5-door), step bars (3-door).			
Electronics Group, XLT and			
Eddie Bauer 5-doors	485	413	460
Remote keyless entry with theft-deterrent system, electrochromatic mirror with autolamp feature.			
Cloth captain's chairs, XL and Sport	280	238	266
Cloth 60/40 split bench seat, XL 5-door	255	216	242
XLT (credit)	(20)	(17)	(17)
Power cloth sport bucket seats, Sport	1020	867	969
upgrade from captain's chairs	750	637	712
XLT	955	812	907
Power leather sport bucket seats, Sport	1600	1360	1520
upgrade from captain's chairs	1326	1127	1259
XLT	1530	1301	1453
Eddie Bauer	NC	NC	NC
Super engine cooling	55	47	52
Privacy glass	220	187	209
Floor-mounted transfer case			
w/manual locking hubs, 4WD (credit)	(105)	(89)	(89)
Bodyside molding	120	102	114
Power Equipment Group, XL 3-door	900	765	855
XL 5-door	*1235*	*1050*	*1173*
Power windows, locks and mirrors, rear defogger, rear wiper/washer, upgraded door trim panels.			
Luggage rack	140	119	133
with manual transmission and			
Pkg. 941A	NC	NC	NC
Power Equipment Group delete,			
Sport with Pkg. 931A (credit)	(190)	(162)	(162)
Power Equipment Group deleted without loss of Pkg. discount.			

FORD

	Retail Price	Dealer Invoice	Fair Price
Tilt-up sunroof	$280	$238	$266
Cruise control and tilt steering wheel	385	328	365
Sport with manual transmission and Pkg. 931A	NC	NC	NC
Deep dish alloy wheels, XL and Sport	250	212	237
XLT and Eddie Bauer	NC	NC	NC
Trailer Towing Pkg.	105	89	99
Rear defogger and wiper/washer, XL	280	238	266
Premium AM/FM cassette	210	178	199
Sport with manual transmission and Pkg. 931A	NC	NC	NC
Ford JBL Audio System	700	595	665
Upgrade from premium cassette	490	416	465
Ford JBL Audio System with CD player	1000	850	950
Upgrade from premium cassette	790	672	750
Limited	300	255	285
Consolette, XL 5-door and XLT	30	26	28
Running boards, 5-door	395	336	375
Delete for credit, Limited	(395)	(336)	(336)
Step bars, 3-doors	245	208	232
Engine block heater	35	30	33
Deluxe tape stripe, 5-doors	55	47	52
Special Appearance Pkg.	285	243	270
Fog lamps, black bodyside molding, tape stripes.			
Deluxe 2-tone paint	120	102	114
Fog lamps, XL and Sport	185	158	175
235/75R15 outline white letter all-terrain tires	230	196	218
Floormats	45	38	42

Ford Mustang	Retail Price	Dealer Invoice	Fair Price
2-door notchback	$13365	$12050	—
GT 2-door notchback	17280	15534	—
2-door convertible	20160	18098	—
GT 2-door convertible	21970	19708	—
Destination charge	475	475	475

Fair price not available at time of publication.

Standard Equipment:

3.8-liter V-6 engine, 5-speed manual transmission, driver- and passenger-side air bags, 4-wheel disc brakes, variable-effort power steering, reclining cloth bucket seats with 4-way power driver-side adjustment, split folding rear seat, armrest storage console with cup holder and CD/cassette storage, visor mirrors, tachometer, trip odometer, coolant temperature and oil pressure gauges, tilt steering wheel, intermittent wipers, tinted glass, rear defogger, 205/65R15 all-season tires, wheel covers. **Convertible** adds: power convertible top, power mirrors, door locks and decklid release, power windows, lighted visor mirrors. **GT** adds to convertible: 5.0-liter V-8 engine, 4-way head restraint and power lumbar support for front seats, GT Suspension Pkg., Traction-Lok Axle, fog lamps, rear decklid spoiler, leather-wrapped steering wheel, shift and brake handles, 225/55ZR16 all-season tires, alloy wheels.

Optional Equipment:

	Retail Price	Dealer Invoice	Fair Price
4-speed automatic transmission	$790	$703	$711
Anti-lock brakes	565	503	508
Air conditioning	780	694	702
Preferred Pkg. 241A, base models	565	503	508
Air conditioning, AM/FM cassette.			
Preferred Pkg. 243A, base 2-door	1825	1626	1642
base convertible	1415	1260	1273
Air conditioning, power windows and door locks (std. convertible), illuminated remote keyless entry system, remote decklid release (std. convertible), cruise control, leather-wrapped shift knob and parking brake handle, cassette player with premium sound, lighted visor mirrors (std. convertible), cargo net, alloy wheels.			
Preferred Pkg. 249A, GT models	1405	1251	1264
Anti-lock brakes, air conditioning, cruise control, AM/FM cassette with premium sound.			
Group 1, base models	505	449	454
Power windows and door locks, remote decklid release.			
Group 2, base 2-door	870	775	783
base convertible	775	690	697
GT models	510	454	459
Cruise control, AM/FM cassette with premium sound, lighted visor mirrors (std. GT and convertibles), alloy wheels (std. GT).			
Group 3	310	276	279
Illuminated remote keyless entry system, cargo net.			
Convertible hardtop	1545	1375	1390
Anti-theft system	235	209	211
Requires Pkg. 243A (base) or 249A (GT).			
Leather upholstery, base models with Pkg. 243A, GT models	500	445	450
Rear defogger	160	143	144
AM/FM cassette	165	147	148
Mach 460 AM/FM cassette	1215	1081	1093
with Group 2	920	819	828

Prices are accurate at time of publication; subject to manufacturer's change.

FORD

	Retail Price	Dealer Invoice	Fair Price
Includes 460 watts peak power, AM stereo, 60 watt equalizer, CD changer compatability, soft touch tape controls, 10 speakers. Requires Group 1.			
CD player	$475	$423	$427
Requires cassette player.			
Optional axle ratio, GT	NC	NC	NC
Alloy wheels, base	265	236	238
17-inch alloy wheels and 245/45ZR17 tires, GT	380	338	342
Bodyside moldings	50	45	47
Front floormats	30	27	27
Engine block heater	20	18	19

Ford Probe

	Retail Price	Dealer Invoice	Fair Price
3-door hatchback	$13685	$12325	$12825
GT 3-door hatchback	16015	14398	15198
Destination charge	350	350	350

Standard Equipment:

Base: 2.0-liter DOHC 4-cylinder engine, 5-speed manual transmission, power steering, driver- and passenger-side air bags, cloth reclining front bucket seats with memory, split folding rear seat, tachometer, coolant temperature and oil pressure gauges, voltmeter, trip odometer, tinted rear and quarter windows, right visor mirror, center console, dual remote mirrors, AM/FM radio, 195/65R14 all-season tires, wheel covers. **GT adds:** 2.5-liter DOHC V-6 engine, 4-wheel disc brakes, full console with armrest and storage, door pockets, multi-adjustable power seats w/driver-side lumbar support and side bolsters, leather-wrapped steering wheel and shift knob, front seatback storage compartment, cargo net, fog lights, lower bodyside cladding, 225/50VR16 tires, alloy wheels.

Optional Equipment:

4-speed automatic transmission	790	703	711
Anti-lock brakes, Base	735	654	661
GT	565	503	508
Includes 4-wheel disc brakes and sport suspension (std. GT).			
Air conditioning	780	695	702
Requires Group 2.			
Preferred Pkg. 251A, Base	370	329	333
Power mirrors, rear defogger, Convenience Group, tilt steering column.			
Preferred Pkg. 253A, Base	2340	2082	2106
Preferred Pkg. 251A plus air conditioning, power windows and door locks, AM/FM cassette with premium sound, color-keyed bodyside moldings, remote keyless entry, cruise control, Light Group, Power Group.			

	Retail Price	Dealer Invoice	Fair Price
Preferred Pkg. 261A, GT	$1385	$1233	$1246

Air conditioning, power mirrors, tilt steering column, cassette player with premium sound, Convenience Group, rear defogger.

Preferred Pkg. 263A, GT	2790	2484	2511

Pkg. 261A plus anti-lock brakes, color-keyed bodyside moldings, remote keyless entry, cruise control, Light Group, Power Group, rear wiper/washer, heated power mirrors.

Group 1	260	232	234

Rear defogger, power mirrors.

Group 2	495	440	445

Tilt steering column, Convenience Group (tinted glass, intermittent wipers, remote fuel door and liftgate releases, battery saver, headlamp warning chime, convenience lights).

Group 3	1105	984	994

Air conditioning, AM/FM cassette with premium sound.

Group 4	1145	1019	1030

Light Group, Power Group, color-keyed bodyside moldings.

Group 5	740	658	666

Anti-lock brakes, rear wiper/washer.

Light Group	395	352	355

Illuminated entry, lighted visor mirrors, remote keyless entry, fade-to-off dome light with map lights.

Power Group	700	623	630

Power windows and door locks, cruise control.

Sport Edition, Base	760	677	684

Body-color bodyside cladding, front fascia, 205/55R15 tires, alloy wheels.

Rear wiper/washer with heated power mirrors	175	156	157
Power driver's seat	290	258	261

Requires Power Group.

Leather seats, GT	500	445	450
Manual driver seat height adjuster, Base	35	31	31
Feature Car, GT	215	191	193

Wild Orchid exterior, unique black GT bucket seats and floormats. Requires Power Group and rear wiper/washer with heated power mirrors.

Cassette player	325	290	292
CD player, Base with Pkg. 251A	800	712	720
Base with 253A, GT with 261A or 263A	475	423	427
Graphic equalizer	135	120	121
Power antenna	80	71	72

Requires cassette or CD player.

Prices are accurate at time of publication; subject to manufacturer's change.

FORD

	Retail Price	Dealer Invoice	Fair Price
Anti-theft system	$190	$169	$171
Console with storage armrest and cup holder, Ease	60	54	54
Color-keyed bodyside moldings	50	45	45
Sliding power roof	615	547	553
Includes dome light with map lights.			
Alloy wheels and 205/55R15 tires	430	383	387
Floormats	30	27	27

Ford Taurus

	Retail Price	Dealer Invoice	Fair Price
GL 4-door notchback	$16140	$14519	$15019
LX 4-door notchback	18785	16874	17374
SHO 4-door notchback	24715	22151	22651
GL 5-door wagon	17220	15481	15981
LX 5-door wagon	20400	18311	18811
Destination charge	525	525	525

Standard Equipment:

GL: 3.0-liter V-6, 4-speed automatic transmission, power steering, driver- and passenger-side air bags, cloth reclining split bench seat with dual center armrests, tilt steering wheel, power mirrors, tinted glass, intermittent wipers, illuminated entry, door pockets, AM/FM radio, digital clock, trip odometer, wheel covers, luggage rack (wagon), 205/65R15 tires. **LX** adds: 3.8-liter V-6 on wagon, variable-assist power steering, air conditioning, reclining front bucket seats with lumbar support, console with with armrest and storage, 6-way power driver's seat, power windows and door locks, remote fuel door and decklid/liftgate releases, tachometer, diagnostic alert lights, automatic parking brake release, automatic on/off headlamps, cornering lamps, bodyside cladding, Convenience Kit (vinyl pouch with fluorescent lantern, tire pressure gauge, gloves, poncho, shop towel, distress flag, headlamp bulb), Light Group, illuminated entry, cargo tiedown net, alloy wheels. **SHO** deletes automatic parking brake release, and adds: 3.0-liter DOHC V-6 with dual exhaust, 5-speed manual transmission, anti-lock 4-wheel disc brakes, automatic air conditioner, cruise control, rear defogger, fog lamps, cloth and leather front bucket seats, rear spoiler, handling suspension, extended range fuel tank, cornering lights, high-level audio system, power antenna, leather-wrapped steering wheel, floormats, 215/60ZR16 tires.

Optional Equipment:

3.8-liter V-6 engine	555	472	500

Standard LX wagon. Requires Group 1. Not available GL with Pkg. 203A or SHO.

	Retail Price	Dealer Invoice	Fair Price
Anti-lock 4-wheel disc brakes (std. SHO)	$565	$503	$509
4-speed automatic transmission, SHO	790	703	711
Includes 3.2-liter DOHC V-6 engine and 215/60HR16 tires.			
Automatic air conditioning, LX	175	156	158
Automatic air conditioning includes outside temperature readout.			
Preferred Pkg. 203A GL	650	579	585
Air conditioning, rear defogger.			
Preferred Pkg. 204A, GL	2070	1842	1863
Air conditioning, rear defogger, power windows and locks, power driver's seat, remote fuel door/decklid/liftgate releases, Light Group, cassette player, cruise control, floormats, deluxe wheel covers, cargo net, GL Equipment Group (variable-assist power steering, dual visor mirrors, driver's secondary visor, deluxe seat trim, striping).			
Preferred Pkg. 208A, LX 4-door	515	458	464
LX wagon	705	628	635
Rear defogger, cruise control, cassette player, power antenna, keyless entry, leather-wrapped steering wheel, floormats. Wagons add: cargo area cover, rear wiper/washer.			
Group 1, GL	960	855	864
LX	160	143	144
Air conditioning, rear defogger.			
Group 2, GL with Pkg. 204A	1115	992	1004
LX	380	338	342
Cruise control, cassette player, power windows and door locks, Light Group, remote fuel door/decklid/liftgate releases.			
Group 3	370	329	333
Power driver's seat, deluxe wheel covers.			
Group 4	405	360	365
Remote keyless entry system, leather-wrapped steering wheel, power antenna.			
Group 5, wagon	195	174	176
Rear wiper/washer, cargo area cover.			
Luxury Convenience Group, SHO	1555	1383	1400
Power front seats, power moonroof, Ford JBL audio system, remote keyless entry system.			
LX Convenience Group	1030	916	927
Power front seats, power moonroof.			
Bucket seats and console, GL with Pkg. 204A	NC	NC	NC
Leather bucket seats and console, GL with Pkg. 204A	595	530	536
LX	495	441	446
Leather bucket seats, SHO	495	441	446
Leather split bench seat, LX	495	441	446

Prices are accurate at time of publication; subject to manufacturer's change.

FORD

	Retail Price	Dealer Invoice	Fair Price
6-way power driver's seat, GL	$290	$258	$261
Power front passenger seat, LX	290	258	261
Rear facing third seat, wagons	150	134	135
AM/FM cassette	165	147	149
High-level audio system, LX	480	427	432
LX with Group 2	315	280	284
CD player (NA GL)	470	418	423
Ford JBL audio system, (NA GL and wagons)	500	445	450
Cellular telephone with storage armrest	500	445	450
Requires split bench seat.			
Cruise control	215	191	194
Remote keyless entry, GL	310	276	279
with Group 2	215	191	194
Power windows	340	302	306
Power locks, GL	257	219	231
Requires power windows.			
Load floor extension "picnic table," wagon	85	76	77
Alloy wheels, GL with Pkg. 204A	230	205	207
Full-size spare tire (NA SHO)	70	62	63
Heavy duty battery (NA SHO)	30	27	28
Front and rear floormats	45	40	41

Ford Tempo	Retail Price	Dealer Invoice	Fair Price
GL 2-door notchback (Central States)	$9465	$8713	$8913
GL 2-door notchback	10735	9869	10069
GL 4-door notchback	10735	9869	10069
LX 4-door notchback	12560	11530	11730
Destination charge	485	485	485

Standard Equipment:

GL: 2.3-liter 4-cylinder engine, 5-speed manual transmission, power steering, motorized front shoulder belts, cloth reclining front bucket seats, tinted glass, consolette, visor mirrors, intermittent wipers, coolant temperature gauge, AM/FM radio, 185/70R14 tires, wheel covers. **LX** adds to GL: touring suspension, illuminated entry, power locks, remote fuel door and decklid releases, tilt steering wheel, power mirrors, front armrest, upgraded upholstery, cargo tiedown net, seatback pockets, Light Group, tachometer and trip odometer, floormats, performance tires, polycast wheels.

Optional Equipment:	Retail Price	Dealer Invoice	Fair Price
3.0-liter V-6 engine	$655	$583	$590
Requires air conditioning.			
3-speed automatic transmission	535	476	482
Air conditioning	465	414	419
Driver-side air bag, GL	325	290	293
LX	224	191	202
Includes passenger-side motorized shoulder belt. Not available with tilt steering wheel (deleted from LX with credit), cruise control, 5-speed manual transmission or 3.0-liter V-6 engine.			
Preferred Pkg. 225A, GL	310	277	279
Air conditioning, Light Group, power mirrors, rear defogger.			
Preferred Pkg. 226A, GL 2-door	1255	1118	1130
GL 4-door	1295	1153	1166
Pkg. 225A plus 3-speed automatic transmission (may be deleted without loss of package discount when ordered with 3.0-liter V-6 engine), cassette player, tilt steering wheel, front armrest, rear defogger, power locks, remote fuel door and decklid releases, cassette player, polycast wheels, floormats.			
SRS Pkg. 227A, GL 2-door	1150	1025	1035
GL 4-door	1190	1060	1071
Driver-side air bag, 3-speed automatic transmission, air conditioning, Light Group, power mirrors, front armrest, rear defogger, power locks, remote fuel door and decklid releases, floormats.			
Preferred Pkg. 233A, LX	960	855	864
Air conditioning, rear defogger, cassette player, 3-speed automatic transmission (may be deleted without loss of package discount when ordered with 3.0-liter V-6 engine), decklid luggage rack, 3.0-liter V-6 engine.			
Front armrest, GL	55	49	50
Rear defogger	160	143	144
Sport Instrument Cluster, GL	85	76	77
Tachometer and trip odometer.			
Light Group, GL	35	31	32
Power Lock Group, GL 2-door	295	263	266
4-door	335	298	302
Power door locks, remote fuel door and decklid releases.			
Power mirrors, GL	115	102	104
Cassette player, GL	150	134	135
Premium sound system	130	116	117
Upgraded speakers and amplifier.			
AM/FM radio delete (credit)	(235)	(209)	(209)
Power driver's seat	290	258	261
Requires power mirrors.			
Cruise control	215	191	194
Not available with air bag.			

Prices are accurate at time of publication; subject to manufacturer's change.

FORD

	Retail Price	Dealer Invoice	Fair Price
Decklid luggage rack	$110	$98	$99
Tilt steering wheel	140	124	120
Not available with air bag.			
Polycast wheels, GL	185	165	167
Power windows, 4-doors	315	280	284
Decklid luggage rack	110	98	99
185/70R14 whitewall tires	80	71	72
Front floormats, GL	25	23	24
Rear floormats, GL	20	17	18
Clearcoat paint	85	76	77
Engine block heater	20	17	18

Ford Thunderbird

	Retail Price	Dealer Invoice	Fair Price
LX 2-door notchback	$16830	$15124	$15624
Super Coupe 2-door notchback	22240	19938	20438
Destination charge	495	495	495

Standard Equipment:

LX: 3.8-liter V-6, 4-speed automatic transmission, driver- and passenger-side air bags, variable assist power steering, air conditioning, cruise control, cloth reclining front bucket seats with power driver's seat, center console with dual cup holders, rear seat center armrest, dual power mirrors, visor mirrors, tinted glass, coolant temperature gauge, tachometer, tilt steering wheel, trip odometer, fog lights, AM/FM cassette, power windows and door locks, leather-wrapped steering wheel and shift knob, illuminated entry system, remote fuel door and decklid release, body-color side moldings, intermittent wipers, 205/70R15 tires. **Super Coupe** deletes cruise control, power locks, power driver's seat and adds: 3.8-liter supercharged V-6 with dual exhaust, 5-speed manual transmission, anti-lock 4-wheel disc brakes, adjustable sport suspension, semi-automatic temperature control, Traction-Lok axle, articulated cloth/leather/vinyl sport seats with power lumbar and side bolsters, seat-back pockets, tachometer, boost gauge, lower bodyside cladding, 225/60ZR16 tires, locking alloy wheels.

Optional Equipment:

4.6-liter V-8, LX	515	459	464
4-speed automatic transmission, SC	790	703	711
Includes Traction-Assist.			
Anti-lock 4-wheel disc brakes, LX	565	503	509
Includes Traction-Assist.			
Preferred Pkg. 155A, LX	NC	NC	NC
Semi-automatic temperature control, rear defogger, lighted visor mirrors, alloy wheels.			

	Retail Price	Dealer Invoice	Fair Price
Preferred Pkg. 157A, SC	NC	NC	NC

Power driver's seat, automatic climate control, rear defogger, cruise control, power door locks, remote fuel door and decklid releases.

	Retail Price	Dealer Invoice	Fair Price
Group 1, SC	$800	$712	$720

Power door locks, remote fuel door and decklid releases, cruise control, power driver's seat.

	Retail Price	Dealer Invoice	Fair Price
Group 2, LX	315	280	284
SC	160	143	144

Semi-automatic temperature control (std. SC), rear defogger.

	Retail Price	Dealer Invoice	Fair Price
Group 3, LX	305	271	275
SC	95	85	86

Lighted visor mirrors, 215/70R15 tires, alloy wheels.

	Retail Price	Dealer Invoice	Fair Price
Luxury Group, LX	580	516	522
SC	555	494	500

Autolamp system, automatic day/night mirror, illuminated entry (SC), Light Group, power front passenger seat, integrated warning lamp.

	Retail Price	Dealer Invoice	Fair Price
Leather seat trim, LX	490	436	441
SC	615	547	554
Anti-theft system	235	209	212
Traction-Assist, LX	210	187	189
Premium cassette player	370	329	333
Includes power antenna.			
Ford JBL audio system	500	445	450
Trunk mounted CD player	785	699	707
Remote keyless entry, LX and SC			
with Luxury Group	215	191	194
SC	295	263	266
Cold Weather Group, LX	300	267	270
LX with Pkg. 155A	140	124	126
LX with 4.6-liter engine	275	245	248
LX with Pkg. 155A and 4.6-liter engine	115	102	104
LX with Traction-Assist and 4.6-liter engine, SC with automatic transmission	180	160	162
SC with automatic and Pkg. 157A, LX with Traction-Assist, Pkg. 155A and 4.6-liter engine	20	18	19
SC with manual transmission and LX with Traction-Assist	205	182	185
SC with manual transmission and Pkg. 157A, LX with Traction-Assist with Pkg. 155A	45	40	41

Includes engine block heater, heavy duty battery (std. SC w/automatic), heavy duty alternator, rear defogger.

	Retail Price	Dealer Invoice	Fair Price
Power moonroof	$740	$658	$666
Voice activated cellular phone	530	472	477
Tri-coat paint	225	201	203
225/60ZR16 all-season performance tires, SC	70	62	63

GEO

Geo Metro

	Retail Price	Dealer Invoice	Fair Price
XFi 3-door hatchback	$7195	$6706	$6906
Base 3-door hatchback	7195	6706	6906
Base 5-door hatchback	7695	7172	7372
Destination charge	295	295	295

Standard Equipment:

XFi: 1.0-liter 3-cylinder engine, 5-speed manual transmission, door-mounted automatic front seatbelts, automatic power locks, cloth and vinyl reclining front bucket seats, one-piece folding rear seatback, temperature gauge, console with cup holders and storage tray, left door pocket, 145/80R12 tires. **Base** adds: left remote and right manual mirrors, intermittent wipers, bodyside moldings, wheel covers.

Optional Equipment:

3-speed automatic transmission, base	495	441	448
Air conditioning, base	720	641	652
UL1 AM/FM radio	301	268	272
Includes seek and scan, digital clock, and four speakers.			
UL0 AM/FM cassette player	496	441	449
Includes seek and scan, theft deterrent, tone select, digital clock, and four speakers.			
XFi Preferred Equipment Group 2	301	268	272
UL1 AM/FM radio.			
With UL0 AM/FM cassette player, add	195	174	176
Base Preferred Group 2	1021	909	924
Air conditioning, UL1 AM/FM radio.			
With UL0 AM/FM cassette player, add	195	174	176
Rear defogger	150	134	136
Rear wiper/washer, base	125	111	113
Requires rear defogger.			
Tachometer	50	45	45

	Retail Price	Dealer Invoice	Fair Price
Left remote and right manual mirrors, XFi	$20	$18	$18
Bodyside moldings, XFi	50	45	45
Cargo security cover	50	45	45

Geo Prizm

	Retail Price	Dealer Invoice	Fair Price
4-door notchback	$10730	$10215	$10515
4-door notchback (California only)	10460	9958	—
LSi 4-door notchback	11500	10603	11103
LSi 4-door notchback (California only)	11230	10354	—
Destination charge	365	365	365

California models' fair price not available at time of publication.

Standard Equipment:

1.6-liter DOHC 4-cylinder engine, 5-speed manual transmission, driver- and passenger-side air bags, left remote and right manual mirrors, reclining front bucket seats, cloth/vinyl upholstery, center console with storage tray and cup holders, remote fuel door release, tinted glass, rear-seat heating ducts, bodyside molding, 175/65R14 tires. **LSi** adds: tilt steering wheel, upgraded full-cloth upholstery, center console with armrest, dual front storage pockets, split-folding rear seat, visor mirrors, wheel covers.

Optional Equipment:

1.8-liter 4-cylinder engine, LSi	352	303	308
Includes rear stabilizer bar and 185/65R14 tires.			
3-speed automatic transmission	495	426	433
Requires 1.6-liter engine.			
4-speed automatic transmission, LSi	775	667	678
Requires 1.8-liter engine.			
Anti-lock brakes	595	512	521
Air conditioning	795	684	696
Cruise control, LSi w/Preferred Equipment Group 2	175	151	153
Rear defogger	170	146	149
Power locks	220	189	193
Power sunroof, LSi	660	568	578
Includes map light.			
Intermittent wipers	40	34	35
Tachometer	60	52	53
AM/FM radio	330	284	289
Includes seek and scan, digital clock, and four speakers.			
AM/FM cassette player	525	452	459

Prices are accurate at time of publication; subject to manufacturer's change.

	Retail Price	Dealer Invoice	Fair Price

Includes seek and scan, theft deterrent, tone select, digital clock, and four speakers.

| AM/FM radio with CD and cassette player, LSi | $568 | $488 | $497 |

Includes seek and scan, theft deterrent, tone select, digital clock, and six speakers.

| Base Preferred Equipment Group 2 | 590 | 507 | 516 |

Power steering and AM/FM radio with digital clock.

| With AM/FM cassette player, add | 195 | 168 | 171 |
| LSi Preferred Equipment Group 2 | 1545 | 1329 | 1352 |

Air conditioning, AM/FM radio with digital clock, dual power mirrors, power steering, remote decklid release, intermittent wipers.

With AM/FM cassette, add	195	168	171
With AM/FM radio, CD, and cassette player, add	568	488	497
LSi Preferred Equipment Group 3	2240	1926	1960

LSi Preferred Equipment Group 2 plus power windows and door locks, cruise control.

With AM/FM cassette, add	195	168	171
With AM/FM radio, CD, and cassette player, add	568	488	497
Alloy wheels, LSi	335	288	293
Front and rear floormats	40	34	35

Geo Tracker

	Retail Price	Dealer Invoice	Fair Price
2-door convertible, 2WD	$10865	$10343	$10543
3-door wagon, 4WD	12295	11705	11905
LSi 3-door wagon, 4WD	13765	13104	13304
2-door convertible, 4WD	12135	11553	11753
LSi 2-door convertible, 4WD	13500	12852	13052
Destination charge	300	300	300

Standard Equipment:

1.6-liter 4-cylinder engine, 5-speed manual transmission, anti-lock rear brakes, rear defogger (wagon only), cloth/vinyl reclining front bucket seats, folding rear bench seat (4WD), center console with storage tray and cup holders, tachometer (4WD), trip odometer, dual mirrors, intermittent wipers, full-size lockable spare tire, spare tire cover, front and rear tow hooks, 195/75R15 tires, (205/75R15 tires 4WD). **LSi** adds: automatic locking front hubs, power steering, AM/FM radio, floormats, tinted glass, upgraded cloth/vinyl upholstery and door trim, adjustable rear bucket seats, rear wiper/washer (wagon only), bodyside moldings, styled steel wheels.

Optional Equipment:

	Retail Price	Dealer Invoice	Fair Price
3-speed automatic transmission	$595	$530	$538
Air conditioning	745	663	674
Tilt steering wheel	115	102	104
UL1 AM/FM radio	306	272	277
Includes seek and scan, digital clock, and four speakers.			
UL0 AM/FM cassette player	501	446	453
LSi	195	174	176
Includes seek and scan, theft deterrent, tone select, digital clock, and four speakers.			
UP0 AM/FM radio with CD			
and cassette player, LSi	897	798	812
LSi	591	526	535
Includes seek and scan, theft deterrent, tone select, digital clock, and four speakers.			
Convertible 2WD Preferred			
Group 2	581	517	526
UL1 AM/FM radio, power steering.			
With UL0 AM/FM cassette, add	195	174	176
With UP0 AM/FM radio, CD,			
and cassette player, add	591	526	535
Base and convertible 4WD			
Preferred Equipment Group 2	581	517	526
UL1 AM/FM radio, power steering.			
With UL0 AM/FM cassette, add	195	174	176
With UP0 AM/FM radio, CD,			
and cassette player, add	591	526	535
Rear seat, 2WD	445	396	403
Transfer case shield, 4WD	75	67	68
Alloy wheels	335	298	303
Floormats, base	28	25	25
Bodyside moldings, base wagon	59	53	53
Convertibles	85	76	77

GMC

GMC Jimmy	Retail Price	Dealer Invoice	Fair Price
3-door wagon, 2WD	$15639	$14153	$14353
3-door wagon, 4WD	17558	15890	16090
5-door wagon, 2WD	16941	15332	15782
5-door wagon, 4WD	19298	17465	17915
Destination charge	475	475	475

Prices are accurate at time of publication; subject to manufacturer's change.

GMC

Standard Equipment:

3-door: 4.3-liter V-6 engine, 5-speed manual transmission, part-time 4WD with electronic transfer case (4WD), 4-wheel anti-lock brakes, power steering, solar-control tinted glass, coolant temperature and oil pressure gauges, voltmeter, trip odometer, AM/FM radio, dual outside mirrors, front highback reclining buckets seats, door map pockets, 205/75R15 tires, full-size spare tire, front tow hooks, wheel trim rings (4WD). **5-door** adds: cloth 60/40 reclining split bench seat with folding center armrest, folding rear 3-passenger bench seat (4WD), mirrors, illuminated entry, reading lights, lighted visor mirrors, seat back convenience net, cupholders, floormats, bodyside moldings, wheel trim rings.

Option Pkgs., 3-door:	Retail Price	Dealer Invoice	Fair Price
SL Pkg. 2	$684	$588	$609
AM/FM cassette, cruise control, tilt steering wheel, folding rear 3-passenger bench seat, deep-tinted glass with light-tinted rear window, luggage carrier.			
SLS Pkg. 2, 2WD	1310	1127	1166
4WD	1278	1099	1137
SL Pkg. 2 contents plus SLS Sport Decor Pkg.			
SLE Pkg. 2	1412	1214	1257
SL Pkg. 2 contents plus SLE Comfort Decor Pkg.			
SLS Pkg. 3	2708	2329	2410
SLS Sport Decor Pkg. plus air conditioning, AM/FM cassette, cruise control, tilt steering wheel, power door locks and windows, rear wiper/washer, alloy wheels, folding rear 3-passenger bench seat, deep-tinted glass, luggage carrier.			
SLE Pkg 3	2662	2289	2369
SLE Comfort Decor Pkg. plus air conditioning, AM/FM cassette, cruise control, tilt steering wheel, power door locks and windows, rear wiper/washer, alloy wheels, folding rear 3-passenger bench seat, deep-tinted glass, luggage carrier.			
SLT Pkg. 4, 2WD	4216	3626	3752
4WD	4441	3819	3952
SLT Touring Decor Pkg. plus air conditioning, cruise control, tilt steering wheel, AM/FM cassette with equalizer, power mirrors, rear defogger, power tailgate release, rear wiper/washer, deep-tinted glass, luggage carrier.			

Option Pkgs., 5-door:			
SLE Pkg. 2, 2WD	410	353	365
4WD (credit)	(25)	(22)	(22)
Cruise control, tilt steering wheel, AM/FM cassette, folding rear 3-passenger bench seat (std. 4WD), deep-tinted glass with light-tinted rear window, luggage carrier.			

	Retail Price	Dealer Invoice	Fair Price
SLE Pkg. 3, 2WD	$2194	$1887	$1953
4WD	1791	1540	1594

SLE Pkg. 2 plus air conditioning, power door locks and windows, rear wiper/washer, rear defogger, power tailgate release, cloth reclining bucket seat and floor console (60/40 split bench seat may be substituted at no additional cost), alloy wheels.

SLS Pkg. 3, 2WD	2248	1933	2001
4WD	1845	1587	1642

SLS Pkg. 2 plus air conditioning, power door locks and windows, rear wiper/washer, rear defogger, power tailgate release, cloth reclining bucket seat and floor console (60/40 split bench seat may be substituted at no additional cost), alloy wheels.

SLT Pkg. 4, 2WD	3735	3212	3324
4WD	3557	3059	3166

SLT Touring Decor Pkg. plus air conditioning, cruise control, tilt steering wheel, AM/FM cassette with equalizer, power mirrors, rear defogger, power tailgate release, rear wiper/washer, deep-tinted glass, luggage carrier.

Individual Options:

Enhanced Powertrain Pkg.	1160	998	1032

Includes high output 4.3-liter V-6, 4-speed automatic transmission, extra capacity cooling.

Optional axle ratio	(NC)	(NC)	(NC)
Locking differential	252	217	224
Manual transfer case, 4WD (credit)	(123)	(106)	(106)

Replaces standard electronic push button shift with manual floor mounted shift.

SLE Comfort Decor Pkg. (std. 5-door),			
3-door 2WD	900	774	801
4WD	868	746	773

Reclining bucket seats, cloth upholstery, upgraded door trim, chrome grille, bodyside and wheel opening moldings, floor console, illuminated entry, lighted visor mirrors, reading lights, floormats, rally wheels (2WD), wheel trim rings (4WD).

SLS Sport Decor Pkg., 3-door	1202	1034	1070

Reclining bucket seats, floor console, leather-wrapped steering wheel, illuminated entry, lighted visor mirrors, reading lights, convenience net (2-door), body-color bumpers and grille, upgraded door trim, bodyside and wheel opening moldings, floormats, alloy wheels.

SLS Sport Decor Pkg. 5-door 2WD	302	260	269
5-door 2WD with bucket seats	513	441	457
5-door 4WD	334	287	297
5-door 4WD with bucket seats	545	469	485

Prices are accurate at time of publication; subject to manufacturer's change.

	Retail Price	Dealer Invoice	Fair Price
Leather-wrapped steering wheel, body-color bumpers, grille, and wheel opening moldings, alloy wheels.			
SLT Touring Decor Pkg., 3-door 2WD	$3325	$2860	$2959
3-door 4WD	3550	3053	3160
5-door 2WD	2844	2446	2531
5-door 4WD	2666	2293	2373
Reclining leather buckets seat with driver- and passenger-side lumbar adjustment, 6-way power driver's seat, folding rear 3-passenger bench seat, floor and overhead consoles, power windows and door locks, remote keyless entry system, illuminated entry, reading lights, lighted visor mirrors, leather-wrapped steering wheel, body-color bumpers, bodyside and wheel opening moldings, upgraded door trim, conventional 2-tone paint, convenience net (3-door), floormats, 205/75R15 all-season tires, alloy wheels. 4WD adds: Bilstein shocks, 235/75R15 all-season tires.			
Air conditioning	780	671	694
Folding rear seat, 3-door	409	352	364
Cloth folding rear seat, 3-door and			
5-door 2WD	435	374	387
Cloth bucket seats, 3-door	76	65	68
5-door	211	181	188
6-way power driver's seat and driver/			
passenger power lumber support	290	249	258
Requires SLE or SLS Decor Pkgs., power windows and locks, reclining bucket seats.			
Floor console	145	125	129
Requires reclining bucket seats.			
Overhead console	83	71	74
Includes reading lights and storage compartments. Requires SLE or SLS decor Pkgs., bucket seats.			
Heavy duty battery	56	48	50
Spare wheel and tire carrier	159	137	142
Cold Climate Pkg., 3-door	179	154	159
SLE, SLS or SLT 3-door,			
5-door	109	94	97
Convenience Pkg. ZQ3	383	329	341
Cruise control, tilt steering wheel.			
Convenience Pkg. ZM8	197	169	175
Remote tailgate release, rear defogger.			
Convenience Pkg. ZQ2, 3-door	367	316	327
5-door	542	466	482
Power windows and locks.			
Deep-tinted glass	225	194	200
with light-tinted rear window	144	124	128
Requires Convenience Pkg. ZM8.			

	Retail Price	Dealer Invoice	Fair Price
Air deflector with fog lamps, 2WD	$115	$99	$102
Rear wiper/washer	125	108	111
Requires ZM8 Convenience Pkg.			
Sliding side window (2WD only)	257	221	229
Electronic instrumentation	195	168	174
Remote keyless entry	135	116	120
Requires ZQ2 and ZM8 Convenience Pkgs., bucket seats, floor console.			
Luggage carrier	126	108	112
Power mirrors	83	71	74
Wheel opening moldings	43	37	38
Special 2-tone paint	172	148	153
Conventional 2-tone paint (NA SL or SLS decor)	172	148	153
AM/FM cassette	122	105	109
AM/FM cassette with equalizer	272	234	242
AM/FM with CD player	406	349	361
AM/FM radio delete (credit)	(226)	(194)	(194)
AM radio (credit)	(131)	(113)	(113)
Credit when AM radio is substituted for standard AM/FM radio.			
Shield Pkg., 4WD (NA SLT Decor Pkg.)	75	65	67
Heavy duty shock absorbers (NA SLT Decor Pkg.)	40	34	36
Heavy duty front springs, 4WD	63	54	56
Softride Suspension, 4WD 5-door	235	202	209
with 235/75R15 WL tires	358	308	319
Off-Road Suspension Pkg., 3-door, 4WD	122	105	109
Bilstein gas shock absorbers, larger torsion bar, jounce bumpers, stabilizer bar, larger body mounted tow hooks. NA SLT.			
Heavy duty trailering equipment	345	297	307
with high output 4.3-liter V-6 engine	210	181	187
Light duty trailering equipment	300	258	267
with high output 4.3-liter V-6 engine	109	94	97
205/75R15 on/off-road WL tires	170	146	151
205/75R15 all-season WL tires	121	104	108
235/75R15 all-season tires	153	132	136
235/75R15 all-season WL tires, 4WD	286	246	255
with SLT	133	114	118
235/75R15 on/off-road WL tires, 4WD	335	288	298
WL denotes white letter; OWL denotes outline white letter.			
Alloy wheels	340	292	303
with SLE	284	244	253
Wheel trim rings, 3-door	60	52	53
Rally wheels, 2WD	92	79	82
Body striping	55	47	49

Prices are accurate at time of publication; subject to manufacturer's change.

	Retail Price	Dealer Invoice	Fair Price
Cargo area security shade	$69	$59	$61
NA 3-door; requires spare tire carrier.			
Front floormats	25	22	22

HONDA

Honda Accord	Retail Price	Dealer Invoice	Fair Price
DX 2-door notchback, 5-speed	$14130	—	—
DX 2-door notchback, automatic	14880	—	—
DX 2-door notchback, 5-speed w/ABS............	15080	—	—
DX 2-door notchback, automatic w/ABS........	15830	—	—
LX 2-door notchback, 5-speed	17030	—	—
LX 2-door notchback, automatic	17780	—	—
LX 2-door notchback, 5-speed w/ABS	17980	—	—
LX 2-door notchback, automatic w/ABS	18730	—	—
EX 2-door notchback, 5-speed	19550	—	—
EX 2-door notchback, automatic	20300	—	—
EX 2-door notchback, 5-speed w/leather	20600	—	—
EX 2-door notchback, automatic w/leather	21350	—	—
DX 4-door notchback, 5-speed	14330	12181	—
DX 4-door notchback, automatic	15080	12818	—
DX 4-door notchback w/ABS, 5-speed	15280	12988	—
DX 4-door notchback w/ABS, automatic	16030	13626	—
LX 4-door notchback, 5-speed	17230	14646	—
LX 4-door notchback, automatic	17980	15283	—
LX 4-door notchback w/ABS, 5-speed	18180	15453	—
LX 4-door notchback w/ABS, automatic	18930	16091	—
EX 4-door notchback, 5-speed	19750	16788	—
EX 4-door notchback, automatic	20500	17425	—
EX 4-door notchback w/leather, 5-speed	20800	17680	—
EX 4-door notchback w/leather, automatic	21550	18318	—
LX 5-door wagon, 5-speed	—	—	—
LX 5-door wagon, automatic	—	—	—
EX 5-door wagon, 5-speed	—	—	—
EX 5-door wagon, automatic	—	—	—
Destination charge	350	350	350

2-door dealer invoice, fair price and wagon prices not available at time of publication.

Standard Equipment:

DX: 2.2-liter 4-cylinder engine, 5-speed manual or 4-speed automatic transmission, variable-assist power steering, driver- and passenger-side air bags, cloth reclining front bucket seats, folding rear seatback, front console with armrest, tachometer, coolant temperature gauge, trip odometer, tinted glass, tilt steering column, intermittent wipers, rear defogger, dual remote mirrors, remote fuel door and decklid releases, door pockets, maintenance interval indicator, 185/70R14 tires. **Models with ABS** add 4-wheel anti-lock disc brakes. **LX** adds: air conditioning, cruise control, power windows and locks, power mirrors, AM/FM cassette, power antenna, rear armrest, beverage holder; wagon has cargo cover, full-size spare tire. **EX** adds: 145-horsepower VTEC engine, anti-lock 4-wheel disc brakes, driver's seat lumbar support and power height adjusters, power moonroof, upgraded audio system, 195/60HR15 tires, alloy wheels; wagon adds remote keyless entry.

Options are available as dealer-installed accessories.

Honda Civic	Retail Price	Dealer Invoice	Fair Price
CX 3-door hatchback, 5-speed	$9400	$8460	$9360
DX 3-door hatchback, 5-speed	10800	9288	10188
DX 3-door hatchback, automatic	11780	10131	11031
VX 3-door hatchback, 5-speed	11500	9890	10790
Si 3-door hatchback, 5-speed	13170	11326	12226
Si 3-door hatchback w/ABS, 5-speed	14020	12057	12957
DX 2-door notchback, 5-speed	11220	9649	10549
DX 2-door notchback, automatic	12200	10492	11392
EX 2-door notchback, 5-speed	13600	11696	12596
EX 2-door notchback, automatic	14350	12341	13241
EX 2-door notchback w/ABS, 5-speed	14450	12427	13327
EX 2-door notchback w/ABS, automatic	15200	13072	13972
DX 4-door notchback, 5-speed	11750	10105	11005
DX 4-door notchback, automatic	12500	10750	11650
LX 4-door notchback, 5-speed	12950	11137	12037
LX 4-door notchback, automatic	13700	11782	12682
LX 4-door notchback w/ABS, 5-speed	13800	11868	12768
LX 4-door notchback w/ABS, automatic	14550	12513	13413
EX 4-door notchback, 5-speed	15740	13536	14436
EX 4-door notchback, automatic	16490	14181	15081
Destination charge	350	350	350

Standard Equipment:

CX: 1.5-liter (70 horsepower) 4-cylinder engine, 5-speed manual transmission, driver- and passenger-side air bags, reclining cloth front bucket seats, 50/50 split folding rear seatback, remote fuel door and hatch releases, tinted glass, rear defogger, dual remote mirrors, 165/70R13 tires. **DX** adds: 1.5-liter (102 horsepower) engine, 5-speed manual or 4-speed automatic

HONDA

transmission, power steering (sedans; hatchbacks and coupes with automatic transmission only), rear wiper/washer (hatchback), tilt steering column, cargo cover (hatchback), intermittent wipers, bodyside moldings, 175/70R13 tires. **VX** adds to CX: 1.5-liter (92 horsepower) engine, tachometer, alloy wheels. **Si** adds to DX: 1.6-liter engine, 4-wheel disc brakes, power steering, dual power mirrors, power moonroof, digital clock, tachometer, sport seats, cruise control, rear wiper/washer, wheel covers, 185/60HR14 tires. **LX 4-door** adds to DX 4-door: power mirrors, power windows and locks, cruise control, digital clock, tachometer, front armrest, wheel covers, 175/65R14 tires. **Models with ABS** add: anti-lock 4-wheel disc brakes. **EX 4-door** adds to LX 4-door: 1.6-liter engine, anti-lock 4-wheel disc brakes, air conditioning, power moonroof, upgraded interior trim. **EX 2-door** adds to DX 2-door: 1.6-liter engine, power windows and locks, power mirrors, power moonroof, cruise control, AM/FM cassette, wheel covers, 185/60HR14 tires.

Options are available as dealer-installed accessories.

Honda Civic del Sol	Retail Price	Dealer Invoice	Fair Price
S 2-door notchback, 5-speed	$14100	$12126	$13626
S 2-door notchback, automatic	15080	12969	14469
Si 2-door notchback, 5-speed	16100	13846	15346
Si 2-door notchback, automatic	16850	14491	15991
VTEC 2-door notchback, 5-speed	17500	15050	16550
Destination charge	350	350	350

Standard Equipment:

S: 1.5-liter 4-cylinder engine, driver- and passenger-side air bags, power steering (with automatic), reclining front bucket seats, center armrest with storage, power windows, rear defogger, intermittent wipers, tilt steering column, tachometer, remote fuel door release, 175/70R13 tires, wheel covers. **Si** adds: 1.6-liter 4-cylinder engine, power steering, 4-wheel disc brakes, cruise control, AM/FM cassette, power mirrors, 185/60HR14 tires, alloy wheels. **VTEC** adds: 1.6-liter DOHC VTEC engine, 195/60VR14 tires.

Options are available as dealer-installed accessories.

Honda Prelude	Retail Price	Dealer Invoice	Fair Price
S 2-door notchback, 5-speed	$18100	$15385	$16085
S 2-door notchback, automatic	18850	16023	16723
Si 2-door notchback, 5-speed	21400	18190	18890
Si 2-door notchback, automatic	22150	18828	19528
Si 4WS 2-door notchback, 5-speed	24160	20536	21236
Si 4WS 2-door notchback, automatic	24910	21174	21874

	Retail Price	Dealer Invoice	Fair Price
VTEC 2-door notchback, 5-speed	$24500	$20825	$21525
Destination charge	350	350	350

Dealer invoice and fair price not available at time of publication.

Standard Equipment:

S: 2.2-liter 4-cylinder engine, 5-speed manual or 4-speed automatic transmission, 4-wheel disc brakes, variable-assist power steering, driver- and passenger-side air bags, cloth reclining front bucket seats, folding rear seat, power moonroof, AM/FM cassette with power antenna, remote fuel door and decklid releases, rear defogger, intermittent wipers, power windows, power mirrors, cruise control, tilt steering column, tachometer, visor mirrors, 185/70HR14 tires, wheel covers. **Si adds:** 2.3-liter DOHC 4-cylinder engine, anti-lock brakes, air conditioning, power locks, driver-seat height and lumbar support adjusters, 205/55VR15 tires, alloy wheels. **Si 4WS** adds: 4-wheel steering, leather seats, rear spoiler. **VTEC** adds to Si: 2.2-liter DOHC VTEC engine, leather seats, rear spoiler.

Options are available as dealer-installed accessories.

HYUNDAI

Hyundai Elantra	Retail Price	Dealer Invoice	Fair Price
4-door notchback, 5-speed	$9749	$8800	$9000
4-door notchback, automatic	11024	9948	10148
GLS 4-door notchback, 5-speed	10959	9669	9869
GLS 4-door notchback, automatic	11684	10320	10520
Destination charge	405	405	405

Standard Equipment:

1.6-liter DOHC 4-cylinder engine, 5-speed manual transmission, power steering, driver-side air bag, motorized front shoulder belts, cloth reclining front bucket seats, center console, digital clock, remote fuel door and decklid releases, rear defogger, variable-intermittent wipers, coolant temperature gauge, trip odometer, tinted glass, dual remote outside mirrors, 175/65R14 tires. **Automatic** adds: 4-speed automatic transmission, 1.8-liter DOHC engine. **GLS** adds: 1.8-liter DOHC engine, 6-way adjustable driver's seat, split folding rear seat, upgraded upholstery, power mirrors, front map pockets, tachometer, power windows and locks, tilt steering column, AM/FM cassette, 185/60R14 tires.

Prices are accurate at time of publication; subject to manufacturer's change.

HYUNDAI

Optional Equipment:	Retail Price	Dealer Invoice	Fair Price
Option Pkg. 2, base	$350	$268	$305
AM/FM cassette.			
Option Pkg. 3, base	1245	998	1108
Pkg. 2 plus air conditioning.			
Option Pkg. 4, base	1465	1178	1305
Pkg. 3 plus cruise control.			
Option Pkg. 10, GLS	1303	1053	1163
Air conditioning, uplevel AM/FM cassette, cruise control.			
Option Pkg. 11, GLS	1643	1330	1468
Pkg. 10 plus alloy wheels.			
Option Pkg. 12, GLS	1813	1469	1621
Pkg. 10 plus sunroof.			
Option Pkg. 13, GLS	2075	1764	1896
Pkg. 10 plus anti-lock brakes.			
Option Pkg. 14, GLS	3120	2605	2827
Pkg. 13 plus high level AM/FM cassette, alloy wheels, and sunroof.			
Option Pkg. 15, GLS	2345	1894	2093
Deletes anti-lock brakes from Pkg. 14.			
CD player	395	290	338
Front console armrest	108	70	88
Door edge guards	36	23	29
Mud guards, front and rear	78	47	62
Sunroof wind deflector	52	30	40
Floormats	58	38	47

Hyundai Excel	Retail Price	Dealer Invoice	Fair Price
3-door hatchback, 5-speed manual	$7190	$6710	$6910
3-door hatchback, 4-speed automatic	7815	7271	7471
GS 3-door hatchback, 5-speed manual	8099	7311	7511
GS 3-door hatchback, 4-speed automatic	8724	7872	8072
GL 4-door notchback, 5-speed manual	8099	7476	7676
GL 4-door notchback, 4-speed automatic	8724	8037	8237
Destination charge	405	405	405

Standard Equipment:

1.5-liter 4-cylinder engine, 5-speed manual or 4-speed automatic transmission, door-mounted front shoulder belts, cloth and vinyl reclining front bucket seats, 60/40 folding rear seatback, dual remote outside mirrors, coolant temperature gauge, trip odometer, center bodyside molding, rear defogger, locking fuel door, intermittent wipers, cargo cover, 155/80R13 tires. **GL 4-door** adds: AM/FM cassette player, tinted glass, door map pockets, remote fuel door and decklid releases, lockable glove box, 175/70R13 tires. **GS 3-door** adds: tachometer, 5-way adjustable driver's seat, full cloth upholstery, digital clock, upgraded door trim, door map pockets, rear heater ducts, rear spoiler, passenger-side visor mirror, console with cassette storage, rear wiper/washer.

Optional Equipment:

	Retail Price	Dealer Invoice	Fair Price
Option Pkg. 2, base	$340	$260	$293
AM/FM cassette.			
Option Pkg. 3, base	660	541	586
Pkg. 2 plus power steering and tinted glass.			
Option Pkg. 4, base	1545	1263	1370
Pkg. 3 plus air conditioning.			
Option Pkg. 5, GL and Option Pkg. 10, GS	260	232	240
Power steering.			
Option Pkg. 6, GL and Option Pkg. 11, GS	1155	994	1048
Pkg. 5, GS and Pkg. 10, GL plus air conditioning.			
Option Pkg. 12, GS	1646	1394	1483
Pkg. 11 plus sunroof.			
Sunroof air deflector	62	30	40
Console armrest	105	64	82
Mud guards, rear	40	26	32
Floormats	62	38	47

Hyundai Scoupe

	Retail Price	Dealer Invoice	Fair Price
2-door notchback, 5-speed	$9499	$8575	$8775
2-door notchback, automatic	10174	9188	9388
LS 2-door notchback, 5-speed	10599	9351	9551
LS 2-door notchback, automatic	11274	9964	10164
Turbo 2-door notchback, 5-speed	11399	10057	10257
Destination charge	405	405	405

Standard Equipment:

1.5-liter 4-cylinder engine, 5-speed manual or 4-speed automatic transmission, door-mounted front shoulder belts, cloth reclining front bucket seats, 60/40 folding rear seatback, tachometer, coolant temperature gauge, trip odometer, remote outside mirrors, rear window defroster, tinted glass, intermittent wipers, remote fuel door and decklid releases, digital clock, door map pockets, rear spoiler, passenger-side visor mirror, 175/70R13 tires. **LS** adds: power steering, power windows and mirrors, 6-way adjustable driver's seat, 4-way adjustable passenger's seat, full cloth upholstery, AM/FM cassette, cup holders, 185/60HR14 tires. **Turbo** adds to LS: turbocharged 1.5-liter engine, LED turbo boost gauge, sport suspension, leather-wrapped steering wheel and shift knob, fog lamps, alloy wheels.

Optional Equipment:	Retail Price	Dealer Invoice	Fair Price
Option Pkg. 2, base	$610	$496	$540
AM/FM cassette, power steering.			
Option Pkg. 3, base	1505	1235	1337
Pkg. 2 plus air conditioning.			
Option Pkg. 10, LS	895	739	797
Air conditioning.			
Option Pkg. 11, LS	1190	983	1060
Pkg. 10 plus sunroof.			
Option Pkg. 12, LS	1715	1405	1522
Pkg. 11 plus high-level AM/FM cassette, air conditioning.			
Option Pkg. 15, Turbo	1385	1132	1228
High-level AM/FM cassette, air conditioning, sunroof.			
CD player	395	290	334
Console armrest	105	64	82
Sunshade	58	38	47
Floormats	58	38	47

INFINITI

Infiniti G20	Retail Price	Dealer Invoice	Fair Price
4-door notchback, 5-speed	$21750	$17835	$19335
4-door notchback, automatic	22750	18655	20155
Destination charge	450	450	450

Standard Equipment:

2.0-liter DOHC 4-cylinder engine, 5-speed manual or 4-speed automatic transmission, anti-lock 4-wheel disc brakes, power steering, driver- and passenger-side air bags, automatic climate control, cloth reclining front bucket seats, tachometer, coolant temperature gauge, trip odometer, power windows and locks, power mirrors, AM/FM cassette, power antenna, leather-wrapped steering wheel, remote fuel door and decklid releases, tinted glass, anti-theft device, 195/65HR14 all-season tires, alloy wheels.

Optional Equipment:	Retail Price	Dealer Invoice	Fair Price
Power glass sunroof	$1000	$820	$910
Leather Appointment Group	2200	1804	2000

Includes leather seats, 4-way power front seats, padded leather center console armrest, remote keyless entry system, power glass sunroof.

Infiniti J30	Retail Price	Dealer Invoice	Fair Price
4-door notchback	$36950	$29930	$32930
J30t with Touring Package	39250	31793	34793
Destination charge	450	450	450

Standard Equipment:

3.0-liter DOHC V-6 engine, 4-speed automatic transmission, anti-lock 4-wheel disc brakes, variable-assist power steering, limited-slip differential, driver- and passenger-side air bags, 8-way heated power front bucket seats, leather upholstery, walnut inlays, automatic climate control, cruise control, tilt steering column, AM/FM cassette and CD player with six speakers, power sunroof, tinted glass, power windows and locks, 8-way power front seats, heated power mirrors, remote fuel door and decklid releases, remote keyless entry and anti-theft alarm systems, intermittent wipers, tachometer, trip odometer, leather-wrapped steering wheel, rear folding armrest, floormats, 215/60HR15 all-season tires, cast alloy wheels. **J30t** adds: Touring Package (Super HICAS 4-wheel steering, rear spoiler, firmer suspension, larger stabilizer bars, 215/60HR15 performance tires, forged alloy wheels).

Infiniti Q45	Retail Price	Dealer Invoice	Fair Price
4-door notchback	$50450	—	—
Q45t with Touring Pkg.	53550	—	—
Q45a with Full-Active Suspension	57050	—	—
Destination charge	450	450	450

Prices include Gas Guzzler Tax.

Dealer invoice and fair price not available at time of publication.

Standard Equipment:

4.5-liter DOHC V-8, 4-speed automatic transmission, anti-lock 4-wheel disc brakes, power steering, limited-slip differential, driver- and passenger-side air bags, cruise control, automatic climate control, leather reclining front bucket seats (wool is available at no charge), wood interior trim, Nissan/Bose AM/FM cassette, power antenna, power sunroof, tinted glass, power windows and locks, remote keyless entry system, power driver's seat with

2-position memory (memory includes tilt/telescopic steering column), power passenger seat, heated power mirrors, fog lights, remote fuel door and decklid releases, intermittent wipers, front and rear folding armrests, theft deterrent system, 215/65VR15 tires, alloy wheels. **Q45t** adds to base: Touring Pkg. (Includes Super HICAS 4-wheel steering, rear spoiler, forged alloy wheels, larger front stabilizer bar, rear stabilizer bar, performance tires, heated front seats). **Q45a** adds to base: Full-Active Suspension, all-season tires, heated front seats, traction control, trunk-mounted CD changer, larger front stabilizer bar, rear stabilizer bar, alloy wheels.

Optional Equipment:	Retail Price	Dealer Invoice	Fair Price
Traction control, base	$1600	—	—
with Touring Pkg.	1500	—	—
Includes all-season tires, heated front seats.			

ISUZU

Isuzu Rodeo	Retail Price	Dealer Invoice	Fair Price
S 4-cylinder 2WD 5-door wagon, 5-speed	$14969	—	—
S V-6 2WD 5-door wagon, 5-speed	17499	—	—
S V-6 2WD 5-door wagon, automatic	18399	—	—
LS V-6 2WD 5-door wagon, automatic	22729	—	—
S V-6 4WD 5-door wagon, 5-speed	19249	—	—
S V-6 4WD 5-door wagon, automatic	20249	—	—
LS V-6 4WD 5-door wagon, 5-speed	23799	—	—
LS V-6 4WD 5-door wagon, automatic	24899	—	—
Destination charge.	375	—	—

Dealer invoice and fair price not available at time of publication.

Standard Equipment:

S: 2.6-liter 4-cylinder engine, 5-speed manual transmission, anti-lock rear brakes, power steering, cloth front bench seat with folding armrest, folding rear seat, rear defogger, tinted glass, day/night mirror, cargo rope hooks, carpet, 225/75R15 all-terrain tires, styled steel wheels with bright center caps. **S V-6** adds: 3.2-liter V-6, 5-speed manual or 4-speed automatic transmission, 4-wheel disc brakes, reclining front bucket seats, center console, tachometer, oil pressure and coolant temperature guages, voltmeter, intermittent rear wiper/washer, carpeted floormats, outside spare tire, wheel trim rings. **LS** adds: air conditioning, tilt steering column, split folding rear seat, power windows and doors, cruise control, cassette player, velour upholstery, map and courtesy lights, intermittent wipers, right visor mirror, leather-wrapped steering wheel, bright exterior trim, roof rack, privacy rear quarter and rear side glass, cargo net, alloy wheels. **4WD** adds: part-time 4WD automatic locking hubs, tow hooks, skid plates, 245/70R16 tires, alloy wheels.

Optional Equipment:

	Retail Price	Dealer Invoice	Fair Price
Air conditioning, S	$850	—	—
Preferred Equipment Pkg., S V-6	1990	—	—
Air conditioning, power windows and locks, cruise control, intermittent rear wiper/washer, roof rack, 4-speaker cassette player, cargo net.			
Alloy Wheel Pkg., S 4WD	990	—	—
16-inch alloy wheels, 245/70R16 tires, limited-slip differential.			
Limited-slip differential, LS 4WD	260	—	—
Sunroof, LS	300	—	—
Rear wiper/washer, S 4-cylinder	185	—	—
Outside spare tire carrier, S 4-cylinder	275	—	—
Brush/grille guard	305	—	—
AM/FM cassette, S	585	—	—
CD player, LS	550	—	—
Aero roof rack, S	195	—	—
Carpeted floormats (std. V-6)	55	—	—

Isuzu Trooper

	Retail Price	Dealer Invoice	Fair Price
S 4-door 4WD wagon, 5-speed	$21250	—	—
S 4-door 4WD wagon, automatic	22400	—	—
LS 4-door 4WD wagon, 5-speed	26850	—	—
LS 4-door 4WD wagon, automatic	28000	—	—
RS 2-door 4WD wagon, 5-speed	24000	—	—
RS 2-door 4WD wagon, automatic	25150	—	—
Destination charge	400	—	—

Dealer invoice and fair price not available at time of publication.

Standard Equipment:

S: 3.2-liter V-6 engine, 5-speed manual transmission, power steering, 4-wheel disc brakes, anti-lock rear brakes, part-time 4WD system with automatic locking front hubs, cloth reclining front bucket seats, folding rear seat, full door trim, AM/FM cassette, center console, dual outside mirrors, rear defogger, tilt steering column, intermittent wipers, rear wiper/washer, skid plates, tachometer, voltmeter, oil pressure gauge, visor mirrors, tinted glass, rear step pad, rear air deflector, 245/70R16 tires, wheel trim rings. **LS** adds: 3.2-liter DOHC engine, 4-wheel anti-lock brakes, limited-slip differential, air conditioning, power windows and locks, cruise control, multi-adjustable driver's seat, split folding rear seat, bright exterior trim, color-keyed bumpers, variable intermittent wipers, headlamp wiper/washer, leather-wrapped steering wheel, heated power mirrors, privacy glass, premium cassette system with six speakers, power antenna, anti-theft alarm, visor mirrors, fog lamps, cargo floor rails, retractable cargo cover, cargo net, alloy wheels. **RS** deletes 4-wheel anti-lock brakes, bright exterior trim and adds: anti-lock rear brakes, sport cloth interior, one-piece folding and reclining rear seat, flip-out quarter windows, color-keyed grille, 2-tone paint, gas shocks.

Optional Equipment:	Retail Price	Dealer Invoice	Fair Price
4-wheel anti-lock brakes, S and RS	$1100	—	—
Limited-slip differential, S	260	—	—
Requires Preferred Equipment Pkg.			
Air conditioning, S	900	—	—
Preferred Equipment Pkg., S	1880	—	—
Air conditioning, power windows and locks, 6-speaker radio, split-folding rear seat, power mirrors, cruise control, retractable cargo cover, cargo net.			
Appearance Pkg., S	750	—	—
Alloy wheels with locks, bright radiator grille and mirrors, color-keyed bumpers. Requires Preferred Equipment Pkg.			
Power sunroof, LS	1100	—	—
Heated leather power seats, LS	2250	—	—
Split folding rear seat, S	250	—	—
CD player, S with Preferred Equipment Pkg., RS and LS	550	—	—
2-tone paint, LS	280	—	—
Retractable cargo cover, S	120	—	—
Cargo net, S	30	—	—

JEEP

Jeep Cherokee	Retail Price	Dealer Invoice	Fair Price
SE 3-door 2WD	$13077	$12355	$12555
SE 3-door 4WD	14562	13721	13921
SE 5-door 2WD	14087	13289	13739
SE 5-door 4WD	15572	14661	15111
Sport 3-door 2WD	15234	13861	14061
Sport 3-door 4WD	16719	15183	15383
Sport 5-door 2WD	16244	14765	15215
Sport 5-door 4WD	17729	16092	16542
Country 3-door 2WD	16871	15301	15551

	Retail Price	Dealer Invoice	Fair Price
Country 3-door 4WD	$18356	$16623	$16873
Country 5-door 2WD	17881	16205	16655
Country 5-door 4WD	19366	17532	17982
Destination charge	495	495	495

Standard Equipment:

SE: 2.5-liter 4-cylinder engine, 5-speed manual transmission, power steering, vinyl front bucket seats, front armrest, folding rear seat, mini console, AM/FM radio with two speakers, tinted glass, dual remote mirrors, 215/75R15 tires; 4WD system is Command-Trac part-time. **Sport** adds: 4.0-liter 6-cylinder engine, cloth reclining front bucket seats, tachometer, trip odometer, oil pressure and coolant temperature gauges, voltmeter, intermittent wipers, Sport Decor Group, spare tire cover, cargo tiedown hooks, 2-tone paint, 225/75R15 outlined white letter all-terrain tires. **Country** adds: front console with armrest and storage, rear seat heater ducts, AM/FM stereo with four speakers, Light Group, leather-wrapped steering wheel, roof rack, rear wiper/washer, dual remote break-away mirrors, Country Decor Group, Extra-Quiet Insulation Pkg., front floormats, bodyside cladding, 225/70R15 tires, lattice-design alloy wheels.

Optional Equipment:

Pkg. 23B/25B/26B, SE	492	418	431

Cloth reclining bucket seats, floor console with armrest, Visibility Group. Pkg. 25B requires 4.0-liter engine. Pkg. 26B requires 4.0-liter engine and automatic transmission.

Pkg. 26E, Sport	897	762	785

Adds 4-speed automatic transmission.

Pkg. 25E/26E, Sport	1169	994	1023

Air conditioning, floor console with armrest, roof rack, leather-wrapped tilt steering wheel, rear wiper/washer, floormats. Pkg. 26E requires 4-speed automatic transmission.

Pkg. 25H/26H, Country	824	700	721

Air conditioning, cruise control, cassette player with four speakers, tilt steering wheel. Pkg. 26H requires 4-speed automatic transmission.

4.0-liter 6-cylinder engine	612	520	536
4-speed automatic transmission	897	762	785
Selec-Trac full-time 4WD, Sport, Country	394	335	345

Requires automatic transmission.

Trac-Lok rear differential	285	242	249

Requires conventional spare tire.

Anti-lock brakes	599	509	524

Requires 4.0-liter engine.

Prices are accurate at time of publication; subject to manufacturer's change.

JEEP

	Retail Price	Dealer Invoice	Fair Price
Heavy Duty Alternator/Battery Group	$135	$115	$118
with rear defogger	63	54	55
Air conditioning	836	711	732
Includes Heavy Duty Alternator/Battery Group.			
Rear defogger	161	137	141
Requires air conditioning or Heavy Duty Alternator/Battery Group .			
Visibility Group, SE	208	177	182
Intermittent wipers, rear wiper/washer.			
Fog lamps, Sport, Country	110	94	96
Requires air conditioning or Heavy Duty Alternator/Battery Group.			
Rear wiper/washer, Sport	147	125	129
Deep-tinted glass, Sport and			
Country 3-doors	305	259	267
Sport and Country 5-doors	144	122	126
Front vent windows	91	77	80
Power Windows and Door Locks Group,			
Sport and Country 3-doors	437	371	382
Sport and Country 5-doors	582	495	509
Power windows and locks, remote keyless entry.			
Dual remote break-away mirrors,			
SE, Sport	22	19	20
Power mirrors, Country	100	85	88
Requires Power Windows and Door Locks Group.			
Tilt steering wheel	132	112	116
SE requires Visibility Group.			
Cruise control	230	196	201
SE requires Visibility Group.			
Leather-wrapped steering wheel,			
SE, Sport	48	41	42
Cassette player with four speakers,			
SE, Sport	291	247	255
Country	201	171	176
Premium speakers (six), Country	128	109	112
Requires Power Windows and Door Locks Group.			
Fabric seats, SE	137	116	120
SE w/Pkgs. 23B, 25B, 26B	NC	NC	NC
Power driver's seat, Country	296	252	259
Leather seats, Country 5-door	831	706	727
Floor console with armrest, SE, Sport	147	125	129
Overhead console, Sport, Country	203	173	178
Includes compass and thermometer, reading lights. Requires Power Windows and Door Locks Group.			
Cargo area cover	72	61	63
Roof rack, SE, Sport	139	118	122

	Retail Price	Dealer Invoice	Fair Price
Light Group, SE, Sport	$195	$166	$171
Headlamp-off delay system, lighted visor mirrors, misc. lights.			
Bright Group, Country	202	172	177
Bright dual power remote mirrors, front and rear bumpers, grille and headlamp bezels, door handle and escutcheons, windshield and drip rail moldings. Requires Power Windows and Door Locks Group			
Trailer Tow Group	358	304	313
4WD models with Off-Road Suspension	242	206	212
Requires 4.0-liter engine, automatic transmission, Heavy Duty Alternator/Battery Group, conventional spare tire.			
Off-Road Suspension (4WD only), SE	761	647	666
Sport	448	381	392
Country	360	306	315
Requires Heavy Duty Alternator/Battery Group, dual remote break-away mirrors (SE and Sport).			
Skid Plates Group, 4WD models	144	122	126
225/75R15 outlined white letter tires			
(four), SE	313	266	274
Spare 225/75R15 tire (required), SE	116	99	102
Conventional (215/75R15) spare tire, SE	71	60	62
Conventional (225/75R15 outlined white letter) spare tire, Sport	116	99	102
Conventional (225/70R15) spare tire, Country	140	119	123
10-hole alloy wheels, SE	435	370	381
Sport	332	282	291
Country	87	74	76
Requires conventional spare tire.			
Matching fifth alloy wheel, Sport	26	22	23
Country	87	74	76
Requires conventional spare tire.			
Front floormats, SE, Sport	20	17	18
Engine block heater (Alaska only)	31	26	27

Jeep Grand Cherokee

	Retail Price	Dealer Invoice	Fair Price
SE 5-door 2WD	$21156	$19242	$19942
SE 5-door 4WD	22096	20109	20809
Laredo 5-door 2WD	22192	20123	20823
Laredo 5-door 4WD	23132	21659	22359
Limited 5-door 4WD	29618	26728	27628
Destination charge	495	495	495

Prices are accurate at time of publication; subject to manufacturer's change.

Standard Equipment:

SE: 4.0-liter 6-cylinder engine, 5-speed manual transmission (4WD) or 4-speed automatic transmission (2WD), driver-side air bag, anti-lock brakes, power steering, cloth reclining front bucket seats, split folding rear seat, air conditioning, leather-wrapped tilt steering wheel, cruise control, tachometer, voltage and temperature gauges, console with armrest and cupholders, AM/FM cassette, tinted glass, rear defogger, intermittent rear wiper/washer, dual outside mirrors, remote fuel door release, trip odometer, map lights, roof rack, striping, 215/75R15 tires, wheel covers. 4WD system is Command-Trac part-time. **Laredo** adds: power windows and locks, power mirrors, remote keyless entry system, lighted visor mirrors, extra sound insulation, floormats, cargo area tie-down hooks and skid strips, cargo area cover and net, 225/75R15 outlined white letter tires, alloy wheels. **Limited** adds: 4-speed automatic transmission, 4-wheel disc brakes, automatic temperature control, leather power front seats, automatic day/night rearview mirror, automatic headlamp system, illuminated entry system, anti-theft alarm, overhead console with compass and temperature display, trip computer, heated power mirrors, fog lamps, deep tinted side and rear glass, 6-speaker AM/FM cassette with equalizer and amplifier, power antenna, 225/70R15 outlined white letter tires, alloy wheels, full-size spare tire. 4WD system is Quadra-Trac permanent 4WD

Optional Equipment:	Retail Price	Dealer Invoice	Fair Price
Pkg. 26F, Laredo 2WD	$3020	$2567	$2869
Pkg. 26F/28F, Laredo 4WD	3464	2944	3291
Luxury Group, Security Group, overhead console, deep-tinted glass, cassette system with equalizer and six speakers. Pkg. 26F (4WD) requires automatic transmission. Pkg. 28F requires 5.2-liter V-8 engine, automatic transmission.			
5.2-liter V-8 engine, 4WD SE			
and Laredo	1176	1000	1117
Laredo w/Pkg. 28F	732	622	695
Includes Trailer Tow Prep Group and Quadra-Trac. Requires 225/75R15 tires or Up Country Suspension Pkg. Requires automatic transmission.			
4-speed automatic transmission,			
SE, Laredo	897	762	852
Selec-Trac full-time 4WD, SE, Laredo	394	335	374
Limited	NC	NC	NC
Requires automatic transmission. Not available with 5.2-liter V-8.			
Quadra-Trac permanent 4WD,			
SE, Laredo	444	377	422
Requires automatic transmission.			
Trac-Lok rear differential	285	242	271
Requires automatic transmission.			
Power Group, SE	616	524	585

steering, dual power/heated outside mirrors, electronic analog instruments, power tilt/telescopic steering column, cloth power driver and front passenger seats, power windows and door locks, walnut wood trim, automatic climate control, automatic on/off headlamps, remote entry system, illuminated entry system, rear defogger, variable intermittent wipers, theft-deterrent system, illuminated visor mirrors, remote electric trunk and fuel-filler door releases, Lexus Premium Audio System with AM/FM/cassette and seven speakers, power diversity antenna, cellular phone pre-wiring, outside temperature indicator, illuminated entry system, tool kit, first aid kit, 215/60VR16 tires, alloy wheels.

Optional Equipment:

	Retail Price	Dealer Invoice	Fair Price
Traction Control System	$1800	$1440	$1710

Includes heated front seats. Requires Leather Trim Package and all-season tires.

Leather Trim Package	1300	1040	1235
Lexus/Nakamichi Premium Audio System	1100	825	1045

Requires Leather Trim Package and remote 12-CD auto-changer.

Remote 12-CD auto-changer	900	720	855
Power tilt and slide moonroof with sunshade	900	750	950
All-season tires	NC	NC	NC

Lexus LS 400

	Retail Price	Dealer Invoice	Fair Price
4-door notchback	$49900	$39920	$46900
Destination charge	470	470	470

Standard Equipment:

4.0-liter DOHC V-8 engine, 4-speed automatic transmission, anti-lock 4-wheel disc brakes, driver- and passenger-side air bags, variable-assist power steering, seatbelt pretensioners, air conditioning with automatic climate control, cloth reclining front bucket seats with 7-way power adjustment, power windows and locks, cruise control, remote entry system, walnut wood trim, heated power mirrors, tachometer, trip odometer, coolant temperature gauge, outside temperature indicator, remote fuel door and decklid releases, lighted visor mirrors, theft-deterrent system, automatic on/off headlamps, power tilt/telescopic steering column, AM/FM cassette with seven speakers and power diversity antenna, intermittent wipers, cellular phone pre-wiring, tool kit, first aid kit, 225/60VR16 tires, alloy wheels.

Optional Equipment:

Power moonroof with sunshade	1000	800	950
Traction control with heated front seats	1900	1520	1805

Prices are accurate at time of publication; subject to manufacturer's change.

LEXUS

	Retail Price	Dealer Invoice	Fair Price
Electronic air suspension	$1000	$1360	$1615
Requires moonroof and memory system.			
Seat memory system	800	640	760
Lexus/Nakamichi Premium Audio System	1100	825	1045
Requires CD changer.			
Remote 6-CD auto-changer	1000	750	950
All-season tires	NC	NC	NC
Wheel locks	50	30	48
Floormats	115	69	109
Carpeted trunk mat	68	41	65

Lexus SC 300/400

	Retail Price	Dealer Invoice	Fair Price
300 2-door notchback, 5-speed	$38000	$31160	$36000
300 2-door notchback, automatic	38900	31898	36900
400 2-door notchback	45100	36080	43100
Destination charge	470	470	470

Standard Equipment:

300: 3.0-liter DOHC 6-cylinder engine, 5-speed manual or 4-speed automatic transmission, anti-lock 4-wheel disc brakes, variable-assist power steering, driver- and passenger-side air bags, air conditioning with automatic climate control, tinted glass, power front seats, tilt/telescoping steering column, rear defogger, heated power mirrors, power windows and door locks, remote entry system, illuminated entry system, cruise control, tachometer, AM/FM cassette with seven speakers and automatic power diversity antenna, automatic on/off headlamps, lighted visor mirrors, remote fuel door and decklid releases, variable intermittent wipers, theft-deterrent system, cellular phone pre-wiring, tool kit, first aid kit, 215/60VR15 tires, alloy wheels. **400** adds: 4.0-liter DOHC V-8 engine, 4-speed automatic transmission, power tilt/telescoping steering column, leather upholstery, driver-side seat memory system, 225/55VR16 tires.

Optional Equipment:

	Retail Price	Dealer Invoice	Fair Price
Traction control system with heated front seats	1800	1440	1710
Requires automatic transmission.			
Remote 12-CD auto changer	1000	750	950
Lexus/Nakamichi Premium Audio System	1100	825	1045
Requires remote CD changer; 300 also requires Leather Trim Pkg. with seat memory system.			

	Retail Price	Dealer Invoice	Fair Price
Leather Trim Pkg. with seat memory system, 300	$1800	$1440	$1710
Power moonroof with sunshade	900	720	855
Heated front seats, 300 with manual transmission	400	320	380
Rear spoiler, 400	400	320	380

LINCOLN

Lincoln Continental

	Retail Price	Dealer Invoice	Fair Price
Executive 4-door notchback	$33750	$29296	$29796
Signature Series 4-door notchback	35600	30886	31386
Destination charge	625	625	625

Standard Equipment:

Executive: 3.8-liter V-6, 4-speed automatic transmission, anti-lock 4-wheel disc brakes, power steering, driver- and passenger-side air bags, automatic climate control, 50/50 leather front seat, power driver's seat with power recliner, tilt steering wheel, cruise control, automatic parking brake release, rear defogger, heated power mirrors, power windows and locks, remote fuel door and decklid releases, power decklid pulldown, AM/FM cassette, automatic power antenna, tinted glass, intermittent wipers, cornering lamps, electronic instruments, coolant temperature and oil pressure gauges, voltmeter, trip odometer, trip computer, service interval reminder, door pockets, rear courtesy lights, leather-wrapped steering wheel, right visor mirror, 205/70R15 tires, alloy wheels. **Signature Series** adds: 6-way power remote memory front seats with power recliners, remote keyless illuminated entry, Headlight Convenience Group, automatic dimmer, lighted visor mirrors, bodyside accent stripe, floormats.

Optional Equipment:

Anti-theft alarm system	290	250	255

Executive requires Preferred Equipment Pkg. 952A.

Comfort/Convenience Group, Executive	700	602	616

Power passenger seat with power recliner, Headlight Convenience Group, lighted visor mirrors, power decklid pulldown, rear floormats.

Preferred Equipment Pkg. 952A, Executive	NC	NC	NC

Comfort/Convenience Group, remote keyless illuminated entry.

LINCOLN

	Retail Price	Dealer Invoice	Fair Price
Preferred Equipment Pkg. 953A, Executive	$1325	$1140	$1166
Power Moonroof, 5-passenger seating with remote memory.			
Overhead Console Group	350	303	308
Includes compass and automatic day/night mirror, electrochromatic outside mirror; Executive requires Preferred Equipment Pkg.			
Remote keyless illuminated entry,			
Executive	300	257	264
5-passenger seating, Executive	890	767	783
Power moonroof	1515	1303	1333
Not available with Overhead Console Group.			
CD player	600	516	528
Ford JBL audio system	565	486	497
Executive requires Preferred Equipment Pkg.			
Voice-activated cellular telephone	690	593	607
White opalescent clearcoat paint	235	201	207

Lincoln Mark VIII

	Retail Price	Dealer Invoice	Fair Price
2-door notchback	$38050	$33034	$34234
Destination charge	625	625	625

Standard Equipment:

4.6-liter DOHC V-8 engine, 4-speed automatic transmission, 4-wheel anti-lock disc brakes, driver- and passenger-side air bags, automatic air conditioning, variable-assist power steering, tilt steering wheel, analog instrumentation with message center and programmable trip functions, service interval reminder, console with cup holder and storage bin, leather seat trim, Autoglide dual reclining 6-way power front seats with power lumbar supports and remote driver-side memory, leather wrapped steering wheel, automatic headlamps, door map pockets, solar-control tinted glass, anti-theft alarm system, cruise control, power windows and locks, heated power mirrors with remote 3-position memory, lighted visor mirrors, rear defogger, remote decklid and fuel door releases, illuminated and remote keyless entry systems, AM/FM cassette stereo with premium sound system, automatic power antenna, intermittent wipers, cargo net, floormats, 225/60VR16 tires, alloy wheels.

Optional Equipment:

Traction Assist	215	184	204
Power moonroof	1515	1302	1439
Voice-activated celluar telephone	690	594	655
Requires JBL Audio System.			
Electrochromatic auto dimming			
inside/outside mirrors	215	184	204

	Retail Price	Dealer Invoice	Fair Price
AM/FM stereo with CD player	290	250	275
Requires JBL Audio System.			
JBL Audio System	565	486	536.
Trunk-mounted CD changer	815	700	774
Requires JBL Audio System.			
Chrome wheels	845	726	802

Lincoln Town Car

	Retail Price	Dealer Invoice	Fair Price
Executive 4-door notchback	$34750	$30166	$30666
Signature Series 4-door notchback	36050	31284	31784
Cartier Designer Series 4-door notchback	38100	33046	33546
Destination charge	625	625	625

Standard Equipment:

Executive: 4.6-liter V-8, 4-speed automatic transmission, 4-wheel anti-lock disc brakes, power steering, driver- and passenger-side air bags, automatic climate control, 6-way power twin-comfort lounge seats with 2-way front head restraints, front and rear folding armrests, power windows and locks, tilt steering wheel, leather wrapped steering wheel, cruise control, automatic parking brake release, heated power mirrors, rear defogger, AM/FM cassette with premium sound, power antenna, solar-control tinted glass, remote fuel door and decklid release, power decklid pulldown, illuminated and remote keyless entry systems, cornering lamps, intermittent wipers, electronic instruments, digital clock, map pockets on front doors, dual lighted visor mirrors, front and rear floormats, dual exhaust, 215/70R15 whitewall tires. **Signature Series** adds: dual shade paint, dual footwell lights, front seat storage with cup holders, map pockets on front seatbacks, striping. **Cartier Designer Series** adds: cloth and leather upholstery, driver's seat position memory and power lumbar support, power front recliners, Ford JBL audio system, upgraded door trim panels.

Optional Equipment:

	Retail	Dealer	Fair
Traction Assist	215	184	193
Leather seat trim (std. Cartier)	555	479	499
Anti-theft alarm system	290	248	261
Programmable memory seat (std. Cartier)	535	460	481
Automatic day/night mirror	110	94	99
Power moonroof	1515	1302	1363
Ford JBL audio system, (std. Cartier)	565	486	508
Trunk-mounted CD changer	815	700	733

Prices are accurate at time of publication; subject to manufacture's change.

	Retail Price	Dealer Invoice	Fair Price
Ride Control Pkg.	$285	$246	$256

Auxiliary power steering fluid cooler. larger front and rear stabilizer bars, firmer front and rear springs. 225/70R15 whitewall tires. Not available with Heavy Duty Pkg.. Livery Pkg.. Trailer Tow III Pkg. or any other tire and wheel combination.

Heavy Duty Pkg.. Executive and Signature	805	692	724

3.55 Traction-Lok axle. heavy duty cooling, transmission oil and and steering fluid coolers. heavy duty suspension, full-size spare tire, heavy duty alternator and battery. 225/75R15 whitewall tires, steel wheels. Not available with Traction Assist. power moonroof, Livery Pkg., Trailer Tow III Pkg.. conventional axle. 225/70R15 or 215/70R15 tires.

Trailer Tow III Pkg.	465	400	418

3.55 axle ratio. heavy duty cooling, transmission oil and steering fluid coolers. heavy duty suspension, larger front stabilizer bar, heavy duty shock absorbers. heavy duty turn signals and flashers, full-size spare tire, trailer wiring harness. Not available with Livery Pkg.

Livery Pkg. Executive and Signature	325	280	292

Same as Heavy Duty Pkg. but with standard cooling system and 215/70R15 tires.

Voice activated cellular telephone	690	594	621
White opalescent clearcoat paint	235	202	211
Engine block heater	60	52	54
Full-size spare tire	220	190	198

MAZDA

Mazda Miata	Retail Price	Dealer Invoice	Fair Price
2-door convertible	$16650	$14931	$16150
Destination charge	395	395	395

Prices are for vehicles distributed by Mazda Motor of America, Inc. Prices may be higher in areas served by independent distributors.

Standard Equipment:

1.8-liter DOHC 4-cylinder engine, 5-speed manual transmission, 4-wheel disc brakes. driver- and passenger-side air bags, cloth reclining bucket seats. tachometer, coolant temperature gauge, trip odometer, intermittent wipers. AM/FM cassette, passenger visor mirror, dual outside mirrors, center console. dual courtesy lights, tinted glass, remote fuel door release, 185/60HR14 tires. alloy wheels.

Optional Equipment:

	Retail Price	Dealer Invoice	Fair Price
4-speed automatic transmission	$850	$739	$765
Requires Pkg. A, B, or C.			
Anti-lock brakes	900	765	810
Requires Pkg. A, B, or C.			
Air conditioning	830	680	765
Detachable hardtop	1500	1215	1350
Requires Pkg. A, B, or C.			
Sensory Sound System	700	560	630
Requires Pkg. B or C.			
Option Pkg. A, 5-speed	1710	1436	1539
Automatic	1320	1109	1188
Power steering, alloy wheels with locks, power mirrors, leather-wrapped steering wheel, headrest speakers, limited-slip differential (5-speed).			
Option Pkg. B, 5-speed	2410	2024	2169
Automatic	2020	1697	1818
Pkg. A plus power windows, cruise control, power antenna.			
Option Pkg. C, 5-speed	3110	2612	2799
Automatic	2720	2285	2448
Pkg. B plus tan interior with leather seating surfaces, tan vinyl top.			
Floormats	65	47	59

Mazda MPV

	Retail Price	Dealer Invoice	Fair Price
4-door van, 5-passenger, 2.6	$18195	$16313	$16813
4-door van, 7-passenger, 2.6	19595	17560	18060
4-door van, 7-passenger, 3.0	20395	18273	18773
4WD van, 7-passenger, 3.0	23395	20947	21447
Destination charge	445	445	445

Prices are for vehicles distributed by Mazda Motor of America, Inc. Prices may be higher in areas served by independent distributors.

Standard Equipment:

5-passenger: 2.6-liter 4-cylinder engine, 4-speed automatic transmission, anti-lock rear brakes, driver-side air bag, power steering, cloth reclining front bucket seats, removable reclining 3-passenger bench seat, remote mirrors, tachometer, coolant temperature gauge, trip odometer, intermittent wipers, rear defogger and wiper/washer, tinted glass, door pockets, remote fuel door release, tilt steering column, AM/FM cassette w/four speakers, digital clock, wheel covers, 195/75R15 tires. **7-passenger:** 2.6-liter 4-cylinder or 3.0-liter V-6, removable reclining 2-passenger middle and flip-fold 3-passenger rear bench seats, AM/FM cassette with six speakers, power mirrors. **4WD** has on-demand 4WD, 215/65R15 tires, alloy wheels.

MAZDA

Optional Equipment:	Retail Price	Dealer Invoice	Fair Price
Single air conditioning	$860	$705	$792
Dual air conditioning	1500	1230	1382
Requires V-6 engine and Pkg. A, B, C, or D.			
Touring Pkg.1, V-6 2WD	570	490	537
8-passenger seating, 3-passenger middle seat with fold-down armrests, cup holders, and outboard armrests.			
Requires Option Pkg. B or D. Cold Pkg.	300	258	283
Heavy duty battery, larger windshield washer solvent reservoir, rear heater.			
Option Pkg. A, 2WD	1050	872	973
Power windows and locks, cruise control, bronze-tinted windshield, rear privacy glass.			
Option Pkg. B, 2WD V-6	1350	1121	1251
Pkg. A plus keyless entry system, body-color grille, rear license plate illumination bar.			
Option Pkg. C, 4WD	1350	1121	1251
Pkg. A plus keyless entry system, body-color grille, rear license plate illumination bar.			
Luxury Pkg. (Option Pkg. D), 2WD V-6	3995	3316	3702
4WD	3550	2947	3290
Pkg. B (2WD), Pkg. C (4WD), leather upholstery, leather-wrapped steering wheel, color-keyed bodyside moldings, 2-tone paint, lace alloy wheels; requires dual air conditioning, Towing Pkg., and moonroof.			
CD player, 2WD V-6, 4WD	700	560	638
Requires Pkg. D.			
Power moonroof, 2WD V6, 4WD	1000	820	922
Requires Pkg. B, C, or D.			
2-tone paint	250	246	276
Towing Pkg., 2WD V-6	500	430	471
4WD	400	344	377
Transmission oil cooler, automatic load leveling, heavy duty cooling fan (2WD), conventional spare (2WD). 2WD requires Alloy wheel Pkg. or Pkg. D; 4WD requires Pkg. C or D.			
Alloy wheel Pkg., 2WD V-6	450	374	417
215/65R15 tires, alloy wheels. Requires Pkg. B.			
Floormats, 5-passenger	65	47	57
7-passenger	90	65	78
8-passenger	95	69	83

Mazda MX-3	Retail Price	Dealer Invoice	Fair Price
3-door hatchback	$13595	$12347	$12747
GS 3-door hatchback	16095	14438	14938
Destination charge	395	395	395

Prices are for vehicles distributed by Mazda Motor of America, Inc. Prices may be higher in areas served by independent distributors.

Standard Equipment:

1.6-liter DOHC 4-cylinder engine, 5-speed manual transmission, driver- and passenger-side air bags, cloth reclining front bucket seats, power steering, tachometer, AM/FM cassette stereo, coolant temperature gauge, variable-intermittent wipers, rear defogger, folding rear seat, power mirrors, tinted glass, tilt steering column, remote fuel door and hatch releases, rear cargo cover, wheel covers, 185/65R14 tires. **GS** adds: 1.8-liter DOHC V-6, 4-wheel disc brakes, rear wiper/washer, front and rear spoilers, 205/55R15 tires, alloy wheels.

Options not available at time of publication.

Mazda MX-6	Retail Price	Dealer Invoice	Fair Price
MX-6 2-door notchback	$17495	$15512	$16012
MX-6 LS 2-door notchback	21495	18818	19618
Destination charge	395	395	395

Prices are for vehicles distributed by Mazda Motor of America, Inc. Prices may be higher in areas served by independent distributors.

Standard Equipment:

2.0-liter DOHC 4-cylinder engine, 5-speed manual transmission, power steering, driver- and passenger-side air bags, cloth reclining front bucket seats, driver's-seat thigh support adjustment, 60/40 folding rear seat with armrest, console with storage, power windows and locks, cruise control, power mirrors, visor mirrors, AM/FM cassette with power antenna, tachometer, coolant temperature gauge, trip odometer, tilt steering column, intermittent wipers, dual remote mirrors, door pockets, tinted glass, remote fuel door and decklid releases, rear defogger, 195/65R14 tires, full wheel covers. **LS** adds: 2.5-liter DOHC V-6 engine, 4-wheel disc brakes, air conditioning, power sunroof, leather-wrapped steering wheel, anti-theft alarm, fog lamps, 205/55VR15 tires, alloy wheels.

Optional Equipment:

4-speed automatic transmission	800	696	760
Anti-lock 4-wheel disc brakes, base	950	808	902
Anti-lock brakes, LS	800	680	760
Air conditioning, base	850	680	807
Popular Equipment Group, base	1250	1000	1188

    Power sunroof, anti-theft alarm, alloy wheels.

Prices are accurate at time of publication; subject to manufacturer's change.

MAZDA

	Retail Price	Dealer Invoice	Fair Price
Leather Pkg., LS	$1000	$800	$950
Leather seats, power driver's seat, heated outside mirrors.			
Rear spoiler	375	300	356
Floormats	70	51	66

Mazda Navajo	Retail Price	Dealer Invoice	Fair Price
DX 3-door 2WD wagon	$17775	$15760	$16060
LX 3-door 2WD wagon	18995	16834	17134
DX 3-door 4WD wagon	19565	17335	17635
LX 3-door 4WD wagon	20785	18410	18710
Destination charge	490	490	490

Prices are for vehicles distributed by Mazda Motor of America, Inc. Prices may be higher in areas served by independent distributors.

Standard Equipment:

DX: 4.0-liter V-6, 5-speed manual transmission, anti-lock brakes, power steering, cloth reclining front bucket seats, split folding rear seat, intermittent wipers, tinted glass, AM/FM radio, skid plates, 225/70R15 tires. **LX** adds: power windows and locks, cassette player, rear window privacy glass, leather-wrapped steering wheel, power mirrors, lighted visor mirrors, upgraded door trim, retractable cargo cover, cargo net, alloy wheels. **4WD** models add part-time 4WD with electronic transfer case.

Options not available at time of publication.

Mazda RX-7	Retail Price	Dealer Invoice	Fair Price
3-door hatchback	$36000	$30760	$32260
Destination charge	395	395	395

Prices are for vehicles distributed by Mazda Motor of America, Inc. Prices may be higher in areas served by independent distributors.

Standard Equipment:

1.3-liter turbocharged rotary engine, 5-speed manual transmission, limited-slip differential, anti-lock 4-wheel disc brakes, variable-assist power steering, driver- and passenger-side air bags, cloth highback sport bucket seats, air conditioning, power windows and locks, dual storage compartments, power mirrors, AM/FM cassette, power antenna, tachometer and gauges, trip odometer, cruise control, tinted glass, intermittent wipers, leather-wrapped steering wheel, anti-theft alarm, remote fuel door and decklid releases, 225/50VR16 tires, alloy wheels.

Optional Equipment:	Retail Price	Dealer Invoice	Fair Price
4-speed automatic transmission	$900	$783	$810
Not available with R-2 Pkg. or Popular Equipment Group.			
R-2 Pkg.	2000	1640	1800
Dual oil coolers, special suspension tuning, front brake air ducts, rear spoiler, front air dam, front shock tower support brace, upgraded cloth upholstery, Pirelli Z-rated tires; deletes cruise control. Not available with Touring Pkg. or Popular Equipment Group.			
Touring Pkg.	4200	3444	3780
Leather seats, power glass moonroof, cargo cover, rear wiper/washer, Bose Acoustic Wave music system with CD player, fog lights, rear cargo cover, additional sound insulation. Not available with R-2 Pkg.			
Popular Equipment Group	1800	1476	1620
Leather seats, power steel sunroof, rear cargo cover. Not available with automatic transmission.			
Floormats	70	51	63

Mazda 323/Protege	Retail Price	Dealer Invoice	Fair Price
323 3-door hatchback	$8395	—	—
Protege DX 4-door notchback	11495	10576	10776
Protege LX 4-door notchback	13195	11992	12192
Destination charge	395	395	395

323 dealer invoice and fair price not available at time of publication.

Prices are for vehicles distributed by Mazda Motor of America, Inc. Prices may be higher in areas served by independent distributors.

Standard Equipment:

323: 1.6-liter 4-cylinder engine, 5-speed manual transmission, motorized front shoulder belts, vinyl reclining front bucket seats, one-piece folding rear seat, left remote mirror, coolant temperature gauge, trip odometer, cargo cover, console with storage, rear defogger, 155SR13 tires. **Protege DX**: 1.8-liter 4-cylinder engine, 5-speed manual transmission, power steering, cloth reclining front bucket seats, 60/40 folding rear seat, remote mirrors, coolant temperature gauge, trip odometer, console with storage, tinted glass, bodyside moldings, door pockets, remote fuel door and decklid releases, intermittent wipers, color-keyed bumpers, right visor mirror, digital clock, rear defogger, 175/70R13 tires. **Protege LX** adds to DX: 1.8-liter DOHC engine, 4-wheel disc brakes, power windows and locks, tilt steering column, cruise control, AM/FM cassette, power mirrors, rear center folding armrest, driver seat adjustable thigh support, trunk light, tachometer, left visor mirror, 185/60R14 tires.

MAZDA

Optional Equipment:	Retail Price	Dealer Invoice	Fair Price
4-speed automatic transmission	$750	$675	$695
Power steering, 323	250	—	—
Air conditioning	850	680	746
Plus Pkg., 323	650	—	—
Cloth upholstery, AM/FM cassette, 60/40 split folding rear seat, full wheel covers.			
DX Convenience Group, Protege DX	650	520	571
Tilt steering column, tachometer, AM/FM cassette with four speakers, trunk light, diagnostic warning lights.			
Power sunroof, Protege LX	560	408	472
Alloy wheels, Protege LX	425	340	373
Floormats	65	47	55

Mazda 626	Retail Price	Dealer Invoice	Fair Price
626 DX 4-door notchback	$14255	$13134	$13634
626 LX 4-door notchback	16540	14737	15237
626 LX V-6, 4-door notchback	18700	16472	17172
626 ES V-6, 4-door notchback	21545	18761	19461
Destination charge	395	395	395

Prices are for vehicles distributed by Mazda Motor of America, Inc. Prices may be higher in areas served by independent distributors.

Standard Equipment:

DX: 2.0-liter DOHC 4-cylinder engine, 5-speed manual transmission, power steering, driver- and passenger-side air bags, cloth reclining front bucket seats, driver's-seat thigh support adjustment, 60/40 folding rear seat with armrest, console with storage, tachometer, coolant temperature gauge, trip odometer, tilt steering column, intermittent wipers, dual remote mirrors, door pockets, tinted glass, remote fuel door and decklid releases, rear defogger, 195/65R14 tires, full wheel covers. **LX** adds: air conditioning, power windows and locks, cruise control, power mirrors, AM/FM cassette with power antenna, map lights. **LX V-6** adds: 2.5-liter DOHC V-6 engine, 4-wheel disc brakes, alloy wheels. **ES** adds: anti-lock brakes, anti-theft alarm, power moonroof, leather seats, heated power mirrors, CD player, fog lamps, 205/55VR15 tires.

Optional Equipment:

4-speed automatic transmission	800	696	760
Anti-lock 4-wheel disc brakes, LX	950	808	902
Anti-lock brakes, LX V-6	800	680	760
Luxury Pkg., LX	1500	1200	1425
Power moonroof, heated power mirrrors, anti-theft alarm, alloy wheels.			

	Retail Price	Dealer Invoice	Fair Price
Premium Pkg., LX V-6	$1875	$1500	$1781
Anti-lock brakes, power driver's seat, power moonroof, heated power mirrors, anti-theft alarm.			
Floormats	70	51	67

Mazda 929

	Retail Price	Dealer Invoice	Fair Price
4-door notchback	$31500	$26943	$27543
Destination charge	395	395	395

Prices are for vehicles distributed by Mazda Motor of America, Inc. Prices may be higher in areas served by independent distributors.

Standard Equipment:

3.0-liter DOHC engine, 4-speed automatic transmission, anti-lock 4-wheel disc brakes, variable-assist power steering, driver- and passenger-side air bags, automatic climate control, cloth reclining front bucket seats, power driver's seat, console with storage, tachometer, coolant temperature gauge, voltmeter, trip odometer, heated power mirrors, analog clock, variable intermittent wipers, cruise control, AM/FM cassette, power antenna, diversity antenna system, power sunroof, tinted glass, remote fuel door and decklid releases, map lights, lighted visor mirrors, rear defogger, 205/65R15 tires, alloy wheels.

Optional Equipment:

Premium Pkg.	4100	3362	3731
Leather Pkg., premium audio system with multi-disc CD changer, keyless entry system, reflective solar-control tinted glass, wood trim, cellular phone pre-wiring.			
Leather Pkg.	1850	1517	1684
Leather upholstery, rear storage armrest, power front passenger seat.			
Cold Pkg.	600	498	549
Heated front seats, all-season tires, limited-slip differential, heavy duty wiper motor, larger washer reservoir, heavy duty battery. NA California.			
Solar Ventilation System	650	533	592
Requires Premium Pkg.			
Floormats	100	77	86

MERCEDES-BENZ

Mercedes-Benz C-Class	Retail Price	Dealer Invoice	Fair Price
C220 4-door notchback	$29900	$25440	—

Prices are accurate at time of publication: subject to manufacturer's change.

MERCEDES-BENZ

	Retail Price	Dealer Invoice	Fair Price
C280 4-door notchback	$34900	$29690	—
Destination charge	475	475	475

Fair price not available at time of publication.

Standard Equipment:

C220: 2.2-liter DOHC 4-cylinder engine, 4-speed automatic transmission, anti-lock 4-wheel disc brakes, driver- and passenger-side air bags, power steering, air conditioning, automatic climate control, cruise control, power windows, heated power mirrors, 10-way power driver's seat, 10-way manual adjustable passenger seat, center console with armrest and bi-level storage, folding rear armrest, cellular phone and CD pre-wiring, tinted glass, fog lamps, AM/FM cassette, automatic power antenna, power steel sunroof, lighted visor mirrors, cup holder, rear defogger, sunroof, first aid kit, 195/65HR15 tires, alloy wheels. **C280** adds: 2.8-liter DOHC 6-cylinder engine, Bose sound system, power passenger seat.

Optional Equipment:

C1 Option Pkg., C220	1560	1295	—
C280	2750	2283	—
ASD automatic locking differential (C220), ASR automatic slip control (C280), headlamp washer/wipers, heated front seats.			
C2 Option Pkg., C220 and C280	320	266	—
Split folding rear seat.			
C3 Option Pkg., C280	1710	1419	—
Leather upholstery, power glass sunroof, retractable rear head restraints.			
ASD automatic locking differential, C220	1110	921	—
ASR automatic slip control, C280	2615	2170	—
Leather upholstery, C280	1580	1311	—
Anti-theft alarm system	575	477	—
Headlamp washer/wipers	310	257	—
Bose sound system, C220	485	403	—
Rear head restraints	330	274	—
Power glass sunroof	220	183	—
Power passenger seat, C220	560	465	—
Heated front seats	550	457	—
Power front seat orthopedic backrests (each)	355	295	—
Split folding rear seat	270	224	—
Metallic paint	560	469	—

Mercedes-Benz E-Class

	Retail Price	Dealer Invoice	Fair Price
E300 Diesel 4-door notchback	$40000	$34030	—
E320 4-door notchback	42500	36160	—
E320 2-door notchback	61600	51130	—
E320 2-door convertible	77300	64160	—
E320 5-door wagon	46200	39310	—
E420 4-door notchback	51000	43390	—
E500 4-door notchback	80800	67060	—
Destination charge	475	475	475
Gas Guzzler Tax, E500	1700	1700	1700

Fair price not available at time of publication.

Standard Equipment:

E300 Diesel/E320: 3.0-liter DOHC 6-cylinder diesel engine (E300 Diesel), 3.2-liter DOHC 6-cylinder engine (E320), 4-speed automatic transmisssion, driver- and passenger-side air bags, anti-lock 4-wheel disc brakes, power steering, cruise control, automatic climate control, cloth power front seats, rear head rests, seat pockets, anti-theft alarm system, power windows and door locks, AM/FM cassette, automatic power antenna, tinted glass, rear defogger, visor mirrors, leather-wrapped steering wheel, cellular phone and CD pre-wiring, power steel sunroof, first aid kit, fog lamps, outside temperature indicator, 195/65R15 tires, alloy wheels. **E320 4-door** adds to E300 Diesel: leather upholstery. **E320 2-door** adds to E320 4-door: high performance sound system, headlamp washers/wipers, rear console storage box, adjustable steering column with memory, memory driver's seat. **E320 convertible** adds to E320 2-door: wind deflector, power convertible top; deletes rear console storage box. **E320 wagon** adds to E320 4-door: cloth upholstery, luggage rack, rear facing third seat. **E420 4-door** adds to E320 4-door: 4.2-liter DOHC V-8 engine, headlamp washers/wipers, high performance sound system, adjustable steering column with memory, memory driver's seat. **E500 4-door** adds to E420 4-door: 5.0-liter DOHC V-8 engine, ASR automatic slip control, rear console storage box, heated front seats, rear reading lamps, rear axle level control, rear window sunshade, metallic paint.

Optional Equipment:

E1 Option Pkg. , E300 Diesel	1560	1295	—
E320 4-door and E320 wagon	2750	2283	—
E320 2-door, E320 Cabriolet and			
E420 4-door	2500	2075	—

ASD automatic locking differential (E320 Diesel), ASR automatic slip control (NA E320 Diesel), headlamp washers/wipers (std. E320 2-door and Cabriolet, E420), heated front seats.

Prices are accurate at time of publication; subject to manufacturer's change.

MERCEDES-BENZ

	Retail Price	Dealer Invoice	Fair Price
E2 Option Pkg., E300 Diesel and E320 4-door	$1050	$872	—
Memory driver's seat, adjustable steering column with memory, high performance sound system.			
E3 Option Pkg., E320 wagon	1000	830	—
Memory driver's seat, adjustable steering column with memory, partition net and luggage cover.			
Sportline Pkg., E320 4-door	1850	1536	—
E320 2-door	1060	880	—
4-place sport seats (4-door), sport suspension and steering.			
Leather upholstery, E300 Diesel and E320 wagon	1580	1311	—
ASD automatic locking differential, E320 Diesel	1110	921	—
ASR automatic slip control (Std. E500; NA E320 Diesel)	2615	2170	—
Rear axle level control (NA 300 Diesel)	675	560	—
Headlamp washers/wipers	310	257	—
High performance sound system	485	403	—
Power adjustable steering column	355	295	—
Heated front seats	550	457	—
Memory driver's seat	450	374	—
Power front seat orthopedic backrests (each)	355	295	—
Not available with Sportline Pkg.			
Rear window sunshade	400	332	—
Rear reading lamps	85	71	—
Metallic paint	645	535	—
E320 2-door, Cabriolet and E420 4-door	NC	NC	NC

Mercedes-Benz S-Class

	Retail Price	Dealer Invoice	Fair Price
S350 Turbodiesel 4-door notchback (NA California and New York)	$70600	$58600	—
S320 4-door notchback	70600	58600	—
S420 4-door notchback	79500	65990	—
S500 4-door notchback	95300	79100	—
S500 2-door notchback	99800	82830	—
S600 4-door notchback	130300	108150	—
S600 2-door notchback	133300	110640	—
Destination charge	475	475	475
Gas Guzzler Tax, S420	1700	1700	1700

	Retail Price	Dealer Invoice	Fair Price
S500	$2100	$2100	$2100
S600 2-door notchback	3000	3000	3000
S600 4-door notchback	3700	3700	3700

Fair price not available at time of publication.

Standard Equipment:

S350 Turbodiesel: 3.5-liter 6-cylinder turbodiesel engine, 4-speed automatic transmission, power steering, anti-lock 4-wheel disc brakes, driver- and passenger-side air bags, anti-theft alarm, power windows and locks, automatic climate control, AM/FM cassette, CD and cellular phone pre-wiring, automatic power antenna, power leather front seats with 3-position memory, power telescopic steering column with memory, leather-wrapped steering wheel and shift knob, rear defogger, cruise control, headlamp wipers/washers, speed-sensitive intermittent wipers, heated windshield washer jets, power sunroof, heated power memory mirrors, automatic day/night memory rearview mirror, outside temperature indicator, tachometer, coolant temperature and oil pressure gauges, trip odometer, first aid kit, lighted visor mirrors, 225/60HR16 tires, alloy wheels. **S320** adds: 3.2-liter DOHC 6-cylinder engine, 5-speed automatic transmission. **S420** adds: 4.2-liter DOHC V-8 engine, 4-speed automatic transmission, 235/60HR16 tires. **S500** adds: 5.0-liter DOHC V-8 engine, ASR Automatic Slip Control, rear axle level control, heated front and rear seats (sedan), power rear seat (sedan), active charcoal ventilation filter, rear storage console (coupe), rear reading lamps (sedan). **S600** adds to S500: 6.0-liter DOHC V-12 engine, ADS Adaptive Damping System, rear air conditioner, 10-disc CD changer, cellular telephone, rear window sunshade, orthopedic front backrests, 235/60ZR16 tires.

Optional Equipment:

Rear air conditioner (std. 600)	1840	1527	—
ADS (Adaptive Damping System),			
350, 320, and 420	2750	2283	—
500	2040	1693	—
ASD (Automatic Locking Differential),			
350	1110	921	—
ASR (Automatic Slip Control),			
320 and 420	2615	2170	—
Rear window sunshade (std. 600)	400	332	—
Orthopedic front backrests, each			
(std. 600)	355	295	—
4-place seating (NA 500 and 600 2-doors)	5220	4333	—
600	3908	3303	—
Power rear seats 350, 320, and 420	1040	863	—

Prices are accurate at time of publication; subject to manufacturer's change.

	Retail Price	Dealer Invoice	Fair Price
Heated front and rear seats, each	$575	481	—
Heated rear seat	580	481	—
Active charcoal filter	500	415	—
Rear axle level control	860	714	—
Power glass sunroof	390	324	—

MERCURY

Mercury Capri	Retail Price	Dealer Invoice	Fair Price
2-door convertible	$13190	$12118	$12618
XR2 2-door convertible	14900	13674	14174
Destination charge	375	375	375

Standard Equipment:

1.6-liter DOHC 4-cylinder engine, 5-speed manual transmission, power steering, 4-wheel disc brakes, driver- and passenger-side air bags, cloth reclining front bucket seats, driver-seat tilt, height and lumbar support adjustments, folding rear seatback, tinted glass, power windows and mirrors, leather-wrapped steering wheel, trip odometer, oil pressure and coolant temperature gauges, voltmeter, front storage console with coin slots and cup holders, door map pockets, rear heater ducts, AM/FM radio, variable intermittent wipers, body-color side moldings, visor mirrors, 185/60R14 tires. **XR2** adds: turbocharged engine, air conditioning, cruise control, sport suspension, AM/FM cassette, turbo boost gauge, power door locks, leather upholstery, body-color grille, fog lamps, rear spoiler, 195/50VR15 tires, alloy wheels.

Optional Equipment:

4-speed automatic transmission, base	790	703	711
Air conditioning, base	780	694	702
Cruise control, base	215	191	194
Leather upholstery, base	500	445	450
Power door locks, base	200	178	180
Preferred Pkg. 651A, base	NC	NC	NC
Air conditioning, AM/FM cassette, cruise control, alloy wheels.			
Alloy wheels, base	335	296	302
AM/FM cassette, base	165	147	149
Premium AM/FM cassette, base	430	383	387
Base with Pkg. 651A and XR2	265	236	239
Tonneau cover	185	165	167

Mercury Cougar

	Retail Price	Dealer Invoice	Fair Price
XR7 2-door notchback	$16260	$14617	$15117
Destination charge	495	495	495

Standard Equipment:

3.8-liter V-6, 4-speed automatic transmission, power steering, driver- and passenger-side air bags, air conditioning, reclining front bucket seats with power lumbar support, cloth and leather upholstery, floor storage console with cup holders, tilt steering wheel, intermittent wipers, tinted glass, power windows, AM/FM cassette, oil pressure and coolant temperature gauges, voltmeter, tachometer, center console with storage, power windows and mirrors, rear armrest, door map pockets, color-keyed bodyside moldings, bumpers and door trim panels, rear heater ducts, visor mirrors, cargo area net, 205/70R15 tires.

Optional Equipment:

4.6-liter V-8 engine	615	548	524
Anti-lock 4-wheel disc brakes	585	503	527
Preferred Pkg. 260A	990	881	891

Cruise control, rear defogger, power driver's seat, AM/FM cassette, Power Lock Group (includes power locks, remote fuel door and decklid releases), Light Group (includes underhood light, courtesy lights, lighted visor mirrors), illuminated entry, leather-wrapped steering wheel, 215/70R15 tires, alloy wheels, front floormats.

Group 1	410	365	369

Rear defogger, illuminated entry, Light Group, front floormats.

Group 2	515	458	464

Cruise control, leather-wrapped steering wheel, alloy wheels, 215/70R15 tires.

Group 3	585	521	527

Power Lock Group, power driver's seat.

Automatic air conditioning	155	138	140

Requires automatic headlamp on/off delay.

Automatic headlamp on/off delay	70	62	63
Keyless entry system	215	191	194
Power moonroof	740	658	666

Includes dual reading lights, pop-up air deflector, sunshade, rear tilt-up. Requires Groups 1, 2, and 3.

Premium electronic AM/FM cassette	370	329	333

Includes power antenna.

Ford JBL audio system	500	445	450

Requires Premium electronic AM/FM cassette, trunk-mounted CD changer, Groups 1, 2, and 3.

10-disc trunk-mounted CD changer	785	699	707

Prices are accurate at time of publication; subject to manufacturer's change.

	Retail Price	Dealer Invoice	Fair Price
Requires Premium electronic AM/FM cassette, Ford JBL audio system, Groups 1, 2, and 3.			
Cellular phone	$530	$472	$477
Requires Premium electronic AM/FM cassette.			
Dual power seats	290	258	261
Requires Pkg. 260A.			
Individual leather seats	490	436	441
Cold Weather Group	140	124	126
with 4.6-liter engine	115	102	104
with Traction-Assist	45	40	41
with 4.6-liter engine and Traction-Assist	20	18	18
Includes rear defogger, Traction-Lok axle, engine block heater, heavy duty battery.			
Traction-Assist	210	187	189
Requires anti-lock brakes.			
Tri-coat paint	225	201	203

Mercury Grand Marquis

	Retail Price	Dealer Invoice	Fair Price
GS 4-door notchback	$20330	$18690	$19190
GS Special Value 4-door notchback	19990	18435	—
LS 4-door notchback	21500	19852	20352
LS Special Value 4-door notchback	21990	20359	—
Destination charge	575	575	575

Special Value fair price not available at time of publication. Special Value prices include destination charge.

Standard Equipment:

GS: 4.6-liter V-8, 4-speed automatic transmission, 4-wheel disc brakes, power steering, driver- and passenger-side air bags, air conditioning, dual reclining seats, 6-way power driver's seat, dual front and rear folding armrests, power windows and mirrors, tinted glass, AM/FM cassette, right visor mirror, intermittent wipers, cargo net, digital clock, tilt steering wheel, trip odometer, Luxury Sound Insulation Pkg., remote fuel door release, automatic parking brake release, 215/70R15 all season whitewall tires. **GS Special Value** adds Preferred Equipment Pkg. 157A. **LS** adds: upgraded upholstery and door trim, luxury reclining twin comfort lounge seats, locking wire spoked wheel covers. **LS Special Value** adds Preferred Equipment Pkg. 172A.

Optional Equipment:

Anti-lock brakes w/Traction-Assist	665	592	599

	Retail Price	Dealer Invoice	Fair Price
Preferred Pkg. 157A, GS	$225	$204	$208

Cruise control, rear defogger, Power Lock Group, floormats.

Preferred Pkg. 172A, LS	1055	966	971

Pkg. 157A plus illuminated entry, bodyside paint stripe, leather-wrapped steering wheel, illuminated entry, Luxury Light Group (includes underhood light, dual dome/map lights, rear reading lights, dual secondary sun visors, lighted visor mirrors), alloy wheels, power antenna, cornering lights, rear license plate frame.

Group 1	205	182	185

Rear defogger, floormats.

Group 2	510	454	459

Power Lock Group (includes power locks, remote fuel door and decklid releases), cruise control.

Group 3, LS	995	886	896

Illuminated entry, Luxury Light Group, bodyside paint stripe, leather-wrapped steering wheel, alloy wheels, power antenna, cornering lights, rear license plate frame.

Luxury Light Group	190	169	171

Includes underhood light, dual dome/map lights, rear reading lights, dual secondary sun visors, lighted visor mirrors.

Electronic Group, LS	515	458	463

Automatic climate control with outside temperature readout, digital instrumentation, tripminder computer. Requires rear window defogger.

Illuminated entry system	80	71	72
Keyless entry system	215	191	193

Requires Group 2.

Handling Pkg., LS	1485	1322	1336
with Pkg. 172A	1065	948	958.

Includes rear air suspension, tuned suspension, larger stabilizer bars, anti-lock brakes with Traction-Assist, dual exhaust, 3.27 axle ratio, 225/70R15 whitewall tires, alloy wheels.

Rear air suspension, LS	270	240	243
Trailer Tow III Pkg., LS	785	699	706

Includes rear air suspension, heavy duty battery, dual exhaust, trailer towing wiring harness, power steering and transmission oil coolers, heavy duty flashers, full-size spare tire, heavy duty U-joint, 3.27 Traction-Lok axle. Requires alloy wheels.

Power front passenger's seat, LS	385	343	346

Includes power lumbar support and recliners for both front seats.

Leather seat trim, LS	530	472	477
Premium electronic AM/FM cassette, LS	315	280	283
Full-size conventional spare tire, LS	185	165	166

Includes alloy wheel.

MERCURY

	Retail Price	Dealer Invoice	Fair Price
Power antenna	$80	$71	$72
Alloy wheels, LS	420	374	378
Locking radial-spoked wheel covers, GS	295	263	265
Front cornering lamps	65	58	58
Leather-wrapped steering wheel	90	80	81
Requires Group 2.			
Bodyside paint stripe	60	54	54

Mercury Sable

	Retail Price	Dealer Invoice	Fair Price
GS 4-door notchback	$17740	$15948	$16448
LS 4-door notchback	20000	17960	18460
GS 5-door wagon	18900	16961	17461
LS 5-door wagon	21110	18948	19448
Destination charge	525	525	525

Standard Equipment:

GS: 3.0-liter V-6, 4-speed automatic transmission, power steering, driver- and passenger-side air bags, air conditioning, cloth reclining 50/50 front seat with armrests, rear center armrest, tinted glass, intermittent wipers, rear defogger, tachometer, coolant temperature gauge, trip odometer, low fuel light, power mirrors, tilt steering wheel, AM/FM radio, Sound Insulation Pkg., dual visor mirrors, front door and seatback map pockets, 205/65R15 tires; **wagon** has 60/40 folding rear seat, tiedown hooks, luggage rack, rear wiper, lockable under floor storage. **LS** adds: anti-lock 4-wheel disc brakes, reclining bucket seats with power lumbar support (4-door), power driver's seat (4-door), cassette player, power windows, automatic parking brake release, remote fuel door and decklid releases, Light Group, bodyside cladding, 50/50 reclining front seats with power driver's seat (wagon), console, cargo net, lighted visor mirrors, alloy wheels.

Optional Equipment:

3.8-liter V-6	530	472	477
Includes heavy duty battery.			
3.0-liter V-6, LS with Pkgs. 461/462A and Group 4 (credit)	(530)	(472)	(472)
Anti-lock 4-wheel disc brakes, GS	565	503	509
Automatic climate control, LS	175	156	158
Preferred Pkg. 450A, GS	800	711	720

Power Lock Group (includes power locks, remote fuel door and decklid/liftgate releases), power windows, cruise control, Light Group (includes underhood light, courtesy lights, lighted visor mirrors), floor-mats, striping.

	Retail Price	Dealer Invoice	Fair Price
Preferred Pkg. 451A, GS	$1100	$978	$990
Pkg. 450A plus power driver's seat, cassette player, alloy wheels.			
Preferred Pkg. 461A, LS	975	868	878
3.8-liter V-6, leather-wrapped steering wheel, cruise control, Premium AM/FM cassette, power antenna, keyless entry system, Power Lock Group, Light Group, striping, floormats.			
Preferred Pkg. 462A, LS	1310	1166	1179
Pkg. 461A plus electronic instruments, autolamp system, air conditioning with automatic climate control.			
Group 1, GS	160	143	144
LS	105	94	95
Light Group, floormats, striping.			
Group 2, GS	895	795	806
LS	460	409	414
Power windows, Power Lock Group, cruise control.			
Group 3, GS (std. LS)	710	632	639
Power driver's seat, AM/FM cassette player, alloy wheels.			
Group 4, LS	1330	1184	1197
3.8-liter V-6 engine, keyless entry system, premium AM/FM cassette, leather-wrapped steering wheel, power antenna.			
Group 5, LS	535	476	482
Automatic climate control, autolamp system, electronic instrument cluster.			
Cargo area cover, wagons	65	58	59
Extended-range fuel tank	45	40	41
Not available with Group 5.			
Remote keyless entry	295	263	266
Includes illuminated entry; requires Group 2.			
Power moonroof, LS	740	658	666
Cassette player, GS	165	147	149
CD player	470	418	423
Requires Group 4.			
Rear-facing third seat, Wagons	150	134	135
Not available with conventional spare tire.			
Power driver's seat, GS	290	258	261
Dual power seats, GS with Pkg. 450A	580	516	522
GS with Pkg. 451A and LS with 461A or 462A	290	258	261
Cloth individual seats, GS	NC	NC	NC
Leather Twin Comfort Lounge seats, LS	495	441	446
Leather individual seats, LS	495	441	446
Cellular telephone	500	445	450
Leather-wrapped steering wheel, LS	90	80	81
Requires Group 2.			
Heavy duty suspension	25	23	23

Prices are accurate at time of publication; subject to manufacturer's change.

	Retail Price	Dealer Invoice	Fair Price
Full-size spare tire	$70	$62	$63
Alloy wheels, GS	255	227	230
Heavy duty battery	30	27	27
Engine block heater	20	18	18

Mercury Topaz

	Retail Price	Dealer Invoice	Fair Price
GS 2-door notchback	$11270	$10361	$10561
GS 2-door notchback (Great Lakes, Central and Southwest regions)	10320	9497	9697
GS 4-door notchback	11270	10361	10561
Destination charge	485	485	485

Standard Equipment:

2.3-liter 4-cylinder engine, 5-speed manual transmission, power steering, motorized front shoulder belts, cloth reclining front bucket seats, tinted glass, intermittent wipers, door map pockets, digital clock, dual visor mirrors, power mirrors, tachometer, coolant temperature gauge, trip odometer, AM/FM radio, center console, 185/70R14 all season tires, floormats.

Optional Equipment:

3.0-liter V-6 engine	655	583	590
Requires air conditioning.			
3-speed automatic transmission	535	476	482
Driver-side air bag	465	414	419
Requires 3-speed automatic transmission. NA with tilt steering wheel, cruise control, or 3.0-liter V-6 engine.			
Air conditioning	780	694	702
Rear defogger	160	143	144
Preferred Pkg. 352A, 2-door	830	739	747
4-door and 4-door Great Lakes, Central and Southwest regions	870	774	783
Automatic transmission, Comfort/Convenience Group, rear defogger, air conditioning, Power Lock Group.			
Preferred Pkg. 353A, 4-door and 4-door Great Lakes, Central and Southwest regions	1245	1108	1121
Pkg. 352A plus power windows, tilt steering wheel, cruise control, cassette player.			
Preferred Pkg. 354A, 2-door	830	739	747
2-door Great Lakes, Central and Southwest regions	NC	NC	NC
Comfort/Convenience Group, rear defogger, AM/FM cassette, air conditioning, luggage rack, alloy wheels.			

	Retail Price	Dealer Invoice	Fair Price
Comfort/Convenience Group	$190	$169	$171
Light Group, remote fuel door and decklid releases, front armrest.			
Power Lock Group, 2-door	295	263	266
2-door with Comfort/ Convenience Group	200	178	180
4-door	335	298	302
4-door with Comfort/ Convenience Group	240	213	216
Includes power door locks, remote fuel door and decklid releases.			
Max Edition Option Group, 4-door with Pkg. 353A	290	258	261
Includes alloy wheels, black luggage rack, black antenna, 2-tone paint.			
Power windows, 4-door	315	280	284
Power driver's seat	290	258	261
Tilt steering wheel	140	124	126
Cruise control	215	191	194
Cassette player	150	134	135
Decklid luggage rack	110	96	99
Clearcoat paint	85	76	77
2-tone paint, 4-door	150	134	135
Polycast wheels	185	165	167
Alloy wheels	265	236	239
185/70R14 performance whitewall tires	80	71	72
185/70R14 performance blackwall tires	NC	NC	NC
Engine block heater	20	18	18

Mercury Tracer	Retail Price	Dealer Invoice	Fair Price
4-door notchback	$10250	$9428	$9628
5-door wagon	10520	9674	9874
LTS 4-door notchback	12560	11530	11780
Destination charge	375	375	375

Standard Equipment:

1.9-liter 4-cylinder engine, 5-speed manual transmission, driver-side air bag, cloth reclining front bucket seats, 60/40 split rear seatback, AM/FM radio, tachometer, trip odometer, digital clock, console, coolant temperature gauge, low fuel warning light, door map pockets, variable intermittent wipers, tinted glass, 175/70R13 tires. **Wagon** adds: power steering, wipers, remote fuel door release, power mirrors, rear defogger, cargo cover, rear wiper/washer, 175/65R14 tires, full wheel covers. **LTS** adds: 1.8-liter DOHC engine, 4-wheel disc brakes, sport suspension, tilt steering column, AM/FM cassette, remote decklid release, Light Group (includes dual map lights, lighted visor mirrors, trunk and engine compartment lights, rear door courtesy light), driver's seat tilt adjustment, cruise control, leather-wrapped steering wheel, 185/60HR14 tires, alloy wheels.

Optional Equipment:

	Retail Price	Dealer Invoice	Fair Price
Preferred Pkg. 550A, base 4-door	NC	NC	NC
Wagon	NC	NC	NC
Power steering, power mirrors, AM/FM radio, rear defogger, driver's seat tilt adjustment, Light Group, remote fuel door release, remote decklid release (NA wagon).			
Preferred Equipment Pkg. 560A, LTS	NC	NC	NC
Power steering, power mirrors, AM/FM cassette, rear defogger, driver's seat tilt adjustment, Light Group, remote fuel door release, remote decklid release (NA wagon).			
4-speed automatic transmission	$790	$703	$711
Air conditioning	725	646	653
Anti-lock brakes, LTS	566	503	509
Power Group	520	463	468
Power door locks and windows.			
Convenience Group	355	316	320
Tilt steering wheel, cruise control.			
Power moonroof, LTS	525	468	473
Cassette player, base	165	147	149
Premium sound system	130	116	117
Requires cassette player.			
CD player and premium sound system, base	445	396	401
LTS	280	249	252
Luggage rack, wagon	110	98	99

1993 Mercury Villager

	Retail Price	Dealer Invoice	Fair Price
GS 4-door van	$17015	$15138	$16215
LS 4-door van	22090	19606	21290
Destination charge	540	540	540

Standard Equipment:

GS: 3.0-liter V-6 engine, 4-speed automatic transmission, anti-lock brakes, motorized front shoulder belts, power steering, cloth reclining front bucket seats, 3-passenger bench seat, AM/FM radio, tachometer, coolant temperature gauge, trip odometer, dual outside mirrors, tinted glass, variable-intermittent wipers, rear wiper/washer, remote fuel door release, cornering lamps, front door map pockets, floormats, 205/75R15 tires. **LS adds:** front air conditioning, 2-passenger middle and 3-passenger rear bench seats, tilt steering column, cruise control, power windows and locks, deep-tinted privacy glass, rear defogger, lighted visor mirrors, luggage rack, 2-tone paint, leather-wrapped steering wheel, rear cargo net, underseat storage bin, striping.

Optional Equipment:	Retail Price	Dealer Invoice	Fair Price
Front air conditioning, GS	$857	$729	$788
Front and rear air conditioning w/rear heater, GS	1323	1125	1217
GS w/Pkgs. 691A or 692A, LS w/ Pkg. 695A	466	396	429
Preferred Pkg. 691A, GS	1507	1281	1386
Front air conditioning, 7-passenger seating, power windows and locks, tilt steering column, cruise control, rear defogger, power mirrors.			
Preferred Pkg. 692A, GS	2549	2166	2345
Pkg. 691A plus power driver's seat, cassette player, luggage rack, underseat storage bin, alloy wheels.			
Preferred Pkg. 695A, LS	345	293	317
Power driver's seat, cassette player, flip open liftgate window, alloy wheels.			
Preferred Pkg. 696A, LS	1748	1485	1608
Pkg. 696A plus: rear air conditioning and heater, power passenger seat, quad bucket seats, keyless entry system, headlamp delay system, electronic instrumentation.			
Handling Suspension, LS	87	74	80
Includes 215/70R15 performance tires, firm ride suspension, rear stabilizer bar. Requires alloy wheels.			
Trailer Towing Pkg.	249	211	229
Includes wiring harness, heavy duty radiator and battery, conventional spare tire.			
7-passenger seating, GS	332	282	305
Quad bucket seats, LS	598	508	550
8-way power driver's seat	394	335	362
4-way power front passenger's seat	194	165	178
Requires 8-way power driver's seat.			
Leather seats, LS	865	735	796
Requires quad bucket seats, power driver's and front passenger's seats.			
Electronic instrumentation, LS	244	207	224
Keyless entry and headlamp delay systems, LS	301	256	277
Tilt steering column and cruise control, GS	372	316	342
Rear defogger, GS	168	143	155
Power windows and locks, GS	530	541	488
Requires 7-passenger seating.			
Flip open liftgate window	90	77	83
Requires rear defogger.			

Prices are accurate at time of publication; subject to manufacturer's change.

	Retail Price	Dealer Invoice	Fair Price
Light Group, GS w/Pkg. 692A	$155	$132	$143
Deep-tinted privacy glass, GS	413	351	380
Requires rear defogger.			
Power mirrors, GS	98	83	90
Power sunroof, LS	776	659	714
AM/FM cassette, GS	239	203	220
High-level AM/FM cassette, LS	332	282	305
AM/FM cassette and CD players, LS ...	899	764	827
Radio delete (credit), GS	(91)	(78)	(78)
Luggage rack, GS	143	121	132
Underseat storage bin, GS	37	31	34
Monotone paint, LS	NC	NC	NC
Striping, GS	43	36	40
Alloy wheels	379	322	349

MITSUBISHI

Mitsubishi Diamante	Retail Price	Dealer Invoice	Fair Price
ES 4-door notchback	$25525	$21431	$21931
5-door wagon	—	—	—
LS 4-door notchback	32500	26006	26506
Destination charge	470	470	470

Wagon prices and options not available at time of publication.

Standard Equipment:

ES: 3.0-liter V-6, 4-speed automatic transmission, 4-wheel disc brakes, power steering, driver- and passenger-side air bags, 7-way adjustable cloth front bucket seats, automatic climate control, power windows, power locks, power mirrors, cruise control, alarm system, automatic shut-off headlamps, rear defogger, console with armrest, tilt steering column, folding rear armrest, dual cup holders, tinted glass, front and rear map lights, remote fuel door and decklid releases, tachometer, coolant temperature gauge, trip odometer, variable intermittent wipers, AM/FM cassette with equalizer and power diversity antenna, steering wheel mounted radio controls, floormats, 205/65VR15 tires, full-size spare tire. **Wagon** adds: rear wiper/washer, 60/40 folding split rear seatback, luggage tiedown hooks, woodgrain interior accents. **LS** adds to ES: 3.0-liter DOHC engine, anti-lock 4-wheel disc brakes, speed-sensitive power steering, leather seats and interior trim, dual power front seats with driver-side memory, Mitsubishi/Infinity audio system with equalizer and eight speakers, heated power mirrors, remote keyless entry system, alloy wheels.

Optional Equipment:

	Retail Price	Dealer Invoice	Fair Price
Anti-lock brakes, ES	$1100	$880	$965
Mitsubishi/Infinity audio system, ES	429	300	355
Includes steering wheel controls, equalizer, and eight speakers.			
CD auto changer	699	488	579
Power sunroof	863	690	757
Leather Seat Pkg., ES	1888	1548	1676
Includes power memory driver's seat, leather seat, door, and console trim.			
Traction control, LS	678	556	601
Power passenger seat with memory, LS	369	295	323
Keyless entry system, ES	242	157	194
Sunroof wind reflector	57	37	45
Trunk mat, ES	71	46	57

Mitsubishi Eclipse

	Retail Price	Dealer Invoice	Fair Price
3-door hatchback, 5-speed	$11979	$10482	$10782
3-door hatchback, automatic	12659	11075	11375
GS 1.8 3-door hatchback, 5-speed	14089	12256	12556
GS 1.8 3-door hatchback, automatic	14769	12849	13149
GS DOHC 3-door hatchback, 5-speed	15819	13764	14164
GS DOHC 3-door hatchback, automatic	16499	14357	14757
GS Turbo 3-door hatchback, 5-speed	18529	16117	16617
GS Turbo 3-door hatchback, automatic	19339	16827	17327
GSX 3-door hatchback, 5-speed	21269	18504	19004
GSX 3-door hatchback, automatic	22089	19214	19714
Destination charge	420	420	420

Standard Equipment:

1.8-liter 4-cylinder engine, 5-speed manual or 4-speed automatic transmission, 4-wheel disc brakes, motorized front shoulder belts, cloth reclining front bucket seats, split folding rear seat, tilt steering column, map lights, remote fuel door and hatch releases, visor mirrors, tachometer, coolant temperature gauge, trip odometer, AM/FM radio, tinted glass, rear defogger, fog lamps, digital clock, remote mirrors, 185/70R14 tires. **GS** adds: power steering, driver-side lumbar support, power mirrors, cargo cover, center storage console with coin and cup holders, AM/FM cassette, rear spoiler, lower body-side cladding, upgraded door trim, alloy wheels. **GS DOHC** adds: 2.0-liter DOHC engine, air conditioning, sport suspension, cruise control, automatic power antenna, intermittent wipers, rear wiper/washer, rear spoiler, wraparound rear spoiler, 205/55HR16 all-season tires, full wheel covers. **GS Turbo** adds: turbocharged intercooled engine, gas-charged

MITSUBISHI

shock absorbers, air conditioning, engine oil cooler, 6-way adjustable driver's seat, power windows and door locks, turbo boost gauge, leather-wrapped steering wheel, AM/FM cassette/CD player with equalizer and diversity antenna, alloy wheels. **GSX** adds: permanent 4-wheel drive, anti-lock brakes, limited-slip rear differential.

Optional Equipment:

	Retail Price	Dealer Invoice	Fair Price
Anti-lock brakes, GS Turbo	$952	$781	$866
Power steering, base	274	225	249
Air conditioning, base, GS	835	685	760
AM/FM cassette, base	178	146	162
AM/FM cassette with equalizer and diversity antenna, GS DOHC	250	205	227
AM/FM cassette with CD player, GS DOHC	740	607	673
CD player (NA Turbo)	642	417	529
Requires AM/FM cassette.			
Power Pkg., GS, GS DOHC	472	387	429
Power windows and locks.			
Keyless entry system, (NA base)	242	157	199
Requires Power Pkg.			
Leather Pkg., GS Turbo, GSX	448	368	408
Leather front seats.			
Lower body paint and graphic accent, GS DOHC	125	105	115
Alloy wheels, GS DOHC	330	271	300
Rear wiper/washer, GS	135	111	123
Cruise control, GS	221	181	201
Sunroof (NA base)	377	309	343
Wheel covers, base	106	87	96
Wheel locks, GS DOHC	33	21	27
Floormats	58	38	48
Mud guards	123	80	101

Mitsubishi Expo

	Retail Price	Dealer Invoice	Fair Price
LRV base 4-door wagon, 5-speed	$13019	$11716	$12216
LRV base 4-door wagon, automatic	13859	12474	12974
LRV Sport 4-door wagon, 5-speed	16799	14619	15119
LRV Sport 4-door wagon, automatic	17489	15219	15719
Base 5-door wagon, 5-speed	15689	13648	14148
Base 5-door wagon, automatic	16379	14248	14748
Base AWD 5-door wagon, 5-speed	17129	14900	15400
Base AWD 5-door wagon, automatic	17819	15500	16000

	Retail Price	Dealer Invoice	Fair Price
Destination charge	$445	$445	$445

Standard Equipment:

LRV base: 1.8-liter 4-cylinder engine, 5-speed manual or 4-speed automatic transmission, driver-side air bag, power steering, tilt steering column, cloth reclining front bucket seats, 50/50 folding rear bench seat, coolant temperature gauge, trip odometer, remote fuel door release, front air dam, color-keyed bumpers and bodyside molding, 2-tone paint, dual outside mirrors, rear window defogger, variable intermittent wipers, wheel covers, 185/75R14 tires. **LRV Sport** adds: 2.4-liter 4-cylinder engine, air conditioning, rear heater ducts, power windows and locks, power mirrors and tailgate lock/release, remote keyless entry, rear intermittent wiper/washer, cruise control, tachometer, digital clock, center armrest, map pockets, cargo cover, AM/FM cassette, 205/70R14 all-season tires, alloy wheels. **Base Expo** adds to base LRV: 2.4-liter 4-cylinder engine, 7-passenger seating with split folding middle and rear reclining bench seats, power mirrors, power tailgate lock/release, tachometer, digital clock, cargo cover, front storage tray, rear intermittent wiper/washer, 205/70R14 all-season tires. **Expo AWD** adds permanent 4-wheel drive.

Optional Equipment:

Anti-lock brakes (NA LRV base)	976	800	866
Air conditioning	829	680	736
Power Pkg., Expo	894	715	784
LRV base	719	575	631
Power windows and locks, cruise control, remote keyless entry. LRV base adds: power mirrors and requires automatic transmission.			
Convenience Pkg., LRV base	596	477	523
Rear cargo cover, digital clock, center armrest, upgraded door trim, power door locks, power tailgate release, rear intermittent wiper/washer.			
Luggage rack	274	178	220
CD player, Expo	626	407	503
Power sunroof (NA LRV Sport or Expo AWD)	685	548	601
Cargo Kit, LRV	99	70	82
Cargo tray and net.			
AM/FM stereo, LRV base	334	217	268
AM/FM cassette	466	312	379
Floormats, LRV	73	47	58
Expo	85	55	68
Mud guards (front and rear)	84	54	67
Wheel locks, Expo	37	24	29
Alloy wheels, Expo	291	233	255

Prices are accurate at time of publication; subject to manufacturer's change.

MITSUBISHI

Mitsubishi Galant	Retail Price	Dealer Invoice	Fair Price
S 4-door notchback, 5-speed	$13600	$12104	—
S 4-door notchback, automatic	14500	12905	—
ES 4-door notchback, automatic	16775	14259	—
LS 4-door notchback, automatic	18215	15483	—
GS 4-door notchback, 5-speed	20494	17420	—
GS 4-door notchback, automatic	21277	18086	—
Destination charge	393	393	393

Fair price not available at time of publication.

Standard Equipment:

S: 2.4-liter 4-cylinder engine, 5-speed manual or 4-speed automatic transmission, driver- and passenger-side air bags, power steering, 5-way adjustable driver's seat, tinted glass, cloth upholstery, rear defogger, tilt steering column, center console armrest with storage, driver-side door map pocket, cup holders, remote fuel door and decklid releases, driver-side visor mirror, intermittent wipers, tachometer, coolant temperature gauge, color-keyed bumpers and bodyside moldings, dual manual remote outside mirrors, day/night rearview mirror, digital clock, 185/70HR14 all-season tires, full wheel covers. **ES adds:** 4-speed automatic transmission, air conditioning, cruise control, power windows and door locks, AM/FM cassette with six speakers, automatic power diversity antenna, color-keyed dual power remote outside mirrors, folding rear seat with center armrest, full cloth upholstery and door trim, passenger-side visor mirror, door map pockets. **LS adds:** power glass sunroof with sun shade, variable intermittent wipers, 6-way adjustable front seats, fog lamps, ETACS-IV (includes ignition key illumination, seat belt warning timer/chime, headlight on warning chime, rear defogger timer, fade out dome light), lighted visor mirrors, front seat-back map pockets, center sunvisor, floormats, 195/60HR15 all-season tires, alloy wheels. **GS adds:** 2.4-liter DOHC 4-cylinder engine, 5-speed manual or 4-speed automatic transmission, 4-wheel disc brakes, AM/FM cassette/CD player with six speakers, rear decklid spoiler, leather-wrapped steering wheel and shift knob, rear stabilzer bar.

Optional Equipment:

Anti-lock brakes, ES, LS, and GS	924	758	—
Air conditioning, S	827	678	—
AM/FM cassette player, S	457	297	—
CD player, S, ES, and LS	641	449	—
S requires AM/FM cassette player.			
Keyless remote entry system, ES, LS, and GS	223	145	—
Mud guards	117	76	—
Sunroof wind deflector, LS and GS	52	34	—

Mitsubishi Mirage

	Retail Price	Dealer Invoice	Fair Price
S 2-door notchback, 5-speed	$8989	$7433	$7633
ES 2-door notchback, 5-speed	10359	8317	8517
ES 2-door notchback, 3-speed automatic	10839	8747	8947
LS 2-door notchback, 5-speed	11879	9551	9751
LS 2-door notchback, 4-speed automatic	12459	9981	10181
S 4-door notchback, 5-speed	11369	8882	9082
S 4-door notchback, 3-speed automatic	11849	9312	9512
ES 4-door notchback, 5-speed	11929	9849	10049
ES 4-door notchback, 4-speed automatic	12579	10431	10631
LS 4-door notchback, 4-speed automatic	14529	11645	11845
Destination charge	420	420	420

Standard Equipment:

S 2-door: 1.5-liter 4-cylinder engine, 5-speed manual transmission, driver-side air bag, front bucket seats with vinyl and cloth upholstery, locking fuel-filler door, rear defogger, center console with storage, coolant temperature gauge, 145/80R13 tires. **ES 2-door** adds: 5-speed manual or 3-speed automatic transmission, power steering, height-adjustable driver's seat, cloth upholstery, day/night rearview mirror, front door map pockets, remote fuel filler and trunk release, trip odometer, radio accommodation package, color-keyed bumpers and grille, tinted glass, manual remote mirrors, wheel covers, 155/80R13 tires. **S 4-door** adds to S 2-door: 5-speed manual or 3-speed automatic transmission, power steering, day/night rearview mirror, door map pockets, color-keyed bumpers and grille, digital clock, cloth upholstery, child-proof rear door locks, low-fuel warning light, radio accommodation package, 175/70R13 all-season tires, wheel covers. **ES 4-door** adds to S 4-door: 1.8-liter engine, 5-speed manual or 4-speed automatic transmission, height-adjustable driver's seat, day/night rearview mirror, tinted glass, manual remote mirrors, upgraded door trim, remote fuel door and trunk release, trip odometer, intermittent wipers, 185/65R13 all-season tires. **LS 2-door** adds to ES 2-door: 1.8-liter engine, split folding rear seat, cloth upholstery, tachometer (with manual transmission), intermittent wipers, tilt steering column, full trunk trim, digital clock, trunk light, AM/FM cassette, rear spoiler, power mirrors, 185/65R13 all-season tires, alloy wheels. **LS 4-door** adds to ES 4-door: 4-speed automatic transmission, split folding rear seat with center armrest, cruise control, variable intermittent wipers, tilt steering column, power mirrors, windows and door locks, cloth upholstery, color-keyed bodyside molding, alloy wheels.

Optional Equipment:

Air conditioning	805	660	732
Cruise control, ES 4-door	225	180	202
Power Pkg., ES 4-door	531	425	478

Prices are accurate at time of publication; subject to manufacturer's change.

	Retail Price	Dealer Invoice	Fair Price
Power windows and locks.			
Convenience Pkg., ES 4-door	$169	$135	$152
Includes luxury front and rear seats, tilt steering column, upgraded upholstery, split folding rear seat with center armrest.			
Convenience Pkg., ES 2-door	215	172	193
Includes digital clock, intermittent wipers, cloth door trim, split folding rear seat, trunk trim, trunk courtesy light.			
CD player	626	407	516
Requires AM/FM cassette player.			
Radio accommodation pkg., S 2-door	76	53	64
AM/FM radio, S and ES	334	234	284
AM/FM cassette, S and ES	446	312	379
Rear spoiler, ES 2-door	213	170	191
Wheel locks, LS	33	21	27
Wheel trim rings, S	68	44	56
Mud guards, 2-doors (NA S)	99	67	83
4-doors	98	64	81
Floormats	64	41	52

Mitsubishi Montero	Retail Price	Dealer Invoice	Fair Price
LS 5-door wagon, 5-speed	$23975	—	—
LS 5-door wagon, automatic	24825	—	—
SR 5-door 4WD wagon, automatic	31475	—	—
Destination charge	445	—	—

Dealer invoice and fair price not available at time of publication.

Standard Equipment:

LS: 3.0-liter V-6, 5-speed manual transmission or 4-speed automatic transmission, full-time 4-wheel drive, 4-wheel disc brakes, driver-side air bag, power steering, tilt steering column, digital clock, trip odometer, cloth reclining front bucket seats, tachometer, oil pressure gauge, voltmeter, inclinometer, AM/FM cassette, front and rear tow hooks, remote fuel door release, front and rear mud guards, storage console with cup holders, power mirrors, power windows and door locks, cruise control, rear defogger, intermittent wipers, rear wiper/ washer, tinted glass, skid plates, map lights, cargo tie-down hooks, rear door mounted tool kit, rear seat heater ducts, passenger-side visor mirrors, front and rear stabilizer bars, reclining and folding rear seat, 235/75R15 tires. **SR** adds: 3.5-liter DOHC V-6 engine, 4-speed automatic transmission, anti-lock brakes, air conditioning, remote keyless entry, driver's suspension seat, LCD compass, altimeter, interior and exterior thermometer, AM/FM cassette with equalizer, power diversity antenna, headlamp washers, wide body fender flares, spare tire cover, 265/70R15 all-weather tires, alloy wheels.

Optional Equipment:

	Retail Price	Dealer Invoice	Fair Price
Anti-lock brakes, LS	$1188	—	—
Rear differential lock, SR	400	—	—
CD auto changer, SR	899	—	—
Includes cargo mat and net.			
Leather and Wood Pkg., SR	1748	—	—
Includes: leather seats, leather-wrapped assist grip, burled wood instrument panel accents, power driver's seat.			
Pkg. A, LS	754	—	—
Air conditioning, remote keyless entry system, single play CD player, roof rack, cargo mat and net, spare tire cover.			
Pkg. B, LS	1337	—	—
Pkg. A plus graphic equalizer, CD auto changer, power diversity antenna.			
Power sunroof	688	—	—
Fog lights	228	—	—
Cargo cover	108	—	—
Side step	335	—	—
Roof rack, SR	277	—	—
Sliding rear quarter window	125	—	—
Chrome wheels, SR	625	—	—
Alloy wheels with locks, LS	331	—	—

Mitsubishi 3000GT

	Retail Price	Dealer Invoice	Fair Price
3-door hatchback, 5-speed	$27175	$22286	$22786
3-door hatchback, automatic	28050	22998	23498
SL 3-door hatchback, 5-speed	31650	25955	26995
SL 3-door hatchback, automatic	32525	26667	27667
VR-4 3-door hatchback, 6-speed	40900	33529	35029
Destination charge	470	470	470

Standard Equipment:

3.0-liter DOHC V-6, 5-speed manual or 4-speed automatic transmission, 4-wheel disc brakes, power steering, driver- and passenger-side air bags, air conditioning, power windows, door locks and mirrors, ETACS alarm control system, cruise control, rear spoiler, 6-way adjustable cloth front bucket seats, split folding rear seat, center storage console with coin and cup holders, tachometer, coolant temperature and oil pressure gauges, voltmeter, trip odometer, remote fuel door and hatch releases, AM/FM cassette with equalizer and anti-theft circuitry, power antenna, tilt steering column, leather-wrapped steering wheel, fog lamps, variable intermittent wipers, rear intermittent wiper, visor mirrors, rear defogger, digital clock, tinted glass, cargo area cover, 225/55VR16 tires, alloy wheels. **SL** adds: anti-lock brakes, electronically controlled suspension, automatic climate control, 7-way adjustable

Prices are accurate at time of publication; subject to manufacturer's change.

driver's seat, rear wiper/washer, remote keyless entry, Mitsubishi/Infinity audio system with external amp, eight speakers and steering-wheel mounted radio controls, heated power mirrors, auxiliary power outlet. **VR-4** adds: turbocharged, intercooled engine, permanent 4-wheel drive, 4-wheel steering, limited-slip rear differential, Active Aero with retractable front air dam extension and motorized rear spoiler, Active Exhaust, leather seats, turbo boost gauge, 245/45ZR17 tires.

Optional Equipment:

	Retail Price	Dealer Invoice	Fair Price
CD auto changer	$799	$530	$687
Sunroof, SL and VR-4	375	300	322
Chrome wheels, VR-4	500	400	430
Leather front seat trim, SL	1120	—	—
Yellow pearl paint, SL and VR-4	313	250	269
Mud guards	142	92	122

NISSAN

Nissan Altima	Retail Price	Dealer Invoice	Fair Price
XE 4-door notchback, 5-speed	$13739	$12122	$12939
XE 4-door notchback, automatic	14699	12696	13899
GXE 4-door notchback, 5-speed	14859	12958	14059
GXE 4-door notchback, automatic	15684	13678	14884
SE 4-door notchback, 5-speed	18179	15761	17379
SE 4-door notchback, automatic	19004	16476	18204
GLE 4-door notchback, automatic	19179	16628	18379
Destination charge	380	380	380

Standard Equipment:

XE: 2.4-liter DOHC 4-cylinder engine, 5-speed manual or 4-speed automatic transmission, driver- and passenger-side air bags, power steering, tilt steering column, rear window defroster, dual cup holders, remote trunk and fuel door releases, cloth seats, center front console, tachometer, coolant temperature gauge, low fuel warning light, digital clock, child safety rear door locks, tinted glass, dual power mirrors, front map pockets, 205/60R15 tires, styled steel wheels. **GXE** adds: power windows with auto down driver's window, power locks, rear seat center armrest with trunk pass-through. **SE** adds: 4-wheel disc brakes, air conditioning, cruise control, front sport seats, AM/FM cassette, power diversity antenna, variable intermittent wipers, alloy wheels, fog lights, front cornering lights, bodyside cladding and rear spoiler, power sunroof, front sport seats, leather-wrapped steering wheel and shift knob. **GLE** adds to GXE: automatic transmission, automatic temperature control, cruise control, variable intermittent wipers, front cornering lights, theft deterrent system, head-up display, AM/FM cassette and CD player, power diversity antenna, power sunroof, adjustable lumbar support, alloy wheels.

Optional Equipment:

	Retail Price	Dealer Invoice	Fair Price
Anti-lock 4-wheel disc brakes, XE	$995	$843	$897
Requires XE Option Pkg.			
Anti-lock brakes with limited-slip differential	1195	1012	1077
Not available XE; GXE requires GXE Value Opt. Pkg.			
Cruise control, XE	230	195	207
Requires automatic transmission.			
Leather Trim Pkg., SE and GLE	1000	847	901
Not available with sport seats.			
XE Opt. Pkg.	1825	1545	1644
Air conditioning, AM/FM cassette, cruise control.			
Power sunroof, GXE	825	699	743
Requires GXE Value Option Pkg. with automatic transmission.			
GXE Value Opt. Pkg.	1200	1016	1081
AM/FM cassette, air conditioning, cruise control, power antenna.			

Nissan Maxima	Retail Price	Dealer Invoice	Fair Price
GXE 4-door notchback, automatic	$22199	$19246	$20046
SE 4-door notchback, 5-speed	23299	20200	21000
SE 4-door notchback, automatic	24234	21011	21811
Destination charge	380	380	380

Standard Equipment:

GXE: 3.0-liter V-6, 4-speed automatic transmission, driver-side air bag, motorized front shoulder belts, power steering, air conditioning, cruise control with steering mounted controls, power windows with auto-down driver's window, power locks with keyless entry, cloth reclining front bucket seats, driver's seat height and lumbar adjustments, fold down rear armrest, door map pockets, heated power mirrors, cruise control, tinted glass, AM/FM cassette with automatic power diversity antenna, theft deterrent system, tilt steering column, variable-intermittent wipers, dual cup holders, rear defogger, remote fuel door and decklid releases, illuminated entry, visor mirrors, dual overhead map lights, tachometer, trip odometer, coolant temperature gauge, digital clock, 205/65R15 tires, alloy wheels. **SE** deletes keyless entry and adds: 3.0-liter DOHC V-6 engine, 5-speed manual or 4-speed automatic transmission, 4-wheel disc brakes, limited-slip differential, Bose audio system, rear spoiler, leather-wrapped steering wheel and shifter, fog lamps.

Prices are accurate at time of publication; subject to manufacturer's change.

NISSAN

Optional Equipment:

	Retail Price	Dealer Invoice	Fair Price
Anti-lock brakes	$995	$843	$897
SE requires sunroof.			
Luxury Pkg., GXE	2595	2197	2338
Power sunroof, 4-way power front seats, Nissan-Bose AM/FM cassette/ CD audio system, automatic climate control, leather-wrapped steering wheel, shift lever, and parking brake handle.			
Leather Trim Pkg., GXE	1025	868	923
SE	1425	1207	1284
SE includes 4-way power front seats and requires sunroof; GXE requires Luxury Pkg.			
Pearlglow paint	350	297	316
Power sunroof, SE	875	741	788
CD player, SE	400	339	360
Requires sunroof; deletes cup holders.			

Nissan Pathfinder

	Retail Price	Dealer Invoice	Fair Price
XE 2WD 5-door wagon, 5-speed	$19429	$17043	$17443
XE 2WD 5-door wagon, automatic	20649	18113	18513
XE 4WD 5-door wagon, 5-speed	21099	18508	18908
XE 4WD 5-door wagon, automatic	22469	19709	20109
SE 4WD 5-door wagon, 5-speed	25009	21938	22338
SE 4WD 5-door wagon, automatic	26109	22903	23303
LE 4WD 5-door wagon, automatic	28999	25438	25838
Destination charge	380	380	380

Standard Equipment:

XE: 3.0-liter V-6, 5-speed manual or 4-speed automatic transmission, anti-lock rear brakes, power steering, part-time 4WD with automatic locking front hubs (4WD), cloth reclining front bucket seats, split folding and reclining rear seat, tachometer, coolant temperature gauge, trip odometer, digital clock, rear wiper/washer, tinted glass, dual outside mirrors, front tow hooks, AM/FM cassette with diversity antenna, tilt steering column, rear defogger, front door map pockets, remote fuel door release, cargo tiedown hooks, skid plates, fender flares and mud guards (4WD), 235/75R15 tires, chrome wheels. **SE** adds: power windows and locks, cruise control, variable-intermittent wipers, heated power mirrors, remote rear window release, voltmeter, rear quarter privacy glass, upgraded upholstery, flip-up removable sunroof, lighted visor mirrors, map lights, driver's seat height and lumbar support adjustments, folding rear armrests, step rail, fog lamps, rear wind deflector, alloy wheels, remote security system. **LE** adds: 4-speed automatic transmission, 4-wheel disc brakes, air conditioning, running board and splash guards, heated leather front seats, CD player.

Optional Equipment:

	Retail Price	Dealer Invoice	Fair Price
Air conditioning, XE and SE	$995	$843	$897
XE Convenience Pkg.	1550	1313	1397

Cruise control, power windows and door locks, heated power mirrors, map lights, variable-intermittent wipers, remote vehicle security system. Requires air conditioning.

XE Sport Pkg.	860	728	775

Includes outside spare tire carrier, spare tire cover, fender flares (2WD), fog lights, limited-slip differential (4WD), cargo net. Requires XE Convenience Pkg.

Leather Trim Pkg., SE	1255	1063	1131

Includes leather seats, leather-wrapped steering wheel, shift knob and parking brake handle, heated front seats with individual controls. Requires air conditioning.

SE Off-Road Pkg.	750	635	676

Limited-slip rear differential, dual-rate adjustable shock absorbers, rear disc brakes, black exterior trim, luggage rack.

2-tone paint, LE	300	254	270

Nissan Quest

	Retail Price	Dealer Invoice	Fair Price
XE 7-passenger	$18529	$16065	$17729
GXE 7-passenger	23039	19975	22239
Destination charge	380	380	380

Standard Equipment:

XE: 3.0-liter V-6 engine, 4-speed automatic transmission, driver-side air bag, motorized front shoulder belts, front air conditioning, power steering, cloth reclining front bucket seats, 2-passenger middle bench seat and 3-passenger rear bench seat, Quest Trac flexible seating, remote fuel door release, rear defogger, tilt steering column, dual mirrors, tachometer, trip odometer, variable intermittent wipers, rear intermittent wiper/washer, color-keyed bodyside moldings, visor mirrors, cornering lamps, door map pockets, AM/FM cassette, tinted glass, carpeted front and rear floormats, console with cassette/CD storage, tilt-out middle and rear quarter windows, cargo area net, cargo area mat, full wheel covers, 205/75R15 all-season tires. **GXE** adds: anti-lock brakes, rear air conditioning, rear heater controls, cruise control, power driver's seat, power locks and windows, power rear quarter windows, upgraded upholstery and door trim panels, power mirrors, illuminated visor mirrors, upgraded radio with rear controls, leather-wrapped steering wheel, power antenna, dual liftgate with opening window, side and rear privacy glass, map light, lockable underseat storage, alloy wheels.

Prices are accurate at time of publication; subject to manufacturer's change.

NISSAN

Optional Equipment:	Retail Price	Dealer Invoice	Fair Price
Extra Performance Pkg., XE	$950	$805	$903
GXE	525	445	499

Heavy duty battery and radiator, tuned springs, shock absorbers and rear stabilizer bar, full-size spare tire, 215/70HR15 tires, alloy wheels (XE), 3500 lb. towing capacity.

Power Pkg., XE	825	699	784

Power windows, locks, and mirrors.

Convenience Pkg., XE	800	677	760

Cruise control, upgraded radio with power antenna, leather-wrapped steering wheel, privacy rear glass, lighted right visor mirror, luggage rack, lockable underseat storage. Requires Power Pkg.

Rear air conditioning, XE	625	529	594

Requires Power Pkg.

Anti-lock brakes, XE	700	593	665
2-tone paint, GXE	300	254	285
Power sunroof, GXE	825	699	784

GXE Extra Performance Pkg. is required when power sunroof and Leather Trim Pkg. are combined.

Leather Trim Pkg., GXE	1000	847	950

Leather uphostery. Requires Luxury Pkg.

Luxury Pkg., GXE	800	677	760

Power passenger seat, middle row captain's chairs, illuminated Digital Touch System, automatic headlamp control.

Premium Audio Pkg., GXE	1015	859	864

AM/FM cassette/CD player, subwoofer, eight speakers.

Nissan Sentra	Retail Price	Dealer Invoice	Fair Price
E 2-door notchback, 5-speed	$10049	$9430	$9630
E 2-door notchback, automatic	11699	10978	11178
XE 2-door notchback, 5-speed	12099	10737	10937
XE 2-door notchback, automatic	12899	11448	11648
SE 2-door notchback, 5-speed	12599	11116	11316
SE 2-door notchback, automatic	13399	11822	12022
SE-R 2-door notchback, 5-speed	13799	12175	12475
SE-R 2-door notchback, automatic	14599	12881	13181
E 4-door notchback, 5-speed	10599	9946	10146
E 4-door notchback, automatic	11899	11166	11366
XE 4-door notchback, 5-speed	12299	10914	11114
XE 4-door notchback, automatic	13099	11624	11824
GXE 4-door notchback, 5-speed	14669	12943	13243
GXE 4-door notchback, automatic	15469	13649	13949
Destination charge	380	380	380

Standard Equipment:

E 2-door: 1.6-liter DOHC 4-cylinder engine, 5-speed manual or 4-speed automatic transmission, door-mounted automatic front shoulder belts, cloth reclining front bucket seats, rear defogger, tinted glass, coolant temperature gauge, dual cup holders, door map pockets, trip odometer, 155/80R13 tires (models with automatic transmission have 175/70R13 tires, power steering and tilt steering column); **4-door** has motorized front shoulder belts, child-safety rear door locks. **XE** adds: air conditioning, cruise control, AM/FM cassette with diversity antenna, power steering, tilt steering column, power mirrors, body-color bumpers, deluxe door trim, intermittent wipers, locking glovebox, remote trunk and fuel-door releases, digital clock, wheel covers, 175/70R13 tires. **GXE** adds to XE: driver-side air bag, power windows and locks, velour upholstery, split folding rear seat, tachometer, alloy wheels. **SE** deletes air conditioning and adds to XE: front air dam, rear spoiler, sport bucket seats, velour uoholstery, leather-wrapped steering wheel, leather-wrapped shift knob (5-speed), rear spoiler, tachometer. **SE-R** adds to SE: 2.0-liter DOHC engine, 4-wheel disc brakes, limited-slip differential, sport suspension, fog lights, 185/60R14 tires, alloy wheels.

Optional Equipment:

	Retail Price	Dealer Invoice	Fair Price
Driver-side air bag (std., GXE)	$575	$487	$531
Anti-lock brakes, GXE and SE-R	700	593	647
Not available with sunroof on GXE. GXE includes rear discs.			
Air conditioning (std. XE and GXE)	995	843	919
Power sunroof, GXE and SE-R	825	699	762
Not available with anti-lock brakes on GXE.			
Power Steering Pkg., E with manual transmission	500	423	462
Power steering, tilt steering wheel, front and rear stabilizer bars, 175/70R13 all-season tires, wheel covers.			
Value Option Pkg., SE and SE-R	1300	1101	1201
Air conditioning, AM/FM cassette with diversity antenna, cruise control.			
Cruise control, SE and SE-R	230	195	213
AM/FM cassette with diversity antenna, SE and SE-R	600	508	554
Metallic paint, E	100	85	93
XE, SE, SE-R and GXE	NC	NC	NC

Nissan 240SX	Retail Price	Dealer Invoice	Fair Price
SE 2-door convertible	$23969	$21025	—
Destination charge	380	380	380

Fair price not available at time of publication.

Standard Equipment:

2.4-liter DOHC 4-cylinder engine, 4-speed automatic transmission, 4-wheel disc brakes, door mounted front shoulder belts, power steering, cloth reclining front bucket seats, power windows and door locks, cruise control, leather-wrapped steering wheel and shift knob, map lights, power convertible top, AM/FM cassette with power diversity antenna, tachometer, coolant temperature gauge, trip odometer, digital clock, tilt steering column, intermittent wipers, remote fuel door and decklid releases, console with storage, door pockets, visor mirrors, rear decklid spoiler, body-color bumpers, tinted glass, 195/60R15 all-season tires, alloy wheels.

Optional Equipment:	Retail Price	Dealer Invoice	Fair Price
Air conditioning	$850	$843	—

OLDSMOBILE

Oldsmobile Achieva	Retail Price	Dealer Invoice	Fair Price
S 2-door notchback	$14075	$12738	$13138
S 4-door notchback	14175	12828	13228
S 2-door and 4-door notchbacks (California Pkg. 1)	13995	—	—
S 2-door and 4-door notchbacks (California Pkg. 2)	14995	—	—
S Special Edition 2-door notchback, Pkg. R7B	13995	13252	—
S Special Edition 4-door notchback, Pkg. R7B	13995	13252	—
S Special Edition 2-door notchback, Pkg. R7C	14995	14197	—
S Special Edition 4-door notchback, Pkg. R7C	14995	14197	—
S Special Edition 2-door notchback, Pkg. R7D	16995	16087	—
S Special Edition 4-door notchback, Pkg. R7D	16995	16087	—
SC 2-door notchback	17475	15815	16215
SC 2-door notchback (California)	16995	—	—
SL 4-door notchback	17475	15815	16215
SL 4-door notchback (California)	16995	—	—
Destination charge	485	485	485

California models' invoice and fair prices not available at time of publication. S Special Edition fair price not available at time of publication. California and

S Special Edition prices include destination charge.

Standard Equipment:

S: 2.3-liter OHC 4-cylinder engine, 5-speed manual transmission, anti-lock brakes, driver-side air bag, power steering, cloth reclining front bucket seats, dual outside mirrors, console with storage armrest, tilt steering wheel, intermittent wipers, AM/FM radio, tinted glass, rear defogger, automatic power locks, remote fuel door and decklid releases, reading and map lights, 185/75R14 tires, wheel covers. **S California Pkg. 1** adds to S: 3-speed automatic transmission, air conditioning. **S California Pkg. 2** adds to S: 4-speed automatic transmission, air conditioning, cruise control, Gage Pkg. with tachometer, power windows, power mirrors, cassette player. **S Special Edition Pkg. R7B** adds to S: 3-speed automatic transmission, air conditioning, floormats. **S Special Edition Pkg. R7C** adds to S: 4-speed automatic transmission, power windows, Pkg. 1SB. **S Special Edition Pkg. R7D** adds to S: 3.1-liter V-6 engine, 4-speed automatic transmission, power windows. **SC and SL** add to S: 170-horsepower 2.3-liter Quad 4 engine, air conditioning, cruise control, power mirrors, leather-wrapped steering wheel, analog gauges, tachometer, voltmeter, coolant temperature and oil pressure gauges, trip odometer, 4-way manual driver's seat, split folding rear seat with luggage compartment pass-through, cassette player, lighted visor mirrors, floormats, trunk cargo net, fog lamps, rear spoiler, touring suspension, dual exhausts, 205/55R16 tires, alloy wheels. **SC and SL California models** add: 3.1-liter V-6 engine, 4-speed automatic transmission, power windows.

Optional Equipment:	Retail Price	Dealer Invoice	Fair Price
155-horsepower 2.3-liter Quad 4 engine, S	$410	$353	$373
Requires 4-speed automatic transmission.			
155-horsepower 2.3-liter Quad 4 engine, SC, SL (credit)	(140)	(121)	(121)
Required with automatic transmission.			
3.1-liter V-6, S	410	353	373
SC, SL (credit)	(140)	(121)	(121)
Requires 4-speed automatic transmission.			
5-speed manual transmission, S Special Edition with Pkg. R7B (credit)	(555)	(477)	(477)
3-speed automatic transmission, S	555	477	505
4-speed automatic transmission S, SC and SL	755	649	687
4-speed automatic transmission, S Special Edition with Pkg. R7B (Calif., Hawaii, N.Y.)	200	172	182
Air conditioning, S	830	714	755
Option Pkg. 1SB, S	1468	1262	1336

Prices are accurate at time of publication; subject to manufacturer's change.

OLDSMOBILE

	Retail Price	Dealer Invoice	Fair Price
Air conditioning, cruise control, analog gauge cluster, power mirrors, cassette player, floormats.			
Option Pkg. 1SC, S 2-door	$1968	$1692	$1791
S 4-door	2033	1748	1850
Pkg. 1SB plus power windows, Remote Lock Control Pkg., 6-speaker stereo, rear window grid antenna.			
Option Pkg. 1SB, SC	400	344	364
SL	465	400	423
Power windows, Remote Lock Control Pkg.			
Power sunroof	595	512	541
Power windows, 2-doors	275	237	250
4-doors	340	292	309
Power driver's seat	270	232	246
Leather seats, SC, SL	425	366	387
Split folding rear seat, S	150	129	137
Remote Lock Control Pkg.,			
Special Edition with Pkg. R7D	125	108	114
Cassette player, S	140	120	127
AM/FM w/CD player	256	220	233
S requires Option Pkg. 1SB or 1SC.			
Decklid luggage rack, S	115	99	105
Alloy wheels, S	391	336	356
Includes 195/65R15 touring tires.			
Floormats, S	45	39	41
Trunk cargo net, S	30	26	27
Engine block heater	18	15	16

Oldsmobile Aurora

	Retail Price	Dealer Invoice	Fair Price
4-door notchback	$31995	—	—

Dealer invoice, fair and option prices not available at time of publication.

Standard Equipment:

4.0-liter DOHC V-8 engine, 4-speed automatic transmission, anti-lock 4-wheel disc brakes, driver- and passenger-side air bags, traction control, variable-assist power steering, automatic climate control system, tinted glass, AM/FM radio with cassette player, power antenna, steering wheel touch controls, leather-wrapped steering wheel, leather upholstery, power front buckets seats with 2-position memory for driver's side, power windows and door locks, power mirrors, intermittent wipers, Pass-Key theft deterrent system, remote keyless entry system, tachometer, temperature, voltage, and oil pressure gauges, trip odometer, oil level sensor, cruise control, rear defogger, folding rear armrest with trunk pass-through, 235/60R16 tires, alloy wheels.

Oldsmobile Bravada

	Retail Price	Dealer Invoice	Fair Price
5-door 4WD wagon	$25995	$23525	$23975
California/Special Edition 5-door 4WD wagon	24995	23891	—
Destination charge	475	475	475

California/Special Edition fair price not available at time of publication. California/Special Edition price includes destination charge.

Standard Equipment:

4.3-liter V-6, 4-speed automatic transmission, permanent 4-wheel drive, anti-lock brakes, power steering, air conditioning, power driver's seat, driver and passenger power lumbar adjustment, center console with cup holders and electrical outlets, overhead console with compass, outside temperature readout and reading lamps, folding rear seat with armrest, solar control tinted windshield and front door glass, deep-tint rear windows, cruise control, power windows, power locks with remote control, power mirrors, rear wiper/washer, intermittent wipers, rear defogger, coolant temperature and oil pressure gauges, voltmeter, trip odometer, fog lamps, remote tailgate release, roof luggage rack, AM/FM cassette with equalizer, tilt steering wheel, leather-wrapped steering wheel, lighted visor mirrors, map lights, floormats, 235/75R15 tires, alloy wheels, full-size spare tire. **California/Special Edition** adds: custom leather trim, electronic instruments, exterior spare tire carrier, towing package.

Optional Equipment:

Custom leather trim	650	559	579
CD player	134	115	119
Towing Pkg.	255	219	227
Electronic instruments	195	168	174
235/75R15 white outline letter tires	133	114	118
Special Edition	NC	NC	NC
Exterior spare tire carrier	159	137	142
Engine block heater	33	28	29
Gold Pkg.	60	52	53
Special Edition	NC	NC	NC

Gold-tinted exterior emblems, gold-tinted cast aluminum wheels with black ports.

Oldsmobile Cutlass Ciera

	Retail Price	Dealer Invoice	Fair Price
S 4-door notchback	$15675	$14029	$14529
S 4-door notchback (Calif.)	13995	—	—
S 4-door notchback (Calif. Pkg. 2)	15995	—	—

Prices are accurate at time of publication; subject to manufacturer's change.

	Retail Price	Dealer Invoice	Fair Price
S Special Edition 4-door notchback, Pkg. R7B	$13995	$13389	—
S Special Edition 4-door notchback, Pkg. R7C	15995	15144	—
Cruiser S 5-door wagon	17175	15372	15872
Cruiser S 5-door wagon (Calif.)	16995	—	—
Crusier S Special Edition wagon, Pkg. R7D	16470	15564	—
Destination charge	525	525	525

California models' invoice and fair prices not available at time of publication. S Special Edition fair price not available at time of publication. California and S Special Edition models include destination charge.

Standard Equipment:

S/Calif.: 2.2-liter 4-cylinder engine, 3-speed automatic transmission, anti-lock brakes, driver-side air bag, door-mounted automatic front seatbelts, power steering, air conditioning, 55/45 bench seat with armrest and power seatback recliners, automatic power locks, tilt steering wheel, AM/FM radio, tinted glass, left remote and right manual mirrors, rear defogger, intermittent wipers, illuminated entry system, reading lights, 185/75R14 whitewall tires, wheel covers. **Calif. Pkg. 2** adds to S: 3.1-liter V-6 engine, 4-speed automatic transmission, power windows, cruise control, power mirrors, cassette player, front storage armrest. **S Special Edition Pkg. R7B** adds to S: floormats. **S Special Edition Pkg. R7C** adds to S: 3.1-liter V-6 engine, 4-speed automatic transmission, power windows, cruise control, power mirrors, cassette player, front storage armrest. **Cruiser S wagon** adds to S: 3.1-liter V-6 engine, split folding rear seat. **Cruiser S wagon California model** adds: rear-facing third seat, front console with armrest, power windows, power mirrors, cruise control, cassette player, roof luggage carrier. **Cruiser S Special Edition** adds to Cruiser S wagon: rear-facing third seat, roof luggage carrier, rear air deflector.

Optional Equipment:

3.1-liter V-6 engine, S 4-door	810	697	713
Includes 4-speed automatic transmission.			
Option Pkg. 1SB, S 4-door	562	483	495
S wagon	717	617	631
Cruise control, power mirrors, cassette player, front storage armrest, floormats. Wagon adds: roof luggage carrier, rear air deflector.			
Option Pkg. 1SC, S	1232	1060	1084
S wagon	1327	1141	1168
Pkg. 1SB plus power windows, Remote Lock Control Pkg., 6-speaker radio, power antenna.			

	Retail Price	Dealer Invoice	Fair Price
Variable-assist power steering, S	$62	$53	$55
Requires V-6 and Pkg. 1SC.			
Power driver's seat, S	305	262	268
Requires Pkg. 1SC.			
Custom leather trim, S	425	366	374
Requires Pkg. 1SC. Wagon Pkg.			
S wagon	328	282	289
Rear-facing third seat, rear vent windows and cargo area cover. Requires Pkg. 1SB or 1SC.			
Power windows, S	340	292	299
Requires Pkg. 1SB.			
Remote Lock Control Pkg. S 4-door	185	159	163
S wagon	125	108	110
Includes door and decklid/tailgate lock releases, illuminated entry and key-chain transmitter. Requires Pkg. 1SB.			
Wire wheel covers, S	240	206	211
Not available with 195/75R14 tires.			
Cassette player, Special Edition	140	120	123
Cassette player with equalizer, S	150	129	132
S requires Pkg. 1SC.			
High-capacity cooling	40	34	35
Requires V-6.			
Decklid luggage rack, S 4-door	115	99	101
Requires Pkg. 1SB or 1SC.			
Woodgrain exterior trim, S wagon	325	280	286
Requires Molding Pkg.			
Engine block heater	18	15	16
Floormats, S	45	39	40
Molding Pkg., S	151	130	133
Lower bodyside moldings, rocker panel and wheel opening moldings, door edge guards.			
Trunk net, S	30	26	26
Striping, S	45	39	40
195/75R14 whitewall tires, S	40	34	35
with alloy wheels	295	254	260

Oldsmobile Cutlass Supreme	Retail Price	Dealer Invoice	Fair Price
S 2-door notchback	$17375	$15203	$15703
S 4-door notchback	17475	15291	15791
2-door and 4-door notchback (California Pkg. 1)	16995	—	—
2-door notchback (California Pkg. 2)	17995	—	—

Prices are accurate at time of publication; subject to manufacturer's change.

OLDSMOBILE

	Retail Price	Dealer Invoice	Fair Price
Special Edition 2-door and 4-door notchback, Pkg. R7B	$16995	$16089	—
Special Edition 2-door and 4-door notchback, Pkg. R7C	17995	17034	—
2-door convertible	25275	22116	23116
Destination charge	525	525	525

California models' invoice and fair price not available at time of publication. Special Edition fair price not available at time of publication. California and Special Edition prices include destination charge.

Standard Equipment:

S: 3.1-liter V-6 engine, 4-speed automatic transmission, anti-lock 4-wheel disc brakes, driver-side air bag, door-mounted automatic front shoulder belts, power steering, air conditioning, cloth reclining front bucket seats, 4-way manual driver's seat, tilt steering wheel, analog temperature gauges, center console with cup holder, automatic power door locks, AM/FM radio, left remote and right manual mirrors, tinted glass, rear defogger, intermittent wipers, illuminated entry system, reading lights, Pass-Key theft-deterrent system, visor mirrors, 205/70R15 tires, wheel covers. **California Pkg. 1** adds to S: sport exterior trim, cruise control, power windows (4-door) power mirrors, cassette player, 16-inch performance tires, alloy wheels. **California Pkg. 2** adds to California Pkg. 1: leather bucket seats, power driver's seat, split folding rear seat, power windows, remote keyless entry, power antenna, lighted visor mirrors. **Special Edition Pkg. R7B** adds to S: Sport Luxury Pkg., Option Pkg., 1SB. **Special Edition Pkg. R7C** adds to S: Option Pkg. 1SC, Sport Luxury Pkg., leather seats, power driver's seat, Custom Trim Pkg. **Convertible** adds to S: leather seats, power driver's seat, 4-way manual passenger's seat, cruise control, leather-wrapped steering wheel, front console with armrest, power windows, power mirrors, power decklid release, fog lamps, floormats, 225/60R16 tires, alloy wheels.

Optional Equipment:

3.4-liter DOHC V-6, S	1520	1307	1322
S with BYP Sport Luxury Pkg., Special Edition	1123	966	977
Conv.	1085	856	944
3.4-liter DOHC V-6 engine, sport suspension, rear spoiler, dual exhausts, special alloy wheels.			
Option Pkg. 1SB, S	487	419	424
Cruise control, power mirrors, cassette player, floormats.			
Option Pkg. 1SC, S 2-door	1203	1035	1047

	Retail Price	Dealer Invoice	Fair Price
S 4-door	$1268	$1090	$1103
Pkg. 1SB plus power windows, Remote Lock Control Pkg., power antenna, lighted visor mirrors, 6-speaker radio.			
Option Pkg. 1SD, S 2-door	2053	1766	1786
S 4-door	2118	1821	1843
Pkg. 1SC plus automatic air conditioning, power driver's seat, Custom Trim Pkg., steering wheel touch controls.			
BYP Sport Luxury (SL) Pkg., S	913	785	794
S with leather seats or Pkg. 1SD	823	708	716
Special front and rear fascias, rocker moldings, body-color wheel opening moldings, fog lamps, leather-wrapped steering wheel, "Cutlass Supreme SL" lettering on doors, 215/60R16 tires, alloy wheels. Requires Option Pkg. 1SB, 1SC, or 1SD.			
Option Pkg. 1SB, conv.	296	255	258
Remote Lock Control Pkg., lighted visor mirrors, power antenna.			
Option Pkg. 1SC, conv.	691	594	601
Pkg. 1SB plus automatic air conditioning, leather-wrapped steering wheel, steering wheel touch controls.			
55/45 front seats, S	NC	NC	NC
Includes storage armrest and seatback recliners. Not available with 3.4-liter V-6, leather seats, or head-up instrument display.			
Custom Trim Pkg., S	150	129	131
Includes split folding rear seat back. Requires Option Pkg. 1SB, 1SC, or 1SD.			
Power driver's seat, S	305	262	265
Requires Pkg. 1SC.			
Astroroof	695	598	605
Requires power driver's seat, Pkg. 1SC, or 1SD.			
Remote Lock Control Pkg., Special Edition	185	159	161
Power windows, S 2-door	275	237	239
S 4-door..	340	292	296
Requires Pkg. 1SB.			
Alloy wheels, S	285	245	248
Not available with BYP Sport Luxury Pkg. or 3.4-liter V-6.			
Cassette player with equalizer,			
S with Pkg. 1SC, conv.	130	112	113
S with Pkg. 1SD, conv. with Pkg. 1SC	100	86	87
AM/FM radio with CD player,			
S with Pkg. 1SC , conv.	256	256	256
S with Pkg. 1SD, conv. with Pkg. 1SC	226	194	197
Custom leather trim, S	665	572	579
S requires Pkg. 1SD or power driver's seat.			
Floormats, S	45	39	40

Prices are accurate at time of publication; subject to manufacturer's change.

OLDSMOBILE

	Retail Price	Dealer Invoice	Fair Price
Head-up instrument display, S, conv.	$250	$215	$218
S requires Pkg. 1SD. Conv. requires Pkg. 1SC.			
Decklid luggage carrier, S	115	99	100
Requires Option Pkg. 1SB, 1SC, or 1SD. Not available with 3.4-liter V-6.			
Bodyside moldings, S, conv.	60	52	53
Engine block heater	18	15	16
Trunk cargo net, S, conv.	30	26	27

Oldsmobile Eighty Eight

	Retail Price	Dealer Invoice	Fair Price
4-door notchback	$20875	$18266	$18866
4-door notchback (California)	19995	—	—
Special Edition 4-door notchback, Pkg. R7B	19995	19121	—
LS Special Edition 4-door notchback, Pkg. R7C	22995	21936	—
LS 4-door notchback	22875	20016	20616
LSS 4-door notchback (California)	22995	—	—
Destination charge	575	575	575

California models' invoice and fair price not available at time of publication. Special Edition fair price not available at time of publication. California and Special Edition models include destination charge.

Standard Equipment:

3.8-liter V-6, 4-speed automatic transmission, power steering, driver- and passenger-side air bags, anti-lock brakes, power steering, air conditioning, 55/45 cloth front seat with armrest and reclining seatback, power windows, left remote and right manual mirrors, tinted glass, solar control rear window, rear defogger, intermittent wipers, AM/FM radio, tilt steering wheel, Pass-Key theft-deterrent system, power locks, trip odometer, visor mirrors, 205/70R15 whitewall tires, wheel covers. **California model** adds: power driver's seat, cruise control, power mirrors, remote decklid release, front console with storage armrest, cassette player, power antenna, reading lights, lighted visor mirrors, trunk cargo net, alloy wheels. **Special Edition** adds: Option Pkg. 1SC. **LS** adds to base: cruise control, power mirrors, cassette player, power antenna, power decklid release, front armrest with storage, reading lights, floormats. **LS Special Edition** adds: Option Pkg. 1SB, LSS Pkg., Comfort Pkg., leather seats. **LSS** adds to base: variable-assist power steering, touring suspension, dual zone air conditioner, Gage Pkg. with tachometer, steering wheel touch controls, reclining power leather bucket seats, uplevel interior trim, front console with storage armrest, cruise control, power mirrors, cassette player, power antenna, Accessory Pkg., illuminated entry system, remote keyless entry, reading lights, lighted visor mirrors, remote decklid release, trunk cargo net, 16-inch blackwall touring tires, alloy wheels.

Optional Equipment:

	Retail Price	Dealer Invoice	Fair Price
Option Pkg. 1SB, base	$1030	$886	$937
Cruise control, front storage armrest, cassette player, power antenna, floormats, alloy wheels.			
Option Pkg. 1SC, base	1667	1434	1517
Option Pkg. 1SB plus power driver's seat, power mirrors, power decklid release, reading lights, lighted visor mirrors.			
Option Pkg. 1SB, LS	1547	1330	1408
with LSS Pkg., without leather seats	1217	1047	1107
with leather seats, without LSS Pkg.	1497	1287	1362
with LSS Pkg. and leather seats	1167	1004	1062
Dual zone automatic air conditioner, Luxury/Convenience Pkg., Reminder Pkg., steering wheel touch controls, rear storage armrest, overhead console, trunk cargo net, alloy wheels.			
LSS Pkg., LS	845	727	769
Reclining front bucket seats, power driver's seat, center console with floor shifter and storage armrest, full analog gauges, coolant temperature gauge, voltmeter, Driver Information Center, touring suspension, dual auxiliary 12-volt outlets, Reminder Pkg., 225/60R16 tires, alloy wheels. Not available with electronic instrument cluster. Requires Option Pkg. 1SB.			
Remote Accessory Control Pkg., base, Special Edition	225	194	205
Illumination Pkg., programmable power door locks, remote keyless entry system. Base requires Option Pkg. 1SC.			
Luxury /Convenience Pkg., LS	725	624	660
Remote Accessory Control Pkg., programmable power door locks, power driver's seat, lighted visor mirrors, reading lights.			
Comfort Pkg., LS	555	477	505
Power passenger's seat with recliner, cornering lamps, automatic day/night rearview mirror with compass. Requires Option Pkg. 1SB.			
Traction control system	175	151	159
Base requires Option Pkg. 1SC. LS requires Option Pkg. 1SB.			
Power driver's seat, base	350	301	319
Requires Option Pkg. 1SB.			
Leather seats, base, Special Edition	610	525	555
LS	565	486	514
LS with LSS Pkg.	475	409	432
Base requires power driver's seat. LS requires Option Pkg. 1SB.			
Striping	45	39	41
Wire wheel covers, base, Special Edition, LS with Pkg. 1SB	NC	NC	NC

Prices are accurate at time of publication; subject to manufacturer's change.

OLDSMOBILE

	Retail Price	Dealer Invoice	Fair Price
LS without Pkg. 1SB	$316	$272	$288
Includes 205/70R15 whitewall tires. Base requires Option Pkg. 1SB or 1SC.			
15-inch alloy wheels, LS	330	284	300
205/70R15 whitewall tires	76	65	69
Electronic instrument cluster, LS	345	297	314
Requires Option Pkg. 1SB.			
AM/FM cassette, base	265	228	241
AM/FM cassette and CD	396	341	360
Base requires Option Pkg. 1SB or 1SC.			
Power antenna, base	85	73	77
Engine block heater	18	15	16

Oldsmobile Ninety Eight

	Retail Price	Dealer Invoice	Fair Price
Regency 4-door notchback	$25875	$22641	$23341
Regency 4-door notchback (Calif.)	24999	—	—
Regency Special Edition 4-door notchback	24995	23898	—
Regency Elite 4-door notchback	27975	24478	25178
Destination charge	625	625	625

California model invoice and fair price not available at time of publication. Special Edition fair price not available at time of publication. California and Special Edition prices include destination charge.

Standard Equipment:

Regency: 3.8-liter V-6, 4-speed automatic transmission, anti-lock brakes, driver- and passenger-side air bags, power steering, automatic climate control, cloth 55/45 reclining front seat with storage armrest, power driver's seat, cruise control, power windows and door locks, power mirrors, AM/FM radio, power antenna, remote fuel door and decklid releases, tilt steering wheel, cruise control, automatic leveling suspension, solar control glass, power mirrors, intermittent wipers, rear defogger, Pass-Key theft deterrent system, visor mirrors, reading lights, floormats, 205/70R15 whitewall tires, wire wheel covers. **Calif. model** adds: dual zone automatic climate control, power passenger seat, leather upholstery, cassette player, alloy wheels. **Regency Special Edition** adds to Regency: Option Pkg. 1SB, leather seats, alloy wheels. **Regency Elite** adds to Regency: dual zone air conditioner, power passenger seat, AM/FM cassette, steering wheel touch controls, programmable power door locks, lighted visor mirrors, Remote Accessory Control Pkg., Reminder Pkg., overhead console storage, trunk cargo net, alloy wheels.

Optional Equipment:

	Retail Price	Dealer Invoice	Fair Price
Supercharged 3.8-liter V-6 Engine Pkg.,			
Elite	$1631	$1403	$1484
Elite with leather seats	1541	1325	1402

Supercharged 3.8-liter V-6 engine, touring car ride and handling suspension, traction control system, tachometer, variable-assist power steering, leather-wrapped steering wheel, 225/60R16 tires, alloy wheels. Not available with electronic instrument cluster or Computer Command Ride System. Requires Option Pkg. 1SB.

Traction control system, Regency, Elite	175	151	159

Requires Computer Command Ride System and Option Pkg. 1SB.

Option Pkg. 1SB, Regency	1448	1245	1318

Dual zone air conditioner, Reminder Pkg., lighted visor mirrors, power passenger seat with power recliner, power front seat lumbar adjusters, steering wheel touch controls, AM/FM cassette, Remote Accessory Control Pkg., trunk cargo net.

Option Pkg. 1SB, Elite	635	546	578

Power trunk pull-down, Twilight Sentinel, heated electrochromatic driver-side outside mirror, electrochromatic day/night rearview mirror with compass, driver-side power seat memory, cornering lamps.

Astroroof, Regency, Elite	995	856	905

Requires Option Pkg. 1SB.

Computer Command Ride System,			
Regency, Elite	470	404	428
with leather seats	380	327	346

Requires traction control system and Option Pkg. 1SB. Not available with traction control system on Elite.

Wire wheel covers, Special Edition,			
Elite	NC	NC	NC

Not available with supercharged V-6.

Alloy wheels, Regency	131	113	119
AM/FM cassette and CD player,			
Regency, Elite	396	341	360

Requires Option Pkg. 1SB.

Electronic instrument cluster,			
Regency, Elite	345	297	314

Includes Driver Information Center. Requires Option Pkg. 1SB. Not available with supercharged V-6.

Custom leather trim, Regency,			
Elite	515	443	469

Requires Option Pkg. 1SB.

Cloth seat trim, Special Edition,			
(credit)	(515)	(443)	(443)
Accent stripe	45	39	41
Engine block heater	18	15	16

OLDSMOBILE

Oldsmobile Silhouette

	Retail Price	Dealer Invoice	Fair Price
4-door van	$20095	$18186	$18586
4-door van (California)	19995	—	—
Special Edition 4-door van	19995	19119	—
Destination charge	530	530	530

California model dealer invoice and fair price not available at time of publication. Special Edition fair price not available at time of publication. California and Special Edition prices include destination charge.

Standard Equipment:

Base: 3.1-liter V-6, 3-speed automatic transmission, anti-lock brakes, driver-side air bag, power steering, front air conditioning, 4-way adjustable driver's seat, 7-passenger seating (front bucket seats, three middle and two rear modular seats), center console with locking storage, power mirrors, tachometer, coolant temperature and oil pressure gauges, voltmeter, trip odometer, AM/FM radio, tilt steering wheel, tinted glass, intermittent wipers, rear wiper/washer, rear defogger, fog lamps, visor mirrors, floormats, 205/70R15 tires, alloy wheels. **California model** adds: 3.8-liter V-6 engine, power windows and locks, cruise control, remote keyless entry system, cassette player, roof luggage carrier, cargo area net. **Special Edition** adds to base: 3.8-liter V-6 engine, 4-speed automatic transmission, Option Pkg. 1SB.

Optional Equipment:

3.8-liter V-6 engine, base	800	688	716
Includes 4-speed automatic transmission.			
Traction control system, base	350	301	313
Requires FE3 Touring Suspension and 3.8-liter V-6, or Option Pkg. 1SC.			
Option Pkg. 1SB, base	1660	1428	1486
Convenience Pkg., AM/FM cassette, Remote Lock Control Pkg., deep-tinted glass, roof luggage carrier, overhead console with compass and temperature readout, cargo area net.			
Option Pkg. 1SC, base	3270	2812	2927
Base with sunroof	3095	2662	2770
Option Pkg. 1SB plus 3.8-liter V-6 engine, 4-speed automatic transmission, power driver's seat, power sliding door, steering wheel touch controls, leather-wrapped steering wheel.			
Convenience Pkg., base	800	688	716
Power windows, programmable power door locks with sliding door delay, cruise control.			
Integrated dual child seats, base	225	194	201
Rear air conditioning	450	387	403
Base requires Option Pkg. 1SB plus 3.8-liter V-6 engine, or Option Pkg. 1SC.			
Deep-tinted glass, base	245	211	219

	Retail Price	Dealer Invoice	Fair Price
Power driver's seat	$270	$232	$242
Base requires Option Pkg. 1SB.			
Power sliding door, base	295	254	264
Requires Option Pkg. 1SB.			
FE3 Touring Suspension, base	205	176	183
Includes eletronic level control, air inflation kit, 205/70R15 touring tires. Requires Option Pkg. 1SB or 1SC.			
Towing Pkg., base	355	305	318
Requires 3.8-liter V-6 engine or Option Pkg. 1SC. Includes FE3 Touring Suspension and traction control system.			
Cassette player, base	140	120	125
Base with Option Pkg. 1SB	30	26	27
AM/FM radio and CD player,			
Base with Option Pkg. 1SB	256	256	256
Base with Option Pkg. 1SC	226	194	202
Roof luggage carrier, base	145	125	130
Sunroof, base	350	301	313
Requires Option Pkg. 1SC.			
Cargo area net, base	30	26	27
Custom leather trim, base and			
Special Edition	870	748	779
Base with Option Pkg. 1SC	780	671	698
Engine block heater	18	15	16
Black roof delete	NC	NC	NC

PLYMOUTH

Plymouth Acclaim	Retail Price	Dealer Invoice	Fair Price
4-door notchback w/Pkg. 21A	$12470	$11339	$11539
4-door notchback w/Pkg. 22D	13649	12376	12576
Destination charge	505	505	505

Standard Equipment:

Pkg. 21A: 2.5-liter 4-cylinder engine, 5-speed manual transmission, power steering, driver-side air bag, cloth reclining front bucket seats, coolant temperature gauge, voltmeter, trip odometer, center console, tinted glass, dual remote mirrors, visor mirrors, narrow bodyside moldings, AM/FM radio with two speakers, intermittent wipers, 185/70R14 tires, wheel covers. **Pkg. 22D** adds: 3-speed automatic transmission, air conditioning, 50/50 split front bench seat, tilt steering wheel, cruise control, rear defogger, floormats.

Optional Equipment:

	Retail Price	Dealer Invoice	Fair Price
Pkg. 24D	NC	NC	NC
Pkg. 22D plus 2.5-liter 4-cylinder flexible fuel engine.			
Pkg. 26D	$725	$616	$638
Pkg. 22D plus 3.0-liter V-6 engine.			
Pkg. 24E	883	751	777
Pkg. 24D plus power windows and locks, heated power mirrors, split folding rear seat, remote decklid release.			
Pkg. 28E	883	751	777
Pkg. 22D plus power windows and locks, heated power mirrors, split folding rear seat, remote decklid release. Requires 3.0-liter V-6 engine, 4-speed automatic transmission.			
3.0-liter V-6 engine, w/Pkgs. 26D, 28E	725	616	638
Includes 195/70R14 tires.			
4-speed automatic transmission, w/Pkg. 28E	173	147	152
Anti-lock 4-wheel disc brakes	699	594	615
Not available with Pkg. 26D.			
Argent Special Equipment Group, w/Pkg. 22D, 26D	200	170	176
Luggage rack, 195/70R14 tires, alloy wheels.			
Gold Special Equipment Group, w/Pkg. 22D, 26D	200	170	176
Includes gold badging and molding inserts, luggage rack, 195/70R14 tires, alloy wheels with gold accents.			
Rear window defogger, w/Pkg. 21A	173	147	152
AM/FM cassette with four speakers	170	145	150
Not available with Pkg. 21A.			
Power door locks, w/Pkg. 22D, 24D, 26D	250	213	220
Power driver's seat, w/Pkg. 24E, 28E	306	260	269
Split folding rear seat	NC	NC	NC
Mini trip computer/message center	93	79	82
Not available with Pkg. 21A.			
195/70R14 whitewall tires, w/Pkg. 22D, 24D, 24E	104	88	92
w/Pkg. 26D or 28E	73	62	64
Conventional spare tire	95	81	84
Extra-cost paint	97	82	85

Plymouth Laser	Retail Price	Dealer Invoice	Fair Price
3-door hatchback	$11542	$10811	$11111
RS 3-door hatchback	13910	12884	13284
RS Turbo 3-door hatchback	15444	14265	14765
RS Turbo AWD 3-door hatchback	17572	16220	16720

	Retail Price	Dealer Invoice	Fair Price
Destination charge	$430	$430	$430

Standard Equipment:

1.8-liter 4-cylinder engine, 5-speed manual transmission, motorized front shoulder belts, 4-wheel disc brakes, cloth reclining front bucket seats, split folding rear seatback, center console, tachometer, coolant temperature and oil pressure gauges, trip odometer, tinted glass, remote fuel door and hatch releases, dual remote mirrors, visor mirrors, map lights, AM/FM radio, tilt steering column, intermittent wipers, 185/70R14 tires. **RS** adds: 2.0-liter DOHC 4-cylinder engine, power steering, driver-seat lumbar support adjustment, rear defogger, power mirrors, cassette player, tonneau cover, rear spoiler, 205/55R16 tires, wheel covers. **RS Turbo** adds: turbocharged, intercooled engine, turbo boost gauge, leather-wrapped steering wheel, 205/55VR16 tires. **RS Turbo AWD** adds: sport suspension, alloy wheels.

Optional Equipment:

Pkg. 21T/22T, base	1099	934	989

Air conditioning, power steering. Pkg. 22T requires automatic transmission.

Pkg. 21B/22B, base	827	703	744

Power steering, cup holder console, rear defogger, rear spoiler, cargo area cover, striping, floormats. Pkg. 22B requires automatic transmission.

Pkg. 21C/22C, base	1654	1406	1489

Pkg. 21B plus air conditioning. Pkg. 22C requires automatic transmission.

Pkg. 21D/22D, base	2070	1760	1863

Pkg. 21C plus cruise control, cassette player. Pkg. 22D requires automatic transmission.

Pkg. 23F/24F, RS	921	783	829

Air conditioning, console cup holder, striping, floormats. Pkg. 24F requires automatic transmission.

Pkg. 23G/24G, RS	1489	1265	1340

Pkg. 23F plus cruise control, cassette player with equalizer, rear wiper/washer. Pkg. 24G requires automatic transmission.

Pkg. 23H/24H, RS	2013	1711	1812

Pkg. 23G plus power windows and locks, fog lamps. Pkg. 24H requires automatic transmission.

Pkg. 25H/26H, RS Turbo	2013	1711	1812

Air conditioning, power windows and locks, cruise control, cassette player with equalizer, console cup holder, rear wiper/washer, fog lamps, striping, floormats. Pkg. 26H requires automatic transmission.

Prices are accurate at time of publication; subject to manufacturer's change.

PLYMOUTH

	Retail Price	Dealer Invoice	Fair Price
Pkg. 25Q, RS Turbo AWD	$2013	1711	1812
Pkg. 26Q, RS Turbo AWD	1956	1622	1760

Air conditioning, power windows and locks, cruise control, cassette player with equalizer, console cup holder, rear wiper/washer, fog lamps (Pkg. 25Q), striping, floormats. Pkg. 26Q requires automatic transmission.

4-speed automatic transmission	716	609	630
Anti-lock brakes (Not available on base)	699	594	615
Cassette player	198	168	174
CD player (Not available on base)	517	439	455
Rear defogger, base	130	111	114
Sunroof	373	317	328
Gold Decor Pkg. (Not available on base)	NC	NC	NC

Gold striping and badging. Requires alloy wheels.

Alloy wheels, RS and RS Turbo	302	257	266

Plymouth Sundance

	Retail Price	Dealer Invoice	Fair Price
3-door hatchback	$8806	$8263	$8453
5-door hatchback	9206	8631	8821
Duster 3-door hatchback	11046	10246	10436
Duster 5-door hatchback	11446	10606	10796
Destination charge	505	505	505

Standard Equipment:

Base: 2.2-liter 4-cylinder engine, 5-speed manual transmission, power steering, driver-side air bag, cloth reclining front bucket seats, mini console with storage, tinted rear window, trip odometer, coolant temperature gauge, voltmeter, left remote mirror, removable shelf panel, 185/70R14 tires. **Duster** adds: 3.0-liter V-6 engine, sport suspension, dual outside mirrors, AM/FM radio, rear spoiler, body-color bumpers and bodyside cladding, 195/60R15 tires, wheel covers.

Optional Equipment:

Pkgs. 21Y, 22Y, 23Y, 24Y, base	1545	1313	1336

Air conditioning, tinted glass, rear defogger, dual remote mirrors, AM/FM radio, visor mirrors, intermittent wipers, Light Group, floormats, wheel covers, body-color fascias, color-keyed instrument panel bezels, bodyside moldings, striping. Pkg. 22Y requires 3-speed automatic transmission; Pkg. 23Y requires 2.5-liter engine; Pkg. 24Y requires 2.5-liter engine and 3-speed automatic transmission.

Pkg. 23H, 24H, 27H, 28H, Duster	978	831	846

	Retail Price	Dealer Invoice	Fair Price

Air conditioning, tinted glass, rear defogger, cassette player, remote hatch release, Light Group, tachometer, intermittent wipers, console with storage armrest and cup holders, fog lamps, floormats, visor mirrors.

	Retail Price	Dealer Invoice	Fair Price
2.5-liter 4-cylinder engine, base	$286	$243	$247
Duster (credit)	(794)	(675)	(675)
3-speed automatic transmission, base	557	473	482
4-speed automatic transmission, Duster	730	621	631
Air conditioning and tinted glass	900	765	779
Anti-lock brakes	699	594	605
Requires automatic transmission.			
Light Group	77	65	67
Overhead console,			
Duster w/Pkgs. 23-28H	265	225	229
Includes temperature readout and compass. Requires power windows and locks, power mirrors.			
Rear defogger	173	147	150
Power locks, Base 3-door w/Pkgs. 21-24Y,			
Duster 3-door	199	169	172
Base 5-door w/Pkgs. 21-24Y,			
Duster 5-door	240	204	208
Intermittent wipers	66	56	57
Dual remote mirrors, Base	69	59	60
Power mirrors, Duster w/Pkgs. 23-28H	57	48	49
Power driver's seat,			
Duster w/Pkgs. 23-28H	306	260	265
Requires power windows, locks, and mirrors.			
Power windows, Duster			
3-door w/Pkgs. 23-28H	265	225	229
Duster 5-door w/Pkgs. 23-28H	331	281	286
Requires power locks and mirrors.			
AM/FM radio, Base	284	241	246
AM/FM cassette, Base w/Pkgs. 21-24W..........	504	428	436
Base w/Pkgs. 21-24Y	170	145	147
Duster	220	187	190
Infinity cassette system with equalizer,			
Duster w/Pkgs. 23-28G	520	442	450
Duster w/Pkgs. 23-28H	300	255	260
Requires power door locks, intermittent wipers.			
Infinity CD system with equalizer,			
Duster w/Pkgs. 23-28G	690	587	597
Duster w/Pkgs. 23-28H	470	400	407
Requires tilt steering wheel, intermittent wipers.			
Cruise control	224	190	194
Requires tilt steering wheel.			

PLYMOUTH

	Retail Price	Dealer Invoice	Fair Price
Light Group	$77	$65	$67
Sunroof	379	322	328
Not available with overhead console.			
Tilt steering wheel	148	126	128
Requires intermittent wipers.			
Remote liftgate release,			
Base w/Pkgs. 21Y-24Y	24	20	21
Alloy wheels, Base	376	320	325
Base w/Pkgs. 21Y-24Y, Duster	328	279	284
Conventional spare tire with steel wheel	85	72	74
with alloy wheel, Duster	213	181	184
Extra-cost paint	97	82	84
Floormats	46	39	40

Plymouth Voyager

	Retail Price	Dealer Invoice	Fair Price
Base SWB	$14919	$13629	$14329
Base Grand	18178	16522	17222
SE SWB	18139	16462	17162
Grand SE	19304	17513	18413
Grand SE AWD	21982	19869	20769
LE SWB	21963	19827	20727
Grand LE	22883	20662	21562
Grand LE AWD	25560	23017	23917
LX SWB	22472	20275	21175
Destination charge	560	560	560

SWB denotes standard wheelbase; AWD denotes All-Wheel Drive.

Standard Equipment:

Base: 2.5-liter 4-cylinder engine, 5-speed manual transmission, driver- and passenger-side air bags, power steering, cloth front bucket seats, 3-passenger middle bench seat, tinted glass, trip odometer, coolant temperature gauge, dual outside mirrors, visor mirrors, AM/FM radio, intermittent wipers, rear wiper/washer, 195/75R14 tires, wheel covers. **Base Grand** adds: 3.0-liter V-6 engine, 3-speed automatic transmission, 7-passenger seating (front buckets and 2-place middle and 3-place rear bench seats), rear trim panel storage and cup holders, 205/70R15 tires. **SE** adds to Base: 3.0-liter V-6 engine, 3-speed automatic transmission, cruise control, power mirrors, cassette player, power remote tailgate release, tilt steering wheel, front passenger lockable underseat storage drawer, striping, dual note horn. **Grand SE** adds to Base Grand: 3.3-liter V-6 engine, 4-speed automatic transmission, cruise control, power mirrors, cassette player, power remote tailgate release, tilt steering wheel, front passenger lockable underseat storage drawer, striping, dual note horn. **LE** adds to SE: front air conditioning, front storage console, overhead console with trip computer, rear defogger, power rear quarter vent windows, power door locks, remote keyless entry system, tachometer, oil pressure gauge, voltmeter, heated power mirrors, lighted visor mirrors, illuminated entry system, headlamp time delay, floormats, 205/70R15 tires. **Grand LE** adds to Grand SE: front air conditioning, front storage console, overhead console with trip computer, rear defogger, power rear quarter vent windows, power door locks, remote keyless entry system, tachometer, oil pressure gauge, voltmeter, heated power mirrors, lighted visor mirrors, illuminated entry system, headlamp time delay, floormats. **LX** adds to LE SWB: LX Decor Group. **AWD** models have permanently engaged all-wheel drive.

Quick Order Packages:

	Retail Price	Dealer Invoice	Fair Price
Pkgs. 21T, 22T, 24T Base SWB and 26T Base SWB, Base Grand	$213	$181	$196

Air conditioning, map and cargo lights, power remote liftgate release, front passenger underseat lockable storage drawer, bodyside molding, dual horns. Pkg. 22T requires 3-speed automatic transmission; Pkg. 24T requires 3.0-liter engine and 3-speed automatic transmission; Pkg. 26T requires 3.0-liter engine and 4-speed transmission.

Pkg. 26B SE SWB and Pkg. 28B SWB, Grand SE, Grand SE AWD	213	181	196

Pkgs. 24-28B add to SE standard equipment: air conditioning, map and cargo lights, rear defogger. SE SWB Pkg. 24B requires 4-speed automatic transmission; SE SWB Pkg. 28B requires 3.3-liter engine and 4-speed automatic transmission.

Pkg. 26D SE SWB, and Pkg. 28D SE SWB, Grand SE, Grand SE AWD	1159	985	1066

Pkgs. 26-28D add to Pkgs. 26-28B forward and overhead consoles, oil pressure and voltage gauges, tachometer, lighted visor mirrors, Light Group, power door locks and rear quarter vent windows, floormats, deluxe insulation. SE SWB Pkg. 26D requires 4-speed automatic transmission; SE SWB Pkg. 28D requires 3.3-liter engine and 4-speed automatic transmission.

Pkg. 26K LE SWB, and Pkg. 28K LE SWB, Grand LE, Grand LE AWD and Pkg. 29K Grand LE, Grand LE AWD	306	260	282

Pkgs. 26K-29K add to LE standard equipment: power driver's seat, power windows, AM/FM radio with cassette player, equalizer and six Infinity speakers, sunscreen glass. LE SWB Pkg. 26K requires 4-speed automatic transmission; LE SWB Pkg. 28K requires 3.3-liter engine and 4-speed automatic transmission; Grand LE and Grand LE AWD require 3.8-liter engine.

Pkg. 28L and 29L Grand LE, Grand LE AWD	962	818	885

	Retail Price	Dealer Invoice	Fair Price

Pkgs. 28L-29L add to 28K-29K: Woodgrain Decor Group (woodgrain trim and moldings, front and rear body-color fascias, luggage rack, whitewall tires, alloy wheels). Requires 3.8-liter engine.

Pkg. 26M-28M LX SWB $431 $366 $397

Pkgs. 26M-29M add to 26K-28K LX SWB: LX Decor Group (body-color fascia, cladding, and grille, fog lamps, alloy wheels), Sport Handling Group (heavy duty brakes, firmer front and rear sway bars and front struts and rear shocks, 205/70R15 tires, alloy wheels). LX SWB Pkg. 26M requires 4-speed automatic transmission; LX SWB Pkg. 28M requires 3.3-liter engine and 4-speed automatic transmission.

Individual Options:

3.0-liter V-6, Base SWB	767	652	706
Requires 3-speed automatic transmission.			
3.3-liter V-6, SE, LE, and ES SWB	102	87	94
Requires 4-speed automatic transmission.			
3.8-liter V-6, Grand LE, and Grand LE AWD	302	257	278
Includes 4-speed transmission.			
3-speed automatic transmission, Base SWB	601	511	553
4-speed automatic transmission, SE, LE, LX SWB and Base Grand	198	168	182
Anti-lock brakes: SE SWB with Pkgs. 26-28B or 26-28D	687	584	632
SE SWB with Pkgs. 26-28B or 26-28D and alloy wheels, Trailer Tow, Sport Handling, Gold Special Edition, or Sport Wagon Groups; Grand SE with Pkgs. 28B or 28D	599	509	551
LE SWB with Pkgs. 26-28K or 26-28M; Grand LE with Pkgs. 26-28K, 26-28L or 26-28M	599	509	551
Front air conditioning, Base SWB and Base Grand	857	728	788
Front air conditioning with sunscreen glass, Base SWB with Pkg. 26T, SE SWB with Pkg. 26-28B and 26-28D, Base Grand with Pkg. 26T and SE Grand with Pkg. 28B and 28D	414	352	381
Not available with Sport Wagon Decor Group.			
Sunscreen glass, Grand SE AWD with Pkg. 28B and 28D	414	352	381

	Retail Price	Dealer Invoice	Fair Price
Rear air conditioning with rear heater and sunscreen glass, Base Grand with Pkg. 26T, Grand SE with Pkg. 28B, Grand SE AWD with Pkg. 28B	$988	$840	$909
Grand SE and Grand SE AWD with Pkg. 28B and Sport Wagon Decor Group	574	488	528
with Trailer Towing Group	925	786	851
with Sport Wagon Decor Group and Trailer Towing Group	511	434	470
Grand SE and Grand SE AWD with Pkg. 28D	880	748	810
with Sport Wagon Decor Group	466	396	429
with Trailer Towing Group	818	695	753
with Sport Wagon Decor Group and Trailer Towing Group	404	343	372
Grand LE and Grand LE AWD with Pkgs. 28-29K, 28-29L, or 28-29M	466	396	429
with Trailer Towing Group	404	343	372
Requires rear defogger.			
Rear bench seat, Base SWB	346	294	318
7-passenger seating with integrated child seat, Base SWB	570	485	524
SE, LE and LX SWB, Grand, Grand AWD	225	191	207
Quad Command Seating, SE, LE and LX	597	507	549
Two front and two middle bucket seats, 3-passenger rear bench seat.			
Converta-Bed 7-passenger seating, SE, LE and LX	553	470	509
Leather trim, LX	865	735	796
Not available with integrated child seat.			
Heavy Duty Trailer Towing Group, SE SWB with Pkgs. 26-28B and 26-28D	556	473	512
with Gold Special Edition Group	442	376	407
LE SWB with Pkgs. 26-28K, Grand SE with Pkgs. 28B and 28D and Grand LE with Pkgs. 28-29K and 28-29L	442	376	407
SE SWB with Pkgs. 26-28B and 26-28D, LE SWB with Pkgs. 26-28K, LX SWB with Pkgs. 26-28M, Grand SE with Pkgs. 28B and 28D, Grand LE with Pkgs. 28-29K and 28-29L	410	349	377
Grand SE AWD with Pkgs. 28B and 28D, Grand LE AWD with Pkgs. 28-29K, 28-29L and 28-29M	373	317	343

	Retail Price	Dealer Invoice	Fair Price

Heavy duty brakes, battery, load suspension and radiator, trailer towing wiring harness, 205/70R15 all-season tires, conventional spare tire.

Sport Handling Group, SWB SE
with Pkg. 26-28B and 26-28D $239 $203 $220
Grand SE with Pkg. 28B and 28D,
Grand LE with Pkg. 28-29L 125 106 115
Heavy duty brakes, front and rear sway bars, 205/70R15 tires. Not available with Sport Wagon Decor Pkg.
LE SWB with Pkg. 26-28K
and Grand LE with Pkg. 28-29K 488 415 449
Heavy duty brakes, front and rear sway bars, 205/70R15 tires, alloy wheels.
Convenience Group I, Base SWB and
Base Grand 372 316 342
Cruise control, tilt steering wheel.
Convenience Group II, Base SWB and
Base Grand 694 590 638
SE SWB with Pkg. 26-28B and
Grand SE with 28B 265 225 244
Convenience Group I plus power mirrors and door locks.
Convenience Group III, SE SWB with
Pkg. 26-28B and Grand SE
with Pkg. 28B 673 572 619
SE SWB with Pkg. 26-28D and Grand SE
with Pkg. 28D 408 347 375
Convenience Group II plus power windows and remote keyless entry system.
AWD Convenience Group I, Grand SE AWD
with Pkg. 28B 265 225 244
Power mirrors and door locks.
AWD Convenience Group II, Grand SE AWD
with Pkg. 28B 673 572 619
with Pkg. 28D 408 347 375
AWD Convenience Group I plus power windows and remote keyless entry system.
Gold Special Edition Group,
SE 250 213 230
Gold striping, moldings and badging, 205/70R15 tires, gold-color alloy wheels.
Sport Wagon Decor Group, SE 750 638 690
Sunscreen glass, front and rear fascias, leather-wrapped steering wheel, fog lamps, Sport Handling Group, alloy wheels.
Rear defogger 168 143 155
Power door locks 265 225 244

	Retail Price	Dealer Invoice	Fair Price
Luggage rack	143	122	132
Cassette player	170	145	156
AM and FM stereo with CD player, equalizer and six Infinity speakers, SE SWB with Pkg. 26-28D, Grand SE with Pkg. 28D, Grand SE AWD with Pkg. 28D	501	426	461
LE SWB with Pkg. 26-28K and 26-28L, Grand LE with Pkg. 28-29K, 28-29L, 28-29M, Grand LE AWD with Pkg. 28-29K, 28-29L, 28-29M	170	145	156
Infinity speaker system, SE	202	172	186
Firm Ride Heavy Load Suspension, 2WD	178	151	129
with Sport Handling Group	146	124	105
Includes conventional spare tire.			
205/70R14 whitewall tires, Base SWB and SE SWB	143	122	132
205/70R15 whitewall tires, SWB SE, SWB LE, Base Grand, Grand SE, Grand LE, Grand SE AWD, Grand LE AWD	69	59	63
Not available with Sport Handling, Gold Special Edition, Sport Wagon Groups.			
Conventional spare tire	109	93	100
15-inch alloy wheels, LE SWB with Pkg. 26-28K, Grand LE with Pkg. 28-29K, Grand LE AWD with Pkg. 28-29K	363	309	334
Extra-cost paint	97	82	89

PONTIAC

Pontiac Bonneville	Retail Price	Dealer Invoice	Fair Price
SE 4-door notchback sedan	$20424	$17871	$18471
SLE 4-door notchback (California)	21795	—	—
SSE 4-door notchback sedan	25884	22649	23249
Destination charge	575	575	575

California SLE dealer invoice and fair price not available at time of publication. California SLE price includes destination charge.

Standard Equipment:

SE: 3.8-liter V-6, 4-speed automatic transmission, anti-lock brakes, power

PONTIAC

steering, driver- and passenger-side air bags, air conditioning, cloth 45/55 reclining front seats, front overhead console with reading lights, tilt steering wheel, power windows with driver-side express down, power door locks, AM/FM radio, tinted glass, left remote and right manual mirrors, fog lamps, trip odometer, intermittent wipers, Pass-Key theft-deterrent system, visor mirrors, floormats, 215/65R15 tires, wheel covers. **SLE** adds: Sport Luxury Edition (SLE) Pkg. 1SD/H4U. **SSE** adds: variable-assist power steering, rally gauges with tachometer, electronic load leveling suspension, 45/45 cloth bucket seats with center storage console and rear air conditioning vents, overhead console with power outlet, 6-way power driver's seat, rear center armrest with cup holders, rear defogger, heated power mirrors, cruise control, cassette player with equalizer, power antenna, Driver Information Center, remote decklid release, Twilight Sentinel, rear spoiler, accessory emergency road kit (includes spot light, first aid kit, air hose, windshield scraper, gloves), Lamp Group (includes rear courtesy lights, rear assist handles, headlamp-on warning, engine compartment light), lighted visor mirrors, deluxe floormats, 225/60R16 tires, alloy wheels.

Optional Equipment:

	Retail Price	Dealer Invoice	Fair Price
Option Group 1SB, SE	$628	$540	$565

Cruise control, rally gauges with tachometer, Lamp Group, illuminated entry, cassette player.

Option Group 1SC, SE	1281	1102	1153

Group 1SB plus variable-assist steering, 6-way power driver's seat, power mirrors, rear defogger, decklid release.

Option Group 1SD, SE	1942	1670	1748

Group 1SC plus remote keyless entry system, 45/55 cloth front seat with storage armrest and cup holders, lighted visor mirrors, Twilight Sentinel, leather-wrapped steering wheel, power antenna.

Sport Luxury Edition (SLE) Pkg. 1SC/H4U, SE	3009	2603	2708

Group 1SC plus 45/45 leather bucket seats with center storage console and rear air conditioning vents, overhead console with power outlet, leather-wrapped steeing wheel and shift knob, power antenna, rear decklid spoiler, monotone side and rocker moldings, 3.06 axle ratio, lighted visor mirrors, trunk net, deluxe floormats, 225/60R16 tires, gold or silver crosslace alloy wheels.

Sport Luxury Edition (SLE) Pkg. 1SD/H4U, SE	3204	2770	2884

Group 1SD plus SLE Pkg.

Option Group 1SB, SSE	1440	1238	1296

6-way power seat, head-up display, automatic climate control, remote keyless entry system, automatic day/night rearview mirror, traction control, 8-speaker sound system, fuel door lock.

Enhancement Group, SE w/Group 1SC	206	177	185

	Retail Price	Dealer Invoice	Fair Price
with cloth bucket seats	$110	$95	$99
with leather bucket seats or SLE 1SC/H4U	60	52	54
with Group 1SD	NC	NC	NC
Lighted visor mirrors, leather-wrapped steering wheel, Twilight Sentinel.			
SE Performance and Handling Pkg.	649	558	584
with SLE Pkg.	225	194	203
225/60R16 touring tires, 5-blade alloy wheels.			
SE Monotone Appearance Pkg.	200	172	180
with SLE Pkg.	NC	NC	NC
Monotone bodyside and rocker moldings.			
SSEi Supercharger Pkg., SSE	1242	1068	1118
with leather bucket seats	1167	1004	1050
Supercharged 3.8-liter engine, boost gauge, driver-selectable shift controls, 2.97 axle ratio, upgraded carpet, SSEi badging and floormats, 225/60ZR16 tires.			
Rear decklid spoiler, SE	110	95	99
Rear decklid spoiler delete, SE with Sport Edition Pkg. and SSE (credit)	(110)	(95)	(95)
Traction control, SE and SSE	175	151	158
SE with Performance and Handling Pkg.	NC	NC	NC
Rear window defogger, SE	170	146	153
Power glass sunroof, SE	995	856	896
SSE	981	844	883
Requires lighted visor mirrors.			
B20/E6 custom interior, SE	235	202	212
45/55 reclining front bench seat with storage armrest and cup holders, upgraded cloth upholstery, trunk net, deluxe floormats.			
B20/E7 custom interior, SE	505	434	455
with Group 1SD	174	150	157
45/55 cloth bucket seats with center storage console and rear air conditioning vents, lighted visor mirrors, overhead console with power outlet, trunk net, deluxe floormats.			
B20/27 custom interior, SE	1409	1212	1268
with Group 1SD	1028	884	925
45/55 leather bucket seats, floor console.			
45/45 leather bucket seats, SSE	854	734	769
45/45 articulating leather bucket seats, SSE	1404	1207	1264
with Group 1SB	1099	945	989
6-way power driver's seat	305	262	275
6-way power passenger seat	305	262	275
Remote keyless entry system	135	116	122
AM/FM cassette player, SE	170	146	153

Prices are accurate at time of publication; subject to manufacturer's change.

PONTIAC

	Retail Price	Dealer Invoice	Fair Price
AM/FM cassette with equalizer, SE	$460	$396	$414
with Sport Edition Pkg., Enhancement Group, or leather bucket seats	401	345	361
with Group 1SD	325	280	293
AM/FM CD player with equalizer, SE	686	590	617
with Sport Edition Pkg., Enhancement Group, or leather bucket seats	636	547	470
with Group 1SD	551	474	408
AM/FM CD player with equalizer, SSE	226	194	167
Computer Command Ride, SSE	380	327	281
Requires traction control.			
Power antenna, SE	85	73	77
16-inch 5-blade alloy wheels, SE	340	292	306
16-inch gold or silver alloy wheels, SE	(NC)	(NC)	(NC)
225/60R16 blackwall touring tires, SE	84	72	76
Engine block heater	18	15	16

Pontiac Firebird

	Retail Price	Dealer Invoice	Fair Price
3-door hatchback	$13995	$12805	—
Formula 3-door hatchback	17995	16465	—
Trans Am 3-door hatchback	19895	18204	—
Trans Am GT 3-door hatchback	21395	19576	—
Destination charge	490	490	490

Convertible and fair prices not available at time of publication.

Standard Equipment:

3.4-liter V-6, 5-speed manual transmission, anti-lock brakes, power steering, driver- and passenger-side air bags, cloth reclining front bucket seats, folding rear bench seat, tilt steering wheel, center console with storage, lamp and cup holder, remote hatch release, AM/FM cassette, intermittent wipers, solar-control tinted glass, front air dam, rear decklid spoiler, left remote and right manual mirrors, coolant temperature and oil pressure gauges, tachometer, trip odometer, Pass-Key theft-deterrent system, day/night rearview mirror with dual reading lamps, covered visor mirrors, front floormats, 215/60R16 tires, alloy wheels. **Formula** adds: 5.7-liter V-8, 6-speed manual transmission, anti-lock 4-wheel disc brakes, air conditioning, performance suspension, 3.42 axle ratio, limited-slip differential, 235/50ZR16 touring tires, bright silver alloy wheels. **Trans Am** adds: cruise control, power windows with driver-side express down, power mirrors, automatic door locks, fog lamps. **Trans Am GT** adds: articulating cloth bucket seats, 4-way manually adjustable driver's seat, leather-wrapped steering wheel and shift knob, cassette with equalizer and 10-speaker sound system, steering wheel radio controls, rear defogger, remote keyless entry system, body-color bodyside molding, rear floormats, 245/50ZR16 tires.

Optional Equipment:	Retail Price	Dealer Invoice	Fair Price
4-speed automatic transmission	$620	$533	—
Air conditioning, base	895	770	—
Air conditioning delete, Formula (credit)	(895)	(770)	(770)
Option Group 1SB, base	1005	864	—
Air conditioning, manual 4-way adjustable driver's seat, bodyside moldings, rear floor mats.			
Option Group 1SC, base	2421	2082	—
Group 1SB plus power windows with driver-side express down, automatic power door locks, cruise control, remote keyless illuminated entry, cassette player with equalizer and 10-speaker sound system, leather-wrapped steering wheel with radio controls.			
Option Group 1SB, Formula	906	779	—
Cruise control, power windows with driver-side express down, automatic power door locks, mirrors, bodyside moldings, rear floormats.			
Option Group 1SC, Formula	1491	1282	—
Group 1SB plus remote keyless illuminated entry system, cassette player with equalizer and 10-speaker sound system, leather-wrapped steering wheel with radio controls.			
Cruise control (std. Trans Am and Trans Am GT)	225	194	—
Rear defogger, (std. Trans Am GT)	170	146	—
Removable locking hatch roof	895	770	—
Hatch roof sunshades	25	22	—
Rear performance axle, Formula, Trans Am GT w/automatic	110	95	—
Includes 3.23 axle ratio, engine oil cooler, 245/50ZR16 tires.			
Body-color bodyside moldings, (std. Trans Am GT)	60	52	—
Power mirrors (std. Trans Am and Trans Am GT)	96	83	—
Automatic power door locks (std. Trans Am and Trans Am GT)	220	189	—
Power windows (std. Trans Am and Trans Am GT)	290	249	—
Includes driver-side express down.			
Cassette player with equalizer (std. Trans Am GT)	450	387	—
CD player, (NA Trans Am GT)	226	194	—
CD player with equalizer, base, Formula and Trans Am	676	581	—

Prices are accurate at time of publication; subject to manufacturer's change.

	Retail Price	Dealer Invoice	Fair Price
Base and Formula with Group 1SC, Trans Am GT	$226	$194	—
Leather articulating bucket seats, base, Formula and Trans Am	780	671	—
Trans Am GT	475	409	—
4-way manual driver's seat (NA Formula, Trans Am; std. Trans Am GT)	35	30	—
6-way power driver's seat, base, Formula and Trans Am	305	262	—
Base with Group 1SB or 1SC	270	232	—
Remote keyless entry system, (std. Trans Am GT)	135	116	—
235/55R16 touring tires, base	132	114	—
245/50ZR16 tires, Formula	144	124	—
Bright white alloy wheels, (NA base)	(NC)	(NC)	(NC)
Rear floormats, (std. Trans Am GT)	15	13	—

Pontiac Grand Am

	Retail Price	Dealer Invoice	Fair Price
SE 2-door notchback	$12514	$11450	$11850
SE 2-door notchback (California)	13995	—	—
SE 4-door notchback	12614	11542	11942
SE 4-door notchback (California)	13995	—	—
GT 2-door notchback	15014	13738	14138
GT 4-door notchback	15114	13829	14229
Destination charge	485	485	485

California models' dealer invoice and fair price not available at time of publication. California models include destination charge.

Standard Equipment:

SE: 2.3-liter 4-cylinder engine, 5-speed manual transmission, anti-lock brakes, driver-side air bag, power steering, cloth reclining front bucket seats, center console with armrest, storage and coin holder, overhead compartment, left remote and right manual mirrors, front door map pockets, AM/FM radio, tinted glass, automatic power locks, decklid release, fog lamps, trip odometer, illuminated entry, visor mirrors, rear seat headrests, 185/75R14 tires, wheel covers. **California models** add: 4-speed automatic transmission, air conditioning, rear defogger, AM/FM cassette player, tilt steering wheel. **GT** adds to SE: 2.3-liter DOHC Quad 4 engine (175 horsepower), air conditioning, rally gauge cluster (includes tachometer, voltmeter, oil pressure and coolant temperature gauges), intermittent wipers, rear decklid spoiler, 205/55R16 tires, alloy wheels.

Optional Equipment:

	Retail Price	Dealer Invoice	Fair Price
2.3-liter DOHC (155 horsepower) 4-cylinder engine, GT (credit)	($140)	($120)	($120)
Includes 4-speed automatic transmission.			
3.1-liter V-6 engine, SE	410	353	373
GT (credit)	(140)	(120)	(120)
Includes 4-speed automatic transmission. Requires air conditioning and 15- or 16-inch tires.			
3-speed automatic transmission	555	477	505
4-speed automatic transmission	755	649	687
Air conditioning, SE	830	714	755
Option Group 1SB, SE	1575	1355	1433
Air conditioning, cruise control, cassette player, intermittent wipers, rear defogger, tilt steering wheel.			
Option Group 1SC, SE 2-door	2086	1794	1898
SE 4-door	2151	1850	1957
Group 1SB plus power windows with driver-side express down, power mirrors, split folding rear seat.			
Option Group 1SB, GT	535	460	487
Cruise control, cassette player.			
Option Group 1SC, GT 2-door	1046	900	952
GT 4-door	1111	955	1011
Group 1SB plus power windows with driver-side express down, power mirrors, split folding rear seat.			
Sport Interior Group, SE and GT	432	372	393
with Group 1SC	282	243	257
with leather upholstery	907	780	825
with leather upholstery and Group 1SC	757	651	689
Driver-seat lumbar adjuster, articulated front headrests, 4-way manual seat adjuster, leather-wrapped steering wheel and shift knob, reading and courtesy lamps, sunvisor extensions, split folding rear seat, passenger assist grips.			
Rally gauge cluster, SE	111	95	101
Cruise control	225	194	205
Rear defogger	170	146	155
Power mirrors	86	74	78
Power driver's seat	340	292	309
with Sport Interior Group	305	262	278
Power windows with driver-side express down, 2-door	275	237	250
4-door	340	292	309
Split folding rear seat	150	129	137
Tilt steering wheel, SE	145	125	132
Intermittent wipers, SE	65	56	59

Prices are accurate at time of publication; subject to manufacturer's change.

PONTIAC

	Retail Price	Dealer Invoice	Fair Price
Remote keyless entry system	$135	$116	$123
AM/FM cassette player	140	120	127
AM/FM cassette player with equalizer	375	323	341
with group 1SB or 1SC	235	202	214
AM/FM CD player w/equalizer	580	499	528
with Group 1SB or 1SC	440	378	400
Rear decklid spoiler, SE	110	95	100
Rear decklid spoiler delete, GT (credit)	(110)	(95)	(95)
195/65R15 tires, SE	158	136	144
205/55R16 tires, SE	223	192	203
Crosslace wheel cover, SE	55	47	50
16-inch alloy wheels, SE	300	258	273

Pontiac Grand Prix

	Retail Price	Dealer Invoice	Fair Price
SE 4-door notchback	$16174	$14475	$14975
SE 4-door notchback (California)	16295	—	—
SE 2-door notchback	16770	15345	15845
SE 2-door notchback (California)	17195	—	—
Destination charge	525	525	525

California models' dealer invoice and fair price not available at time of publication. California models include destination charge.

Standard Equipment:

4-door: 3.1-liter V-6 engine, 4-speed automatic transmission, 4-wheel disc brakes, driver- and passenger-side air bags, power steering, air conditioning, power windows with driver-side express down, automatic power door locks, 45/55 cloth reclining front seat with folding armrest, AM/FM radio, Pass-Key theft-deterrent system, tachometer, trip odometer, coolant temperature gauge, tilt steering wheel, left remote and right manual mirrors, tinted glass, intermittent wipers, fog lamps, day/night rearview mirror, door map pockets, 205/70R15 tires, wheel covers. **California 4-door model** adds: anti-lock brakes, cruise control, rear defogger, AM/FM cassette player, power mirrors, remote decklid release, visor mirrors, floormats, 215/60R16 touring tires, alloy wheels. **2-door** adds: cruise control, cloth reclining bucket seats with storage console, AM/FM cassette player, leather-wrapped steering wheel with radio controls, power mirrors, rear defogger, remote decklid release, covered visor mirrors, front and rear floormats, 215/60R16 tires, alloy wheels. **California 2-door model** adds: anti-lock brakes, front and rear fascias with integral fog lamps, lower bodyside moldings, chrome grille, dual exhaust.

Optional Equipment:	Retail Price	Dealer Invoice	Fair Price
3.4-liter DOHC V-6	$1125	$968	$1011

Includes sport suspension and dual exhaust. Requires 225/60R16 tires, alloy wheels.

Anti-lock brakes (std. Calif. models)	450	387	404
Option Group 1SB, SE 4-door	717	617	644

Cruise control, rear defogger, power mirrors, AM/FM cassette player, remote decklid release, covered visor mirrors.

Option Group 1SC, SE 4-door	1912	1644	1718

Group 1SC plus anti-lock brakes, 6-way power driver's seat, leather-wrapped steering wheel with radio controls, remote keyless entry, power antenna, front and rear floormats.

GT Performance Pkg. with			
Group 1SB, SE 4-door	2198	1890	1975
with Group 1SC	2103	1809	1890

3.4-liter DOHC V-6 engine, sport suspension, dual exhaust, GT name-plates, 225/60R16 tires, alloy wheels.

6-way power driver's seat	305	262	274
Cruise control	225	194	202
Remote decklid release (std. 2-door)	60	52	54
Rear defogger (std. 2-door)	170	146	153
Power glass sunroof	695	598	625
with Custom Interior Trim Group	646	556	581
Trip computer	199	171	179
Head-up display	250	215	225
Remote keyless entry	135	116	121
Covered visor mirrors (std. 2-door)	14	12	13
B20/C6 Custom Interior Trim with			
Group 1SB, 4-door	488	420	439
with Group 1SC	393	338	354

45/55 reclining front bench seat with storage armrest, upgraded cloth upholstery, leather-wrapped steering wheel, front overhead miniconsole with front and rear reading lights, door courtesy lights, rear seat pass through, rear folding armrests, lighted visor mirrors, trunk net, deluxe floormats.

B20/C3 Custom Interior Trim			
with Group 1SB, 4-door	628	540	565
with Group 1SC	533	458	480
with GT Performance Pkg.	(NC)	(NC)	(NC)

Replaces 45/55 front bench seat with custom bucket seats.

B20/23 Custom Interior Trim			
with Group 1SB, 4-door	1103	949	993
with Group 1SC	1008	867	907
with GT Performance Pkg.	475	409	428

Adds leather upholstery.

	Retail Price	Dealer Invoice	Fair Price
UN6 AM/FM cassette player, 4-door	$170	$146	$153
UT6 AM and FM stereo cassette player			
with Group 1SB	400	344	359
with 1SB and Custom Interior			
Trim Group	350	301	315
with Group 1SC	225	194	202
Includes equalizer and steering wheel radio controls.			
U1C AM and FM stereo with CD player	396	341	356
with Group 1SB or 1SC	226	194	203
Includes equalizer and steering wheel radio controls.			
UP3 AM and FM stereo with CD			
player with Group 1SB	626	538	563
with Group 1SB and Custom			
Interior Group	576	495	518
with Group 1SC	451	388	405
Includes equalizer and steering wheel radio controls.			
Steering wheel radio controls	175	151	157
with Custom Interior Group	125	108	112
Requires UT6, U1C, or UP3 radio.			
Power antenna	85	73	76
Dual exhausts	90	77	81
Alloy wheels	275	237	247
215/60R16 touring tires	112	96	101
225/60R16 performance tires	150	129	135
Cellular phone provisions	35	30	31
Front and rear floormats	45	39	40
Engine block heater	18	15	16

Pontiac Sunbird

	Retail Price	Dealer Invoice	Fair Price
LE 2-door notchback	$9764	$9129	$9329
LE 2-door notchback (California)	9995	—	—
LE 4-door notchback	9764	9129	9329
LE 4-door notchback (California)	9995	—	—
LE 2-door convertible	15524	14515	15015
SE 2-door notchback	12424	11244	11444
Destination charge	475	475	475

California models' dealer invoice and fair price not available at time of publication. California models include destination charge.

Standard Equipment:

LE: 2.0-liter 4-cylinder engine, 5-speed manual transmission, anti-lock brakes, power steering, door-mounted automatic front seatbelts, cloth reclining front bucket seats, center storage console, automatic power locks, tinted glass, trip odometer, left remote and right manual mirrors, illuminated entry, rear courtesy lights, day/night rearview mirror, AM/FM radio, 185/75R14 tires, wheel covers. **California models** add: air conditioning. **Convertible** has power top, power windows with driver-side express down, rear decklid spoiler, intermittent wipers, front storage armrest, visor mirrors, 195/65R15 touring tires, crosslace wheel covers. **SE** adds: 3.1-liter V-6 engine, ride and handling suspension, rally gauges (includes tachometer, coolant temperature and oil pressure gauges, trip odometer), rear decklid spoiler, front and rear fascias, visor mirrors, front and rear floormats, 195/65R15 touring tires, crosslace wheel covers.

Optional Equipment:	Retail Price	Dealer Invoice	Fair Price
3.1-liter V-6 (std. SE)	$712	$612	$627
Includes rally gauges.			
3-speed automatic transmission	495	426	436
Air conditioning	785	675	691
Option Group 1SB, LE and SE	1234	1061	1086
Air conditioning, cassette player, tilt steering wheel, intermittent wipers, front storage armrest, remote decklid release.			
Option Group 1SC, LE 2-door	1974	1698	1738
LE 4-door	1969	1693	1733
SE 2-door	1904	1637	1676
Group 1SB plus cruise control, power windows with driver-side express down, split folding rear seat, trunk net, rear decklid spoiler (LE 2-door).			
Option Group 1SB, LE convertible	1366	1175	1202
Air conditioning, cruise control, cassette player, tilt steering wheel, remote decklid release, trunk net.			
Special Appearance Pkg.,			
LE convertible	316	272	278
Includes white convertible top, white vinyl interior, color-keyed bodyside moldings, door decals, front and rear fascias, white alloy wheels. Requires Group 1SB.			
Cruise control	225	194	198
Rear defogger	170	146	150
Power windows, 2-door	265	228	233
4-door	330	284	290
Cassette player	170	146	150
CD player, LE, LE convertible and SE	396	341	349
with Group 1SB or 1SC	226	194	199
White vinyl bucket seats and			
interior trim, LE convertible	75	65	66
Split folding rear seat (NA convertible)	150	129	132
Decklid spoiler, LE 2-door	70	60	62
Tilt steering wheel	145	125	128

Prices are accurate at time of publication; subject to manufacturer's change.

PONTIAC

	Retail Price	Dealer Invoice	Fair Price
Removable glass sunroof, LE 2-door and SE	$350	$301	$308
195/70R14 touring tires, LE	141	121	124
LE convertible (credit)	(17)	(15)	(15)
195/65R15 touring tires (std. LE convertible and SE)	158	136	139
15-inch crosslace wheelcovers (std. LE convertible and SE)	55	47	48
14-inch alloy wheels, LE	275	237	242
LE convertible and SE	220	189	194

Pontiac Trans Sport

	Retail Price	Dealer Invoice	Fair Price
SE 4-door van	$17639	$15719	$16219
SE 4-door van (California)	19495	—	—
Destination charge	530	530	530

California model dealer invoice and fair price not available at time of publication. California model price includes destination charge.

Standard Equipment:

SE: 3.1-liter V-6 engine, 3-speed automatic transmission, anti-lock brakes, driver-side air bag, power steering, 4-way adjustable driver's seat, front reclining bucket seats, 3-passenger middle seat, cloth upholstery, tinted glass with solar-control windshield, tachometer, coolant temperature and oil pressure gauges, voltmeter, trip odometer, AM/FM radio, Lamp Group (includes overhead console map lights, rear reading lights, cargo area lights, underhood light), left remote and right manual mirrors, door and seatback pockets, intermittent wipers, fog lamps, rear wiper/washer, visor mirrors, front and rear floormats, 205/70R15 tires, wheel covers. **California model** adds: 3.8-liter V-6 engine, 4-speed automatic transmission, cruise control, front air conditioning, AM/FM cassette player, power door locks, windows and mirrors, remote keyless entry system, 7-passenger seating, 6-way power driver's seat, cargo area net, deep-tint glass, luggage carrier, 205/70R15 touring tires, alloy wheels.

Optional Equipment:

3.8-liter V-6 engine	819	704	734
Includes 4-speed automatic transmission.			
Front air conditioning	830	714	744
Front and rear air conditioning			
with rear heater	1280	1101	1147
with Group 1SB, 1SC, 1SD, or 1SE	450	387	403
Requires automatic level control and deep-tint glass.			

	Retail Price	Dealer Invoice	Fair Price
Automatic level control	$200	$172	$179
Includes rear saddle bags.			
Option Group 1SB	1248	1073	1118
Front air conditioning, cruise control, cassette player, power mirrors, tilt steering wheel.			
Option Group 1SC	2383	2049	2135
Group 1SB plus automatic power door locks, power windows with driver-side express down, rear defogger, 7-passenger seating, deep-tint glass.			
Option Pkg. 1SD	2933	2522	2628
Group 1SC plus 6-way power driver's seat, remote keyless entry system, luggage rack.			
Option Pkg. 1SE	3908	3361	3502
Group 1SD plus automatic level control, cassette player with equalizer, self-sealing touring tires, alloy wheels.			
Rear defogger	170	146	152
Deep-tint glass	245	211	220
Pop-up glass sunroof	300	258	269
Luggage rack	175	151	157
Includes rear saddle bags.			
Power mirrors	48	41	43
Automatic power locks	300	258	269
6-way power driver's seat	270	232	242
Power windows with driver-side express down	275	237	246
Requires automatic power door locks.			
Power sliding side door	295	254	264
Requires automatic power door locks.			
Remote keyless entry system	135	116	121
Cassette player	140	120	125
Cassette player with equalizer, with Group 1SD	315	271	282
Includes steering wheel radio controls and leather-wrapped steering wheel.			
CD player with equalizer, with Group 1SD	541	465	485
with Group 1SE	206	177	185
Includes steering wheel radio controls and leather-wrapped steering wheel.			
7-passenger seating	705	606	632
Three second row and two third row modular seats, cargo area net.			
7-passenger seating with leather upholstery, with Group 1SD or 1SE	870	748	780
Integral child seat	125	108	112
Requires 7-passenger seating.			

Prices are accurate at time of publication; subject to manufacturer's change.

	Retail Price	Dealer Invoice	Fair Price
Two integral child seats	$225	$194	$202
Requires 7-passenger seating.			
Traction control	350	301	314
Trailer towing provisions	150	129	134
205/70R15 touring tires	35	30	31
Self-sealing touring tires	185	159	166
Alloy wheels	275	237	246
Engine block heater	18	15	16

SAAB

Saab 900	Retail Price	Dealer Invoice	Fair Price
S 5-door hatchback	$20990	—	—
S 2-door convertible	33275	28750	29550
SE 5-door hatchback	—	—	—
Turbo 2-door convertible	38415	32730	33530
Commemorative Edition Turbo 2-door convertible	40415	—	—
Destination charge	460	460	460

S dealer invoice and fair price not available at time of publication. SE price not available at time of publication.

Standard Equipment:

S: 2.3-liter 4-cylinder engine, 5-speed manual transmission, anti-lock 4-wheel disc brakes, driver- and passenger-side air bags, front seatbelt pretensioners, power steering, air conditioning, cruise control, power door and trunk locks, theft alarm system, power windows, automatic power antenna, telescopic steering wheel, front fog lamps, rear fog lamp, dual heated power mirrors, rear defogger, intermittent wipers, solar-control tinted glass, AM/FM cassette, trip computer, cellular phone and CD pre-wiring, cloth heated reclining front bucket seats, folding rear seat, front console with storage, headlamp wipers/washers, rear wiper/washer, tachometer, analog clock, front spoiler, front and rear stabilizer bars, tool kit, bodyside moldings, floormats, 195/60VR15 tires, full wheel covers. **S convertible** deletes passenger-side air bag and adds: 2.1-liter engine 4-cylinder, power top, power heated front bucket seats, leather upholstery, leather-wrapped steering wheel, 185/65TR15 tires, alloy wheels. **SE** adds to S: 2.5-liter V-6 engine, traction control, automatic climate control, 8-way power front seats with driver-side memory, leather upholstery, leather-wrapped steering wheel, shift knob and boot cover, premium AM/FM cassette, Saab Car

Computer, alloy wheels. **Turbo convertible** adds to S convertible: 2.0-liter turbocharged 4-cylinder engine, engine oil cooler, turbo boost gauge, AM/FM cassette/CD player with equalizer, 195/60VR15 tires.

Optional Equipment:

	Retail Price	Dealer Invoice	Fair Price
2.5-liter V-6 Pkg., S	$2295	—	—
Includes traction control and spoke alloy wheels.			
4-speed automatic transmission, S and SE	895	—	—
3-speed automatic transmission, convertible	705	576	620
Leather Upholstery Pkg., S	1195	—	—
Leather upholstery, leather-wrapped steering wheel, shift knob and boot cover.			
Power front seats with driver-side memory, S	820	—	—
Sunroof, S	980	—	—

Saab 9000	Retail Price	Dealer Invoice	Fair Price
CS 5-door hatchback	$28725	—	—
CS Turbo 5-door hatchback	31780	—	—
CSE 5-door hatchback	33045	—	—
CSE Turbo 5-door hatchback	36100	—	—
CDE Turbo 4-door notchback	36685	—	—
9000 Aero, 5-door notchback	38690	—	—
Destination charge	460	460	460

Dealer invoice and fair price not available at time of publication.

Standard Equipment:

CS: 2.3-liter DOHC 4-cylinder engine, 5-speed manual transmission, anti-lock 4-wheel disc brakes, driver- and passenger-side air bags, power steering, automatic climate control, removable AM/FM cassette player, cruise control, power glass sunroof, cloth reclining heated bucket seats, folding rear seat, power door locks and windows, dual heated power mirrors, automatic power antenna, remote decklid release, tachometer, trip odometer, intermittent wipers, headlamp wipers/washers, rear wiper/washer, solar-control tinted glass, dual visor mirrors, rear defogger, locking center console with storage, overhead console with swivel map light, front and rear fog lamps, courtesy lights, dual rear reading lights, lighted visor mirrors, front spoiler, analog clock, floormats, 195/65TR15 tires, alloy wheels. **CS Turbo** adds: 200-horsepower 2.3-liter turbocharged engine with intercooler, turbo boost gauge. **CSE** adds to CS: power front seats with driver-side memory, leather upholstery, leather-wrapped steering wheel and shift boot cover, Saab Car Computer with digital clock, removable CD player and equalizer, CD changer pre-wiring, 195/65VR15 tires. **CSE Turbo** adds to CSE: 200-horsepower 2.3-liter turbocharged engine with intercooler, turbo boost gauge. **CDE Turbo** deletes rear fog lamp, adds to CSE Turbo: wood interior trim, rear seat pass-through, 205/60ZR15 tires. **Aero** adds: 225-horsepower 2.3-liter turbocharged engine, aerodynamic body trim, sport suspension, rear spoiler, 205/55ZR16 tires.

Optional Equipment	Retail Price	Dealer Invoice	Fair Price
4-speed automatic transmission	$945	—	—

SATURN

Saturn SC1/SC2	Retail Price	Dealer Invoice	Fair Price
SC1 2-door notchback, 5-speed	$11695	$10175	—
SC1 2-door notchback, automatic	12495	10871	—
SC2 2-door notchback, 5-speed	12895	11219	—
SC2 2-door notchback, automatic	13695	11915	—
Destination charge	330	330	330

Fair price not available at time of publication.

Standard Equipment:

SC1: 1.9-liter 4-cylinder engine, 5-speed manual or 4-speed automatic transmission, driver-side air bag, motorized front shoulder belts, power steering, cloth/vinyl reclining front bucket seats, 60/40 rear seatback, tachometer, trip odometer, tilt steering column, intermittent wipers, rear defogger, AM/FM radio, remote fuel door and decklid releases, door pockets, digital clock, right visor mirror, front and rear consoles, dual remote outside mirrors, color-keyed bumpers, wheel covers, 175/70R14 tires. **SC2** adds: 1.9-liter DOHC engine, driver's seat height and lumbar support adjustments, sport suspension, upgraded upholstery, retractable headlamps, 195/60R15 tires.

Optional Equipment:

Anti-lock brakes (includes rear discs), 5-speed	675	587	—
Anti-lock brakes (includes rear disc brakes and traction control), automatic	725	631	—
Air conditioning	885	770	—
Option Pkg. 1, SC1	1640	1427	—
Air conditioning, cruise control, power windows and locks.			

	Retail Price	Dealer Invoice	Fair Price
Option Pkg. 2, SC2	$1840	$1601	—
Option Pkg. 1 plus sawtooth alloy wheels.			
Power sunroof	650	566	—
AM/FM cassette radio	195	170	—
AM/FM cassette with equalizer	355	309	—
AM/FM with CD player and equalizer	600	522	—
Coaxial speakers	70	61	—
Cruise control	240	209	—
Leather upholstery, SC2	660	574	—
Rear spoiler	175	152	—
Sawtooth alloy wheels, SC1	400	348	—
Includes 195/60R15 tires.			
Teardrop alloy wheels, SC2	200	174	—

Saturn Sedan/Wagon

	Retail Price	Dealer Invoice	Fair Price
SL 4-door notchback, 5-speed	$9995	$8696	—
SL1 4-door notchback, 5-speed	10795	9392	—
SL1 4-door notchback, automatic	11595	10088	—
SL2 4-door notchback, 5-speed	11795	10262	—
SL2 4-door notchback, automatic	12595	10958	—
SW1 5-door wagon, 5-speed	11695	10175	—
SW1 5-door wagon, automatic	12495	10871	—
SW2 5-door wagon, 5-speed	12595	10958	—
SW2 5-door wagon, automatic	13395	11654	—
Destination charge	330	330	330

Fair price not available at time of publication.

Standard Equipment:

SL: 1.9-liter 4-cylinder engine, 5-speed manual transmission, driver-side air bag, cloth/vinyl reclining front bucket seats, 60/40 folding rear seatback, tachometer, trip odometer, tilt steering column, intermittent wipers, rear defogger, AM/FM radio, remote fuel door and decklid releases, door pockets, digital clock, right visor mirror, front console, child-safety rear door locks, wheel covers, 175/70R14 tires. **SL1** adds: 5-speed manual or 4-speed automatic transmission, power steering, upgraded interior trim. **SL2** adds: 1.9-liter DOHC engine, driver's seat height and lumbar support adjustments, dual outside mirrors, sport suspension, upgraded upholstery, color-keyed bumpers, 195/60R15 tires. **SW1** adds to SL1: dual mirrors, cargo area net. **SW2** adds to SW1: 1.9-liter DOHC engine, color-keyed bumpers, driver's seat height and lumbar support adjustments, sport suspension, upgraded upholstery, 195/60R15 tires.

Prices are accurate at time of publication; subject to manufacturer's change.

Optional Equipment:

	Retail Price	Dealer Invoice	Fair Price
Anti-lock brakes (includes rear discs), 5-speed	$675	$587	—
Anti-lock brakes (includes rear disc brakes and traction control), automatic	725	631	—
Air conditioning	885	770	—
Option Pkg. 1, SL1	1800	1566	—
SW1, SW2	1765	1536	—
Air conditioning, cruise control, power windows and locks, right outside mirror (SL1).			
Option Pkg. 2, SL2	2065	1797	—
Option Pkg. 1 plus sawtooth alloy wheels.			
Power sunroof, SL1, SL2	650	566	—
AM/FM cassette radio	195	170	—
AM/FM cassette w/equalizer	355	309	—
AM/FM w/CD player and equalizer	600	522	—
Power door locks, SL1, SW1	245	213	—
Coaxial speakers	70	61	—
Cruise control (NA on SL)	240	209	—
Right outside mirror, SL1	35	30	—
Fog lamps, SL2, SW2	150	131	—
Leather upholstery, SL2, SW2	660	574	—
Rear spoiler, SL2	175	152	—
Sawtooth alloy wheels, SL2, SW2	300	261	—

SUBARU

1993 Subaru Impreza

	Retail Price	Dealer Invoice	Fair Price
4-door notchback, 5-speed	$10999	$9877	$10377
L 4-door notchback, 5-speed	11499	10262	10762
L AWD 4-door notchback, 5-speed	14499	12627	13127
L 5-door Wagon, 5-speed	13399	11677	12177
L AWD 5-door Wagon, 5-speed	14899	12972	13472
LS 4-door notchback, automatic	15699	13687	14187
LS AWD 4-door notchback, automatic	17199	14804	15304
LS 5-door Wagon, automatic	16099	13854	14354
LS AWD 5-door Wagon, automatic	17599	15499	15999
Destination charge	445	445	445

Prices are for vehicles distributed by Subaru of America. Prices may be higher in areas served by independent distributors.

Standard Equipment:

Base: 1.8-liter 4-cylinder engine, 5-speed manual transmission, driver-side air bag, power steering, reclining front bucket seats, rear defogger, dual manual outside mirrors, tinted glass, tilt steering column, analog gauges with tachometer, intermittent wipers, cup holders, center console, remote trunk and fuel door releases, 165/80R13 tires. **L** adds: front- or all-wheel drive (AWD), 5-speed manual or 4-speed automatic transmission, upgraded interior trim, body-color grille, wheel covers, 175/70R14 all-season tires (AWD). **Wagon** adds: 60/40 folding rear seatback. **LS** adds: 4-speed automatic transmission, anti-lock 4-wheel disc brakes, air conditioning, dual power mirrors, power windows and locks, 80-watt AM/FM cassette, cruise control, trunk/cargo area light, 60/40 folding rear seatback (4-door), velour upholstery, front and rear stablizer bars, 175/70R14 all-season tires.

Optional Equipment:	Retail Price	Dealer Invoice	Fair Price
4-speed automatic transmission, L models	$800	$721	$751
Air conditioning, base and L 4-door	969	872	901

1993 Subaru Legacy	Retail Price	Dealer Invoice	Fair Price
L 4-door notchback	$16250	$14405	$14605
L 5-door wagon	16950	15025	15225
L AWD 4-door notchback	17850	15824	16024
L AWD 5-door wagon	18550	16444	16644
LS 4-door notchback	19150	16829	17029
LS AWD 4-door notchback	20750	18234	18434
LS 5-door wagon	19850	17444	17644
LS AWD 5-door wagon	21450	18850	19050
LSi AWD 4-door notchback	21650	19026	19226
LSi AWD 5-door wagon	22650	19904	20104
Sport Sedan AWD 4-door	20850	18323	18523
Touring Wagon AWD 5-door	22650	19904	20104
Destination charge	445	445	445

Prices are for vehicles distributed by Subaru of America. Prices may be higher in areas served by independent distributors.

Standard Equipment:

L: 2.2-liter 4-cylinder engine, 5-speed manual transmission, front-wheel drive or permanent all-wheel drive (AWD), 4-wheel disc brakes, driver-side air bag, air conditioning, power windows and locks, power steering, Hill-Holder clutch (5-speed), cloth reclining front bucket seats, split folding rear seat, driver's-seat lumbar support adjustment, dual power mirrors, bodyside moldings, rear defogger, tinted glass, tachometer and gauges, AM/FM cassette with equalizer, center console with storage bin, remote fuel door and decklid releases, dual cup holders, cruise control, child-safety rear door locks, tilt steering column, intermittent wipers, 185/70HR14 tires. **LS** adds: 4-speed automatic transmission, anti-lock brakes, driver's seat height adjustment, variable-intermittent wipers, power antenna, power moonroof, lighted visor mirrors, rear wiper/washer (wagons), leather-wrapped steering wheel and shift knob, adjustable air suspension (AWD wagon and FWD wagon with automatic), alloy wheels. **LSi** adds: permanent AWD, leather upholstery, CD player. **Sport Sedan** adds to LS: turbocharged engine, 5-speed manual transmission, permanent AWD, sport seats, front air dam, rear spoiler, 195/60HR15 tires. **Touring Wagon** adds: 4-speed automatic transmission.

Optional Equipment:	Retail Price	Dealer Invoice	Fair Price
4-speed automatic transmission, L and Sport Sedan	$800	$721	$742
Anti-lock brakes, L AWD wagon	995	873	911

SUZUKI

Suzuki Sidekick	Retail Price	Dealer Invoice	Fair Price
JS 2WD 2-door conv., 5-speed	$11449	$10762	$10962
JS 2WD 2-door conv., 5-speed (New York and California)	11749	11044	11244
JS 2WD 2-door conv., automatic	12049	11326	11526
JS 2WD 2-door conv., automatic (New York and California)	12349	11608	11808
JX 4WD 2-door conv., 5-speed	12849	11821	12021
JX 4WD 2-door conv., 5-speed (New York and California)	13149	12097	12297
JX 4WD 2-door conv., automatic	13449	12373	12573
JX 4WD 2-door conv., automatic (New York and California)	13749	12649	12849
JS 2WD 5-door, 5-speed	12849	11693	12093
JX 4WD 5-door, 5-speed	14079	12531	12931
JX 4WD 5-door, automatic	15039	13385	13785
JLX 4WD 5-door, 5-speed	15429	13732	14132
JLX 4WD 5-door, automatic	16369	14568	14968
Destination charge, 2-door	330	330	330
5-door	350	350	350

Standard Equipment:

JS 2-door: 1.6-liter 4-cylinder engine, 5-speed manual transmission or 3-

speed automatic transmission, rear-wheel drive, anti-lock rear brakes, cloth reclining front bucket seats and folding rear seat, center console, front door map pockets, fuel tank skid plate, folding canvas top, tinted glass, dual outside mirrors, intermittent wipers, trip odometer, carpeting, 195/75R15 tires. **JX 2-door** adds: part-time 4WD, 5-speed manual or 3-speed automatic transmission, automatic locking front hubs, 2-speed transfer case, power steering, power mirrors, tachometer, 205/75R15 tires. **JS 5-door** adds: 1.6-liter DOHC engine, 5-speed manual transmission, rear-wheel drive, power steering, power mirrors, rear defogger, child-safety rear door locks, carpeting, center console, locking fuel door, tinted glass, front map pockets, AM/FM cassette, reclining front bucket seats, cloth upholstery, split folding rear seat, fuel tank skid plate, tachometer, intermittent wipers, 195/75R15 tires. **JX 5-door** adds: 5-speed manual or 4-speed automatic transmission, part-time 4WD, automatic locking front hubs, 2-speed transfer case, 205/75R15 tires. **JLX 5-door** adds: tilt steering column, power windows and locks, cruise control, map lights, rear wiper/washer, remote fuel door release, deluxe upholstery, locking spare tire case, 205/75R15 outline white letter mud and snow tires, chrome wheels.

Options are available as dealer-installed accessories.

TOYOTA

Toyota Camry	Retail Price	Dealer Invoice	Fair Price
DX 2-door notchback, 5-speed	$16148	$13645	$14648
DX 2-door notchback, automatic	16948	14321	15448
LE 2-door notchback, automatic	18938	16003	17438
LE V-6 2-door notchback, automatic	21218	17929	19718
SE V-6 2-door notchback, automatic	22238	18791	20738
DX 4-door notchback, 5-speed	16438	13890	14938
DX 4-door notchback, automatic	17238	14566	15738
DX 5-door wagon, automatic	18648	15758	17148
LE 4-door notchback, automatic	19228	16248	17728
LE 5-door wagon, automatic	20618	17422	19118
XLE 4-door notchback, automatic	21258	17857	19758
SE V-6 4-door notchback, automatic	22528	19036	21028
LE V-6 4-door notchback, automatic	21508	18174	20008
LE V-6 5-door wagon, automatic	22918	19366	21418
XLE V-6 4-door notchback, automatic	23578	19806	22078
Destination charge	385	385	385

Prices are for vehicles distributed by Toyota Motor Sales, U.S.A., Inc. The dealer invoice, fair price, and destination charge may be higher in areas served by independent distributors.

Prices are accurate at time of publication; subject to manufacturer's change.

TOYOTA

Standard Equipment:

DX: 2.2-liter DOHC 4-cylinder engine, 5-speed manual or 4-speed automatic transmission, driver- and passenger-side air bags, power steering, tachometer, coolant temperature gauge, trip odometer, cloth reclining front bucket seats, split folding rear seat with armrest, remote fuel door and trunk releases, rear defogger, dual remote outside mirrors, front door pockets, tilt steering column, cup holders, auto-off headlamps, intermittent wipers, rear wiper (wagon), AM/FM radio, tinted glass, 195/70HR14 all-season tires. **LE** adds: 2.2-liter DOHC 4-cylinder or 3.0-liter DOHC V-6 engine, 4-speed automatic transmission, 6-way manual driver's seat, air conditioning, cruise control, power windows, door locks, and mirrors, cassette player, power antenna, upgraded interior trim, door courtesy lights (2-door), 205/65HR15 all-season tires, alloy wheels (2-door). **SE** adds to DX: 3.0-liter DOHC V-6 engine, 4-speed automatic transmission, air conditioning, cruise control, 7-way power driver's seat, cassette player, power antenna, power windows, door locks and mirrors, sport suspension, rear spoiler, leather-wrapped steering wheel and parking brake handle, passenger-side visor mirror, 205/65VR15 all-season tires, alloy wheels. **XLE** adds to LE: power moonroof, 7-way power driver's seat, illuminated entry, map light, lighted visor mirrors, variable-intermittent wipers, alloy wheels. V-6 models have 4-wheel disc brakes.

Optional Equipment:

	Retail Price	Dealer Invoice	Fair Price
Anti-lock brakes, 4-cyl. models	$1100	$902	$1045
Includes rear disc brakes.			
V-6 models	950	779	903
Anti-lock brakes and third seat,			
4-cyl. wagon	1415	1154	1344
Includes rear disc brakes.			
V-6 wagon	1265	1031	1202
Air conditioning	975	780	926
Power Seat Pkg., LE 2-door	340	272	323
7-way power driver's seat.			
Folding third seat, 4-cyl. wagon	465	375	442
V-6 wagon	315	252	299
Leather trim, XLE and LE 2-door	1030	824	979
SE	975	780	926
Cruise control, DX	265	213	252
Power moonroof, SE and LE	960	760	903
Includes map lights and sunshade.			
Power door locks, DX 4-door and wagon	260	208	247
DX 2-door	220	176	209
AM/FM cassette, DX	170	127	162
Premium AM/FM cassette, (NA DX)	405	304	385
CD player, SE and XLE	1205	904	1145

	Retail Price	Dealer Invoice	Fair Price
Mud guards	$50	$40	$48
Alloy wheels, LE	400	320	380
LE V-6	420	336	399

Toyota Celica

	Retail Price	Dealer Invoice	Fair Price
ST 2-door notchback, 5-speed	$16168	$13824	—
ST 2-door notchback, automatic	16968	14508	—
GT 2-door notchback, 5-speed	18428	15664	—
GT 2-door notchback, automatic	19228	16344	—
ST 3-door hatchback, 5-speed	16508	14114	—
ST 3-door hatchback, automatic	17308	14798	—
GT 3-door hatchback, 5-speed	18898	16063	—
GT 3-door hatchback, automatic	19698	16743	—
Destination charge	385	385	385

Fair price not available at time of publication. Prices are for vehicles distributed by Toyota Motor Sales, U.S.A., Inc. The dealer invoice, fair price, and destination charge may be higher in areas served by independent distributors.

Standard Equipment:

ST: 1.8-liter DOHC 4-cylinder engine, 5-speed manual or 4-speed automatic transmission, driver- and passenger-side air bags, power steering, cloth 4-way adjustable front sport seats, center console with armrest, split folding rear seat, dual cup holders, digital clock, rear defogger, remote fuel door and trunk/hatch releases, map lights, coolant temperature gauge, tachometer, trip odometer, intermittent wipers, auto-off headlamps, tinted glass, dual outside mirrors, AM/FM radio with four speakers, visor mirrors, cargo area cover (hatchback), 185/70R14 all-season tires. **GT adds:** 2.2-liter DOHC 4-cylinder engine, 4-wheel disc brakes, AM/FM cassette with six speakers, power antenna, power windows and door locks, tilt steering column, intermittent rear wiper (hatchback), upgraded door and interior trim, engine oil cooler (5-speed), 205/55VR15 all-season tires.

Optional Equipment:

Anti-lock brakes	825	676	—
Air conditioning	975	780	—
Power Pkg., ST	510	408	—
Power windows and locks.			
Leather trim, GT	1045	836	—
Includes power driver's seat, leather-wrapped steering wheel, shift knob and parking brake lever. Requires Power Pkg.			
Leather Sport Pkg., GT 3-door hatchback	1565	1252	

Prices are accurate at time of publication; subject to manufacturer's change.

	Retail Price	Dealer Invoice	Fair Price

Leather sport seats, leather-wrapped steering wheel, shift knob and parking brake lever, front sport suspension, alloy wheels.

	Retail Price	Dealer Invoice	Fair Price
Fabric Sport Pkg., GT 3-door hatchback	$905	724	—

Cloth sport seats, leather-wrapped steering wheel, shift knob and parking brake lever, front sport suspension, alloy wheels.

Rear spoiler, hatchbacks	375	300	—
Intermittent rear wiper, ST hatchback	155	127	—
Tilt steering column, ST	155	133	—
Sunroof	740	592	—
Cruise control	265	212	—
Cassette player, ST	170	127	—
Premium cassette player with six speakers, GT	365	273	—
Premium audio system with CD player, GT	1205	903	—
Alloy wheels, GT	420	336	—

Toyota Corolla	Retail Price	Dealer Invoice	Fair Price
4-door notchback, ...	$11918	$10607	$11107
4-door notchback, automatic	12418	11052	11552
DX 4-door notchback, 5-speed	12998	11177	11677
DX 4-door notchback, automatic	13798	11865	12365
LE 4-door notchback, automatic	16088	13787	14287
DX 5-door wagon, 5-speed	14088	12114	12614
DX 5-door wagon, automatic	14888	12804	13304
Destination charge	385	385	385

Prices are for vehicles distributed by Toyota Motor Sales, U.S.A., Inc. The dealer invoice, fair price, and destination charge may be higher in areas served by independent distributors.

Standard Equipment:

1.6-liter DOHC 4-cylinder engine, 5-speed manual or 3-speed automatic transmission, driver- and passenger-side air bags, cloth reclining front bucket seats, console with storage, coolant temperature gauge, trip odometer, remote decklid and fuel door release, auto-off headlights, cup holders, color-keyed bumpers, wheel covers, tinted glass, 175/65R14 all-season tires. **DX** adds: 1.8-liter DOHC 4-cylinder engine, 5-speed manual or 4-speed automatic, power steering, dual remote mirrors, passenger visor mirror, cloth door trim with map pockets, full cloth seats with headrests, rear seat headrests, 60/40 split rear seat, bodyside moldings, rear luggage lamp, digital clock, intermittent wipers, rear cargo cover and power hatch lock (wagon), 185/65R14 all-season tires. **LE** adds: 4-speed automatic transmission, air conditioning, power windows and door locks, cruise control, 4-way adjustable driver's seat, power mirrors, dual visor mirrors, tachometer, variable intermittent wipers, AM/FM cassette radio with four speakers, tilt steering column.

Optional Equipment:

	Retail Price	Dealer Invoice	Fair Price
Anti-lock brakes	$825	$676	$743
Air conditioning, base and DX	920	736	828
Power steering, base	260	222	234
Alloy wheels, LE	400	320	360
Value Pkg., base	845	761	803
Air conditioning, power steering, floormats.			
Value Pkg., DX 4-door	1615	1454	1534
Air conditioning, tilt steering column, Power Pkg., deluxe AM/FM cassette player with four speakers, floormats.			
Value Pkg., LE	1640	1476	1558
Anti-lock brakes, sunroof, deluxe AM/FM cassette player with four speakers, alloy wheels, floormats.			
Convenience Pkg., base	1180	958	1062
Includes power steering, air conditioning.			
Tilt steering column, DX	155	133	140
Power sunroof, DX 4-door, LE	580	464	522
Includes map lights.			
Rear wiper, wagon	175	143	158
Radio Prep Pkg., base and DX	100	75	90
Includes two speakers, wiring harness, antenna.			
AM/FM radio with four speakers, base and DX	385	289	347
AM/FM cassette with four speakers, base and DX	555	416	500
LE	170	127	153
Power Pkg., DX	620	496	558
Power windows and locks.			
Tachometer, DX with 5-speed	65	52	59
Cruise control, DX	265	212	239
Includes variable intermittent wipers.			
All Weather Guard Pkg., base, 5-speed	235	191	212
Base, automatic	245	199	221
DX	65	55	59
Rear defogger, heavy duty battery, heater and wiper motor.			
Rear window defogger, base	170	136	153
Mud guards, DX	50	40	45

Prices are accurate at time of publication; subject to manufacturer's change.

TOYOTA

Toyota Land Cruiser

	Retail Price	Dealer Invoice	Fair Price
5-door 4WD wagon	$34268	$28614	—
Destination charge	385	385	385

Fair price not available at time of publication. Prices are for vehicles distributed by Toyota Motor Sales, U.S.A., Inc. The dealer invoice, fair price, and destination charge may be higher in areas served by independent distributors.

Standard Equipment:

4.5-liter DOHC 6-cylinder engine, 4-speed automatic transmission, permanent 4-wheel drive, power steering, air conditioning, cruise control, cloth reclining front bucket seats, middle seat center armrests, folding rear seat, power windows and locks, power mirrors, rear step bumper, console with storage, rear defogger and intermittent wiper/washer, remote fuel door release, tinted glass, rear heater, AM/FM cassette, digital clock with stopwatch and alarm, auto-off headlamps, skid plates for fuel tank and transfer case, tilt steering column, front and rear tow hooks, tachometer, voltmeter, oil pressure and coolant temperature gauges, trip odometer, variable intermittent wipers, passenger-side lighted visor mirror, transmission oil cooler, trailer towing wiring harness, 275/70R16 tires.

Optional Equipment:

Anti-lock disc brakes	1180	968	—
Premium AM/FM cassette w/CD player	800	600	—
Leather Trim Pkg.	4030	3224	—

Leather seats and door trim, leather-wrapped steering wheel, headrests, transmission lever, transfer case knob, leather covered center console, power seats, Third Seat Pkg.(Requires AM/FM cassette with CD.)

Differential locks	1930	1568	—

Lockable front and rear differentials, viscous coupling transfer case, full floating axle, anti-lock disc brakes.

Power moonroof	1150	920	—
Third Seat Pkg.	1395	1116	—

Includes split folding rear third seat, rear 3-point seat belts, cloth headrests, privacy glass, rear assist grips, sliding rear quarter windows.

Alloy wheels	515	412	—
2-tone paint	260	208	—

1993 Toyota MR2

	Retail Price	Dealer Invoice	Fair Price
2-door notchback, 5-speed	$18948	$16011	$16511
2-door notchback, automatic	19748	16687	17187
2-door notchback w/T-bar roof, 5-speed	20838	17608	18108
Turbo w/T-bar roof, 5-speed	24728	20895	21895

	Retail Price	Dealer Invoice	Fair Price
Destination charge	$325	$325	$325

Prices are for vehicles distributed by Toyota Motor Sales, U.S.A., Inc. The dealer invoice, low price, and destination charge may be higher in areas served by independent distributors.

Standard Equipment:

2.2-liter DOHC 4-cylinder engine, 5-speed manual or 4-speed automatic transmission, 4-wheel disc brakes, driver-side air bag, cloth reclining bucket seats, driver's seat height adjuster, tilt steering column, AM/FM cassette, tachometer, coolant temperature gauge, voltmeter, power mirrors, tinted glass, trip odometer, intermittent wipers, remote fuel door and decklid releases, 195/55VR15 front and 225/50VR15 rear tires, alloy wheels. **Turbo** adds: turbocharged 2.0-liter DOHC 4-cylinder engine, air conditioning, cruise control, 7-way adjustable driver's seat, leather-wrapped steering wheel, center storage box, fog lamps, rear spoiler, power windows and locks, cruise control, variable intermittent wipers, illuminated entry/exit fade-out system, premium AM/FM cassette with eight speakers, power antenna.

Optional Equipment:

Anti-lock brakes	1030	845	975
Limited-slip differential, Turbo	400	320	380
Electro-hydraulic power steering	600	513'	570
Air conditioning, base	915	732	869
Pop-up/removable sunroof, base	380	304	361
Power Pkg., base	530	424	503
Power windows and locks, illuminated entry/exit fade-out system.			
Cruise control, base	265	212	252
Includes variable intermittent wipers.			
Rear spoiler, base	300	240	285
Theft-deterrent system	165	132	157
Requires Power Pkg. or Leather Trim Pkg.			
Leather Trim Pkg., base w/T-bar	1705	1364	1620
Turbo	810	648	770
Turbo: leather seats, headrests, door trim and steering wheel. Base w/T-bar adds: 7-way adjustable driver's seat, leather-wrapped parking brake lever and shift knob, power windows and locks, console with storage, illuminated entry/exit fade-out system, passenger-side seatback map pocket.			
Premium AM/FM cassette, base	515	386	489
Base w/T-bar roof	450	337	427
Includes eight speakers, power antenna.			
Premium AM/FM cassette w/CD player, base..	1215	911	1154
Base w/T-bar roof	1150	862	1092
Turbo	700	525	665

Prices are accurate at time of publication; subject to manufacturer's change.

TOYOTA

Toyota Paseo

	Retail Price	Dealer Invoice	Fair Price
2-door notchback, 5-speed	$12468	$10847	$11247
2-door notchback, automatic	13268	11543	11943
Destination charge	385	385	385

Prices are for vehicles distributed by Toyota Motor Sales, U.S.A., Inc. The dealer invoice, fair price, and destination charge may be higher in areas served by independent distributors.

Standard Equipment:

1.5-liter DOHC 4-cylinder engine, 5-speed manual or 4-speed automatic transmission, power steering, driver-side air bag, cloth reclining bucket seats, door map pockets, tinted glass, tachometer, trip odometer, digital clock, variable intermittent wipers, AM/FM radio, rear defogger, cup holders, remote trunk and fuel door releases, folding rear seat, 185/60R14 tires.

Optional Equipment:

Anti-lock brakes	825	676	784
Air conditioning	900	720	855
Cruise control	265	212	252
Pop-up glass moonroof	400	320	380
Includes sunshade and storage pouch.			
AM/FM cassette with four speakers	315	236	299
All Weather Guard Pkg.	65	54	62
Heavy duty battery, rear defogger with timer, heater.			
Alloy wheels	400	320	380
Rear spoiler	375	300	356

Toyota Previa

	Retail Price	Dealer Invoice	Fair Price
DX 2WD, automatic	$22148	$18937	$19437
LE 2WD, automatic	25793	21928	22428
DX All-Trac, automatic	25388	21580	22080
LE All-Trac, automatic	28848	24521	25021
Destination charge	385	385	385

LE S/C prices not available at time of publication. Prices are for vehicles distributed by Toyota Motor Sales, U.S.A., Inc. The dealer invoice, fair price, and destination charge may be higher in areas served by independent distributors.

Standard Equipment:

DX: 2.4-liter DOHC 4-cylinder engine, 4-speed automatic transmission, driver- and passenger-side air bags, power steering, tilt steering column, cloth reclining front bucket seats, 2-passenger center seat, 3-passenger split-folding rear seat, AM/FM radio, rear defogger, variable intermittent wipers, rear intermittent wiper/washer, auto-off headlamps, tinted glass, digital clock, dual outside mirrors, tilt-out rear quarter windows, wheel covers, 215/65R15 all-season tires, full-size tire. **LE** adds: dual air conditioners, 4-wheel disc brakes, cruise control, power windows and door locks, power mirrors, AM/FM cassette, upgraded upholstery and interior trim, passenger-side lighted visor mirror. **All-Trac** adds permanently engaged 4-wheel drive.

Optional Equipment:	Retail Price	Dealer Invoice	Fair Price
Anti-lock brakes, DX	$1100	$899	$1000
Includes rear disc brakes.			
Anti-lock brakes, LE	950	779	865
Dual air conditioners, DX	1685	1348	1517
Power Pkg., DX	745	596	671
Power windows and locks, power mirrors.			
Privacy glass, LE	385	308	347
Cruise control, DX	275	220	248
AM/FM cassette, DX	170	127	149
Premium AM/FM cassette, LE	435	326	381
Premium AM/FM cassette with CD, LE	1275	956	1116
Dual power moonroofs, LE 2WD	1550	1240	1395
Captain's chairs with armrests, LE	790	632	711
Theft deterrent system, DX	945	756	851
Includes Power Pkg.			
Theft deterrent system, LE	200	160	180
Alloy wheels, LE	420	336	378

Toyota Supra	Retail Price	Dealer Invoice	Fair Price
Base 3-door hatchback, 5-speed	$35800	$29356	—
Base 3-door hatchback, automatic	36700	30094	—
Turbo 3-door hatchback, 6-speed	42800	35096	—
Base Sport Roof 3-door hatchback, 5-speed	36900	30258	—
Base Sport Roof 3-door hatchback, automatic	37800	30996	—
Turbo Sport Roof 3-door hatchback, 6-speed	43900	35998	—
Turbo Sport Roof 3-door hatchback, automatic	42800	35096	—
Destination charge	385	385	385

Fair price not available at time of publication. Prices are for vehicles distributed by Toyota Motor Sales, U.S.A., Inc. The dealer invoice, fair price, and destination charge may be higher in areas served by independent distributors.

TOYOTA

Standard Equipment:

3.0-liter DOHC 6-cylinder engine, 5-speed manual or 4-speed automatic transmission, anti-lock 4-wheel disc brakes, driver- and passenger-side air bags, speed sensitive power steering, cruise control, automatic air conditioning, power windows and locks, color-keyed heated power mirrors, AM/FM cassette player with six speakers and power diversity antenna, anti-theft system, tinted glass, 3-way power adjustable driver's seat, leather-wrapped steering wheel, shift knob, and parking brake handle, folding rear seat, tilt steering column, remote fuel door and hatch releases, variable intermittent wipers, rear intermittent wiper, rear defogger, tachometer, coolant temperature gauge, digital clock, dual digital trip odometers, auto-off headlamps, illuminated entry, front spoiler with integrated fog lamps, passenger-side visor mirror, color-keyed bumpers, cargo area cover, 225/50ZR16 front and 245/50ZR16 rear tires, alloy wheels. **Supra Turbo** adds: turbocharged 3.0-liter DOHC 6-cylinder engine, 6-speed manual or 4-speed automatic transmission, sport-tuned suspension, engine oil cooler, traction control, limited-slip differential, 235/45ZR17 front and 255/40ZR17 rear tires. **Sport Roof** adds removable roof panel.

Optional Equipment:	Retail Price	Dealer Invoice	Fair Price
Leather Trim Pkg.	$1100	$880	—
Leather upholstery and armrests.			
CD player with seven speakers	870	652	—
Limited-slip differential, base	460	368	—
Rear spoiler, Turbo	420	336	—

Toyota Tercel	Retail Price	Dealer Invoice	Fair Price
Standard 2-door notchback, 4-speed	$8698	$7958	$8158
DX 2-door notchback, 5-speed	10148	9133	9333
DX 2-door notchback, automatic	10648	9583	9783
DX 4-door notchback, 5-speed	10248	9223	9423
DX 4-door notchback, automatic	10748	9673	9873
Destination charge	385	385	385

Prices are for vehicles distributed by Toyota Motor Sales, U.S.A., Inc. The dealer invoice, fair price, and destination charge may be higher in areas served by independent distributors.

Standard Equipment:

Standard: 1.5-liter 4-cylinder engine, 4-speed manual transmission, driver-side air bag, vinyl reclining front bucket seats, coolant temperature gauge, left outside mirror, center console, 145/80R13 tires. **DX** adds: 5-speed manual or 3-speed automatic transmission, cloth reclining seats, dual outside mirrors, trip odometer, tinted glass, cup holders, color-keyed grille, 155/80SR13 tires, full wheel covers (2-door).

Optional Equipment:

	Retail Price	Dealer Invoice	Fair Price
Anti-lock brakes	$825	$616	$721
Air conditioning	900	720	810
Rear defogger	170	144	157
Power steering, DX	260	222	241
Value Pkg., DX 2-door	1495	1346	1421
DX 4-door	1395	1256	1326

Air conditioning, power steering, AM/FM cassette player with four speakers, intermittent wipers, dual manual mirrors, digital clock, remote fuel door and decklid releases, split folding rear seat.

Convenience Pkg., DX	330	264	297

Intermittent wipers, digital clock, remote mirrors, 60/40 folding rear seatback, remote fuel door and decklid releases.

Appearance Pkg., DX	130	104	107

Color-keyed bumpers, black bodyside molding.

AM/FM radio with two speakers	240	180	210
with four speakers, DX	385	289	337
AM/FM cassette with four speakers, DX	555	416	486
All Weather Guard Pkg.	235	201	218

Heavy duty battery, rear defogger, heater.

Toyota 4Runner

	Retail Price	Dealer Invoice	Fair Price
2WD 5-door wagon, V-6, automatic	$21028	$17769	$18269
4WD 5-door wagon, 5-speed	19998	16998	17498
4WD 5-door wagon, V-6, 5-speed	21938	18538	19038
4WD 5-door wagon, V-6, automatic	22988	19425	19925
Destination charge	385	385	385

Prices are for vehicles distributed by Toyota Motor Sales, U.S.A., Inc. The dealer invoice, fair price, and destination charge may be higher in areas served by independent distributors.

Standard Equipment:

2.4-liter 4-cylinder engine, 5-speed manual transmission, 4WDemand part-time 4WD (4WD models), power steering, cloth reclining front bucket seats with center console, split folding rear seat, tachometer, coolant temperature and oil pressure gauges, voltmeter, trip odometer, remote fuel door release, dual outside mirrors, tinted glass, power tailgate window, rear wiper/washer, digital clock, 225/75R15 all-season tires. **V6** models add: 3.0-liter V-6, 5-speed manual or 4-speed automatic transmission, anti-lock rear brakes, intermittent wipers, rear defogger, AM/FM radio, tilt steering column, passenger-side visor mirror.

TOYOTA

Optional Equipment:	Retail Price	Dealer Invoice	Fair Price
Anti-lock rear brakes, 4-cylinder	$300	$255	$278
4-wheel anti-lock brakes, V-6	660	541	601
Air conditioning	955	764	860
Tilt steering column, 4-cylinder	215	183	199
Rear heater	160	128	144
Chrome Pkg., 4-cylinder and V-6	245	196	221
Chrome grille, windshield molding, bumpers, and door handles.			
Cruise Control	375	300	338
Includes Lighting Pkg., leather-wrapped steering wheel.			
Power Pkg.	790	632	711
Power windows and locks, chrome power mirrors. Requires Cruise Control Pkg; Chrome Pkg. or alloy wheels.			
Sports Pkg.	450	360	405
with bronze glass	290	232	261
Cloth sport seats, rear privacy glass. Requires Chrome Pkg., or Value Pkg. 1 or 2 or alloy wheels.			
Bronze glass	160	128	144
Leather Seat Pkg., 4WD V-6	1680	1344	1512
Includes rear privacy glass, leather trimmed seats and door trim, 4-way adjustable headrests, Lighting Pkg., cruise control, variable intermittent wipers, leather-wrapped steering wheel.			
Value Pkg. 1, V-6.	1436	1292	1364
4-cyl.	1991	1792	1892
Air conditioning, Chrome Pkg., Power Pkg., Lighting Pkg., cruise control, AM/FM cassette (4-cyl.), variable intermittent wipers, leather-wrapped steering wheel (4-cyl.), floormats.			
Value Pkg. 2, 4WD V-6	2281	2053	2167
Value Pkg. 1 plus alloy wheels, chrome rear bumper for wider tires.			
Value Pkg. 3, 4WD V-6	3586	3227	3407
Value Pkg. 2 plus Leather Trim Pkg.			
All Weather Guard Pkg., 4-cylinder	235	191	213
V-6	65	55	60
Includes rear defogger (std. V-6) and heavy duty battery (V-6 only), heavy duty wiper motor, distributor cover, starter motor. Requires rear heater.			
Power moonroof, V-6	810	648	729
AM/FM cassette, 4-cylinder	555	416	486
V-6	270	207	234
Premium AM/FM cassette, V-6	675	506	591
Includes power antenna, six speakers.			
Cassette and CD player, V-6	1475	1106	1291
Includes power antenna.			
Alloy wheels and 31-inch tires, 4WD V-6	1090	872	981
Includes Chrome Pkg.			
Alloy wheels, V-6	470	376	423

VOLKSWAGEN

Volkswagen Golf/Jetta	Retail Price	Dealer Invoice	Fair Price
Golf GL 5-door hatchback	$11900	$10953	—
Jetta GL 4-door notchback	13125	11866	—
Jetta GLS 4-door notchback	15700	—	—
Destination charge	390	390	390

Dealer invoice and fair price for Jetta GLS and Golf 3-door, GTI, and Jetta GLX prices not available at time of publication.

Standard Equipment:

Golf GL: 2.0-liter 4-cylinder engine, 5-speed manual transmission, 4-wheel disc brakes, driver- and passenger-side air bags, power steering, cloth reclining bucket seats, driver's seat height adjustment, 60/40 split folding rear seat, anti-theft alarm, central power locking system with remote hatch and fuel door releases, tachometer, coolant temperature gauge, trip odometer, intermittent wipers, digital clock, center console with storage, cup holders, dual manual remote mirrors, tinted glass, rear defogger and wiper/washer, front door map pockets, passenger-side visor mirror, body-color bumpers and grille, front and rear spoilers, front floormats, 185/60HR14 all-season tires, full wheel covers. **Jetta GL** adds tilt steering column, driver- and passenger-side lighted visor mirrors, variable intermittent wipers. Deletes rear wiper/washer and spoiler. **Jetta GLS** adds to Jetta GL: air conditioning, cruise control, power windows, AM/FM cassette with theft-deterrent system, height adjustable front passenger seat, adjustable front seat lumbar supports, folding rear armrest, body-color outside mirrors. **Jetta GLX** adds to Jetta GLS: 2.8-liter V-6 engine, close-ratio 5-speed manual transmission, anti-lock brakes, sport suspension, heated front sport seats with leather trim, leather-wrapped steering wheel, shift knob and parking brake handle, heated front door locks, front fog lamps, multi-function trip information computer, brake wear indicator, body-color side moldings, black rocker panel covering, upgraded door trim, 215/50HR15 tires, alloy wheels.

Optional Equipment:

Anti-lock brakes, Jetta GL and GLS..............	NA	NA	NA
4-speed automatic transmission	875	856	—
Air conditioning, GL models	850	742	—
Power glass sunroof with sunshade	575	502	—
AM/FM cassette player, GL models	350	291	—
Clearcoat metallic paint	175	153	—

Prices are accurate at time of publication; subject to manufacturer's change.

VOLVO

Volvo 850

	Retail Price	Dealer Invoice	Fair Price
Level I 4-door, 5-speed	$24300	$22100	$23100
Level I 4-door, automatic	25200	23000	24000
Level II 4-door, 5-speed	26695	23495	24495
Level II 4-door, automatic	27595	24395	25395
Level II wagon, 5-speed	27695	24495	25495
Level II wagon, automatic	28595	25395	26395
Turbo 4-door, automatic	29985	29985	30985
Turbo wagon, automatic	30985	26785	27785
Destination charge	425	425	425

Standard Equipment:

Level I: 2.4-liter DOHC 5-cylinder engine, 5-speed manual or 4-speed automatic transmission, driver- and passenger-side air bags, seat-belt tensioners, anti-lock 4-wheel disc brakes, air conditioning, power steering, tilt/telescoping steering wheel, tinted glass, rear-window defroster, digital clock, intermittent wipers, fold-down rear seat with armrest, power windows and locks, heated power mirrors, cruise control, AM/FM cassette with anti-theft circuitry, cloth upholstery, 195/60R15 tires. **Level II** adds to Level I: power glass sunroof, 3-position driver's seat memory, automatic climate control, remote entry/security system, power antenna (4-doors), integrated window antenna (wagons), cargo net (wagons), alloy wheels. **Turbo 4-door/wagon** adds to Level II: turbocharged 2.3-liter 4-cylinder engine, 4-speed automatic transmission, Alpine AM/FM cassette with anti-theft circuitry, wood instrument panel trim, trip computer, rear head restraints, leather-wrapped steering wheel, leather upholstery, 205/50R16 tires, 5-spoke alloy wheels.

Optional Equipment:

Leather upholstery, Level I and II	995	795	945
Traction control	385	305	366
Power driver's seat, Level I	495	395	470
Power front passenger seat, Level I	495	395	470
Nordic Pkg.	450	360	428
Heated front seats, headlamp wiper/washer, ambient temperature gauge.			
Heated rear seat, wagons	400	320	380
Rear facing third seat, wagons	725	—	—
Automatic climate control, Level I	350	280	333
Sport suspension, 4-doors	150	120	143
Self-leveling rear suspension, wagons	400	320	380
Wood instrument panel trim, Level II	600	480	570

Prices are accurate at time of publication; subject to manufacturer's change.